Everyman, I will go with thee,
and be thy guide

Sophokles

FOUR DRAMAS
OF MATURITY

AIAS, ANTIGONE,
YOUNG WOMEN OF TRACHIS
OIDIPOUS THE KING

Edited by
MICHAEL EWANS
University of Newcastle, Australia

Translated by
MICHAEL EWANS
GRAHAM LEY
GREGORY McCART

EVERYMAN
J. M. DENT · LONDON
CHARLES E. TUTTLE
VERMONT

Translation from the Greek
© Michael Ewans, Graham Ley, Gregory McCart, 1999
Introduction and other critical material © J. M. Dent 1999

This edition first published in Everyman Paperbacks in 1999

J. M. Dent
Orion Publishing Group
Orion House
5 Upper St Martin's Lane
London WC2H 9EA
and
Charles E. Tuttle Co., Inc.
28 South Main Street
Rutland, Vermont 05701, USA

Printed in Great Britain by The Guernsey Press Co. Ltd,
Guernsey, C.I.

British Library Cataloguing-in-Publication Data
is available on request

ISBN 0 460 87743 7

CONTENTS

NOTE ON THE AUTHOR, EDITOR
AND TRANSLATORS

SOPHOKLES was born at Kolonos, a northern suburb of Athens, around 496 BC. At the age of sixteen he was selected to lead the dance, playing the lyre, at the celebrations for the Athenian victory over the Persian navy at Salamis, which ended Xerxes' hopes of conquering Greece. He won the prize with his first entry in the tragedy competition, at the age of twenty-eight. He had a distinguished public career at Athens; he was elected to serve two terms as a general, one as State Treasurer and one as Special State Commissioner. He was selected to compete at the annual Festival of Dionysos on approximately thirty occasions, and won the first prize eighteen times. He lived almost to the end of the twenty-four-year Peloponnesian War between Athens and Sparta; he died in 406 BC, at the age of ninety, leaving *Oidipous at Kolonos* to be produced posthumously by his grandson.

MICHAEL EWANS read Classics at Oxford and wrote his Cambridge PhD thesis on Aischylos. He was appointed in 1973 to a Lectureship in Classics at the University of Newcastle, Australia, and began teaching Drama when the discipline was introduced there in 1974. He became Associate Professor of Drama in 1982, was Head of the Department of Drama from 1982 to 1985, and is now Associate Professor of Drama and Music, with special responsibility for developing postgraduate studies. His publications include scholarly articles and programme notes on Greek tragedy and opera, his other main research field, and five books: *Janáček's Tragic Operas* (1977), *Wagner and Aeschylus* (1982), *Georg Büchner's 'Woyzeck'* (1989), and the Everyman Classics editions of *Aeschylus: 'Oresteia'* and *Aeschylus: Suppliants and other Dramas*. He has directed and supervised numerous productions of Greek tragedy, twentieth-century drama (especially expressionist plays) and opera.

GRAHAM LEY read Classics at Oxford and took his MPhil in Renaissance Historical Studies at the Warburg Institute in London. From 1977 he was Lecturer in Drama at the University of London, Goldsmiths' College, and was Australian Studies Fellow in Drama at the University of New South Wales in 1984. In 1986 he took up the post of Lecturer in Greek Literature in the University of Auckland, where he founded a training company, Sigma Theatre. From 1990 he became a text-writer and editor for Hutchinson Reference (Helicon), and was a supervisor for the faculties of English and Classics at Cambridge from 1994 to 1995. In 1995 he was appointed to a Lectureship in Drama at the University of Exeter. He has adapted and translated a number of Greek tragedies, directed in Auckland and Cambridge, and published many studies of ancient performance, including *A Short Introduction to the Ancient Greek Theater* (1991). He also writes on theatrical theory, in *From Mimesis to Interculturalism: Readings of Theatrical Theory Before and After Modernism* (1999) and, with Jane Milling, *Performance and Theory* (2000). He has been a consultant to professional productions of Greek tragedy, to the director John Barton, and to the Theatre Museum in London.

GREGORY MCCART studied English Literature and Classics at the University of Queensland, Australia. His involvement in the university drama society led him to a career training theatre practitioners and lecturing on Theatre Studies. He has been an actor and a playwright and has directed over forty university productions for the stage. He has translated, directed and performed ancient Greek drama and his commissioned translation of Euripides' *Medeia* was premiered by the Sydney Theatre Company in 1996. In recent years, he has explored the design, manufacture and use of the Greek tragic mask in performance and has conducted numerous workshops on the mask. He currently teaches at the University of Southern Queensland where, after serving as Head of Theatre Department and Associate Dean (Resources) in the Faculty of Arts for many years, he is currently Associate Professor, Director of the Performance Centre (www.usq.edu.au/performancecentre) and Chair of the University's Academic Board.

CHRONOLOGY OF SOPHOKLES' LIFE

Year	Age	Life
c. 496		Sophokles born at Kolonos, a northern suburb of Athens
480	16	Leads the *choros* for the victory sacrifice at Salamis
468	28	Wins with his first entry in the tragedy competition

CHRONOLOGY OF SOPHOKLES' TIMES

Year	Artistic & Historical Events
508	Reforms of Kleisthenes initiate democracy at Athens
501	Performances of tragedy incorporated into the Festival of Dionysos
490	First Persian Invasion of Greece, repelled by Athenian victory at Marathon
480	Second Persian invasion of Greece under Xerxes; unsuccessful defence of Thermopylai by King Leonidas of Sparta; sack of Athens by the Persians; decisive Greek victory at Salamis; withdrawal of Xerxes
478	Athenians form the Delian League, the basis for their developing empire
472	Aischylos, *Persians*
469	Delian League victory over the Persians ends their threat to the Aigeian
467	Aischylos, *Laios, Oidipous, Seven against Thebes, Sphinx*
463	Aischylos, Danaid tetralogy
462	Ephialtes and Perikles curtain the powers of the Areopagos
461	Ephialtes assassinated; unsuccessful siege of Ithome by Sparta; the pro-Spartan statesman Kimon leads Athenian support troops, and is ostracized after his return; alliance between Athens and Argos
460–45	First Peloponnesian War
458	Aischylos, *Oresteia*

Year	Age	Life
c. 450–30	46–66	*Aias*
443/2	53	State Treasurer
441–39	55–7	General against Samos. Sails to fetch reinforcements from Chios and Lesbos
438	58	Wins the tragedy competition, probably with *Antigone*
438/7	59–60	General against the Samian dissidents at Anaia
431	65	Second in tragic competition
430	66	?*Young Women of Trachis*
425	71	?*Oidipous the King*
421	75	Instals cult of Asklepios at his home

Year	Artistic & Historical Events
456/5	Aischylos dies at Gela in Sicily
455	Euripides competes for the first time
449	Peace of Kallias ends hostilities with Persia
443	Ostracism of Thoukydides, son of Milesisas; Perikles becomes Athens' leading politician
441	Samian revolt from the Athenian Empire
439/8	Revolt on Samos put down by Perikles
438	Euripides second with four dramas including *Alkestis*, his first surviving drama
432	Athenian alliance with Kerkyra
431	Attika invaded by Peloponnesians; start of the (second) Peloponnesian War Aischylos' son Euphorion wins; Euripides is last with *Medeia*, his (lost) *Philoktetes*, and other dramas
430	First outbreak of the great plague at Athens
429	Euripides, *Hippolytos*, first version (not performed) Death of Perikles
428	Euripides, *Hippolytos*; second version performed
425	Kleon becomes Athens' leading politician Aristophanes, *Acharnians* (his first surviving comedy)
424	Aristophanes, *Knights*
422	Death of Kleon Aristophanes, *Wasps*
421	Peace of Nikias between Athens and Sparta Aristophanes, *Peace*
420	Athens/Argos alliance
416	Athenians sack Melos
415	Euripides, *Women of Troy* Athenian expedition to Sicily

Year	Age	Life
413	83	*Elektra*? Serves as magistrate (Special State Commissioner)
409	87	*Philoktetes*
406	90	Dies
401		*Oidipous at Kolonos* produced posthumously

Year	Artistic & Historical Events
c.414	Euripides, *Iphigeneia among the Taurians*
414	Aristophanes, *Birds* Sparta resumes hostilities against Athens
413	Athenian defeat by Syracuse
412	Euripides, *Helene*
411	(January) Aristophanes, *Lysistrata* (March) Aristophanes, *Thesmophoriazousai* (May) Right-wing coup at Athens; government of 'The Four Hundred'; (August) 'Four Hundred' expelled and replaced by moderate oligarchy of 'The Five Thousand'
410	Restoration of full democracy at Athens
408	Euripides, *Orestes*
408/7	Euripides leaves Athens for the court of Archelaos in Makedonia
406	Euripides dies, leaving *Bakchai* and *Iphigeneia at Aulis* unperformed
405	Aristophanes, *Frogs* Final defeat of Athens at Aigispotamoi
404	Surrender of Athens and installation of Spartan-backed Junta, 'The Thirty'
403	Restoration of democracy and general amnesty

INTRODUCTION

Sophokles was recognized in his own lifetime as a master of tragic performance. He beat Aischylos in the first year he competed, at the age of twenty-eight. The Athenian judges never placed him third (last) in the competitions, and he won first prize eighteen times. Since each tragedian presented four dramas each time he was selected to compete, seventy-two out of the one hundred and twenty-three dramas that Sophokles is known to have written were regarded as outstanding. He also won elected political offices five times in his middle and old age – once (in 413) during a major crisis – which suggests that he was well known, and well liked, in a highly volatile and faction-ridden democracy. This was all the more a remarkable achievement, because the conservative view of Sophokles as loftily detached, concerned with 'timeless' or 'universal' themes is mistaken; all seven surviving dramas engage with issues central to contemporary Athenian political, social and religious life. We must therefore also shed views of Sophokles that see him writing at a distance from controversy.

For most of the period since his rediscovery in the Renaissance, Sophokles has been celebrated for his sublime poetry and his portrayal of character. Many literary critics have concurred with Aristotle's view that he is the finest Athenian tragedian,[1] and some have openly displayed a preference for his work on the grounds that it is supposedly less theatrical – or at least less dependent for its impact on theatrical effects – than the surviving dramas of Aischylos and Euripides. However, German scholarship throughout the twentieth century has taken a signifi-

---

[1] *Poetics* 55a18, 56a27. Aristotle repeatedly uses *OKing* (see p. lxxx for the key to the abbreviations) as his favourite example of ideal tragic procedures, and his strong focus on plot as the primary element in tragedy (esp. 50a37) also reflects a high regard for this particularly plot-centred tragedy.

cant interest in these aspects of tragedy;[2] and in 1977 Taplin's influential *The Stagecraft of Aeschylus* placed the visual dimension firmly on the agenda of English-speaking scholarship. Subsequently, Seale's *Vision and Stagecraft in Sophocles* attempted to treat Sophokles in similar terms. However, this book is limited by its predominant focus on the use of words for seeing and vision; and by the fact that his many suggestions on staging were not tested in production.[3]

The present volume is the first of two designed to place Sophokles' texts firmly in their original theatrical context, as scripts for performance.[4] This Editor's Introduction provides an overview of his cultural context, aims, and use of the theatre space, followed by an examination of the subject-matter for each drama, and the main devices used to dramatize it.[5] The translators' Notes to each individual drama provide a more detailed consideration of the objectives of each Scene and Choros, together with proposals about the ways in which Sophokles used the actors to realize these in the performance space.

Sophokles the Athenian

Sophokles' seven surviving dramas date from one of the most turbulent and significant places and times in the history of western civilization. His native city was the world's first democracy; in 480 BC, when Sophokles was sixteen, the Athenian navy secured the independence of Europe from the Middle East, when it delivered the decisive blow to Xerxes' attempt to conquer mainland Greece.[6] Over the next fifty years Athens gradually

[2] Dramatic technique plays a major part in the work of Tycho von Wilamowitz, Reinhardt, Lesky, Steidle and Melchinger. Unfortunately, of all their books only Reinhardt's 1933 *Sophokles*, less impressive than his *Aischylos als Regisseur und Theologe*, has been translated into English (Reinhardt 1979).

[3] Seale 1982. Seale's adherence to the now discredited idea of a raised stage would have made many of his suggestions almost impossible to reconcile with the script – and sometimes with each other – in workshop or production.

[4] These two books develop the approach initiated in the two-volume translation of Aischylos, Ewans 1995 and 1996a. For the second Sophokles volume see Further Reading under Ewans (ed.) 2000.

[5] Below, pp. xxxv ff.

[6] Sophokles was chosen to lead the victory dance after the Battle of Salamis (see Chronology above, p. viii). The Persian invasion, which Aischylos drama-

reformed the Delian League, at first an alliance of Aigeian naval cities against the remaining threat of Persian aggression, into an empire of subject 'allies' who paid tribute to Athens and were required to adopt political and social institutions acceptable to the Athenians. During this period Athens evolved an extraordinarily radical democracy, became the richest city in Greece, and was the site of breathtaking achievements in tragedy, architecture, sculpture and painting. The city also became a magnet for Greek intellectuals, many from smaller cities, and it was the centre for rapid advances in the new fields of history, medicine, mathematics and philosophy.

These achievements were bought at an enormous price. The arrogance of the Athenians and their domination of the Aigeian Sea provoked revolts by subject allies, and bred increasing fear in Korinth, Sparta, Thebes and other, smaller cities with less democratic political systems and more conservative governments. These led to two sustained wars between Athens and Sparta. The alliance in 461 between Athens and the other major democratic state, Argos, provoked the inconclusive first war (460–45 BC); but the second, protracted war with Sparta and its Peloponnesian allies, which broke out in 431, was fought continuously (with the exception of the 'Peace of Nikias' from 421 to 414) until it ended with the total defeat and surrender of Athens in 404, shortly after Sophokles' death.

The contemporary Athenian historian Thoukydides argued that Athens had the resources and the potential to win the war with relative ease, but dissipated its opportunities after the death of Perikles due to systemic weaknesses of the democracy and poor leadership.[7] The internal politics of Athens were polarized during the war; many well-born Athenians became increasingly nervous about the directions in which democracy was leading them, and the massive defeat of the expedition to Sicily in 413 precipitated action from the right. First came the temporarily successful coup of 411, in which democratic government was replaced by 400 selected individuals of aristocratic blood; then, after the surrender in 404, Sparta installed a vindictive and ruthless junta. Although a democracy was subsequently

tized in *Persians*, later formed the subject of the *Histories* by Sophokles' contemporary and friend, Herodotos.

[7] *Histories* 2.65.

restored, it was muted in comparison with the achievements of the fifth century.

Tragedy and comedy were directly affected by, and responded to, these events. Aischylos celebrated democratic Argos in the Danaid trilogy of 463;[8] his most famous work, the *Oresteia* of 458, tackled the issues raised by a major recent constitutional crisis, and ends both with a prophecy of future glory for Athens and a warning – which went unheeded later in the century – against excesses either of anarchy or oligarchy. Similarly, Sophokles in *Antigone* condemned by obvious implication an atrocity against Samian rebels, which was committed on Perikles' orders at Miletos in 439.[9] Although the drama won first prize, the Athenian record on what we would now call basic human rights deteriorated further during the Peloponnesian War, and in 415 Euripides used his contribution to the festival to make a searing indictment of further Athenian atrocities committed during the sack of Melos in the previous year (*Women of Troy*). In domestic politics, several later dramas by both Sophokles and Euripides (especially Sophokles' *Elektra* and Euripides' *Orestes*) delivered scathing critiques of the 'new amorality' of utterly ruthless aristocrats who valued nothing else but their own profit.

The work of all three tragedians presupposes an open democracy in which the dramatist could use all his theatrical powers to illuminate dilemmas, moral issues and debates for his fellow-citizens.[10] Tragedy and comedy went into decline after the extinction of democracy at Athens in 404. The next generation failed to continue tragedy at the level achieved by Sophokles and Euripides; Aristophanes' genius is muted in the two comedies that survive from after the fall of Athens (*Wealth* and *Assemblywomen*); and the politically and socially bland 'New

---

[8] The first drama of this trilogy, *Suppliants*, survives; see Ewans 1996a.

[9] For the date and context of *Ant* see below, p. liv.

[10] The same is true of comedy; but this more direct medium, in which even leading contemporary politicians could be portrayed, and subjected to savage lampoons (e.g. Aristophanes, *Knights*), occasionally cut too close to home. Although they are both masterly comedies, there is noticeably less bite to Aristophanes' satire in *Lysistrata* and *Thesmophoriazousai*, which were created during the brief period when a law was in force prohibiting direct attack on named Athenians.

Comedy' evolved later in the fourth century as the preferred medium of entertainment.

In the tragedies of Aischylos (and the victory songs of his contemporary Pindar), men and women move on earth surrounded by divine powers. It is implied, as it is in Homer, that the great personages of early myth, some of whom were sons and daughters of gods, were in closer contact with the divine than the Greeks of the early fifth century, and the gods sometimes appeared to them in visible form; but it is also implied that in their daily life the poets and their audiences were surrounded and sometimes possessed by many invisible gods and *daimones*[11] who react to human behaviour; they are propitiated by worship, and are angered by neglect or defiance of their powers. Their reactions have effect in turn on subsequent events, and sooner or later *dike* will be achieved – a concept that does not possess the righteous overtones of the nearest English word 'justice', but does at least imply that in the long run actions have consequences, and wrongdoers receive their deserts.[12]

In the later fifth century these assumptions were eroded. Pressure came from three directions: first, the tendency to marvel at and celebrate the powers of human beings, as the Greeks began to appreciate the greatness of their own military and scientific achievements;[13] second, the scepticism about anthropomorphic gods, divine causation of human events and divine justice, which was a natural result of scientific enquiry;[14] and third the events of the Peloponnesian War, with their sudden reversals of situation and the demolition of former certainties. The Greek world seemed to have suffered a drastic acceleration

---

[11] All italicized Greek terms are defined in the Glossary.

[12] This theme is fundamental to the *Oresteia*; Ewans 1995, xxvii–xxxiv. Sophokles' contemporary Herodotos maintained basically this structure of belief into the next generation. His subject was the defeat of Persia's greatness by relatively insignificant Greek forces, and the events of 480–79 may well have led many other Greeks to join Aischylos (*Persians*) in speculating that the gods must have opposed Xerxes' venture, and asking why.

[13] 'Man is the measure of all things' said the philosopher Protagoras; Sophokles memorably appropriated for mankind the word *deinos*, previously used only of the gods and of divinely caused natural phenomena, in *Ant* Choros 2 (see Notes below, p. 215).

[14] Cf. Barnes 1982, esp. 82ff., 136ff., 450ff.

of pace, akin in some ways to that created by our own contemporary information explosion; and while the Athenians, with their seemingly boundless energy, spirit of enquiry and innovative skill, were better placed than any other city to work within the new climate, the bases of their political and social morality were undermined.

In Thoukydides' analysis, the plague of 431 began this process:

> The catastrophe overwhelmed people so much that, not knowing what might happen to them, they became indifferent to all that was sacred and holy. Past funeral practices were disrupted, and each buried his dead as best he could. Many turned to utterly shameless methods, because they lacked the necessities for decent burial, having already had to cope with many other deaths . . .
>
> This plague was also the beginning of a greater disregard for law and custom throughout the city. Seeing the sudden changes in fortune of the rich who died suddenly, and of others who had previously had no possessions, but immediately inherited their wealth, people now dared to seek their own pleasure in ways they had previously repressed. They decided to spend their money quickly and on enjoyment, since they reckoned both their bodies and their possessions were ephemeral. Nobody was eager to strive after a reputation for nobility; they felt it was unclear whether you would live long enough to get one. The pleasure of the moment and anything which might contribute to it were now established as being 'noble' and 'valuable'. Neither fear of the gods nor human laws prevented this; people judged that it did not matter whether you worshipped the gods or not, seeing that death came equally to everyone; and nobody expected to live long enough to be tried and punished. They felt that a far graver sentence had already been passed and hung over them, and it was perfectly reasonable to get some pleasure out of life before it fell.[15]

Our sources for Athenian life and thought in the remainder of the century are the richest for any time and place in ancient Greek history, and they all confirm that there was increasing

---

[15] Thoukydides, *Histories* 2.52–3 (Editor's translation).

scepticism about the existence or the efficacy of the gods. Partly in consequence, a ruthlessly selfish amorality developed.[16]

Sophokles' surviving dramas are totally enmeshed with the complex and highly confrontational shifts of perspective that engulfed Athenian society during his adult life. The four tragedies collected here belong to his full maturity, a period when Athens was still at or near the peak of its prosperity; the three reserved for the second volume belong to a different period, in which politics and society were more polarized – the ruthless paraded themselves with less fear of sanction, new arguments were devised to justify more extreme actions, and the search for any basis for morality had become more difficult.[17]

These four dramas revolve almost obsessively around five themes, which reflect central problems in contemporary Athenian society:[18] the suddenness with which situational change may occur – the concept which since Jones' classic analysis[19] has been known as 'mutability' (especially *Young Women of Trachis, Oidipous the King*); the tensions between loyalties to *philoi* and loyalty to the *polis* (especially *Antigone*); the importance even in wartime of some fundamental human decencies – in particular, the right to burial (*Aias, Antigone*); the destructive power of human emotions – in particular hatred (*Aias*) and physical love (*Young Women of Trachis, Antigone*); and the question whether the gods ever intervene in human affairs.

To this last question Sophokles says yes; but the interventions of the gods in these four dramas are so unpleasant that Thoukydides' cynical atheism seems almost easier to live with.[20] Aias,

---

[16] Cf. e.g. Orestes and Elektra in *El*; Orestes in Euripides, *Andromache*; Philokleon in Aristophanes, *Wasps*, the Athenians in Thoukydides' Melian Dialogue, 5. 84ff. Further discussion in Ewans 2000, Introduction.

[17] We have deliberately separated between the two volumes the three dramas set at Thebes. Far from being a 'trilogy' of linked dramas (as they have often, wrongly, been described), *Ant, OKing* and *OKol* represent three distinct uses of the same body of myth, at widely separated periods in Sophokles' life, to reflect quite different attitudes to the world.

[18] Four of them feature in Thoukydides' analysis, quoted above; for erotic passion cf. Euripides, *Medeia* and *Hippolytos*, Plato, *Symposion*.

[19] 1962, esp. 174–7 on *YWT*.

[20] Thoukydides' *History*, unlike any of its predecessors, has no place for gods in its analysis of human behaviour – except when men superstitiously allow religious beliefs to determine their actions, e.g. Nikias at 7.50. Williams (1993, 163–4) rightly draws out the affinity between the historian and our playwright,

the greatest Greek hero after Achilleus, once claimed not to need the help in battle of the goddess of wisdom; for having slighted Athena, he is maddened for twenty-four hours (750ff.). During this time he attempts vengeance on the sons of Atreus, fails, slaughters animals instead, and feels that he then has no option but to abandon his *philoi* and commit suicide. In *Antigone*, the gods indicate their displeasure with Kreon, and he pays a terrible price for preventing the burial of Polyneikes; but the gods do nothing to save the young woman who gives her life for their 'unwritten laws';[21] three lives and two families are destroyed.

In the first words of *Young Women of Trachis* Deianeira tells the audience that she knows her whole fate before she is dead. She is cruelly undeceived; her inability to welcome into the house her husband's new, younger mistress leads to her suicide, and his death in intolerable agony. In this drama the gods do not even indicate their displeasure, as Athena does in *Aias* by maddening the hero, and as the protectors of the dead do in *Antigone* by sending the dust-storm, and the omens which alert Teiresias. The death of Herakles is, appropriately, the result of the poisoned vengeance of another, equally highly sexed creature whom he once killed. But it merely fulfils some oracles from long ago. Particular point is made of the gods' indifference both by the sick pun in the words given from the sacred oak at Dodona (1169ff.), and by Hyllos' justifiably bitter complaint that Zeus is shamed by ignoring the painful death of his own son (1272).

Finally we confront Sophokles' extraordinary reinflection of the myth of Oidipous. At the start of *Oidipous the King* the gods send a plague, which indicates their displeasure with Thebes for continuing to harbour an incestuous parricide; by

---

and contrasts them both with the philosophers (Plato and Aristotle believed that if properly understood the world can yield a pattern that makes sense of human life): 'Each of them represents human beings as dealing sensibly, foolishly, sometimes catastrophically, sometimes nobly, with a world that is only partially intelligible to human agency and in itself is not necessarily well adjusted to ethical practices. In this perspective the difference between a Sophoclean obscurity of fate and Thucydides' sense of rationality at risk to chance is not so significant.'

[21] Antigone herself points this out bitterly, just before she is led off to death; 921ff.

taking steps to avert this plague, Oidipous begins to discover his hidden past. Apollo once simply prophesied that – for no reason at all – Laios' son will kill his father and marry his mother (711ff.). Oidipous has in fact done this; but the Elders are so perturbed, as the action of the drama misleadingly seems to indicate that this appalling oracle has not come true, that they pray for it to be fulfilled.

In each of the surviving dramas the plot gradually leads the characters through to a moment of revelation, when – as Ezra Pound put it, translating the climax of *Young Women of Trachis* extremely freely to bring out Sophokles' central point – 'IT ALL COHERES';[22] in Homeric terms, a *moira* has taken shape.[23] Gradually, freely chosen human actions and interactions lead to a point where a particular oracle or divine prophecy is proved to be true (*Aias, Young Women of Trachis, Oidipous the King*), or an action which is deeply offensive has incurred the terrible consequences which a prophet foresaw (*Antigone*). The gods stand aloof, remote from human affairs – Athena's startling appearance at the opening of *Aias* always excepted. If a particular mortal action offends them, they may give an indication of their displeasure: twice by sending a plague, and once by sending madness; elsewhere their role is confined to prophecy.

These dramas present a singularly bleak world-view,[24] very far from the 'comfortable' Sophokles whom many older critics adopted from a joke in Aristophanes.[25] The dramatist pictures life as in constant flux, and human beings as extremely limited in their power and their knowledge. The immanent gods of Aischylos' integrated universe are no longer present, and the gods intervene in Sophokles only when a human action has offended against one of a few fundamental taboos. This was a

---

[22] Pound 1969, 66.

[23] *Iliad* 6.489. Ewans 1996b analyses the fundamental role of this pattern in Homer, Sophokles and Shakespeare.

[24] Charles Segal (1981, viii) was the first to give due recognition to the savage, almost nihilistic elements in Sophoklean tragedy.

[25] *Frogs* 82; 'Dionysos' says that Sophokles (who had died about a year before the performance) 'was comfortable ['*eukolos*'] on earth, and is comfortable down there [i.e. in Haides]'. I suspect that Aristophanes refers to Sophokles' character, not his dramas; there is anecdotal evidence that Sophokles was one of those creative artists whose work presents a grim vision, but who are genial and relaxed in private life. Ion of Chios, Fragment 6; cf. Plato *Republic* 329b–c.

time when rationalist, 'enlightened' thought at Athens was particularly severe in its attacks on both oracles and prophets. Apparently Sophokles, in this period of his maturity, expected his audiences to find consolation in the reassurance that in his dramas prophecies turn out to be true, and there is some limited pattern in the universe – even if the consequences seem, from a human point of view, to be monstrously disproportionate (Herakles) or totally unjustified (Oidipous).

A generation ago, some critics tried to counteract this grim picture by claiming that Antigone, Aias, Oidipous and Herakles accept their fates with a redeeming, heroic endurance.[26] It is perhaps understandable that readers should want something positive to cling to in middle-period Sophokles; but the blunt fact is that only one of these four characters, Aias, says any words that might remotely justify this consoling vision. Antigone goes to her death protesting the injustice of her fate; Oidipous and Herakles remain agonized, and they are not consoled by the knowledge that their excruciating sufferings fulfil oracles given long ago. All three characters' final scenes stretch actors to the limits; but in rehearsal and performance their angry responses seem absolutely right.

Sophokles in his theatre

Sophokles was a dramatist; he used performance to express his meaning. His medium was a poetic tragedy, in which lyric and spoken verse alternated according to the degree of intensity of the action and of the characters' emotions;[27] his dramas were performed in the Theatre of Dionysos at Athens, a large open-air performance space whose *theatron* seated around 17,000 spectators, arranged by tribal affiliation on five banks of steeply raked tiers of wooden benches.[28] Their seating surrounded two thirds of the circumference of a flat circular *orchêstra*, around twenty metres in diameter, on which up to three solo male

[26] E.g. Whitman 1951, Knox 1964.

[27] This series of translations marks the difference by double-indenting all verses that were sung in the original performance.

[28] The theatre was not equipped with the expensive rows of curved marble seating, familiar from the appearance of the well-preserved theatre at Epidavros, until the fourth century. Newcomers to Greek tragedy should not be misled in this respect by the references in older textbooks to a 'Periklean' reconstruction.

actors (playing the parts of the individual characters) and a *choros* of fifteen actors (playing the part of a collective character), sometimes with silent extras, enacted the dramas.[29]

Athenian actors wore masks, to communicate to spectators up to a hundred metres distant the age and gender of the character portrayed. Acting in mask imposes restraints on the actor, by negating the face as the principal tool for communication. It also liberates the actor's body, through its demands for a very physical form of performance in which the mask, limbs and torso combine to tell the story and delineate character. Working in a replica of that space rapidly demonstrates, to anyone not prejudiced by the traditional view of Greek tragedy as stylized, static and word-bound, that these texts demand a great deal of movement for their effective realization. The size of the *orchêstra* and the outdoor venue both require athletic performance; posture and gesture are important, but the primary means for communicating meaning was relative positioning and movement in the circular performance space.[30]

This round performance space lay in front of a *skene*, a wooden building with one pair of double doors – the only place from which sudden entrances could be made.[31] There were two flanking *parodoi*, entrance ways which by convention led either (actor right, audience left) to the countryside and/or overseas, or (actor left, audience right) to the downtown area of the place in which the action was set.

The *skene* building was equipped with the *ekkyklêma*, a device for displaying tableaux preset indoors, used by Sophokles

[29] Since publication of the standard work on the Theatre of Dionysos (Pickard-Cambridge 1946) there has been vigorous debate, in particular on the shape of the *orchêstra*. I argued at Ewans 1995, xviii for a circular *orchêstra*, and added more bibliography at Ewans 1996, xxiii. See now also the comprehensive discussion in Wiles 1997, 23–62, which should settle the issue.

[30] Ewans 1995, xxvi. In masked acting, the actor must be aware that, although the mask is a theatrical tool in performance, it is also a unique artifact itself which needs to be 'read' and appreciated by the spectators. Calame (1986, 141) considers that the mask was used as an essential intermediary between actor and spectator so that myth could be enacted.

[31] I cannot accept Wiles' unorthodox view (1997, 52) that the *skene* did not lie at a tangent on the circumference of the *orchêstra*, but cut across and occupied a segment of the back of the circle. The archaeological evidence does not require this assumption, and performance considerations militate strongly against it.

in *Aias* and *Elektra*, and possibly in *Antigone*.[32] Just beside or behind the *skene* was the base of the *mechane*, a crane for the appearance of gods; this was installed in or before 431 BC, when Euripides almost certainly used it in the Finale of *Medeia*. Sophokles did not use it in a surviving tragedy until *Philoktetes* (409).

The performance space was circular because it was a dance-floor;[33] in all other respects it was designed to symbolize the dynamics of the meeting-spaces of real life. The open air was the centre for encounter, dialogue and debate; in Athens, the political assembly, the law-courts, the business of the executive and some religious ceremonials all took place in the *agora* or market-place. The audience encircled and looked down into the *orchêstra*; with its three access points, this playing space symbolized the point of encounter between people coming from outside the *polis*, inside the *polis* and from inside the principal characters' *oikos*.[34]

The dialogue between these three means of entry is often central to Sophokles' meaning. In *Aias* a dynamic opening is achieved when two characters enter one from each *parodos*, and meet in front of Aias' tent; the action then crystallizes around the issue of whether Aias should be brought out from inside the *skene* to join them. The second half of the drama is refocused around the centre of the *orchêstra*, where Aias' body now lies;[35] the *skene* is ignored, since the scene is now a deserted seashore, and the last scenes are a dialogue between *philoi* of Aias, who enter from the direction of his tent and territory, and seek to take his body back there, and characters entering from the

[32] See Notes below, pp. 183 and 240.

[33] On circular dancing see Davidson 1986; also Wiles 1997, 87ff. Wiles goes too far when he attempts to argue *ibid.* that all choreography consisted simply of movements of a *choros* arranged in a segment of a circle, first anti-clockwise in each *strophe* and then back clockwise in the *antistrophe*; but it is almost certain that the dance for an *antistrophe* matched that of its previous, corresponding *strophe*; for a worked example from Aischylos cf. Ewans 1995, 133–4.

[34] There is further discussion of the performance implications of the configuration of the Theatre of Dionysos at Ewans 1995, xviii ff. We do not accept the model developed by Wiles 1997 (cf. e.g. 131 on *YWT*). It is too simple in one way, since the audience members were *not* all positioned behind the *orchêstra*; and too complex in another, since it obscures the fundamental dialogue between the three means of access to the performance space.

[35] For this (surprisingly controversial) staging see below, pp. 191–3.

foreign part of the camp, who dem
out unburied.

Antigone makes even more striking u
between right, centre and left entrances, pa
handling of Kreon, who despite being the (new) ru
is disempowered from full possession of the royal pa
contrast both *Young Women of Trachis* and *Oidipous the*
leave the left *parodos* virtually unused. These dramas lack a
effective political dimension, since in neither is the audience
made to feel the presence to their right of a downtown camp or
city, as in *Aias* and *Antigone*. The dramatic focus is skewed, to
become a two-way interplay between arrivals from the countryside or from other cities, and the impact that their presence
makes on the inhabitants of the principal characters' *oikos*.[37]

The front–back axis joins three areas of different strength: the
relatively weak extreme front, where the actor's mask can only
be seen by a small segment of the audience; the dominant, focal
centre point;[38] and the *skene* doors, which draw focus backwards when a character makes an entrance or exit through
them. Sophokles frequently exploits this polarization in specific
scenes;[39] he also uses the front–back axis to realize in performance the implications of the development of his plots. *Aias* is
polarized between a *skene*-focused first half, and a second half
that revolves around the corpse of Aias at the centre; but the
other three tragedies collected here gradually narrow their focus
in performance, from the full *orchêstra* in the opening scenes
towards a concentration near the *skene* building in the closing
scenes.[40]

[36] See below, pp. lii ff.

[37] See below, pp. lx and lxxiii.

[38] Ley and Ewans 1985; Wiles 1997, 63ff.

[39] E.g. the silent exits to suicide of Eurydike, Deianeira and Iokaste. All three
are written so as to be best played with a substantial exit walk, from the centre
or even further forward up to the *skene* doors, to emphasize the finality of their
departure and the way in which they have literally turned their backs on the life
outside.

[40] Although the overall pattern is different, *Ai* also uses, in the Finale, a
concentration of the Sailors, Tekmessa, Eurysakes and finally Teukros in the
rear segment, behind the corpse. Compare the Finale of *YWT*, with the
traumatized Herakles lying at the centre, and Hyllos behind him in the rear
segment; cf. Ley's Notes below, p. 263.

...ous the King, which
...nt and a priest at the
...rds them. There are of
...hich focus is drawn back
...intervention of Iokaste at
...een Kreon and Oidipous;[41]
...oints of focus, in active use,
...where Iokaste prays to Apollo
...moment the action is steadily
...first the Servant, then the blind
...sister-daughters emerge from it,
...ack into it at the close.

...features of Athenian dramatic tech-
nique o...   made special use: *agones*, *kommoi*,
'messenger-sp...   tableaux.[42]

The *agon* was a ... st between antagonists; it replicates, in
stylized form, the manner of debate which was at the heart of
Athenian political and judicial life. In the text these contests are
highly formal: usually a pair of matching speeches, one for each
antagonist (often in accusation and defence), is divided and
sometimes concluded by a deliberately bland two-line comment
from a member of the *choros*. It then ignites a *stichomythia*,
which in Sophokles almost always becomes an inflamed
exchange of insults leading to the departure of one character.
Antigone provides three exceptionally powerful such encounters, between Kreon and first Antigone, then Haimon and finally
Teiresias, which increasingly display Kreon's extremism and his
isolation.[43]

[41] Here a close female *philos*, played by the third actor, intervenes from the
skene to break up and refocus a quarrel in *stichomythia* between two other
principal characters. Sophokles had used this technique before, with enormous
power, in *Ant* Scene 3.

[42] Sophokles' use of the *choros* is not discussed in this general introduction,
partly because it has been the subject of two extended monographs (Burton
1980, Gardiner 1987; see also Scott 1996), and partly because our Notes engage
closely with the specific roles played by the *choros* character in individual Scenes
and Choroses.

[43] His isolation is emphasized by the way in which the *choros* of Councillors,
whom both Antigone and Kreon use in places as an audience in the first *agon*,
are completely marginalized in the exchanges with Teiresias. This increases the
shock after Teiresias has departed. When Kreon has finally been broken, he puts

To stage the long speeches in *agones*, directors and actors need to consider whether at any one point the speaker or the listener is predominant, and block accordingly. Very often the focal strength of the centre point is called for, and its special capacity for turning a character from powerless to powerful (or *vice versa*) is significant.[44] For example, the conflict between Haimon and Kreon requires the silent character in each speech to be placed at the centre, while the unsuccessful attempts of the other to persuade him are symbolized by increasingly agitated movements around the rest of the *orchêstra*. By contrast Teiresias requires the full power of the centre point for his final denunciation of Kreon.[45]

Sophokles sometimes uses *stichomythia* non-aggressively, to bring out facts;[46] but it is regularly employed at the climax of an *agon*, to dramatize the most intense part of the confrontation, crystallizing the irreconcilable opposition and (usually) forcing a departure. These sections demand a blocking in which each character moves one step closer to the other during his or her lines. One of the best examples is *Antigone* 508ff., which becomes an increasingly violent shouting match until Antigone turns the argument with the clinching, unanswerable line 523. This subsection requires an increasing invasion of personal space,[47] with each actor moving closer to the other until Antigone breaks out, turns and moves away to deliver 523 out, away from Kreon. Sophokles then symbolizes the deadlock formally; Kreon cannot rationally answer 523, so he is given two lines

himself in the hands of the Councillors he has ignored, threatened and despised for so long; 1091ff.

[44] The classic example is Aischylos, *Agamemnon* Scene 4, where Klytaimestra converts Agamemnon's central position on arrival from strength to weakness (Ewans 1995, 142ff.). The technique was vital to our realization of *Ant* Scene 3; pp. 217 below.

[45] Below, pp. 226 and 236. Cf. also e.g. Tekmessa and Aias, below pp. 185. The rare occasions when speakers are evenly balanced require symmetrical positioning; but this must be at an equal distance from the front, e.g. BR and BL. (If two characters are positioned e.g. BR and FL, the BR character is in the more powerful position, as his/her mask can be read by more of the audience.)

[46] E.g. *Ai* 36ff., *OKing* 726ff.

[47] Personal space intrusion works on a large scale in a twenty-metre circle. One actor looks as if he is intruding into another's space if he comes within 2.5 metres of him, rather than the one metre with which most modern directors work in smaller indoor theatres.

instead of one, chasing after her to try to have the last word; this finalizes the exchange in total deadlock. This deadlock is very strikingly broken, not by the expected departure but by the entry of a third character, Ismene, which takes the scene to a new and even more unpleasant climax before the two sisters are led away.[48]

Some exchanges become so emotional that at the climax the unit becomes even smaller than one line. For example at the climax of the *agon* between Aias and Tekmessa (*Aias* 591ff.), the exchanges break into half-lines; here the formal closure is symbolized by a one-and-a-half line final speech instead of two, before the unresolved clash is concluded by a departure.

When seeking resolution, Sophokles chooses the *kommos*, a formal lament in which the normal division between choral odes and spoken scenes is deliberately broken. In a *kommos*, a solo actor sings and dances, interacting with the *choros*, to communicate the enormity of his character's grief. In Greek society, public lamentation was normally the role of women and girls; it was therefore natural for Sophokles to compose a short *kommos* when Tekmessa brings out the news of Aias' madness to his Sailors (*Aias* 201ff.), and a longer one to explore Antigone's emotions, when she comes out from the *skene* on her way to death (*Antigone* 801ff.). Sophokles also uses the *kommos* to symbolize the disintegration of the male code of silent grief; four of his male principal characters break into lyric expression, three of them at the end of the drama, all suffering intensely: Aias at 348ff., Kreon at *Antigone* 1261ff., Herakles at *Young Women of Trachis* 984ff., and Oidipous at 1308ff.[49] In all these *kommoi* the stanzas vary in length and coherence to match the ebb and flow of the character's emotion;[50] directors and actors also need to be aware of the ways in which the responses of the *choros* character vary – sometimes supportive, sometimes detached, sometimes critical.

Every Sophoklean *kommos* is followed by a shift to spoken

[48] Cf. *OKing* 631ff. and 989ff. for other third actor interventions.

[49] At *YWT* 1072–5, Herakles makes explicit the fact that his 'moaning and crying' defy Greek gender norms.

[50] Different metres were used for dances of different degrees of intensity, so we occasionally draw attention in our Notes to the metre used in the original Greek lyrics, where it is significant.

dialogue; this usually begins with a long speech by the character who has just sung and danced, in which he or she calms down and reflects on his or her predicament.[51] The emotional but formally structured *kommos* is followed by a reflective, rational but free-form speech; this sequence encapsulates perfectly the constant dialogue and tension between expressions of emotion and of reason, which is at the heart of Greek tragedy.

One of the least understood procedures in Greek tragedy is the convention known as the 'messenger-speech'. This has seemed, both to modern critics and to theatre practitioners, to present the Athenians at their most logocentric, preferring extended speech to enactment.

The practice needs understanding rather than defence. All Athenians, both male and female, had far more exposure to the violence endemic in human life than most inhabitants of first-world countries today. Every male from the age of eighteen fought regularly, usually each year, hand to hand to defend his country; every female from the age of around thirteen became initiated into the realities of childbearing, in a society where medicine was primitive by modern western standards. The ancient Greeks saw far more bloodshed and human suffering than most modern westerners do; it is no surprise that their epic poetry, their vase-painting and their comedy depict directly, objectively and realistically all aspects of human life. They include quite naturally scenes of violent death and serious injury, sexuality and (in Aristophanes) even excretion, which many later western societies have censored, or voluntarily omitted from their art.

For this reason, I have long believed that the tragedians' preference for messenger-speeches over enacted violence was not due (as used to be alleged) to squeamishness or a sense of decorum. The actions described in these speeches happened indoors or across a broad panorama, and were in any case so horribly violent that they could not be credibly enacted.[52] Where

---

[51] Again, *Ant* provides a striking variant. Antigone's *kommos* does 'end' with a speech in that she comes to terms with her fate (891ff.); but suddenly the music resumes (929), and she is dragged off to her death.

[52] Characteristically, Sophokles risked a blatant violation of this aesthetic, when the suicide of Aias took place in plain sight of the audience. See below, p. 192.

possible, tableaux showing the consequences of such violence could be prepared inside the *skene* and exhibited on the *ekkyklêma*, and Sophokles on one occasion made extremely radical use of this convention, when he exhibited Aias surrounded by the bloody carcasses of slaughtered animals.

To evoke violence in action, no medium before the major advances in cinematic illusion since the 1950s could compete with the power of ordered, structured narration. It is quite wrong to suppose that Sophokles' great narratives could have been delivered as static rhetorical displays. The descriptions of self-inflicted death in three of these dramas – by the Bodyguard in *Antigone* (1192ff.), the Nurse in *Young Women of Trachis* (899ff.), and the Servant in *Oidipous the King* (1237ff.) – all require a whole-hearted immersion of the actor's body in the story, and subtle movement around the *orchêstra*. The actor must also possess a flair for impersonation, since these speeches contain passages of direct speech, where the narrator must throw himself or herself into the characters of people, most of whom the audience have previously seen for themselves. The narratives also frequently demand enactment in mime of the postures and gestures taken up by the subject of the story, as he or she prepares to commit suicide.[53]

The 'messenger-speech' is a vital part of Sophokles' dramatic technique. Just as *agones* climax in *stichomythia*, so too on a larger scale these speeches are preparatory to a climax, and designed to work the emotional temperature up towards it. They are always followed by the entry or re-entry for a *kommos* of a broken man, the survivor of the suicide that has just been narrated (Kreon, Herakles, Oidipous); the actor playing this role must be able to take over the impetus of the previous speech and make the suffering, which his character has incurred as a result of the events narrated, real to the audience. It is precisely because 'messenger-speeches' were so powerful in their own evocation of the horrors that have taken place that the demands in the Finale on the actor playing the principal role are so enormous.[54]

---

[53] For the specific performance requirements of these three speeches see our Notes below: pp. 237–8, 261 and 296–8 respectively.

[54] Narrative is of course not only confined to characters whose sole function is to be messengers. Over and over in these dramas the past bears in on the

Drama is the ideal medium for a creative artist who wishes to portray mutability; stage pictures can be formed and re-formed to reflect constant flux. Sophokles therefore sometimes deliberately crystallizes the states of his characters, at particular stages in each drama, in memorable tableaux and stage pictures.[55] He also varies the appearance of characters who leave and re-enter, to convey the changes in their situation. For example, Aias is seen first maddened, covered in blood and brandishing a whip, then dejected, lying among the slaughtered animals on the *ekkyklêma*. He next appears still bloodstained, and carrying – ominously – the sword of Hektor; on his final reappearance he still has the sword, but both he and it are now cleansed. After his death, his corpse remains central to the action, and a further tableau is formed when Tekmessa and Eurysakes take up positions behind it, ritually guarding Aias while the argument rages between Teukros and the sons of Atreus. Only at the end is the procession finally formed, which enacts the successful removal of Aias' body for burial.

Change in the principal characters' appearance is also fundamental to registering the changes in their state throughout *Antigone*. We found it desirable to vary Antigone's appearance to match her condition at each of her three entries: first proudly confident, then bloodied but still defiant, and finally pathetic;[56] and it was essential to change Kreon from the crisp, commanding figure of the earlier scenes to a broken man, covered in dirt and in his son's blood, when he carries in Haimon's body for the Finale. Sophokles has kept the stage picture in more or less constant flux;[57] now in the Finale it takes solid form. Kreon is trapped literally between the corpses of his son and his wife, and faced symbolically with the permanent reality that his family has been completely destroyed.

Tableaux dominate two scenes of *Young Women of Trachis*. In Scene 2 Sophokles creates another literal representation of

---

present, and principal characters too must enact and make vivid an account of other events. Cf. e.g. Tekmessa (*Ai* 284ff.), the Guard (*Ant* 407ff.), Deianeira (*YWT* 555ff.), and Oidipous (*OKing* 771ff.).

[55] Cf. Taplin 1978, 108ff.

[56] See Notes, pp. 204 and 217.

[57] See however the suggestion for Antigone's position, in the long part of Scene 3 before she speaks, p. 217 below. Lying at the centre point, her prone body become the focus of the action, and the centre of attention.

symbolic reality when he places Deianeira between two images
that convey a picture of womanhood suffering unwanted
change: the free young women of Trachis, played by the *choros*,
are set against the desolation of the captives from Oichalia,
played by mute extras; then the tableau refocuses, in the extraordinary moment when Deianeira singles out Herakles' raped
mistress Iole from among them, and feels compassion for her.
Flux is again symbolized in the Finale, where the audience's
images from legend of the supremely powerful, monster-killing
Herakles are cruelly displaced by the tableau of Herakles crippled by his agony.

Sophokles provides a further illustration of mutability in
Oidipous the King, in the contrast between the opening and
closing images of Oidipous. For the first scene he once again
employs silent masks – this time children, symbolizing the
helplessness of the Thebans, in contrast with the regal, almost
god-like strength of Oidipous (32). Child extras are used again,
just before the climax of the drama, when Oidipous brings out
Antigone and Ismene in Scene 4; this prepares for the Finale, in
which Oidipous, now blinded, gropes for the comfort of clinging
to just these two child extras, in absolute contrast with his
domination of the crowd of children in Scene 1. In both scenes
there is another adult present: the Priest's deference to Oidipous
the King at the opening contrasts with Kreon's firm reminders
at the end that Oidipous' royal power is over.

Sophokles uses tableaux and properties[58] with consummate
skill; but it is vital not to privilege them in an analysis of
performance, and so neglect scenes in which they are not used.
In any performance of a Greek drama, the visual dimension is
in constant interaction with the verbal; we possess one of these
elements of Sophokles' tragedies, and we have to reconstruct
the other.[59] This procedure must be followed even-handedly,
throughout each Scene and Choros.

---

[58] E.g. Aias' sword, Deianeira's casket, Iokaste's offerings.

[59] It is now generally accepted that implicit stage directions were incorporated
in the texts of tragedy. Chancellor (1979), in arguing that this is the case for
the benefit of readers rather than spectators, perhaps failed to appreciate
that the first beneficiary was the actor. On implied stage directions, cf. McCart
1991.

Aias

Story

In Homer's *Iliad*, Aias was an independent commander who brought twelve ships from Salamis to the war against Troy. He occupied the second place of honour at the left flank of the Greek camp, and was universally held to be the greatest warrior after Achilleus, who held the right. Although he could be mulishly obstinate, and is once accused of being a clumsy braggart, even his greatest enemy Hektor conceded that Aias was prudent, as well as being physically the largest of the warriors.[60] The presumption of self-sufficiency, and arrogant rejection of divine help, which bring him down in Sophokles' drama, were not present in Homer's hero;[61] but the careful handling that Achilleus and the others bestow on him, when he is in danger of being defeated during the Funeral Games for Patroklos, shows that Aias' extreme touchiness about having due recognition paid to his excellence was already present in the *Iliad*.[62]

Two subsequent epic sequels to the *Iliad* (both now lost) told the story of how Achilleus' golden weapons, forged by the god Hephaistos, were awarded after his death not to Aias but to Odysseus. In the *Aithiopis* by Arktinos, Trojan prisoners were the judges, guided by the goddess Athena, and Aias committed suicide out of resentment at the award to Odysseus.[63] Aias' maddened attempt at revenge originates in the other epic version, the *Little Iliad*. On Nestor's advice the Greeks send spies to gather Trojan comments on the rival Greek heroes. They overhear two Trojan girls talking about Aias and Odysseus; inspired by Pallas Athena, the second argues persuasively that Odysseus was the greater hero.[64] Hearing the report, the Greek chieftains awarded the arms to Odysseus. Aias, maddened by this, slaughtered the Greeks' flocks and herds, and then committed suicide himself. Agamemnon angrily decreed that the body

---

[60] Second only to Achilleus, *Iliad* 2.768; obstinate, 11.558–68, braggart, 13.824; prudent, 7.288; size, 3.227 etc.

[61] Winnington-Ingram 1980, 18.

[62] 23. 708ff., 811ff.

[63] *Odyssey* 11. 547 + ancient commentaries. Cf. Jebb 1907, xii ff.

[64] Ancient commentary on Aristophanes, *Knights* 1056.

should not receive honourable cremation, but should be placed in a coffin and buried.[65]

Fifth-century treatments were influenced by both accounts. Pindar rehabilitates Aias; in three of his victory odes inferior, jealous Greeks spoke persuasively, a secret ballot awarded the armour 'to the supple liar', and the shame made Aias commit suicide, as in the *Aithiopis*.[66] Pindar's songs do not include any mention of Aias' madness, or the slaughter of animals.

Aischylos wrote a trilogy about Aias: *The Judgment of the Arms, Women of Thrakia, Women of Salamis*. The third drama dealt with Teukros' unhappy return to Salamis (an event that is foreshadowed in Sophokles' *Aias* at 1004ff.). In the first drama clearly Aischylos dramatized the dispute itself – presumably with an *agon* of opposing speeches for Aias and Odysseus; the judges were Greeks (as in the *Little Iliad*) so perhaps Aischylos – like Pindar and Sophokles (1135ff.) – developed the idea that the sons of Atreus cheated, and rigged the ballot in favour of Odysseus.

We know that in *Women of Thrakia* Aischylos' Aias committed suicide offstage, and his death was reported by a messenger. He needed the assistance of a goddess, to guide him to the one spot where he was vulnerable.[67] What we crucially do not know is whether Aischylos' Aias killed himself simply in humiliation because he had failed to win the armour, or in humiliation and shame because he had tried to avenge himself, and had failed, slaughtering animals instead through madness.

Sophokles transforms the material simply by adopting the second of these alternatives (from the *Little Iliad*), while keeping Pindar's tradition that corrupt Greek chieftains awarded the arms to Odysseus. He discarded the myth of Aias' near-invulnerability and created a single drama, devoted to the movement of Aias from the moment of his greatest failure – the delusion of triumph seen together with the humiliation of maddened delusion – down to his decision to commit suicide, which unlike Aischylos he decided to portray live in the theatre. The drama then moves upwards to the point when Aias has been rehabili-

---

[65] Proklos, *Abstract of the Little Iliad;* Eustathios commentary on *Iliad* 2.557.

[66] *Nemean* 8.23ff., 7.23ff., and *Isthmian* 4.38ff.

[67] He had been wrapped as a baby in the lion-skin of Herakles, which conferred invulnerability on all the parts of Aias' body that it had covered.

tated. His greatness is recognized once more by all except the sons of Atreus, and his body can then be removed for the honourable burial, which inaugurates his status as an Athenian *heros*.[68]

To create this plot Sophokles had to make small but important changes to the story. He blends those versions in which lesser men cheat Aias out of the armour of Achilleus, and Aias reacts with a revenge attempt which goes horribly wrong; but he adds for balance a more noble Odysseus, who can both begin and end the drama with the lesson he learns from the suddenness of Aias' destruction.

Sophokles rejects the legend of Aias' invulnerability, and with it the need for divine intervention. As in all his other surviving tragedies, gods do not directly cause men's downfall. Athena's appearance in Scene 1 simply reveals the maddened Aias to Odysseus – and to the audience. And the anger of Athena, who can take wisdom away as well as granting it – an anger that lasts only for this one day – is easily understood in psychological terms: it represents the period of extreme vulnerability that follows immediately after recovery from total delusion. Together with some radical stage techniques – the *ekkyklêma* filled with dead animals, and the change of location so Aias can commit suicide alone with Hektor's sword – these modifications to the traditional story made possible a remarkable new drama. It was deservedly Sophokles' most popular work in later antiquity.

Drama

Today, however, *Aias* is Sophokles' least understood surviving tragedy. Some readers believe that Sophokles eccentrically chose to dramatize a 'post-action',[69] rather than treating what they regard as the real story of Aias – the rejection of his claim to Achilleus' armour, followed by his suicide. The simple, sometimes forthright and 'unpoetic' language of many lines after 973 has also bemused many readers;[70] together with Aias' death a little over halfway through the action, this has led to accusations that *Aias*, like *Young Women of Trachis* and *Antigone*, is to be

---

[68] Cf. Stanford 1963, xxxvi.
[69] Seale 1982, 144.
[70] E.g. Waldock 1951, 51.

considered a 'diptych play', broken at the centre and fundamentally incoherent.

That is not the effect that *Aias* makes in performance. In our production, with a talented young actor in the role of Teukros, audiences found the scenes after Aias' suicide most enjoyable, and instinctively understood the logic of the dramatic structure. Sir Richard Jebb had made the same discovery, when he saw a production in Cambridge in 1882.[71]

The drama is set in a military/naval camp; scholars who expect high poetry at all times in tragedy will not find it in the language of Menelaos, Teukros and Agamemnon; but Greek *tragoidia* involves a much wider range of emotions than (for example) the tragedies of Racine, and we should no more expect Teukros to speak like Aias than Shakespeare's Enobarbus like Antony.

The subject of *Aias* is the death and eventual burial of the title figure. Unlike most dramas staged at Athens, *Aias* dramatizes the death of an Athenian *heros*; since the incorporation of Salamis into Attika in the sixth century, and the political reforms of Kleisthenes in 508, one-tenth of Sophokles' audience belonged to the tribe Aiantis – were literally 'descendants of Aias'.[72] Sophokles shows the day of his downfall and burial; the drama begins by showing the madness, inflicted by Athena, which in this version of the story deflects his attempt at revenge. The scenes then explore the inexorable consequences of this, unfolding seamlessly through his recovery, escape from his *philoi* and suicide to the conflicts between Teukros and the sons of Atreus about whether he should be buried.

The whole drama leads up to the moment at which Odysseus' intervention resolves that tension, and Aias is formally carried out by his *philoi* to receive the burial that he deserves. Aias himself is central throughout. After his extraordinary appearance in Scene 1, he holds the spectators' attention first in Tekmessa's dance and narrative and then in his own three successive appearances. After his death his body remains in the

---

[71] 1907, xlv.

[72] The drama stresses Aias' Athenian status e.g. at 202, 861, 1217–22. His notorious touchiness about his excellence was commemorated in the custom that Aiantis was never to be placed last in the inter-tribe choral competitions (Ploutarchos, *Moralia* 628b–9a).

centre of the *orchêstra*, and – as the focus of the dispute – is literally central to the remainder of the drama.

Aias was worshipped at Athens in the hope that he would give the citizens the excellences of his male strength, size, physical prowess and military intelligence.[73] These were key components of *arete* for the ancient Greeks, simply because the survival of their cities depended on these virtues.[74] Technologically advanced weaponry has increasingly marginalized such abilities in modern western culture and society. Central components of the ancient Greek value system, which were exhibited and celebrated annually on the battlefield and in sporting contests, have now become confined to commercialized sport; and our professional armies rarely demonstrate their lethal advanced combat skills. We celebrate heroic skills and values in our popular culture – but nostalgically, ambiguously, and often ironically, when our creative artists set their books, comic strips, films and computer games in periods and places where heroic values possessed an importance that they do not have in our own real lives.[75]

Aias is marked out from the other warrior-kings, in Sophokles' drama as in the *Iliad*, by his superior strength and heroic stature;[76] but Sophokles deliberately removes at the outset any implication that while he is superior in physical strength, he is less intelligent than his rival Odysseus (119–21). This Aias has been brought low by a fully justified over-confidence in his own mental and physical self-sufficiency (757ff.). The *agathos'* role was to compete to the utmost to provide stability and security to his *philoi*; and ancient Greek ethics provided no excuses for

---

[73] The Athenians invoked Aias and Telamon to help them in the naval battle at Salamis. After their victory, the Greeks dedicated a captured Phoinikian trireme to Aias; Herodotos 8. 64, 121.

[74] Adkins 1960, 31ff. and 153ff.

[75] The genre – inspired by Goethe's *Götz von Berlichingen* – began early in the Industrial Revolution. Dumas' *Musketeer* trilogy is far more than just a romanticized view of the courts of Louis XIII and XIV; the author celebrates and farewells a military nobility that was irretrievably lost in the embourgeoisement of France under Colbert. More recent 'invented worlds' which deliberately reinvoke heroic values include the James Bond novels and films and the *Star Wars* trilogy, and indeed all the fictionalized combat zones of Hollywood, from the earliest westerns to and beyond the Rambo films.

[76] March 1991–3, 12–13; she especially notes the contrast between Aias' and Teukros' attitudes to Telamon.

failure.[77] But heroic life was filled with interventions by gods and *daimones*, which could easily prevent the *agathos* from fulfilling his duty.[78]

The core of the myth is Aias' decision to commit suicide. Suicide was not for Greek *agathoi* a noble departure into the Void, as in the code of Japanese samurai.[79] In Greek ethics before Sokrates, success in protecting your *philoi* and harming your enemies, and the avoidance of shame or public humiliation, were everything; there would have been no way of effectively condemning Aias if he had succeeded in killing the Atreidai and Odysseus. As Athena herself reminds the audience, 'the sweetest of all laughter is to laugh at enemies' (79). This is most easily done when they or their *philoi* are dead and/or in your power.

Aias' position when he returns to sanity was therefore for the original audience one of the most powerful dilemmas a man could face. On the one hand, his failure to succeed in his enterprise has shamed him so greatly that it is incompatible with his *arete*, his former greatness as a warrior, and so continued life has become unendurable; on the other hand, Aias' status as an *agathos* requires that he should live on, and fulfil his obligations to his *philoi* - his wife, his son, and the Sailors who depend on him. If he dies, they will be at the mercy of his enemies; so will his corpse, to which those enemies have good reason to deny burial.

Sophokles shaped the story of Aias' suicide and burial around his own intense perception of the mutability of human affairs, the idea that 'one day can weigh down everything a human being is and has/or lift it up again' (Athena; 130–1). The world of *Aias* is in a continuous, inexorable flux; no emotion or situation, not even joy or grief, is stable or lasting,[80] and the most bitter enemy can become a friend – as Odysseus does. Aias

[77] Such pleas began to emerge towards the end of the fifth century; Adkins 1960, 102–6.

[78] This is the fundamental theme of Homer's *Odyssey*, which only reaches its conclusion when Odysseus has – against overwhelming odds – returned home and successfully avenged the looting of his *oikos* by Penelopeia's suitors. The epic ends when he has restored his position as her husband, Telemachos' father and the head of the chief household of Ithaka.

[79] Golder 1990, 14. As he notes, 'suicide was a desperate act, restricted [elsewhere!] in tragedy solely to women.'

[80] Aias himself expresses this thought, in memorable imagery, at 669ff.

moves in the course of the drama from heroic greatness to utter humiliation and then, towards the end, back to the full restoration of his *time*; as we watch this movement, the drama sinks down to the memory of his death, and then rises to the celebration of his greatness.[81] Here especially Jones' warning against 'preconceptions about downfall, retribution, the tale of woe . . . the expectation of Greek Tragedy's heavy downward trudge from Hubris to Nemesis' still needs reiteration; 'lost [in such readings] are those blazing moments in play after play, where a man is marvellously saved – "beyond my best hope" he will say, dazed with joy as he sees the sky ripped open for him. Or if not lost, they are placed in a Wheel-of-Fortune antithesis to the moments of disaster. And then the tune of the circling Bear is never heard, which is the symphonic double movement of Sophoclean action and the reversals of a single day.'[82] If we are to understand the dramatic structure of *Aias*, we must absorb this fundamental rhythm of Sophokles' action. And our performances must find images that link modern spectators to the values of the classical Greek warrior-culture.

Performance

In *Aias* Sophokles made comprehensive use of the physical resources of the Athenian theatre. The drama is framed around the two appearances of Odysseus – Aias' enemy at the opening, his friend in the Finale; and it is launched on its way by the extraordinary spectacle of Aias deluded, played with by the goddess Athena – but also seen in heroic triumph, as if he were still a victorious warrior. This double image, achieved through the goddess' appearance in Scene 1, allows her to spell out for Odysseus and the audience at 118ff. the suddenness of change, the impermanence of all human conditions. This pattern will underlie the drama.

The focus in the rest of the first half is on the increasing grief of Aias and his *philoi*, as he recovers sanity and comes to the decision that his only course of action now is to die. Before the change of scene, the *skene* represents the tent of Aias, and this is the focus round which the action unfolds. As usual, the *skene*

[81] Cf. March 1991–3, 22–23.

[82] Jones 1962, 176–7, quoting *OKol* 607ff. The Bear image underlies *YWT* Choros 1, q.v.; for some moments of marvellous escape Jones cites *Ai* 1382, *El* 1262, *Phil* 1463 and *OKol* 1105, 1120.

right *parodos* leads away from, and the left *parodos* towards, the 'downtown' of the place where the action is set. Since Aias has 'the last position on the flank' (4) of the camp, the right *parodos* leads in the first half of the drama straight out to the plain of Troy and to the lonely seashore; the left *parodos* leads to the camp. Aias' enemy Odysseus enters from the right, his friends the Sailors from the left; both want to know what has happened to Aias, and they induce the audience, once their curiosity has been stimulated by Aias' maddened appearance in Scene 1, to desire to search inward. This becomes the underlying movement of the first half of the drama, a progressive journey of discovery in which the spectators gain more and more insight into the horror inside the *skene*.

The bloodstained, half-naked, maddened whip-bearing Aias of the opening scene is a terrifying sight; but when the Sailors call for him to come out, Sophokles cheats their expectation, and that of the audience, in preparation for an even greater revelation.[83] Tekmessa first dances Aias' situation, and then tells what she knows in an extended spoken narrative. Only then does Sophokles reveal visually the horrors inside the tent, which have been foreshadowed in her words and action; in an extraordinary *coup de théâtre*, the *ekkyklêma* appears, disclosing Aias slumped among slaughtered animals. And Aias is so stricken that he too, departing from normal male behaviour in tragedy, sings and dances to express his grief. The impact of this tableau is then sharpened by an additional element of pathos – the introduction of the child actor playing Eurysakes, whom Aias places among the dead animals on the *ekkyklêma*.

Sophokles has deliberately withheld from sight one prop that is essential to his story: the sword of Hektor, with which Aias slaughtered the animals. In Scene 3 Aias re-enters from the *skene*, bearing this weapon for the first time, and exploring its significance to him. He now brings it into the light of day, and successfully deceives his *philoi* into letting him take it away to the seashore, ostensibly to cleanse himself of *miasma* and dispose of the sword.

This is the halfway point. The appearance of the bloodstained sword concludes the sequence of revelations from inside the *skene*, which began in Scene 1. And Aias' words in Scene 3

---

[83] See Notes below on Scene 2.

clearly indicate to an audience which knew the story that he is now determined to die. The Soldier's appearance from the other *parodos* now clinches that feeling. To the right, Aias has gone into savage space with the sword to make his preparations; from the left, the Sailors – and then Tekmessa – learn that if he goes out today, he will die. And he has.

First Aias and then Tekmessa have now been finally separated from his tent. It is superfluous in the remainder of the drama, so Sophokles changes the scene, following the normal procedure of first removing the *choros*, then presetting a prop at the centre before their return.[84] At Tekmessa's entry (787), the *skene* doors close for the last time. Sophokles then clears the *orchêstra* of actors and *choros*, and stage-hands set some bushes around the centre of the *orchêstra*. This pulls the focus forward, away from the *skene*, to indicate that it will not be used in the rest of the drama. All is then ready for Aias' re-entry for the suicide scene. The right and left continue to represent the directions of outwards, towards savage or hostile territory, and 'home' respectively: right now leads direct to the remainder of the camp, and left leads back to his tent.

With the *skene* now out of use, the rest of the drama revolves around the body of Aias, which is thematically central, and therefore must be literally central in the circular playing space as well.[85] The action is complete when the body can be raised and Aias' burial procession can begin;[86] his rehabilitation after death to the point at which this takes place is the guiding thread in the second half of the action. The theme of mutability is enacted in the change of scene itself, in the transformation of Aias in the sight of the audience from living man to corpse, and in the final transformation of that corpse from a despised, 'dead nothing' (Agamemnon, 1231) to a body that deserves a hero's burial.

Aias' prayer to Zeus at 823ff. and Tekmessa's wish at 921–2 are answered. Teukros does come – though not at once; Tekmessa does the best she can alone, shrouding his body and pronouncing a moving elegy. Then Teukros raises his brother off the sword, fends off Menelaos, and sets Eurysakes and

[84] See Ewans 1995, 174–5 and 201.
[85] Cf. Notes below, p. 192.
[86] March 1991–3, 24–5.

Tekmessa in place, initiating by the rituals of family offering and supplication a reciprocal relationship of protection between the corpse and its *philoi*, which is the next stage towards Aias' burial.[87] Against Agamemnon Teukros argues to an impasse, threatening that all three of them will die rather than yield; but Odysseus' return resolves the issue, and in the last moments Teukros can order the Sailors to take Aias out to an honourable burial. And so the procession leaves, taking the corpse out not by the hostile right *parodos* to remain unburied as the sons of Atreus would have desired, but back towards the left, which symbolizes a return home.[88]

Date

Scholars have often placed *Aias* earliest among the surviving dramas of Sophokles, chiefly because it uses 'spectacular' staging devices – a divine appearance, the *ekkyklêma* and a change of scene – in a manner that is supposedly more Aischylean than the visual austerity that many believe to be characteristic of mature Sophokles. In view of the small number of surviving dramas, such generalizations have little force.[89] Other arguments for an early date for *Aias* have been based on alleged incompetences in dramatic technique and form that do not exist, once the text is properly understood as a script for performance.

March argued for an early date, around 460. This would make *Aias* perhaps the first drama to use the new *skene* building, which is not certainly attested until Aischylos' *Oresteia* of 458 BC, but was possibly used in 463 in the second and third

[87] Taplin 1978, 108–9.

[88] Homeric heroes were normally cremated, and in the *Little Iliad* the fact that Aias was buried symbolized dishonour; but in Sophokles' fifth-century drama Aias' burial both pays him due honour (1163ff.) and is suitable to his status as a hero with a cult. Easterling 1988, 97.

[89] For what it is worth, in the three surviving dramas from his old age Sophokles used all three stage machines available to him: the *ekkyklêma* in *El*, the *mechane* in *Phil* and the *bronteion* in *OKol*. And to judge from the surviving dramas of Euripides and from *Prometheus Bound*, there was plenty of use of spectacular visual effects after 440. Since no surviving drama can certainly be dated between 458 and 440, for all we know visual effects of different kinds may have been popular right through the period after the construction of the *skene* in the Theatre of Dionysos – from the *Oresteia* to *Bakchai*, *OKol* and *Frogs*.

dramas of his Danaid trilogy; and almost the first to use the *ekkyklêma*. But her argument is not compelling;[90] and linguistic analysis suggests that *Aias* could have been written at any time between 460 and 430.

The use of *antilabe*, which is not found in *Antigone*, is a technical detail that might place this drama after 438 – but only if you believe that the Athenian playwrights only gradually introduced new dramatic techniques and writing styles, and continued to use them in all their subsequent dramas once they had been introduced. These are questionable assumptions, made very dangerous by the small number of surviving tragedies.

In the absence of firm evidence, I am reluctant to place a drama of such great power and bold conception as early as the 460s, when Sophokles had only just begun to compete. I would therefore accept a date somewhere between 450 and 430 BC.

Antigone

Story

Antigone, and her decision to defy the rulers of Thebes and bury the dead body of her brother Polyneikes, do not appear in the early epic versions of the story of the royal house of Thebes. Aischylos was almost certainly responsible for the main innovation that made Sophokles' treatment in *Antigone* and *Oidipous the King* possible: in Aischylos' Theban trilogy Oidipous had children incestuously by his mother before discovering who he is and what he had done.[91] It was therefore long thought that the last phase of the story of the house of Labdakos, Antigone's defiance of an edict against burying Polyneikes, first appeared in Aischylos' Theban dramas; in the closing part of

---

[90] March 1991–3, 33–4. She claims that two vase paintings, one from *c.* 460, are based on Sophokles' drama. This is not necessarily true; and her view that Sophokles' portrait of Aias is designed to evoke the Athenian statesman Kimon is not particularly plausible.

[91] Cf. below, p. lxv. In the epic version Oidipous lived on after the death of Epikaste (Iokaste in Sophokles), and had children only by a subsequent wife. The claim at Steiner 1984, 107 (unfortunately prominent at the start of a chapter) that Antigone appears in Homer, *Odyssey* 11. 271ff. is presumably a lapse of memory. Steiner himself had conjectured one year earlier (1983, 87) that Sophokles invented the story of Antigone.

the third, surviving drama *Seven against Thebes*, Antigone insists on burying her brother regardless of the consequences for herself.

However, almost all scholars now believe that this final scene is a spurious ending, added by a later author, possibly so *Seven* could be played as a 'prequel' either to Sophokles' surviving *Antigone* or to Euripides' lost drama of the same title. The language and style echo scenes from Euripides' *Phoinikian Women* (c.411–9); so it dates from twenty or more years after Sophokles' *Antigone*.[92]

Antigone's name is therefore not attested in any source earlier than Sophokles' drama.[93] Scholars have tended to discount the possibility that an Athenian dramatist might have taken a pre-existing legend – in this case the mutual fratricide which up to and including Aischylos' version extinguished the royal house of Thebes – and graft onto it new characters and a wholly new and surprising plot of his own.[94] Antigone's name literally means 'opposed to offspring'; it reflects the fact that her devotion to burying her brother prevented her from reaching the normal goal of young womanhood in ancient Greece: marriage and the creation of children. The setting and plot of *Antigone* are designed to create a sequence of conflicts – first between sisters, and then across gender, class and age boundaries – which echo some of the most central issues affecting Athenian society in the 430s. Sophokles probably invented the title figure, and certainly invented her decision to bury Polyneikes, to create these conflicts and raise these issues. His plot

[92] Translation, discussion and references on the ending of *Seven* at Ewans 1996a, 164–8.

[93] Euripides' lost *Antigone*, in which she survived and has children by Haimon, seems likely to have been a characteristic Euripidean gloss like *Orestes*, inventing new and startling plot strands to contrast with Sophokles' pre-existing, more 'orthodox' version of the story. We know that Sophokles' contemporary, Ion of Chios, wrote a *dithyramb* in which Antigone and Ismene lived on until the siege of Thebes by the Epigonoi, during which they were burned to death by Eteokles' son Laodamas; but there is no means of knowing whether this poem was composed before or after Sophokles' tragedy.

[94] Aristotle's statement about the uniqueness, and unpopularity, of Agathon's wholly fictitious plot for *Antheus*, and his insistence on the value of the old stories in themselves – a characteristically post-classical perspective – have been unduly influential (*Poetics* 51b20–25).

unleashes some of the most powerful tensions imaginable inside
Greek society.[95]

Antigone's name is significant, like that of Elektra
('unmarried') in the story of the house of Atreus; but she is not
the only character whose name has symbolic significance.
Ismene is named, neutrally, after one of the two rivers of
Thebes; but Kreon means 'ruler', and Haimon clearly echoes
haima, blood;[96] and Eurydike's name (literally 'wide in her
judgement') is a title of the Queen of the Dead.[97]

Drama

The proper disposal of the dead is a fundamental right in most
known societies. In classical Greece there were few 'human
rights' recognized as extending even to enemies; so the defence
of this right by the gods, and the reversal of attempts by
vengeful human beings to prevent it, were of great importance
from Homer's *Iliad* onwards. The epic is only resolved when
Achilleus relents, and returns the body of Hektor to Priam for
the Trojan men to bury him, while their women cry the lament
for him; this lament forms the moment of peace that concludes
the poem. The particular horror of the unburied body is also
used for pathos by both Aischylos and Euripides.[98]

Only seven tragedies by Sophokles survive, out of a total of
over ninety; it would therefore be unsafe to claim that he was
obsessed with any one subject. However, the right even of an
enemy to burial is the central issue in two out of the seven –
Antigone and *Aias*; and the right to a proper burial is important
in the closing phase of three others (*Young Women of Trachis*,
Elektra and *Oidipous at Kolonos*). We can at least assert that
Sophokles was particularly concerned with this theme; and this

[95] And especially Athenian society in 438 BC, if this is the right date for the
drama (below, p. liv).

[96] Sophokles plays on this assonance at 794 and 1175. Unlike Ismene, these
two names are attested from an earlier source. In the Homeric epic poem
Oidipodeia, 'godlike' Haimon, Kreon's most handsome son, was killed by the
Sphinx – long before the events dramatized in *Ant*. Interestingly, the fragment
that narrated this event (quoted by a scholiast on Euripides, *Phoinikian Women*
line 1760), describes Kreon as 'noble' or splendid, using the same word
('*amumôn*') as the *Odyssey* uses for Aigisthos. Like Aigisthos, Kreon lost his
epic nobility when reinterpreted by the fifth-century tragedians.

[97] Segal 1981, 180ff.

[98] Cf. e.g. Aischylos, *Persians* 567ff. and Euripides, *Suppliants, passim*.

is not surprising, given the political context in which he created his dramas.

Few debates are as sterile as the academic discussions that were once devoted to the question whether Antigone or Kreon is the central figure in this drama.[99] *Antigone*, like *Young Women of Trachis*, provides a powerful reminder that the Greeks viewed individual tragedy not in isolation, but in the context of its impact on the *oikos* and the *polis*. In performance, without the benefit of hindsight leafing through the text in the study, the drama is neither Antigone's tragedy nor Kreon's. It simply unfolds, with one or other of the two characters predominant at different times.

Antigone commands the playing space in the three scenes in which she appears; but by the end Kreon is the central character: the final image is his exit broken by the loss, in one day, by his own folly, of both son and wife. Antigone deserves the title role because her courage and conviction, her absolute and self-sacrificing defiance of Kreon's edict is the catalyst that creates the whole tragedy; but as the drama unfolds in performance, Kreon's incapacity to handle the political and familial situation that he has created becomes more and more central.

The attempt to place Antigone at the centre is partly the result of a long tradition of male worship of the martyred, virginal heroine;[100] but it also grows, more justifiably, from a feeling that her absolute stance is morally right, and a reluctance to allow Kreon to dominate because he is not an acceptable 'tragic hero' – if Aristotle was right, when he declared that true tragedy is not to be found in the spectacle of a wicked or stupid man encountering his deserts.[101]

Kreon in his final agonies has none of the nobility of Oidipous in the Finale to *Oidipous the King*, and he ignores his Councillors' repeated admonitions that silence, rather than self-indulgent lamentation, is the proper response to the deaths of his son

---

[99] The subject has (hopefully) been laid to rest by Segal 1964 and Hogan 1972.

[100] E.g. Shelley, de Quincey and von Hofmannsthal, cited at Steiner 1984, 4–7; among scholars cf. Jebb 1907, xxv, von Wilamowitz 1923, 342 and Müller 1967, esp. 11–14.

[101] *Poetics* 52b36ff., discussed at Ewans 1996a, xxxi.

and wife.[102] Nobility in a female character who goes to her death long before the end, followed by ignoble agony in an unworthy man who holds the focus to the end, have severely puzzled many (predominantly male) literary critics; and they have headed in three equally misguided directions. Some classical scholars have picked away at Antigone's nobility, trying to see her as just too extreme and single-minded;[103] others have attempted to make Kreon into an archetype of true statecraft tragically subverted by events;[104] a third group diagnoses flaws in them both.[105] Only a few critics have had the courage to argue for the only reading that responds to the text in performance.[106] As the drama unfolds, it becomes clear that Kreon is a paranoid autocrat, and Antigone was right to transgress against the role expected of a woman in fifth century Athens, and bury her brother herself.

Antigone has often been glorified for its supposedly noble theme: the exalted conflict between Kreon's firm defence of the civic values of the Periklean *polis* and the absolute demands of

---

[102] Singing to lament the dead was in Greek ritual the function of women. Aischylos brought out the profoundly 'other' nature of Persian society by allowing Xerxes and his Elders a Finale of unrestrained lamentation for their military disaster in *Persians* (Ewans 1996, 183–5); like Xerxes, Kreon in the original Greek sang several stanzas in the Finale.

[103] E.g. Perotta 1935, 112–14, Lloyd-Jones 1971, 116–17, Gellie 1972, 31–2, Winnington-Ingram 1980, 128ff., and especially Sourvinou-Inwood 1989, who attempts to assimilate *Ant* to the post-modern concern with complexity and ambivalence – showing as much subjectivity as the earlier treatments that she criticizes; cf. esp. 134–6. Her interpretation is sometimes totally perverse; cf. esp. 144–6 on Scene 4, and the desperate closing attempt (149) to force a distinction between Antigone's cause ('right and vindicated') and the character herself ('wrong, and punished accordingly').

[104] Cf. esp. Calder 1968, in which Kreon's name is tendentiously replaced wherever possible by 'the government' or 'the state', against which Antigone and Ismene are allegedly 'conspiring' in Scene 1 (392). 'The State' also gains a prominence which the Greek text does not justify in Taylor's free translation (1986) and in the décor of the BBC production which he based on it.

More pernicious, because less obviously totalitarian, is Oudemans and Lardinois 1987, 165ff., a structuralist 'reading' with very little sensibility either to human feelings or to how Sophokles' drama might actually work in performance.

[105] Knox 1964, 61–116, and Nussbaum 1986, esp. 63ff.

[106] Waldock 1951, Kitto 1956, Segal 1964 and Vickers 1973.

the 'unwritten laws' that Antigone upholds.[107] During the production process we came to reject this idealized view. *Antigone*
is a bleak drama, placed in a city which is starting, falteringly,
to recover from the horrors of war. Sophokles' plot first sets
sister in bitter hatred against sister, and then develops an horrific
situation in which the head of a household confronts his niece
(and prospective daughter-in-law) and coldly replies to her
question 'Do you want to do more than kill me?' with 'No;
that's all I want.'[108] But it is not; Kreon menaces Ismene at
531ff., nearly kills her as well as Antigone (769), and even
threatens to execute Antigone himself, in public, in front of his
son who is her fiancé (758ff.). We then see a young woman
going to a horrible death for giving her brother burial as the
gods require; and finally Kreon drives his son and wife to suicide
by failing – even when he finally yields to good advice – to do
exactly as he is advised.

Kreon sets out some of the principles of good government in
his first long speech; but his degeneration is very fast.[109] He
invents conspiracy theories the moment he finds his edict has
been defied, reacts violently to having his authority challenged
by a woman[110] and fully deserves by Scene 4 his son's unforget-
table quip (739) 'you'd make a very good king – on a desert

---

[107] This is the Hegelian tradition (Steiner 1984, 19ff.) It is part of the tendency
up until the 1980s to idealize Sophokles' themes and principal characters – often
to create an unjustified contrast with Euripides' more overtly negative view of
contemporary Athenian political and moral behaviour.

[108] Fifth-century Athenians set great store on practical wisdom and political
advantage; their word for wisdom, and its cognates, echo through this drama
(Goheen 1951 75–200; Nussbaum 1986, 51–63 and 436; Cropp 1997, 143ff.).
Antigone is the last person Kreon should even think of killing (for any reason
whatever), since Sophokles' new story has her betrothed to Haimon, and
marrying back into the house of Labdakos would confer on his regime and on
his son's succession the legitimacy that Kreon clearly desires, and knows he does
not himself possess since the loss of his own connection to the royal house
through his sister's marriage to Oidipous (see Notes to the opening of Scene 2).
He has also, since the death of Eteokles, become *kyrios* over both Antigone and
Ismene, and is therefore responsible for their welfare until they are married (cf.
Segal 1981, 178).

[109] This controversial point is argued in detail in the Notes to Scenes 2 and 3.

[110] And by anyone else who in his view is inferior to himself: young men,
slaves, even his Councillors – not to mention imaginary left-wing malcontents
and corrupt prophets; cf. Vickers 1973, 533.

island.' Fifth-century Athenian democrats could only see Kreon as a tyrant, opposed to everything that all but the extreme right would desire in a ruler.

Once we placed the central focus on the horrific damage caused by Kreon's ill-conceived attempt to consolidate his newly inherited power, we were led to reappraise traditional images of the principal characters. Kreon was divested of the all-too-frequent image of an ageing, noble patriarch;[111] and Antigone was not played by an aspiring great actress as a woman in her late twenties or early thirties. It is crucial to the plot, and to the pathos of her final scene, that Antigone is a *parthenos* who will now never be married. Greek *parthenoi* were normally married as soon as possible after they began to menstruate.[112] In our production a petite but strong-featured young woman of nineteen was cast as Antigone,[113] and Kreon was played as a middle-aged, vigorous and powerful warlord, who started to rant and rave as soon as he knew he had been defied, rapidly degenerated into a sadistic tyrant, and remained over-emotional even when his resolve was broken after Teiresias' departure. Although a minority of audiences, and viewers of the video-recording, found this approach to performance uncomfortable, it is true to Sophokles' drama. Kreon's self-serving and self-deluding perversion of fine-sounding principles and cultural prejudices, and the appalling consequences when he destroys Antigone for her youthful intensity of belief and her acceptance of the consequences, have as intense a relevance to us today as they had for Athenians of the early 430s.

[111] Cf. e.g. the Actors of Dionysos production imaged in *Didaskalia* 1.5 (1994).

[112] Without the benefits of modern medical science, childbirth was of course progressively more dangerous the further a woman advanced into her twenties. Greek doctors also believed that once a girl's womb started to be fertile hysteria (literally, 'womb-disease') was likely to develop if she were not promptly married, so her womb could be used for its proper function of hosting male seed and producing children (references and discussion at Ewans 1996a, l). The Councillors effectively accuse Antigone of hysteria at 929–30.

[113] This also had the advantage, like my controversial 1986 casting of a relatively slightly statured woman as Klytaimestra in *Agamemnon*, of making the actress work hard with her voice and body to create the immense power of the character, instead of being able to take her authority for granted, as many actresses in these parts have done, simply through physical presence.

Performance

Spatially, this is one of the most powerfully expressive of all the surviving tragedies.[114] In *Antigone*, Sophokles uses the *skene* to represent a royal palace located between arrivals from a relatively safe downtown area of Thebes (left *parodos*), and from a more dangerous, unknown world beyond the city gates, represented by entries from the right *parodos*. And he uses the arrangement of the playing area to sharpen one particular aspect of his script – Kreon's isolation and vulnerability – in three ways.

First, the right *parodos* leads out to the hills overlooking Thebes (1110), hills from which the enemy has only recently departed, and on which the body of Polyneikes still lies. Not one character who enters from this direction brings good news.[115] Before *Antigone* begins it is already the way to the dead body of Polyneikes; by the time the drama ends, it is established simply as the way to death.

Second, the safety of the downtown entry, which leads away from the field of battle and the decaying corpse, also rapidly becomes delusory. The three characters who enter from this direction are the Councillors of Thebes, Haimon and Teiresias. All are people on whom Kreon has good reason, from past experience, to depend; and in the present situation, all three become totally opposed to his decision to kill Antigone – in the case of the two individuals, in the course of one scene.[116]

Finally and most subtly, Kreon does not, like the title figure in *Oidipous the King*, make his first entrance through the palace

---

[114] See Taplin 1984. There is also a discussion of Sophokles' use of space in *Ant* in Wiles 1997, 151ff.; but it is weakened by the lack of a diachronic focus on how the spatial parameters change as the drama unfolds.

[115] The Guard's joy when he brings back Antigone at the opening of Scene 3 is of course delusory for all the other characters; by the end of that scene, Kreon's determination to kill Antigone (and, at that stage, Ismene as well) has effectively sealed his own fate.

[116] The Councillors as a whole take longer to convert. This is a deliberate choice on Sophokles' part, to emphasize by contrast with their hostility Antigone's utter isolation in Scene 5, her final scene. Elsewhere in surviving tragedy only in Euripides' *Bakchai* does a principal character go to his or her death, like Antigone, in the face of a hostile *choros* character of the opposite gender – and Pentheus is so deluded that he does not realize what is going to happen to him.

doors to confirm his royal power.[117] On the contrary, the *skene* doors are first opened by Antigone, and a remark of hers in Scene 1 (33) confirms that Kreon will enter from the city for the start of Scene 2. In this way the palace – though it has in legal fact been Kreon's own residence since the previous evening – is immediately defined as being primarily the domain of girls and women (cf. also 531ff.). Kreon faces female hostility within his own house right from the start of the drama, as Antigone leaves the women's world of the interior and enters the male-dominated, public arena of the *polis* to defy his decree and bury Polyneikes.

As the drama unfolds, the staging continues to reinforce the fact that the entrance leading through the doors into the *skene* is the disputed threshold between the normal worlds of females and of males. Six of the fourteen entrances and exits from the building in this drama are violent, with a female character or characters being dragged, pushed or carried through the entrance. By contrast, Kreon himself goes into the house only twice.

Female dominance of the interior is finally reasserted by the appearance of Eurydike from inside it – a third, new and unexpected woman;[118] and when she hears of Antigone's death and Haimon's, Eurydike changes her intention of going downtown to the security of the temple of Pallas, returns inside the palace and kills herself there, so polluting Kreon's residence with the *miasma* of kindred blood. Kreon then brings the body of Haimon back from the right *parodos*, which has already been established as the place of death – only to be confronted with a second place of death, when the body of Eurydike is brought out from within his own *oikos*. When he himself enters it for the last time, he goes as a broken man who has nowhere else to hide from the horror of the deaths now visible in the public arena, except an *oikos* that he has never truly possessed. In this way the drama creates a compelling theatrical metaphor for

---

[117] *Pace* the stage directions in e.g. Fagles 1984, 66. Calder (1968, 393) would buttress Kreon's authority even further, by having him enter from the right *parodos* 'as though directly from the battlefield and in full panoply'. But Antigone's description at line 27 makes plain that he has already gone downtown to the *agora* to issue his edict.

[118] Cf. Wiles 1997, 167.

Kreon's progressive detachment from what should have been his proper role as the new *kyrios* of the royal house and of all who live in it. If this use of the entrances is not understood and recreated in a modern production, an important part of Sophokles' meaning is lost.

Date

There is a story that Sophokles' success with *Antigone* led to his election as general 'in Samos'.[119] This dates the drama to 438 (or less likely 437); the Athenians were then campaigning, using Samos as their base, against Samian oligarchs who had been expelled in 439, and were continuing their resistance from a base at Anaia on the Ionian mainland.[120]

This date would also give the drama direct contemporary relevance at Athens. The local historian Duris records[121] that in 439 Perikles ordered some captured Samian captains and marines to be strapped to boards for ten days, then clubbed to death and thrown out unburied. If Sophokles invented the story of Antigone and Kreon for a drama first performed in 438, his chosen subject, and his treatment of it, comment adversely on this atrocity.

This period would also sit well with the style of the Greek, which places *Antigone* nearer to *Aias* and *Young Women of Trachis* than to the other four surviving dramas.

Young Women of Trachis

Story

We know very little about the forms taken by the legend of Deianeira's marriage to Herakles before *Young Women of Trachis*. The only sources that survive intact are this drama, Bakchylides *Poem* 16 and Ovid's Latin version in *Metamorphoses* Book IX. Lost poems by Archilochos (in the seventh century BC) and Pindar (a fifth-century contemporary of Aischylos and Sophokles) are known to have told how Herakles won Deianeira in combat with the river-god Acheloos; and we know that the eighth-century epic poet Kreophylos of Samos wrote *The Cap-*

---

[119] Ancient 'Hypothesis' (Preface) to *Ant*, §1.

[120] Lewis 1988; his arguments rule out the traditional dating to 442 or 441 BC.

[121] Ploutarchos, *Life of Perikles* 28; see Lewis *ibid*.

ture of Oichalia, dealing with Herakles' sack of that city when King Eurytos refused to give him his daughter Iole. Deianeira and the robe are also mentioned (but with no statement of why she sent it to Herakles) in a fragment of the Hesiodic *Catalogue of Women*.

Some conjectures are possible. A principal theme of Sophokles' drama is the destructive power of beauty and of sexual passion.[122] Sophokles made this emphasis possible by changing the myth. He placed Herakles' marriage to a young Deianeira in his early manhood, so that she is approaching ancient Greek middle age – i.e. around thirty-five – at the time of the sack of Oichalia; this version of the legend enables the arrival of Iole to cause Deianeira's predicament.[123] And Sophokles made Deianeira meet Iole. This does not happen in the versions preserved by later handbooks of mythology, which probably follow the epic accounts; so Sophokles' second scene, where Deianeira's sixth sense picks out Iole from among the group of silent captives, is likely to be his own innovation.

This is true regardless of whether Bakchylides *Poem* 16 is earlier or later than the drama. Since Bakchylides' traditional date of mature activity is *c*. 467, and reasons are given below for dating *Young Women of Trachis* over thirty years later than that, at about the time of Bakchylides' death, his poem is likely to be earlier than Sophokles' drama. Indeed, the final stanza may have given Sophokles his inspiration, since the lyric poet saw the tragic potential of the arrival of Iole in Deianeira's house:

And then an untameable *daimôn* . . .

wove for Deianeira a shrewd device rich in tears,
when she learnt the news which broke her heart,
that the son of Zeus, unwearied by the fray,

[122] Cf. esp. 24–5, 295–302, 441ff., 464ff., 488–9, Choros 3 (498ff.), and 544+ff. Note how in several of these passages love is imaged as a disease; cf. Easterling 1982, 5–6.

[123] In Pindar's lost poem, Herakles married Deianeira after the last Labour, that of bringing the dog Kerberos back from Haides (ancient commentator on Homer, *Iliad* 21.94). A Phlian tradition placed the marriage before one of the middle Labours, the journey to seek the apples of the Hesperides (Pausanias 2.13.8). For a concise account of the relevant myths in literature before Sophokles see Easterling 1982, 15–19. Also Jebb 1908, xff.

> was sending white-armed Iole
> to his shining house to share his bed.
> Unfortunate, miserable woman!
> Great was her contrivance;
> Jealousy, whose power reaches far, destroyed her,
> and the murky veil that hid
> the future, when at Lykormas' rose-strewn bank
> she accepted from Nessos that marvellous,
> terrible gift.

One other feature of the drama is unusual. Sophokles intensified the suffering of Herakles in the Finale because he does not ascend to heaven, raised to immortal status as the husband of the goddess Hebe, as in some versions of the myth, but dies like any other mortal.[124]

Drama

Young Women of Trachis has at times been severely underrated. This was in part because it does not have the one 'tragic hero' beloved of theorists; instead, it has a hero and heroine whose characters are totally opposed to each other. Its stress on the power of sexuality may also have caused problems to earlier critics;[125] and an additional obstacle may have been that, after appalling suffering has culminated in separate, painful deaths for wife and husband, Hyllos openly challenges the gods at the end. This is an exceptionally uncomfortable tragedy. There is no question of either Herakles or Deianeira being 'punished' for anything. A noble and likeable woman kills her husband accidentally, through fear that she will lose him, and then dies, like a man, by the sword, stabbing her naked belly on her marriage bed;[126] a great hero is reduced to weeping pitiably, like a girl, in

---

[124] 1202. He died, descending to Haides, in Homer, *Iliad* 18.117–19, and in the Hesiodic *Catalogue*. His immortality first occurs in the *Odyssey* (11.601–5) and in Hesiod's *Theogony* (950–55). Though this is controversial, I firmly believe – *pace* e.g. Segal 1981, 99–100 – that the exclusion from *YWT* of all reference to immortality is deliberate and significant. See Ley's discussion at n. 54 below, p. 265. (The absence of the Furies at the end of Sophokles' *El* has caused similar critical concerns; see Ewans 2000, Introduction.)

[125] For Winnington-Ingram (1980, 75), *YWT* is simply 'a tragedy of sex'.

[126] Winnington-Ingram (1980, 81 n. 28) rightly drew attention to the sexual symbolism of Deianeira's choice not to die by hanging, which was the normal means for women both of suicide (e.g. Iokaste in *OKing*) and of execution (the disloyal maidservants in Homer, *Odyssey* 22.461ff.).

public (1072ff.), because he has been enslaved to his passion for Iole (352ff., 488–9). This passion led to the fulfilment of an oracle (1159ff.), bringing down on Herakles the long-delayed revenge of Nessos (cf. 851ff., 151–64).

Young Women of Trachis is central to Sophokles' world-vision, at least as evidenced in the seven surviving dramas. The story of Herakles, Deianeira and Iole enabled Sophokles to create his most complex and compelling dramatization of muta-bility – the idea of the impermanence and lack of security in any current human situation, the constant state of flux in which success and failure, glory and shame, life and death ebb and flow like the waves, and circle like the Plough around the North Pole (129–31). As Deianeira, faced with the newly enslaved women from the sack of Oichalia, says in a telling understate-ment, 'success . . . can end'.[127]

By crystallizing this theme around the fall of Herakles, the epitome of male *arete* brought low by a woman and by sexual desire, Sophokles positions his surviving principal character for an extraordinary attack on Zeus. In all four of the tragedies collected in this volume, Sophokles' gods merely predict that particular events will happen (often if/when something else has happened), or indicate divine disapproval of specific human behaviour. The gods then stand back; mortals create their own disasters, because of their own limitations.

The Greek gods could not be held to blame, any more than Greek *agathoi* could be, if they were indifferent to the death of an unrelated human being; but when Zeus in this drama appar-ently takes no action while his own son Herakles dies in agony, he has violated the basic duty of care implicit in *philos*-relation-ships, and has therefore done something which is shameful for him. Hence the force of Hyllos' unique rebuke to the gods (1267ff.); what is happening 'for us is pitiful,/ shameful for them . . .'; the supreme god apparently does not care even about the fate of his own children. However, even this outcry is subsumed beneath the calm of Hyllos' final insight, that of all

---

[127] 297. Cf. Choros 1 (94ff.), *passim*; 295–306, 460ff., 543ff., 943ff., 1270. Jones 1962, 174–7; cf. Easterling, 1982, 23 and Winnington-Ingram 1980, 330–31. The opening allusion (1–3; cf. 945–6) to the Solonian proverb 'count no man happy until he is dead', like the closing allusion in O*King*, is designed to reinforce this vision; cf. Easterling 1982, 71.

this 'great pain and suffering in the strangest shape', 'there is nothing . . . which is not Zeus'. What does that mean?

Young Women of Trachis is the surviving tragedy that most clearly demonstrates the pattern of a *moira* taking shape, which is central to the plot of the *Iliad* and of every surviving tragedy by Aischylos and Sophokles.[128] In the plot the theme of sexual passion as destroyer, and the vision of human existence as precarious and constantly subject to change, are exhibited through the use of a story-pattern,[129] and dramatized by super-imposing on that pattern an oracle which is gradually narrowed down and made specific.

The pattern is the sequence of events surrounding the *nostos*, the homecoming of a king.[130] Sophokles' story shows how the normal pattern of events, from the first rumours that Herakles is about to return after his Labours, via the arrival of the advance herald Lichas through to the king's actual return, is perverted by Herakles' infatuation with Iole. Her presence rein-flects Lichas' arrival in a literally fatal direction, when it induces Deianeira to welcome her husband with the gift of the (poisoned) robe.

As these events unfold, Herakles' *moira* becomes more fully formed and his moment of death becomes fixed by the gradual revelation of the oracles about his homecoming. Deianeira mentions at 46ff. the tablet that Herakles left behind, and tells Hyllos a loose version of the main oracle at 79ff.; then, after the entry of the Young Women, Deianeira gives them a fuller, more explicit version (155ff.), in which Herakles instructed her to divide up his property, because he had learned from Zeus' oracle at Dodona that he would now either die 'or if he managed to survive that particular term,/he would live free from pain for the rest of his days' (167–8).

The drama shows the action of the critical time during which this 'either/or' is becoming clarified.[131] The oracle is the frame-work within which Sophokles requires us to understand the

[128] Ewans 1995, xxvii ff.; 1996b *passim*.

[129] For this phrase cf. Lattimore's pioneering study (1964).

[130] Cf. e.g. Aischylos' *Persians* and *Agamemnon*; see Taplin 1977, 84. For a detailed analysis of how the *nostos* pattern is used in *Agamemnon*, Ewans 1982.

[131] Cf. the twenty-four-hour period of Athena's wrath inside which the action of *Ai* takes place; *Ai* 719ff.

subsequent action: the return of Lichas with Iole, Deianeira's decision to use the 'love-potion', and its appalling consequences.[132] Once those are known – with Deianeira dead, and Herakles dying – the prediction is brought to the surface once again to explain the action. The Women of Trachis gain full wisdom, and are able to realize how – and how completely – the ambiguous oracle, which appeared to offer two alternatives, has come true (824ff.); Herakles' labours are indeed complete:

> For how could a man who no longer
> sees the light, a dead man,
> still be a slave to labour?

When Hyllos tells him about Nessos, Herakles at once reads this oracle in the same way, and realizes that he is the victim of a sick pun by the gods on the Greek phrase '*apallagê ponôn*' – 'release from labours' (1168ff.):[133]

> the many voices that come
> from my father's oak ... told me that in this living
> and present time now I should obtain release
> from my imposed labours. I hoped for good success.
> But the meaning was only that I should die;
> there is no further labour for the dead.

As Herakles acknowledges in the next line, all has now become clear. Clarity and coherence are finally achieved because two alternatives have narrowed to one, as the principal characters and the audience come to realize how and why terrible events have happened. Elsewhere and earlier in the drama, men and women move in the dark, imprisoned by the limitations of human knowledge (cf. esp. 392–3); the emphasis throughout is on the cycles of change, and the sequence of characters learning the truth too late.[134]

This drama is deployed around extreme contrasts, crystallized

---

[132] Sophokles emphasizes her freedom of choice by having her first resist and then (after exit and re-entry) succumb to temptation: 436ff., 531ff. On the use of the casket as a prop, cf. Seale 1982, 199–200.

[133] The joke is not even mediated through Apollo at Delphi, like the prophecy given to Laios in O King, but given directly by Zeus' own oracle at Dodona. Its sickness is worthy of Aristophanes at his most macabre; cf. Frogs 117ff.

[134] 710–11, 934; Easterling 1982, 2–3. The theme of the limits of human knowledge is one of the main affinities between YWT and OKing.

around the opposition between the two characters played by the First Actor: the gentle heroine with the ominous name (Deianeira means 'husband-killer'), who tries deperately to live up to *sophrosyne*, the Greek ideal of female virtue, inside the civilized world of her *oikos*; and the hero, a supreme manifestation of male *arete*, who lives in the world of beasts and monsters, unlike any other hero in tragedy.[135]

Performance

The plot of *Young Women of Trachis* reflects its dominant theme of mutability. What should be the ordered sequence of a hero's return to his home – an advance herald sent as soon as he has landed, followed by his own return after sacrificing at an altar near his point of landfall – is disrupted by a sequence of surprises. These include Hyllos' running entry and exit; the arrival not of one messenger to herald Herakles' arrival, but of two (the Old Man and then Lichas); Lichas' arrival not alone but with soldiers herding the captive women from Oichalia; Deianeira's attraction to the silent Iole; the Old Man's speech revealing Lichas' account as false; Deianeira's apprehension when the tuft of wool, which she used to anoint the robe, crumbles in the sunlight; Hyllos' return with the account of Herakles' agony; Deianeira's silent departure and her suicide; perhaps even Herakles' insistence that Hyllos marry Iole;[136] certainly the absence of any hint at the legend of his apotheosis.

Young Women of Trachis, like *Oidipous the King*,[137] makes a deliberately lopsided use of the performance space. The left *parodos* is used only for the entrance of the *choros*; apart from their arrival the potential for interaction between the *orchêstra* (which represents the area in front of the *oikos* of Deianeira and Herakles) and the left *parodos* leading to downtown Trachis is

---

[135] The Levi-Straussian ('raw/cooked') antitheses in *YWT* have been particularly explored by Charles Segal (1981; cf. also Segal 1977, included in Segal 1995). As he notes (60), this drama exemplifies his particular preoccupation – liminality, the thresholds that demarcate civilization from brutish violence – more clearly than any other surviving tragedy by Sophokles.

[136] Dorian Greeks traced their descent from Herakles through the marriage of Hyllos and Iole (cf. Easterling 1982, 17), so this may not have been a surprise for the audience.

[137] Below, p. lxxiii.

completely ignored. The reason is the same in both dramas;
Sophokles deliberately narrows the geography of his theatre
down from the normal interaction between three entrances (used
to the full in both *Aias* and *Antigone*) to a simple binary
opposition. Sophokles uses the right *parodos* to represent the
path to a fierce and violent world; the world of Herakles' great
deeds, from which come first the victims of Herakles and then
at last the man himself. By contrast the *skene* door leads into
the *oikos*, and the domestic territory controlled by Deianeira,
who tries to epitomize *sophrosyne*, the excellences of a good
wife and mother; but by supreme irony, Nessos' poison, the
most lethal product of the world of beasts and monsters, has
resided quietly in its civilized depths, and she will give it back
to the light.

While Deianeira is alive, the drama exhibits a sequence of
incursions from the wild into the civilized, until she sends back
to Herakles the poison which symbolizes both his subjection of
bestiality (when he shot the lustful kentaur), and the 'disease' of
erotic passion that is within him – and her – no less than it was
in the beast. After her death, superhuman suffering invades the
orchêstra, when Herakles is brought back in his agony, and the
lead actor performs the extraordinary and demanding Finale.
He is placed at the centre point, and therefore pulls focus
forward, away from the *skene*. He never enters it; the household
has been completely destroyed, by Deianeira's death within and
by his impending death on Mount Oita. One of the few insolu-
ble staging problems in this drama is the direction in which the
choros departs;[138] but if Ley is right in his stage directions to
prefer them to leave not left, back to their homes, but right,
forming a portion of the cortège, this symbolizes the totality of
the disruption. Nobody goes home. Everyone must return to the
wild for the death of Herakles, which will be as fierce and
savage as was his life; and, most uncharacteristically for Greek
mourners, they must stifle their laments, as he will stifle his
groans. They therefore all depart with the silent determination
that he has demanded (1259ff.).

The greatest of this drama's many surprises is also one of the
most remarkable scenes – and certainly the most effective use of
silent extras – in surviving Greek tragedy. When Lichas brings

---

[138] See Ley's Notes, below, n. 56 on p. 266.

back the captive women, they must be placed in symmetrical opposition to the *choros*, and contrasted with them in their costumes.[139] I would conjecture a visual opposition between black clothes of mourning and slavery, for the victims of savage conquest, destruction and rape, and white for Deinaneira's young friends from Trachis, unmarried and sexually inexperienced (NB 142ff.). Here, then, *Young Women of Trachis'* normal binary opposition between *oikos* and wild is abandoned, and this one scene actualizes the Athenian theatre's normal ternary division. Deianeira, who has come from the central *oikos*, is surrounded on her left by the untroubled girls from Trachis and on her right by the suffering women from Oichalia. She is trapped between the two images which together make real in the *orchêstra* Sophokles' central theme of mutability (what one group of women still is, the other group until very recently were, cf. 282–3). This picture symbolizes that she herself – in tragic contrast to her own naïve certainty at 4–5 – is diachronically trapped in the middle of the sequence of mutability, just as she is synchronically trapped in the antithesis between barbarism and civilization.

Date

Young Women of Trachis is a mature and powerful Sophoklean drama; the linguistic style associates it loosely with *Aias* and *Antigone*, and it could therefore have been first performed at any time between around 445 and 425 BC.[140]

The drama is close in subject-matter and dramatic techniques to *Oidipous the King*, which is almost certainly to be dated after 431 BC;[141] and there is one other attractive reason to suggest a relatively late date. There have been many discussions of dramas by different tragedians based on the same myth, and using the audience's knowledge of previous versions for comparison and contrast;[142] Aristophanes' comic uses of recent, and even less recent, tragedies are also well known. Might it not

---

[139] See Ley's Notes, below, p. 252.

[140] The arguments for this time bracket are summarized at Easterling 1982, 20–23. There is no good reason for the traditional belief that it is a dramatically flawed and therefore an early work (cf. e.g. Hoey 1979).

[141] Below, p. lxxv.

[142] Cf. e.g. Baldry (1971) Vickers (1973) and Walton (1980) on the Elektra dramas of Aischylos, Sophocles and Euripides.

have been possible for one tragic playwright to use a different myth, but one that treated obviously similar themes and events, to mount a critique of an opponent's vision of the same aspects of human experience?

The destructive power of sexual passion is central in two tragedies of Euripides: *Medeia* of 431 BC, and *Hippolytos*, which was written in its first version in 429, but generated controversy, and only achieved performance, in the revised version that has survived to us, in 428. In both dramas the plot explores the reactions of a wife whose love is scorned; and in *Medeia*, revenge is achieved through a poisoned robe, which is delivered to the victim in an enclosed casket so it may not react with the sunlight until it has been taken out and worn. It is at least possible that Euripides' *Medeia* – an extremely innovative treatment of a previously neglected part of the Medeia/Iason legend – inspired Sophokles to create *Young Women of Trachis*.[143] His totally opposed heroine – Greek, and striving to the female excellence of *sophrosyne* – created the same terrible revenge by identical means (but unintentionally and in ignorance) as Euripides' barbarian Medeia, aspiring to the revenge code of male *arete*, achieved deliberately.[144]

The first *Hippolytos* might then have been Euripides' reply to *Young Women of Trachis*; a further meditation on the same theme of sexual passion as destroyer, this time with a woman as the central figure who is neither completely opposed to the norms expected by Athenian male society (like Medeia), nor completely in conformity with them (like Deianeira). Phaidra – if we can judge from the revised *Hippolytos* that survives (373ff.) – attempted valiantly to live up to a standard of morality of which she was all too well aware, but was defeated by the power of Aphrodite, and directly propositioned her

---

[143] Kreophylos' epic poem *The Capture of Oichalia* is known to have mentioned Medeia – perhaps for contrast with Deianeira? If so, this may have brought the relationship between the myths of Medeia and Deianeira to Sophokles' mind.

[144] Parallels (and differences) are explored in Ley 1994, 38–40. Deianeira even has a cautionary Nurse, like Medeia. Note also that the 'otherness' of Medeia (her barbarian associations, her superhuman powers and her superior status as the child of a god) is also present in *YWT* – transferred to Herakles.

stepson to commit incest with her.[145] The surviving *Hippolytos* even alludes to Iole (545–54) in a way that presupposes some recent literary treatment. This could very well have been Sophokles' drama, since no other work on the Herakles myth is known from the period. I therefore tentatively conjecture that *Young Women of Trachis* was first performed in 430 BC.[146]

Oidipous the King

Story

Oidipous, the king of Thebes who married his own mother, first appears in Homer.[147] Oidipous' mother/wife[148] committed suicide by hanging herself when the truth was revealed, but Oidipous lived on.[149] There is no mention of children from their incestuous union.

The legend of Oidipous was the central subject of a trilogy by Aischylos, first performed at Athens in 467 BC.[150] Aischylos' version of the myth was different in several essentials from previous accounts; Sophokles in turn accepted some of Aischylos' new features, when he came to retell the story, and made further innovations of his own.

Aischylos' Laios had committed some crime – perhaps, as in other traditions, the abduction and homosexual rape of Pelops' son Chrysippos, who committed suicide in shame. In retaliation, Pelops cursed him 'that the evil should descend to his chil-

---

[145] This was the chief aspect of the first *Hippolytos* that led to its being condemned. In the surviving version Phaidra has a Nurse, who takes as consent Phaidra's failure to forbid her, and propositions Hippolytos on her mistress' behalf.

[146] Short fragments from a *Phaidra* by Sophokles survive; they show – characteristically? – that his Phaidra was much less obviously blameworthy than Euripides'. Perhaps this *Phaidra* was a further member of the same sequence of dramas and counter-dramas.

[147] *Odyssey* 11.271–90.

[148] Epikaste; the name Iokaste is not attested before Sophokles.

[149] In one version of the story, which is probably also early, Oidipous remarried after Epikaste's death and had children by his second wife, Eurygeneia (cf. Pausanias 9.5.110).

[150] *Laios, Oidipous* and the surviving *Seven against Thebes*, with the concluding *satyr-drama Sphinx*.

dren'.[151] After Laios became king of Thebes, Apollo's oracle told him that he must die childless to keep the city safe.[152] None the less, 'thoughtless desire for children conquered him,/ and he created his own fate/ the father-killer Oidipous . . .'.[153] At birth Oidipous was exposed (in Aischylos, in a jar) on the mountainside, but somehow saved.

The remainder of the story appears to have been much as in Sophokles. Laios went on a journey, was involved in a quarrel with a stranger, and was killed together with most, but not all, of his retinue.

Oidipous arrived at Thebes, and rescued the city from the Sphinx. His reward was the hand in marriage of the former king's widow, and he had children by her. The children in his version were sons – Eteokles and Polyneikes;[154] the sisters Antigone and Ismene, who appear in *Oidipous the King*, were probably invented by Sophokles himself, in *Antigone*.[155]

In Homer, Oidipous discovered almost immediately that he had committed incest; his wife Epikaste hanged herself, but Oidipous lived on as king of Thebes. Aischylos' major creative innovation was to give Oidipous a long period of prosperity before the discovery. When he found out what he had done he blinded himself, as in Sophokles; subsequently he cursed his sons that they would divide their inheritance with iron. In the surviving third drama *Seven against Thebes*, Aischylos dramatized how they fought to the death, and so destroyed the royal house of Thebes.

Sophokles omitted Oidipous' sons (except for a glancing reference at 1459); but he made the two daughters, who are still children at the time of the action, play an important part in his Finale. The crucial difference from Aischylos is that Sophokles' drama provides no reason for the oracle given to Laios; it now takes the form of a simple prediction by Apollo that Laios must

---

[151] Ancient commentary on Euripides *Phoinikian Women* line 60; cf. Aischylos *Seven against Thebes* 744ff.

[152] *Seven against Thebes* 742ff. Note that in Aischylos the oracle is conditional; if Laios had abstained from sex, he would have survived.

[153] *Seven against Thebes* 750ff.

[154] The story of Eteokles and Polyneikes probably dates back to a lost post-Homeric epic poem.

[155] Above, p. xlvi.

die at the hands of his child by Iokaste (711ff.).[156] In *Oidipous the King* the story of the Theban royal house is not a tragedy of crime and horrendous punishment. In this version of the story, neither divine command nor human wrongdoing is responsible for Oidipous' unknowing violation of two of western society's greatest taboos.

Drama

Like Aischylos, Sophokles chose to begin his action on the last day of Oidipous' rule at Thebes, long after his murder of Laios, conquest of the Sphinx and wedding to Iokaste. This is the story not of Oidipous' deeds but of how he came to discover the truth about himself, and lose the throne of Thebes.[157] The essence of the drama is contained in the mutability shown by the contrast between the first and last images – the great, problem-solving king and the blinded, powerless beggar – which fills with meaning the closing, 'Solonian' proverb: 'don't be happy till/ you pass life's boundary without suffering grief'.[158]

Sophokles created this drama at a time when increasing numbers of Greeks no longer believed that worshipping the gods was justified; and the plague-ridden city shown in Scene 1 would remind every Athenian of the recent plague which had led many of them to open disbelief in gods, oracles and prophets.[159] *Oidipous the King* begins in an atmosphere of reverence and piety, as the characters all react to the plague as an indication of divine displeasure with Thebes, whose cause only the Delphic oracle and the prophet Teiresias can clarify. The plot is shaped to emphasize a movement from initial piety, through increasing disbelief, to a terrible, sudden reversal in which the whole truth becomes known; as the drama unfolds, circumstances lead the Elders, Iokaste and Oidipous increasingly

[156] Did Iokaste mentally suppress a second half of this oracle which foretold incest, matching Apollo's prediction to Oidipous when he came to Delphi? Or did the first oracle withhold this part of the future from her? Cf. Vickers 1973, 497 + refs.

[157] Vickers (1973, 501–7) provides a useful table, detailing the events in the story in chronological order, together with the points at which Sophokles introduces them into his plot. It demonstrates that all interpretations that criticize Oidipous for being unduly slow to realize the truth are misguided, in the light of the order in which the key facts become available to him.

[158] Cf. Seale 1982, 254.

[159] Thoukydides *History* 2.53, quoted above, p. xx.

towards scepticism. Doubts about prophets – though not yet about the gods themselves – are voiced by the Elders in Choros 2; Iokaste denies the truth of oracles at 711–12 and 848ff.; and her outburst, and Oidipous', when they hear the news from Korinth are openly contemptuous of prophets and of the Delphic oracle (946ff., 964ff.). Just before this the Elders have sung Choros 3 (863ff.) with its extraordinary, desperate desire for even this horrible oracle to be fulfilled. If it is not, there will be no pattern or order in the universe, and no point in worshipping the gods. Indeed, not even any point in dancing the dances of tragedy, as the *choros*, stepping temporarily out of role, sing to the Athenians at 893ff.[160]

Sophokles gives one more twist to the plot before the revelation. At the end of Choros 3, two false beliefs alone sustain Oidipous against the weight of the prophecies, and of the rough coincidence between the time and place of the murder of Laios and his own encounter with an elderly king and his entourage; the beliefs that many robbers attacked Laios, not one; and that Laios' son died at birth. Before the Herdsman comes, and is forced to demolish both these beliefs, the Korinthian arrives, and provides yet another reassuring false belief – that because Polybos is dead, Oidipous' father is dead. But the Korinthian turns out also to be the unintentional bearer of the hidden truth; when he tells Oidipous that Merope was not his mother, Iokaste knows what she has done.

And so the oracle is revealed as all too true. Sophokles – very much like Euripides in *Hippolytos*, another major tragedy from the same period – seems to be asserting that even in a time where the complex interaction between the divine and the human, which is evident in the surviving work of Aischylos, has been lost, there are still some individual gods and goddesses whose power remains strong, and terrible.[161] However, the Aischylean pattern of actions and inexorable consequences, spreading across the world with human acts linked together by

[160] Cf. Knox 1984, 137ff. and Segal 1981, 235–6. Rehm 1993, 115–16 is excellent on the dangers for Sophokles and the mid- to late-fifth-century audience of a random, *tychê*-dominated universe. Cf. also the detailed analysis of 898ff. in Winnington-Ingram 1980, 197ff.

[161] Apollo (backed by Zeus, 904ff.) in O*King*; Aphrodite and Artemis in *Hippolytos*. In one of his two last tragedies, Euripides was to remind his audience also of the powers of Dionysos (*Bakchai*).

the gods and *daimones*, is no longer present; Sophokles' gods stand aloof from human affairs. They merely predict isolated events; they certainly do not control our actions.[162]

Oidipous has often been found wanting by critics determined to detect in him either *hybris* (mistranslated as 'arrogant pride' – the classical meaning is 'wanton violence') or *hamartia*, in the New Testament sense of 'moral flaw' rather than the classical sense of 'error or mistake of fact', to justify his fate.[163] The impulse to find such faults is caused by the most provocative aspect of Sophokles' story, his refusal to supply any reason why these almost incredible misfortunes were visited on this one man before he was even born. But the impulse must be resisted, since precisely that is the point of this singularly bleak tragedy. Oidipous has done, and does, nothing to deserve his appalling misfortune, and he discovers the truth through his distinctive excellences, not through any vices. Oidipous acts exactly as any Greek king would, confronted with a plague on his city; all the aspects of his character noted by modern commentators – his energy, self-sufficiency, pride, daring and practical intelligence – are fundamental, defining components of the fifth century Athenian ideal of male human *arete*.[164]

Oidipous the King has no villains. All the other characters are good men and women, who are doing their best to help the city to escape from the plague and to free their hitherto completely admirable king from the dreadful fear, which increasingly grips him as the drama develops. Each of them acts naturally, and justifiably in the light of the false or inadequate information that they possess; but because of the human limitation of their lack of knowledge, their well-intentioned action generates further disaster, moving the drama one step closer to revelation of the apalling truth. This pattern is seen especially towards the centre of the drama; one of the main examples is Iokaste's attempt to dispel Oidipous' fear of oracles and prophets, by telling him about the prophecy that had been given to

---

[162] This vital point, which renders irrelevant most of the theological and philosophical speculation about *OKing*, is well made by Vickers 1973, 497.

[163] Including even e.g. Jones 1960, 211–12. For a robust demolition of Bowra's attempt to create this kind of 'moral' for *OKing*, see Waldock 1951, 143–58.

[164] Cf. Winnington-Ingram 1980, 203–4.

her and to Laios (707ff.). The other is the Korinthian's desire to help; he is so overjoyed at having been able to give Oidipous and Iokaste welcome news that he tries to soothe their fears, by telling them that Merope was not Oidipous' mother (989ff.). Then at the climax we learn that this pattern was central even in the past, when Oidipous was a baby. The oracle's fulfilment was made possible by yet another well-intentioned emotion, disastrous because of human ignorance of the full facts: the compassion that the Herdsman showed for the infant Oidipous (1178ff.).

As the spectators watch, they know more than the characters, and can foresee the traps which they blunder into because of their ignorance. Behind the audience, up in the sky, looking down on them as they look down on the figures in the *orchêstra*, are the gods, whose superior knowledge gives them exactly the same position in relation to the spectators as that of those spectators in relation to the characters. The audience watches, but cannot intervene in, the tragedy of Oidipous; so too – in Sophokles' vision – the gods merely spectate, and do not interfere in our lives. Few dramas ever written expose so pitilessly the isolation, and the limitations, of human existence:[165]

> ELDERS: Oh you mortal generations, I must count
> your life no life at all.
> For who of you is really happy,
> rather than appearing happy?
> And appearing so soon falls away. (1187ff.)

Oidipous the King is akin to *Young Women of Trachis*: in both dramas a *moira* gradually takes shape, and the events become more and more coherent to the characters through a sequence of discoveries which they make as the action unfolds. This drama begins with a clear indication of divine displeasure with Thebes: the plague. Its general cause is soon clarified by Kreon's message from Delphi – the Thebans must punish the killers of Laios; then it is specified precisely, as a result of the quarrel between Oidipous and Teiresias, in the hideously explicit forecast of the events that the prophet unleashes in his departing lines (447ff.). After that the divine recedes, and human choices lead to the revelation of the truth – just as they

---

[165] Cf. Knox 1957, 77; Segal 1981, 247.

did in the past, as narrated by Oidipous at 787ff. Oidipous' free choice led him to parricide and incest when, horrified by the oracle's prediction, he forgot why he originally came to Delphi, headed north (away from Korinth, where his supposed parents were) – and so encountered Laios on the road to Thebes.[166]

Aischylos and Sophokles frequently provide only broad initial hints at what will actually happen in their dramas.[167] In *Oidipous*, however (like *Aias*), the cause of *miasma* is narrowed down rapidly; before a third of the drama is over, Teiresias has made clear to the audience the truths that will later be revealed to Iokaste and Oidipous. This pattern places the main theme of the drama – Oidipous' movement to the discovery of who he is and what he has done – within a framework that ensures that the successive results of his attempt to disprove the truth of Teiresias' accusations only intensify the searing credibility of the prophet's exit speech. After that it seems as if Oidipous is being coralled in, herded towards the point where he cannot escape the hideously ironic truths – the 'stranger' is a native Theban, the healer is himself the city's sickness, the detective is himself the criminal.[168]

The action reaches its climax at a point of revelation where all the elements cohere: the myth of Oidipous, the Sophoklean rhythm of sudden change or mutability, the *miasma* and the steps towards its removal, the story-pattern of riddle and decipherment, and the momentum created by the plot. Oidipous' search becomes increasingly fanatical as his resistance to the truth becomes increasingly untenable; and the climax (1169ff.) is an archetypal moment at which Oidipous, by the strange paradox that is at the heart of 'the tragic', recognizes the inevitability of choosing to know:

---

[166] Oidipous' freedom of choice still needs emphasis, given the propensity of earlier critics, and of many students, to see him as doom-laden and predestined (brilliantly countered by Dodds 1983). As soon as that is implied, the tragic effect is lost, and a comic dimension intrudes even on this appalling myth; cf. Aristophanes' skittish fun with the opening lines of Euripides' *Oidipous* (*Frogs* 1182ff.), and Berkoff's brilliant rehandling of the myth in *Greek*.

[167] Cf. e.g. the opening scene of Aischylos, *Agamemnon*, especially 11, 34–5 and 248ff.

[168] Cf. Knox 1964, 138; 1984, 131.

OIDIPOUS: A slave, or born of the same line as Laios?
HERDSMAN: Oh, I'm close to speaking of the horror.
OIDIPOUS: And I to hearing of it. But it must be heard.

In that 'must' lies all the force of the tragedy.[169] What Oidipous accepts is not an externally imposed necessity, but a now irresistible human compulsion to know. His search is over, and suddenly the tempo changes, as he slows, and chooses to accept into himself the truth. He takes the step that the audience by now deeply expects – and indeed, almost perversely, desires.[170]

And then the consequences. Few critics have much to say about the scenes after Oidipous has learned the truth;[171] but in performance, the account of Iokaste's death and the sight of the self-blinded Oidipous occupy at least a quarter of the drama's playing time. All the consequences of the action, and of the appalling *miasma* now revealed in the royal house, are remorselessly worked out and shown to the audience. Sophokles dramatizes the death of Iokaste and the self-blinding of Oidipous, in one of his most powerful surviving messenger-speeches; a lyric scene follows, in which Oidipous is seen trying to think out and accept the reality that he has in ignorance violated two of the deepest taboos of almost all human societies. Interactions with Kreon, and with Antigone and Ismene, bring out the extent of his fall, and the destruction of his family in the face of indelible *miasma*, as he first clings to his sister-daughters, and is then forcibly separated from them and driven into the house.[172] The drama closes with a summary by the Elders, which reminds the

[169] Cf. Lattimore 1964, 41; also 7–8 where, writing about Aischylos' *Seven against Thebes*, Lattimore amplified his concept of a 'right order – a sense of necessity, of must-be-so' in tragedy; when Eteokles leaves to confront his brother – choosing to accept the opponent given to him by the sequence of speeches – 'the curse, the fate, the action and the choice coincide'.

[170] In Aristotelian terms, it would be offensive ('miaron'), if at this point Oidipous decided not to know, and broke off his enquiry. Cf. Aristotle's point (*Poetics* 53a36–9) that it will not do for myths to be changed so that e.g. Aigisthos and Orestes go off as friends; by the climax of *El*, both story and plot demand that Orestes *must* murder the usurpers. See further Ewans 1995, esp. xxix ff., on the *Oresteia*.

[171] The honourable exception is Vickers 1973, 512–515. Cf. also Rehm 1992 and Gould 1996, 231–2.

[172] On the implications of his final exit back into the *skene*, cf. Taplin 1983, 169–74.

audience of what the plot has demonstrated so powerfully, the precariousness of any human situation, the possibility of sudden, unexpected and total change at any time before we are dead. Deliberately echoing in reverse the blind Teiresias of Scene 2, who can 'see' more than other mortals, Oidipous at the close is a man alone, literally blind in a way that images the metaphorical blindness of all human beings.[173]

Performance

Many scholars have asserted that *Oidipous the King* is dramatically static.[174] The property list is slight even by the economical standards of Athenian tragedy: suppliant wands for the children and a wreath for Kreon in Scene 1, and wreaths and other offerings for Iokaste's handmaid in Scene 4; but the charge of lack of action can hardly be sustained for a drama which begins with a spectacular crowd scene, and later makes highly effective use (twice) of child extras clinging to a central character. Several scenes demand considerable, vigorous movement for their proper realization in the *orchêstra*.[175] In Scene 5 Oidipous has his servants prepare an old slave for torture (1152ff.), and he appears for the Finale staggering around, blind – possibly wearing a mask with blood streaming from its eye sockets.[176]

However, the power of this drama in its theatre rests on something far more fundamental than spectacle and movement. Sophokles evolves a significant pattern in his use of the *orchêstra*, as the drama unfolds.

Oidipous the King begins, like Aischylos' *Seven against Thebes*, with the king coming from the palace to confront a crowd played by extras. In Aischylos the extras play men of various ages from the city, and all remain silent. Sophokles' more dynamic *mise en scène* makes the extras children of the city, with a spokesman (an aged Priest) played by the second actor.

After their exit, the downtown entrance is only used by the

---

[173] On blindness in *OKing* see Buxton 1980 and Seale 1982, 215–60.

[174] Cf. e.g. Gardiner 1987, 107, cited and discussed by McCart below, n. 43 p. 279. It is deeply unhelpful when a critic of Segal's stature writes (1981, 241) that 'no play is more about language' than *OKing*.

[175] Especially Scene 2. See McCart's Notes below, pp. 278–9.

[176] So e.g. Taplin 1979, 89. But *contra* McCart below, n. 92 p. 298. On the implications see Buxton 1996, 38–39.

actor playing Kreon, for his second and third entries. Although this drama is not as absolute in its neglect of the left *parodos* as is *Young Women of Trachis*, Sophokles' basic spatial technique is the same; once again the normal ternary dialogue between left *parodos*, *skene* doors and right *parodos* is narrowed to a binary opposition: between characters entering from the right – bringing news from Delphi and from Korinth – and the king and queen who receive that news from near the threshold of the central *oikos*. Symbolically, news from abroad invades and destroys the royal household.[177]

This is reinforced in performance by a steady movement from playing in the front and centre of the *orchêstra* to a concentration of both solo actors and *choros* nearer to the *skene*. The altar of Apollo (either C or, better, FC) is used in the opening scene, and then again by Iokaste at 911ff., when she tries to take her own and the Elders' minds off the trouble inside the *oikos* and pray to Apollo. But this is the last point at which the action focuses in the front segment of the *orchêstra*. The arrival of the Korinthian sends her back inside, and she brings Oidipous out to just in front of the *skene*; the altar is never used again; and at the end of this scene and the next first Iokaste (with the children) and then Oidipous exit in haste and agony into the *skene*, unable to face the light of day as each successively realizes the truth. Their suicide and self-mutilation inside the palace lead to a revelation of what is inside the *skene*. This is not achieved, as often in the surviving dramas, by means of a tableau on the *ekkyklêma*.[178] None the less the whole Finale needs to be played in the rear half of the *orchêstra*, and at the end Kreon takes both Oidipous and his daughters back inside the *skene*.

Oidipous the King is remarkable for its cumulative sequence of more and more disastrous entries; these all take their place in a precise and terrifying sequence of events which is surprising – showing how, apparently, the plot is taking shape purely by *tychê*; but for the Athenian audience, aware of the legend of

---

[177] Fanciful theories, which create complex binary oppositions between imaginary offstage spaces, have been developed from the written text by Segal (1981, 227) and Wiles (1997, 177ff.).

[178] Cf. e.g. Aischylos *Agamemnon, Libation-Bearers*; Sophokles *Ai, Ant, El*; Euripides *Hippolytos*. An exception, interesting because it is probably close in date to *OKing*, is *YWT*.

Oidipous, each of these entrances answers a deeper, subconscious need for revelation. Both Kreon and Teiresias come by Oidipous' will, anticipating the Elders' requests; between them they narrow down the opening indication of divine displeasure to the precise denunciation and prophecy at the climax of the Teiresias scene (447ff.). Kreon's almost parenthetical return, to defend himself against the accusations first levelled in the Teiresias scene by Oidipous, is important less for itself than for its consequences; it brings Iokaste from the *skene* for the first time, and here the characteristic pattern of the middle stages of the drama – willing help which turns out to be unhelpful – forces Oidipous to seek further revelation; he sends for the Herdsman who survived the massacre of Laios' men (859ff.), and retreats once more with Iokaste to wait inside the palace.

Sophokles next contrives a fatal meeting (*tychê* again). Iokaste returns from the household, bringing offerings for Apollo; she is met from the right *parodos* not by the expected Herdsman, but by the Korinthian. His news is designed to please Oidipous, but is in fact the beginning of the end, since it precipitates Iokaste's final exit. And the Korinthian's eager presence ensures that the Herdsman, when he arrives – delayed after his expected time[179] because his news, when it comes, is hesitant and reluctant – is able to make the final revelation which proves incest as well as parricide. After the revelation, the Korinthian and the Herdsman both return to the country. News from abroad and from his past has destroyed Oidipous and his household, and the next two entries – first the Servant, and then Oidipous himself – are made from the *skene* to reflect this.

Kreon's third and final entry is from the left *parodos*. It therefore reasserts the role of the city (in the person of its new leader)[180] for the first time since Scene 1.[181] The entrance from the *skene* of Antigone and Ismene once again brings the consequences for the *oikos* into the public domain; it both increases the pathos and allows full exploration of the violations of taboo.

---

[179] In contrast to Kreon and Teiresias, who were hastened; so rightly Seale 1982, 237.

[180] Cf. Macleod, quoted by Taplin 1978, 46.

[181] We should therefore regard his second entry for Scene 3 as a premature attempt to orient Oidipous' world back to tragedy's normal mode, in which the palace is placed evenly between an equally important outside world and *polis*.

Then Kreon rejects Oidipous' plea to be allowed to die on Mount Kithairon. In Scene 1 Oidipous came from the *skene* and moved out, as a powerful and responsible king, to meet on equal terms the suffering people of his *polis*; he controlled a crowd fanned out around the front of the *orchêstra*. At the end that image is reversed, to enforce in theatrical presentation the drama's central theme of the transience and mutability of human life. Kreon chastens Oidipous' vestiges of regal behaviour (1515, 1522), and drives him inside the *skene*, locking the source of *miasma* back away from the light. During this scene the Elders, far from being an audience for Oidipous, are huddled at the perimeter of the *orchêstra*.

Date

There is no firm evidence for the date of *Oidipous the King*. However, most classical scholars are agreed that this drama, on the basis of its linguistic style, falls in the middle of the surviving seven – after *Aias, Antigone* and *Young Women of Trachis*, and before *Elektra, Philoktetes* and *Oidipous at Kolonos*. This would place it between around 430 and 420, or at latest 413 BC. Scene 1 evokes the plague in a way that seems very much drawn from life; this would suggest the drama was written after the plague that afflicted Athens in 430 BC – perhaps even after its recurrence in 426/5.[182] Similarly the figure of Oidipous has seemed to have many affinities with the Athenian national character as described by Thoukydides, both in the analysis in Book 1 and in Perikles' speeches in Book 2.[183] Both these points are obviously subjective and unproveable, but if well taken they would indicate a first performance while both the plague and Perikles' leadership were in recent memory, i.e. within two or three years on either side of 425.

MICHAEL EWANS

[182] See Knox 1956; he detects particular parallels between Sophokles' language and aspects of the recurrence of the plague (Thoukydides 3.87 and Diodoros 12.58). He also claims to see echoes of *OKing* in Aristophanes' *Knights* (January 424), and would therefore date *OKing* precisely to 425.

[183] Thoukydides, *Histories* 1.70; 2.35ff. and 60ff. See Knox 1964, 116ff. and 1984, 138ff., esp. 140: 'Oidipous is the dramatic embodiment of the creative vigour and intellectual daring of the fifth-century Athenian spirit.'

NOTE ON THE TRANSLATION AND NOTES

Translation

The contributors to this book were all initially trained as scholars of the Greek language, but we teach, and direct productions, in Departments of Drama or Performance Studies. We have translated these dramas for performance; our scripts have been modified in workshop or rehearsal to make them fully actable. We also attempt to render the meaning(s) of the text into English as closely and accurately as possible.

The style of our translations varies, to reflect the way in which Sophokles adapted his own Greek style to reflect the very different subject-matter of the four dramas – the rough military/naval vocabulary and occasional sublime imagery of *Aias*, the sometimes disconcerting blend of archaic and colloquial, familial and formal in *Young Women of Trachis*, the different kinds of interaction between political and personal tragedy in *Antigone* and *Oidipous the King*. As translators we have tried to be alert to what we find in each drama, rather than imposing some kind of uniform English style on Sophokles.

The attribution of speeches, and all stage directions in any translation from Greek tragedy, are modern. The directions in this edition are for the Greek theatre shape, and based on the experience gained in our workshops and productions. Modern directors who need to modify these directions to suit a differently shaped performace space must still be aware of Sophokles' own practice and the reasons for it. Only those directions that we regard as certain are printed in the text; further suggestions will be found in the Notes.

Characters enter either actor right – from the countryside/abroad – actor left – from the downtown district of the place in which the action is located – or through the single set of double doors in the centre of the *skene* façade.[1] A character entering down a *parodos* is in the sight of some of the actors and audience, on the opposite side from where he is making his entry, long before he steps into the *orchêstra*. Presumably the convention was that the actor was in character from the moment he became visible to any of the audience, but engaged in interaction with the players already there only after he stepped into the *orchêstra*. Accordingly in these texts the direction *Enter X* is positioned at the moment where X enters the *orchêstra*, not when the actor first comes into sight of some of the audience.

The text is divided into Scenes (predominantly consisting of spoken dialogue) and Choroses (passages sung and danced by the *choros* alone). These are numbered in separate consecutive series for each drama. Sometimes a choral ode is too short to interrupt the development of a scene as a whole (e.g. *Young Women of Trachis* Choros 2); these are numbered as new odes, but the number is placed in parentheses, and the scene is not ended when they begin.

Alternation between Choroses and Scenes is the basic structural feature of Greek tragedy; we have therefore not obscured it by importing the later technical terms found in the twelfth, probably interpolated, chapter of Aristotle's *Poetics*.[2]

Notes

The Notes in this book are framed around the units of Greek dramatic structure: Scenes and Choroses. They are designed to help readers towards an understanding of how, as the original production unfolded through time, each individual drama made its effect on the audience. We believe that modern theatre companies and students can only render these dramas into contemporary theatrical terms by understanding how they used their original performance space and its conventions; and we

[1] We draw readers' attention to the fact that this series follows normal theatrical practice, and gives stage directions from the viewpoint of the actor, since a recent book on Athenian staging (Wiles 1997) gives all directions from the spectator's viewpoint.

[2] 'Prologos', 'parodos', 'stasimon', 'epeisodion' and 'exodos'; *Poetics* 52b14–27. We also do not accept the over-ingenious theory of Act-dividing and non-Act-dividing odes with which Taplin (1977, 49ff.) sought to replace this terminology.

have found that insights gained through study can only be tested and augmented through workshop or production in a replica of the original performance space.

Because we adopt a common approach, we have been able to cross-reference similarities and parallels between Sophokles' dramatic techniques in different dramas. However, a uniform methodology does not imply that we are in monolithic agreement on all aspects of his stagecraft; we therefore also note some specific points on which our views differ.

Positions in the *orchêstra* are described in the Notes by a combination of letters: F = front (nearest to the Priest of Dionysos at the centre of the front row of spectators), B = back (nearest to the *skene*); L = (actor) left, R = (actor) right; C = centre; E = extreme (i.e. at the perimeter).[3]

Lyric and Spoken Verse

The interplay between lyric, sung verse and spoken verse in the Greek text is marked in this edition by double-indenting all verses that were sung in the original performances.

Strophic responsion in lyrics is denoted by numbering the first *strophe* (A1) and its matching *antistrophe* (A2); if there is a concluding *epode* that is marked (A3). The second pair in a system is marked (B1), (B2) – and so on.

Choral dialogue was almost certainly divided between different members of the group. Accordingly we prefix lines spoken by 'the *choros*' with e.g. 1 Sailor, 1 Councillor; directors will choose who is to speak each line as they develop their interpretation of each scene.

Transliteration, Glossaries

In this edition, following the practice of an ever-increasing number of classical scholars, proper names are transliterated directly from the Greek original, and the traditional Latinized spellings (e.g. Oedipus for Oidipous) are not employed. *Upsilon* is transliterated by *y*, not *u*; and *chi* by *ch*, not *kh*.

Two Glossaries are provided, one of all the Greek names that

---

[3] There is further discussion of this notation, with a diagram, in Ley and Ewans 1985.

occur in the text, and the other of all the Greek words italicized in the Introduction and Notes.

Line Numbering

These dramas are translated from the corrected second edition of the Oxford Classical Text edited by H. Lloyd-Jones and N. G. Wilson. For uniformity in referencing, all modern scholars use the line numbering of one of the early editions of Sophokles. However there has been much research, particularly in the last fifty years, on the nature of Greek lyric verse; this has led to revisions of the line structure. Our translations follow the Oxford text's presentation; accordingly in lyric sections there are sometimes more, sometimes less than ten lines of English verse between the line-markers.

Where there is reason to believe that a line or lines are missing from the Greek text, we add a suggested text for performance in square brackets. Where lines have been interpolated into Sophokles' Greek text, we omit them from the translation, and draw attention to this by supplying a line number for the line immediately preceding and that immediately following the omission (cf. e.g. *Ai* 838ff.).

Abbreviations

In the footnotes we abbreviate the titles of Sophokles' seven surviving dramas *Ai* (*Aias*), *Ant* (*Antigone*), *YWT* (*Young Women of Trachis*), *OKing* (*Oidipous the King*), *El* (*Elektra*), *Phil* (*Philoktetes*) and *OKol* (*Oidipous at Kolonos*).

AIAS

Translated by Michael Ewans

THE ACTORS AND THEIR ROLES

ODYSSEUS	Actor 3
ATHENA	Actor 2
AIAS	Actor 1
SAILORS FROM SALAMIS	Choros
TEKMESSA	Actor 3, later a Silent Face
EURYSAKES	Silent Face
A SOLDIER	Actor 2
TEUKROS	Actor 2
MENELAOS	Actor 3
AGAMEMNON	Actor 4

The skene *represents Aias' tent*

SCENE I

(*Enter* ODYSSEUS *right; he searches the ground for footprints.*
Enter ATHENA *left*)

ATHENA: Son of Laertes! I have always seen you hunt
to seize some quick advantage over enemies;
and now I see you at the seashore house
of Aias, where he has the last position on the flank.
Doglike you've hunted down and measured out
his new-imprinted tracks, to find out if
he is inside or not. Your course has brought
you to your goal, keen-scented like a Spartan hound.
The man has just gone back inside; sweat drips
down from his face and from his murderous hands.   10
But you no longer need to try to peer inside
this tent; just tell me why you search
so eagerly. I'm wise, and you can learn from me.
ODYSSEUS: Athena's voice – dearest to me of all the gods –
how easily I hear your call, although you are
invisible to me, and seize it to my soul,
just like a trumpet with its mouth of bronze!
You are quite right; I'm hunting on the track
of my old enemy, Aias the famous shield-bearer.
I have been tracking him, and no one else, for a long time.   20
This night he has accomplished something unbelievable
against us – if indeed he is the man (we know
nothing for certain, we are wandering in the dark);
I volunteered to take the burden of the search.
We recently discovered all our livestock

dead – slaughtered by human hand
together with their guards.
Now, everyone believes that Aias did this deed;
one of our scouts saw him alone,
leaping across the plain with a new-blooded sword,   30
and told me where; I rushed at once
onto his trail, and sometimes I am sure, but then
I'm thrown off course, and don't know where he is.
You came just when I need you; your hand
always steered my path – and always will.

ATHENA: Odysseus, I know; I came some time ago,
eager to guard the path and help your chase.

ODYSSEUS: Dear mistress, is there any point in my hard
   work?

ATHENA: Yes; Aias did those things.

ODYSSEUS: Why did he act so crazily?   40

ATHENA: Anger about Achilleus' armour weighed him down.

ODYSSEUS: Why did he turn in fury on the flocks?

ATHENA: He thought his hand was stained with blood by
   killing you.

ODYSSEUS: What? This plan was aimed against the Greeks?

ATHENA: He would have done it too, if I'd been careless.

ODYSSEUS: How could he get such daring and such
   confidence?

ATHENA: He went against you by himself, at night, and
   stealthily.

ODYSSEUS: Did he come near us? Did he reach his goal?

ATHENA: He reached the doors of our two generals' tents.

ODYSSEUS: How was his hand, so eager for the slaughter,
   stayed?   50

ATHENA: *I* stop him from achieving that irreparable joy;
I cast upon his eyes delusions which he could not overcome,
and turn aside his fury to your flocks, the undivided
spoils, mixed together, which the cowherds guarded.
He fell upon the beasts, and hacked horned animals to death,
cleaving them in a circle round him; sometimes he believed
he had the sons of Atreus and was killing them himself,
then that he was attacking all the other generals in turn.
And while he stalked in maddened frenzy I
encouraged him, and cast him in a net of suffering.   60
At last he rested from his work;

he tied up all the cattle that were still alive with ropes
and brought the whole herd back here to his tent,
as if he'd captured men, and not just animals with horns.
Now he has tied them up and tortures them in there.

I'm going to show this madness to you openly,
so you can tell it out aloud to all the Greeks.
Be brave, and wait to see the man; you won't
be hurt. I will deflect the piercing vision
of his eyes, so he won't see your face.

70

(*facing the doors of the* skene)

You there – tying your captives' hands
behind their backs – I summon you to come to me.
Aias, I'm calling you; come here, out from your house!
ODYSSEUS: Athena, what are you doing? Do not call him out.
ATHENA: Be quiet, or you will be called a coward.
ODYSSEUS: Please don't do it; he is quite enough staying
   inside.
ATHENA: What could happen? Was he not a man before?
ODYSSEUS: Yes, my enemy both then and now.
ATHENA: The sweetest of all laughter is to laugh at enemies.
ODYSSEUS: It is enough for me if he stays in his house.   80
ATHENA: Are you afraid to see a madman in full view?
ODYSSEUS: If he were sane, I would not shrink in fear.
ATHENA: He will not see you now, though you'll be near to
   him.
ODYSSEUS: How can that happen, if he sees with the same
   sight?
ATHENA: I will put darkness on his eyes, although they are so
   bright.
ODYSSEUS: Everything can happen when a god contrives.
ATHENA: So stand in silence; stay exactly where you are.
ODYSSEUS: I'll stay – but I wish I was somewhere else!
ATHENA: Aias, I call you out a second time;
   why do you slight your closest ally, me?

90

(*Enter* AIAS *from the* skene, *covered in blood and carrying a
bloodstained whip*)

AIAS: Athena, welcome; daughter born of Zeus, welcome!
   I'm glad you're here; I'll see that you are crowned
   with golden offerings in thanks for my successful hunt.
ATHENA: Well said. But tell me this; did you
   dye your sword red in the Greek camp?
AIAS: That I can boast; I won't deny the fact.
ATHENA: Did you raise your armed hand against the sons of
   Atreus?
AIAS: Yes; they will never disrespect Aias again.
ATHENA: They're dead – that's what you mean.
AIAS: They're dead – now let them take my weapons from
   me!   100
ATHENA: Good; what about Laertes' son?
   What have you done to him? Did he escape?
AIAS: You ask me where that cursèd fox has gone?
ATHENA: I do. I mean your enemy, Odysseus.
AIAS: He sits inside, mistress – the prisoner who gives me
   the greatest joy; I do not want him dead just yet.
ATHENA: What will you do first? What great profit do you
   seek?
AIAS: First I will bind him to a pillar of my tent –
ATHENA: How will you torment that poor man?
AIAS: I'll whip his back until it is all red before he dies.   110
ATHENA: Do not torture the poor man quite so much.
AIAS: In other things, Athena, I tell you you can have your
   way;
   but he will pay this penalty and nothing else.
ATHENA: All right – since you can do this, and it pleases you,
   go on, do not restrain yourself from any of your plan.
AIAS: I will get back to work. I only tell you this;
   be always on my side just as you are today.

[*Exit* AIAS *into the* skene]

ATHENA: Odysseus, do you see the great strength of the gods?
   Could you find anyone who was more careful than
   this man, or better at responding to a situation's needs?   120
ODYSSEUS: I know of no one else. I pity him
   as he is now, although he is my enemy, because
   he has been bound fast to a terrible downfall.
   In this I think no more of him than of myself.

I see that all of us who live are nothing else
but phantoms, empty shadow.

ATHENA: Now you have seen this, you must never speak
a word of arrogance against the gods,
and do not swell with pride because you're greater
than another in your strength of hand or depth of wealth. 130
One day can weigh down everything a human being is and
    has
or lift it up again; the gods love prudent men
and hate those who are not.

[*Exit* ATHENA *right, followed by* ODYSSEUS]

CHOROS I

(*Enter* SAILORS, *left*)

I SAILOR: Son of Telamon, you are the lord
of Salamis, surrounded by the sea.
When you are doing well, I'm glad;
but when a blow from Zeus falls on you, or
a raging storm of slander from the other Greeks,
I'm very much afraid; you can see terror
in my eye as in a wingèd dove's.   140

I SAILOR: In the night just ended, big
rumours assailed us and
humiliated us – that you had gone out to
the pastures where our horses graze, and killed
all the Greek cattle, spoils
which had not yet been shared,
with blazing sword.

I SAILOR: Odysseus moulded lying whispers about this
and puts them into everybody's ears;
many believe him. What he says about   150
you now is credible, and everyone who hears
rejoices even more than he who tells them;
they exult in your misfortunes!

I SAILOR: Aim arrows at great souls, and you
won't miss; if someone said such things
about me no one would believe him.

1 SAILOR: Jealousy creeps up only towards the rich man.
            Little men without the great
            give bad protection, cannot save the walls;
            best if we work together with the great,   160
            and they will prosper with our help.
            Still, it's not possible to teach
            these truths to foolish men.
1 SAILOR: They're making all this noise
            against you, and we do not have the strength,
            my lord, to answer them.
1 SAILOR: When they have run away from your fierce eye,
            they chatter like a flock of birds;
            but they would surely cringe before
            the mighty vulture, if you suddenly appeared,   170
            and cower, stricken dumb.

SAILORS (A1):   Oh terrible Rumour,
            mother of my shame,
            did Artemis, the savage bull-goddess,
            drive you against the army's herds
            because you gave no tribute after victory,
            cheated either of glorious battle-spoils
            or of due thanks after a stag was shot?
            Or did the war-god hurt you for
            despising help he gave you with his spear
            by making you do this last night?   180

   (A2):   Aias, in your right mind
            you never would have gone so far astray
            as to attack the flocks.
            God-sent diseases can't be stopped; may Zeus
            and lord Apollo make the rumours not be true.
            If the great kings tell lies, and spread
            false rumours – and Odysseus,
            bastard son of sex-mad Sisyphos –
            don't stay inside your seaside tent   190
            like this, and let the rumour grow.

   (A3):   Stand up, wherever you
            have fixed yourself for all
            this time out from the battle, letting flames

of your destruction leap sky-high.
The angry violence of your enemies now speeds
unchecked through windswept glens,
and everyone runs riot
with the worst insults;
I am paralysed by grief.   200

SCENE 2

(*Enter* TEKMESSA *from the* skene)

TEKMESSA: Sailors, supporters of Aias,
        sons of the native soil of Athens,
        all of us who care about the distant house
        of Telamon have reason to lament.
        Aias the terrible, Aias the great, Aias the man
        of savage strength lies motionless;
        a storm sickens his mind.

I SAILOR: What heavy troubles has
        this night exchanged for yesterday's?
        Child of Phrygian Teleutas, Tekmessa,   210
        tell us. Fierce Aias loves you constantly,
        his spear-won bedmate;
        you must know, and could tell us something.

TEKMESSA: How can I tell you the unspeakable?
        He might as well be dead.
        In the night a madness seized
        our glorious Aias, and he's been destroyed.
        Inside the tent you could see corpses
        soaked in blood,
        the victims of his hand.   220

SAILORS (AI):   We cannot bear what you have shown
        about this great man – and we can't escape from it.
        This is what the Greeks all said,
        the Rumour their big story spreads around.
        I fear for what will happen; he will die
        in sight of all, if in this madness his hand killed   230
        with black swords herds
        and shepherds.

TEKMESSA: No! It's there, it's there he came from
                back to us, leading a flock of prisoners;
                inside, he cut the throats of some onto the floor;
                others he tore apart, hacking their sides.
                Then he picked up two whitefoot rams;
                he cuts the head and tongue-tip from the first,
                throws them away; he stands the other one
                upright, ties it to a pillar, takes   240
                a huge leather horse-rein, and flogs
                the animal with hissing double scourge,
                abusing it with words so foul no man –
                it must have been a daimon who taught him.

SAILORS (A2):   Now it is time for us to veil
                our heads and run away to hide,
                or sit on swift oar-benches,
                free the ship and sail to sea.   250
                The two kings, sons of Atreus, are stirring up
                such threats against us; I'm afraid we'll suffer death
                by stoning here with Aias, who is bound
                to a fate no one can go near unscathed.

TEKMESSA: No longer! There is no more lightning-flash;
                after a fierce attack, like southerlies he has eased off,
                and now he's sane again he has new suffering.
                Looking at injuries you've caused yourself,   260
                when no one else contributed,
                creates great suffering.

I SAILOR: If he has stopped, I think all may be well;
            the greater part of our torment is gone.

TEKMESSA: If someone gave the choice, which would you
                take –
            to hurt your friends, while you yourself were happy,
            or be together with your friends and share their grief?

I SAILOR: Lady, a double suffering is worse.

TEKMESSA: Then we're destroyed now his madness is gone.

I SAILOR: What do you mean? I do not understand.   270

TEKMESSA: When he was mad, Aias himself found joy
            in those perverted fantasies that bound him fast,
            while he hurt us, who were sane, being here like that;
            but he has been released, and now, recovered from disease,

he's utterly prostrated by a dreadful grief
 – and we are too, just as we were before.
Is this not double suffering instead of one?
1 SAILOR: You're right; I fear a blow from god has struck.
It must, if his mind is no happier now that
the sickness has gone than when it plagued him.   280
TEKMESSA: Believe me, that is how it is.
1 SAILOR: How did this madness first fly down on him?
We share your suffering; tell us.
TEKMESSA: You will learn everything, as you are part of this.
At dead of night, when evening braziers
had no more light in them, he took a sword,
and started to creep out on empty paths.
I tried to stop him, saying 'Aias, what
are you doing? Why fly off on this sortie
without a summons from a messenger or sound   290
of trumpet? The whole army is asleep.'
He said few words to me – an old, familiar song:
'woman, silence is best for women.'
I learned my lesson and gave up; he rushed outside alone.
I do not know what suffering happened out there;
he brought back prisoners, tied to each other
 – bulls, sheepdogs, and fleecy sheep.
He cut the heads off some, pulled back the necks
of others, cut their throats and hacked them up; some, still
    tied up,
he tortured, mutilating animals as if they were men.   300
At last he leaped out through the doors, talked wildly to
someone invisible, abusing both the sons
of Atreus, and Odysseus, and laughing frequently
about the violence he'd inflicted on them in the night.
Then he rushed back into the house, and somehow,
over time, he painfully recovered sanity.
He looked around the tent, full of his wretched work,
and struck his head and screamed; then he crashed down
and sat among the bloody, shattered corpses of the sheep,
clutching his hair, with fingernails clenched tight.   310
He sat without a word for a long time;
then he threatened to torture me,
if I did not tell everything.
My friends, I was so terrified,

I told him all I knew.
He broke at once into most bitter groans,
such as I never heard from him before.
He always taught me cries like those
were only for the coward and the heavy-hearted man.   320
He never made shrill sounds of grief –
just deep and sullen moans, as from a wounded bull.
He has now fallen into such a miserable state
he will not eat or drink; he's sitting silently
just where he fell among the slaughtered animals,
and plainly he is plotting something terrible.   326
My friends, I came out here to ask –   328
please go inside and help him, if you can.
Words can persuade people in such a state.   330

1 SAILOR: Tekmessa, it is terrible to hear
his sufferings have driven our lord mad –

AIAS: (*cries out inside the* skene)

TEKMESSA: There's worse to come; did you not hear
that great, resounding cry from Aias?

AIAS: (*cries out inside the* skene)

1 SAILOR: Either he is still sick, or grieves about
his recent sickness, as he sees what he has done.

AIAS: (*still inside*) Oh, my boy, my boy!

TEKMESSA: Help! Eurysakes, he's crying out for you.   340
What does he want? Where are you? I am desperate.

AIAS: Teukros! Where is Teukros? Will he go on searching
all this time for plunder, while I'm destroyed?

1 SAILOR: He's not insane. Open the doors. Perhaps even
seeing his friends will make him more restrained.

TEKMESSA: Look, I am opening. Now you can see
what he has done, and how he is.

(*Doors open. Enter* AIAS *on the* ekkyklêma, *surrounded by
dead sheep, sheepdogs and cattle*)

AIAS   (AI): Oh,
my sailors, you alone,
alone of all are still my loyal friends.   350
Look at this wave of blood,
see how it's surged in
and surrounded me!

1 SAILOR: (to Tekmessa) What you said's all too true!
    This shows he's gone insane.

AIAS   (A2):   Oh!
        Skilled sailors, who
        have rowed my ship across the sea,
        you, you alone of all
        can help defend me now;
        kill me at once!   360
1 SAILOR: Don't say that! Don't add suffering to suffering
    and make the pain of this disaster worse.

AIAS   (B1):   D'you see the brave, strong-hearted man,
        fearless in battle with the enemy –
        how terribly I slaughtered unsuspecting animals?
        I've been humiliated, made absurd.
TEKMESSA: Aias, my lord, I beg you, do not say such things.
AIAS: Get out! Just go away!
    Aiai! Aiai!   370
TEKMESSA: For gods' sake, listen to me; learn some sense.
AIAS: Look at my fate! I let
        those bastards go; I fell instead
        on horned cattle and noble goats
        and made their dark blood flow.
1 SAILOR: Why grieve yourself about what has been done?
    You cannot ever change what's happened.

AIAS   (B2):   All-seeing, all-hearing,
        contriver of wickedness, Odysseus –
        filthiest swine in this whole camp,   380
        I bet you're laughing long and loud for joy.
1 SAILOR: The gods give us laughter and tears.
AIAS: If only I could see him, even stricken as I am –

(He cries out in grief)

1 SAILOR: No big ideas; do you not realize what you have
            done?
AIAS: Zeus, father of my ancestors,
        if only I could kill that sneak,
        that vicious swine, and both

          the brother-kings,   390
          then die myself!
TEKMESSA: If you must pray for that, then pray for me to die
     as well; why should I live when you are dead?

AIAS   (C1):   Darkness, my only light;
          Haides, for me the brightest place of all,
          take me, take me to live with you;
          take me! I am no longer
          worthy to get any help
          from gods or mortal men.   400
          Athena,
          mighty goddess,
          tortures me to death.
          Where could I flee?
          Where find some rest?
          My friends, if all
          my former glory perishes
          together with these animals,
          and I became addicted to a madman's quest,
          then all the army will lift up their swords
          and strike me dead!
TEKMESSA: It hurts to hear this great man say such words 410
     who never would have said them in the past.

AIAS   (C2):   Straits of the sea,
          sea-caves, and pastures by the shore;
          long, long have you
          kept me near Troy;
          no more, no more while I
          am still alive. Let everyone know this;
          streams of Skamander
          near to us, river
          that hates all Greeks,   420
          you will not ever see this man
          again – the greatest soldier,
          I will boast,
          that Troy
          has ever seen come here
          from Greece; now I lie utterly
          humiliated on the ground.

I SAILOR: I do not know if it is worse in such misfortunes if
    I hold you back or let you speak.

AIAS: Aiai! Who would have ever thought my name   430
    would be so utterly appropriate?
    Now I can truly twice cry out 'aiai'!   432
    My father went back home from Troy   434
    covered in glory, since his excellence
    in battle won a gorgeous prize.
    I am his son, and I came to this land
    of Troy with no less strength;
    my hands gave equal service to the Greeks, and now
    I am destroyed, humiliated in their sight.   440
    But still, I think I know one thing;
    if Achilleus were still alive, and judging who
    was first in courage and deserved to have his arms,
    no one but me would have grasped hold of them.
    Instead the sons of Atreus, rejecting my great worth,
    procured the weapons for a worthless rogue.
    And if my eyes and brain had not been twisted,
    turned away from my resolve, they never would again
    have got a judgement like this against anybody else.
    But as it is fierce-eyed, invincible Athena   450
    foiled me, about to strike them down;
    she hurled a plague of madness on me, so my hands
    were covered in these creatures' blood instead.
    They have escaped me, and they celebrate.
    I could not stop them; when a god sends harm,
    a lesser man can get away from someone greater.

    What shall I do? Clearly I'm hated by
    the gods, the whole Greek army loathes me;
    Troy and its plains hate me as well.
    Should I go home across the sea,   460
    desert this naval camp, abandon Atreus' sons?
    When I get there, how can I show my face
    to Telamon my father? How could he bear to look at me,
    naked, stripped of my honour as a soldier –
    he who himself won glory's highest crown?
    No; it is intolerable. Should I then go against
    the Trojan stronghold, tackle single-handed

their whole army, do some worthwhile deed before I die?
That way I'd please the sons of Atreus;
it won't happen. I must find some way   470
to show my agèd father that his son
is not a gutless nobody.

It's shameful for a man to want long life,
who sees unchanging misery.
Day follows day, pushing us on, pulling us back;
what joy is there, except in death?
I would not give the slightest value to someone
who warms his heart with empty hopes;
a man of noble birth must live a glorious life,
or die in glory. That is all.   480

1 SAILOR: Aias, no one could tell us you have said
a false word; all this comes from your own heart.
Still, you must stop. Let your friends change
your mind; abandon thoughts like these.

TEKMESSA: Aias, my lord, humans suffer most
from fortunes imposed by Necessity.
I was the daughter of a free-born father,
probably among the wealthiest of all the Phrygians;
now I'm a slave. That's what the gods decided;
your hand was their instrument. So now, because I have   490
been made to lie with you in bed, I care for you;
I pray by Zeus, god of our hearth,
and by the bed in which you have made love to me,
do not condemn me to the bitter taunts
of all your enemies, as someone else's prisoner.
When you die and leave me alone,
you know that on that very day
the Greeks will seize me forcibly
together with your son, to live as slaves.
One of my masters will speak scornfully,   500
hurling these words at me: 'look at the concubine
of Aias, once our greatest warrior; now she
does menial labour, who lived then in bliss!'
That's what they'll say; a god will torment me –
and words like this will shame you and your family.
No! Show you care about your father in painful
old age – and your mother (she too has

lived long); she often begged the gods
for you to come back to their home alive.
My lord, pity your son, if he's deprived   510
of proper care and has to live without
a father, fostered by his enemies. Think what
you'll do to him – and me – if you choose death.
For me, there's nothing else to look to
except you. Your spear destroyed my native land:
another cruel fate seized both my mother
and my father; they are now in Haides, dead.
I have no other home except your house,
no money; my whole life depends on you.
Remember me as well; a man should not forget   520
if he's been given pleasant memories.
Kindness always gives birth to kindness; but
if someone lets the memory of pleasure
flow away, he's lost his honour and nobility.

1 SAILOR: Aias, I hope you have some pity in your heart
like me; then you would praise what she has said.

AIAS: I certainly will praise her – only if
she's strong enough to do what I command.

TEKMESSA: Aias, my love, I will do anything you say.

AIAS: Bring me my son right now, so I may look at him.   530

TEKMESSA: When I was anxious, I sent him away.

AIAS: You mean while I was mad?

TEKMESSA: In case the poor boy had met you, and died.

AIAS: That would have been . . . just typical of my cruel fate.

TEKMESSA: At least I stopped it happening.

AIAS: I praise your actions and your foresight.

TEKMESSA: How can I help you now?

AIAS: Let me see him and speak to him.

TEKMESSA: Of course; servants are looking after him nearby.

AIAS: Then why is he not here?   540

TEKMESSA: My child, your father's calling for you; bring him
here,
whoever's now responsible for minding him.

AIAS: Is he coming? Or can he not hear your words?

TEKMESSA: A servant's bringing him to us right now.

(*An attendant guides* EURYSAKES *in from the left to* TEKMESSA)

AIAS: Lift him, lift him to me; he'll show no fear
in looking at this new-shed blood and gore,
if he's truly a son of mine.
He must be broken now into his father's
savage ways, and mould his character like mine.
My son, may you have better fortune than your father;   550
otherwise, be just like me, and you will turn out fine.
I envy you right now, because
you do not understand my misery.
Life's sweetest when you cannot think,
before you learn about both joy and pain.
When you are grown up, you must show your father's
enemies that you're my son and have my strength.
Meanwhile, feed on light breezes, and enjoy
your childhood, give your mother joy.
None of the Greeks, I know, will dare to violate   560
or harm you, even when you don't have me.
I shall leave a great man to guard you; Teukros,
who won't fail to nurture you – even though right now
he's gone away to hunt our enemies.

My warriors, my comrades on the sea, I lay
this charge to love my son on all of you as well;
tell Teukros my command, that he
must take this boy back to my home,
show him to Telamon and to my mother Eriboia,
so he may feed and cherish them in their old age.   570
As for my weapons, no one may make them games-prizes 572
for the Greeks – especially not Odysseus, who ruined me.
No! You, my son, must take the mighty shield,
from which you take your name, Eurysakes. Hold it and turn
    it by
the leather thong, that seven-thickness shield no spear can
    pierce!
All of my other armour will be buried in my grave with me.
(to TEKMESSA) No more delay! Take this child back inside,
and fasten up the house; don't weep or moan
out here in front. Women are very prone to tears.   580
Close up! A wise doctor does not sing songs
of grief over a sore that needs the knife.

1 SAILOR: Your eagerness makes me afraid.

Your tongue is sharpened, and I do not like the sound.
TEKMESSA: Aias, my lord, what are you going to do?
AIAS: Don't ask, don't question me; restraint is good.
TEKMESSA: You're hurting me! I beg you by your child
and all the gods – do not abandon us.
AIAS: You are annoying me; do you not know
that I no longer owe the gods a thing?   590
TEKMESSA: Don't say that!
AIAS: I'm not listening.
TEKMESSA: You won't let me persuade you?
AIAS: You have said too much already.
TEKMESSA: My lord, I am afraid.
AIAS: Close the doors, right now!
TEKMESSA: By the gods, relent!
AIAS: I think you've just become
a fool, if you think you can teach me what to do.

[*Withdraw* ekkyklêma, *with* AIAS *and the slaughtered animals,*
followed by TEKMESSA *and* EURYSAKES. *The* skene *doors close*]

CHOROS 2

SAILORS (A1):   Wonderful Salamis, you must still be
a happy land surrounded by the waves,
a joy for everyone to see;
but I am miserable. It's so long,   600
I've lost count of the months spent
camping in the grassy fields of Ida;
Time has worn me down,
as I sit waiting for the day when I
shall go to hateful nothingness in Haides.

(A2):   Now a new torment lies in reserve for me –
Aias impossible to cure, forced   610
to live with madness sent by gods;
in better days you once sent him to feats
of bravery in war. But now he nurses
lonely thoughts, and gives his friends great grief;
what his hand once achieved,
all his deeds of great courage have

        fallen upon the ground, unloved by the
        unloving sons of Atreus.   620

(B I):   His mother has lived to old age,
        her hair is grey; when she hears he's
        been stricken with disease that eats the mind,
        she will raise cries of grief –
        not plaintive like the pitiable nightingale.
        Poor woman, she will shriek out bitter cries,   630
        her hands will beat her breasts,
        and tear her old grey hair.

(B2):   He's better dead, now madness has struck down
        this man who by his lineage is best
        of all the Greeks who've suffered here;
        he does not stay constant inside
        his character, but wanders out, away.   640
        Poor father, you still have to hear about
        your son's unbearable misfortune,
        such as never struck
        one of your noble family before.

SCENE 3

(*Enter* AIAS *from the* skene, *with Hektor's sword in his hand,
followed by* TEKMESSA)

AIAS: The long march of immeasurable Time brings all things
     out
      from darkness into light, then hides them back again.
      There's nothing which can't happen; even mighty oaths
      are overcome, and the most stubborn minds.
      Me too. Not long ago I was as strong and terrible   650
      as tempered steel; now my hard edge
      has been made female by this woman – for I pity her
      left to my enemies, a widow with an orphan.
      I will go to the bathing place and meadows
      by the shore: I hope by cleansing my pollution off
      to break free from the heavy anger of the goddess.
      Then I'll go to some untrodden place

and bury this my sword, most hateful of all weapons,
digging it into earth no one will ever see;
let Night and Haides keep it underground!   660
For ever since I took it from the hand
of Hektor as a gift, my greatest enemy,
I have had no good luck among the Greeks.
Yes, the proverb's all too true: 'the gifts
of enemies are not true gifts, and will bring harm'.
So in the future we will learn to yield
to gods, and reverence the sons of Atreus.
They are the rulers; others must submit. How else?
Even the most terrible and strong bow down
to higher powers: that is why the snows   670
and winter storms make way for summer fruits;
the endless circling of the night gives place
for white-horsed day to blaze with light;
the blast of savage winds allows the groaning sea
to rest; and even Sleep, who conquers all,
releases captives, does not bind them for eternity.
So how could we not learn good sense as well?
I have! I now know that an enemy
should only be so hated, as a man who will
become a friend again; and I will wish   680
only to help a friend so far – because I know
he won't always be true. For most men
friendship is a fickle, unsafe anchorage.
All this will turn out well; Tekmessa, go inside
and pray the gods that what my heart
desires may be fulfilled completely.

[*Exit* TEKMESSA *into the* skene]

My friends, honour my wishes
just like her; tell Teukros, when he comes back,
he must care for me, and be loyal to you.
I'm going to the place where I must go;   690
do what I say, and soon – perhaps – you'll learn,
though I am suffering more, that I've been saved.

[*Exit* AIAS, *right*]

CHOROS 3

SAILORS (AI):   I thrill with passion, fly away on wings
                of joy! Oh Pan, Pan,
                Pan, appear – sea-wanderer,
                from craggy ridge of Mount Kyllene
                beaten by snow; king, creator
                of the dances of the gods –
                to make me dance the pounding steps
                of Mysia and Krete inspired by you.   700
                I want to dance now!
                Lord of Delos, king Apollo, come
                across the sea of Ikaros;
                be with me, visible and
                ever kind.

      (A2):   The War-god's lifted that dread trouble from our
                eyes.
                Oh joy! Now, oh Zeus,
                now bright white days
                can come back to
                our swift ships, because Aias has   710
                forgotten all his pain, and has performed
                the rites and sacrifices needed by the gods,
                obeying them with greatest reverence and loyalty.
                Great Time destroys all things;
                and I would say nothing is unbelievable,
                now that beyond our hopes
                Aias has been turned from his fits
                of passion, and his fight with Atreus' sons.

SCENE 4

(Enter a SOLDIER, left)

SOLDIER: My friends, I want to tell you first
           Teukros has just come back here from the hills   720
           of Mysia; he has gone to the middle of the camp
           where all the Greeks are cursing him at once.

They saw him coming from a long way off, and they
surrounded him, and then assaulted him
with angry words from all sides – every one of them –
abusing him as 'brother of that maniac who tried
to kill us all', and saying he could not escape
from being torn to shreds in death by stoning.
They'd come to this; swords had been pulled
with angry haste from scabbards – but
the Elders eased the strife, when it   730
had run its course, with soothing words.

Where is our Aias, so I can tell him?
This news concerns him; he must learn it all.
1 SAILOR: He is not here; he's just gone out;
he's yoked new plans to a new mood.
SOLDIER: No!
Then either he who sent me here
sent me too late, or I have proved too slow.
1 SAILOR: What have we failed to do?   740
SOLDIER: Teukros forbad us to let Aias go
outside the house, until he has come here himself.
1 SAILOR: Well, he has gone – and bent on doing what is best
for him, to find release from anger of the gods.
SOLDIER: What you say is completely stupid, if
Kalchas has any wisdom when he prophesies.
1 SAILOR: What prophecy? What do you know?
SOLDIER: I know this much – for I was there.
Kalchas left the circle of the seated kings,
and drew apart, alone, from Atreus' sons;   750
Then he clasped Teukros' right with his own hand
in all goodwill, and laid a charge on him to use
all means he could to keep Aias inside his house
for this whole day, and not let him go out,
if he wanted to see him still alive again.
For this day only will the anger of the goddess
Athena strike him – that's what he said.
'If people are excessive, and of no more use' –
so spoke the prophet – 'they're struck down
with great disasters sent by gods,
whenever someone born a mortal man   760
forgets this, and thinks thoughts too high for men.

Aias, the very moment he left home,
showed great folly; his father spoke well.
Telamon told him: "son, strive to win
your battles – but always with help from gods."
Aias answered haughtily and foolishly:
"Father, with help from gods even a nobody
might gain a victory; I know that I can win
great glory even with no help from them."
That was his boast. Then once, facing   770
divine Athena, when she urged him on
and told him he must turn a bloody hand against his
    enemies,
he gave her this reply – dreadful, unheard-of:
"Queen, go and support the other Greeks;
where Aias stands the enemy will not break through."
Such words brought down on him the goddess'
implacable hatred, for thoughts greater than men may have.
But if he's still alive today, perhaps
with lord Apollo's help we could save him.'
That's what the prophet said. Teukros   780
got up at once and sent me to make you
keep him inside. But if we've failed,
Aias is dead, or Kalchas has no skill.

(*A* SAILOR *goes up towards the* skene *doors*)

I SAILOR: Your parents were ill-fated – so are you –
Tekmessa, come and see what this man says.
We're at the razor's edge of suffering.

(*Enter* TEKMESSA *from the* skene, *wrapped in a long cloak*)

TEKMESSA: Have I not suffered enough? Why make me get
    up,
when I have only just been freed from unrelenting grief?
I SAILOR: Listen to this man; he's brought some news about
the state of Aias which gives me great pain.   790
TEKMESSA: What are you saying, man? Are we destroyed?
SOLDIER: I don't know what you mean by state; but as for
    Aias,
if he's outdoors, I fear for his life.

TEKMESSA: He is outdoors; I'm terrified; tell me at once.
SOLDIER: Teukros has ordered us to keep Aias inside
  the shelter of this house, and not let him go out.
TEKMESSA: Where is Teukros? Why has he said this?
SOLDIER: He has just come back; he is afraid
  that going out today condemns Aias to death.
TEKMESSA: Oh god! Who told him that?   800
SOLDIER: Kalchas the prophet told him something would
  bring life or death to Aias on this very day.
TEKMESSA: My friends, protect me from this fate.
  Some of you hurry and bring Teukros here;
  some go west, to the curve in the shore; others
  look east for my man who should not have gone.
  I realize that he's deceived me, and has cast aside
  the favour he once showed to me.
  My child, what shall I do? We can't sit here.
  I'll search as well, as far as I can go.   810
  Let's go, let's rush; this is no time to stay.   811
I SAILOR: I'm ready to go too; I'll prove it now.   813
  I'll go, as quickly as I can.

      [*Exeunt* TEKMESSA *and* SAILORS *right; exit* SOLDIER
                left]

Change of scene; set some bushes around the centre of the
orchêstra

SCENE 5

(*Enter* AIAS, *left. He fixes his sword in the ground behind the
bushes*)

AIAS: My executioner now stands where he will cut
  most sharply. If you have time to waste on thought,
  it's Hektor's gift – the guest-friend whom
  I hated most, and could not bear to see.
  And it is fixed in hostile, Trojan soil,
  just sharpened on the whetstone;   820
  I've stuck it in most carefully,

so it will be kind, kill me instantly.
Our preparations are complete, and now it's right
for me to call first on you, Zeus,
my ancestor; I only ask a small favour.
Please send a messenger for me to take
the bad news to Teukros, so he may lift me first
when I have fallen on this bloodstained sword,
and do not let me first be seen by enemies
and thrown out as a prey for dogs and birds.   830
This much I ask of you; I also call on Hermes,
escort of dead souls, to take me quickly down
in one swift leap, without convulsions,
when I drive this sword into my side.
I also call for help to the immortal virgins
who see all the sufferings of mortal men,
the solemn Furies who are swift of foot, to learn
how Atreus' sons are ending my poor life.   838
Come, swift avenging Furies, do not spare,   843
but feast upon the entire army of the Greeks.

Now you, whose chariot climbs the heights of heaven,
Sun-god, when you look down on my native land,
pull up your golden reins, and tell
of my misfortunes and my death
to my old father and my miserable mother.
Poor woman! When she hears of this   850
she'll cry out loud and everyone will hear.

But there's no point in vain regrets.
Now for the end, as quickly as I can.   853
Oh sunlight! Sacred soil of Salamis   859
my native land, hearth of my ancestors,   860
and famous Athens, home of my kinsmen;
springs and rivers here, and plains of Troy, I speak
to you, who have sustained my life; farewell!
This is the last word Aias says to you;
from now on I will speak only among the dead.

(AIAS *falls on his sword. Re-enter just over half the* SAILORS,
right)

SAILORS: Pain, endless pain.
            Where, where,
            where have I not gone?
            No place draws me to find him.
            Hey, hey!   870
            I hear a sudden noise.

(The rest of the SAILORS *enter, left)*

1 SAILOR: It's us, your shipmates.
1 SAILOR: Well?
1 SAILOR: We've searched everywhere west of the ships.
1 SAILOR: Found anything?
1 SAILOR: A lot of pain, and no success.
1 SAILOR: Clearly they haven't found him on
            the eastward path either.

SAILOR (A1):   If only some seaman, who works
            sleeplessly to catch fish,   880
            or goddess from Olympos, or
            from rivers which flow into Bosporos,
            could tell us if they've seen
            that fierce man roaming
            somewhere? It is terrible
            that I should wander painfully so long
            and not run into him,
            but cannot see where poor Aias has gone.   890

(Enter TEKMESSA, *left; she sees* AIAS *behind the bushes and runs straight to him)*

TEKMESSA: *(cries out)*
1 SAILOR: Who's screaming from the bushes over there?
TEKMESSA: *(cries out again)*
1 SAILOR: It's Tekmessa, the wretched captive bride
            of Aias, utterly immersed in grief.
TEKMESSA: I'm lost, my friends – completely finished.
1 SAILOR: What is it?
TEKMESSA: Aias lies here, just dead,
            impaled upon a buried sword.
SAILORS: We'll never get back home!   900

My lord, you've killed
me – your own comrade.
Poor, suffering woman.
TEKMESSA: He's dead; now we must cry 'aiai'!
1 SAILOR: Who killed him?
TEKMESSA: Clearly it's suicide; this sword,
fixed in the ground, accuses him; he fell on it.
1 SAILOR: The blindness of my mind! You killed yourself
alone; your friends could not protect you.   910
I was completely dumb and stupid;
I let you do it. Where, where
is stubborn Aias whose name is so ominous?
TEKMESSA: He must not be seen. I shall wrap
this cloak around and shroud him completely;
no friend could bear to look at him like this,
with dark blood pouring from his nose
and from the awful, self-inflicted wound.

What shall I do? What friend will lift you up?   920
Where's Teukros? He should come here now
to tend his fallen brother.
Unfortunate Aias, you were so great – and now like this;
even your enemies should mourn for you.

SAILOR (A2):   Poor man, you were so stubborn,
you were bound eventually to find
a cruel fate and endless pain; so great
was your fierce rage
all day and night against   930
the sons of Atreus –
a hatred which has killed you.
The day the golden armour stood
as prize for the best fighter
has caused endless suffering.
TEKMESSA: (cries out aloud)
1 SAILOR: I know, the anguish pierces to your faithful heart.
TEKMESSA: (cries out aloud)
1 SAILOR: I understand why you cry more than once,   940
so recently torn from this man you loved.
TEKMESSA: You can think about it; I am suffering.
1 SAILOR: I know.

TEKMESSA: My child, we will be yoked to slavery;
  think who will be our overseers.
I SAILOR: Yes, you're right to grieve;
        the sons of Atreus
        are ruthless, and would be
        brutal beyond belief.
        So may the god prevent it!
TEKMESSA: But for the gods, this never would have
  happened.
                                                                    950
I SAILOR: Yes, they've made our burden far too great to
  bear.
TEKMESSA: Athena, Zeus' fearsome daughter, gives
  us all this suffering to help Odysseus.
I SAILOR: In his black heart that much-
        enduring man rejoices now
        and laughs aloud at sufferings
        which madness caused;
        so will the kings, the sons
        of Atreus, when they are told.
                                                                    960
TEKMESSA: Then let them laugh, and jump for joy at Aias'
  sufferings; perhaps, if they did not want him alive,
  now he is dead they may lament his absence from the war.
  Men of no judgement do not know they have
  a good thing in their hands until it's lost.

  His death is bitter for me, as it's sweet for them,
  but it has brought him joy; he has now found
  all he desired – the kind of death he wanted.
  So why then should they laugh?
  He died because of gods, not them.
                                                                    970
  Odysseus' boasts are empty.
  For them, Aias does not exist; from me
  he's gone, and left me grief and mourning.
TEUKROS: *(in the distance)* AIAS!!
I SAILOR: Quiet! I think I hear Teukros' voice
  crying in grief about this awful death.

(*Enter* TEUKROS, *right*)

TEUKROS: My dearest Aias, brother whom I loved,
  are you dead, as rumour says?

1 SAILOR: Teukros, know this, he's dead.
TEUKROS: My fate is heavy.   980
1 SAILOR: That is how it is –
TEUKROS: I'm wretched.
1 SAILOR: – you must grieve.
TEUKROS: A fierce and sudden shock.
1 SAILOR: Too much, Teukros.
TEUKROS: All wretchedness; but what
    about his son; where in the land of Troy is he?
1 SAILOR: Alone at the tent.
TEUKROS: (to Tekmessa)   Then you must go
    and bring him here at once, to stop his enemies
    from taking him, like the whelp from
    a lioness who's lost her mate.
    Go quickly, rescue him! Everyone loves
    to triumph over stronger men – once they are dead.

                                        [Exit TEKMESSA, left]

1 SAILOR: Teukros; while he was still alive, Aias asked
    you   990
    to give protection to his son – as you are doing now.
TEUKROS: This is the worst of all
    the sights that I have ever seen,
    and the path to this place is the most
    bitter of all paths that I've ever walked,
    oh my beloved Aias, since I heard
    that you were dead while I was looking for you.
    A rumour you had died spread fast throughout
    the army, as if sent by god.
    I heard it far away, and grieved at once;   1000
    but now I see you I'm destroyed.
    Come, lift the cloak, and let me see the worst.

(A SAILOR removes the cloak covering AIAS)

    This is a wretched sight; how cruel was your courage, and
    how many sorrows you have sown for me.
    Where can I go, who will want me, since I
    have failed to help you in your time of need?
    Oh, I am sure our father Telamon

will be so happy and rejoice to see me
coming back without you. Yes, of course! – a man   1010
who never even smiles when he is happy.
He won't hold back! There is no insult he
won't hurl against his bastard by a captive girl;
I betrayed you, dearest Aias, by my cowardice –
or weakness, or through treachery, so when
you're dead I would acquire your power and your house.
That is the sort of thing he'll say; he is bad-tempered,
peevish in old age, and quarrels about nothing.
Then finally he will reject and exile me,
regarding me not as a free man but a slave.   1020
That's what I'll get back home, while here in Troy
I've many enemies, and very little help;
all vanished when you died.
What should I do? How draw you from the bitter point
of Hektor's gleaming sword – the murderer who took
your breath from you? D'you see how, even dead,
your enemy managed to cause your death?   1027

I SAILOR: Do not go on; you must work out   1040
how you can bury him, and what to say right now.
I see an enemy; he's probably come here to gloat
over our sufferings, as you'd expect from such a scoundrel.

TEUKROS: Whom from the army have you seen?

I SAILOR: Menelaos, the reason why we sailed here.

TEUKROS: I see him; he's not hard to recognize when he is
near.

(*Enter* MENELAOS, *right*)

MENELAOS: Hey, you, I'm telling you you cannot raise
that corpse; it must be left right here.

TEUKROS: Why waste your breath in saying that?

MENELAOS: It is my will, and Agamemnon's too.   1050

TEUKROS: And could we hear your reasoning?

MENELAOS: Yes; when we brought him here we hoped
that he would be an ally to the Greeks and friend,
and then we found him more our enemy than any Trojan;
he planned to murder the whole army, ventured out
at night to kill us with his spear.
If some god had not quenched this move,

we would have had the same fate he has now,
and would be lying dead in a most shameful way,
while he lived on. But as it is a god has turned   1060
his violence, so it fell onto sheep and cows.
Because of that there's nobody with strength enough
to lay this body in a tomb; he will
be thrown out somewhere on the yellow sand
and become food for seabirds.
Do not get in a mighty rage;
if we could not control him while he was alive,
we'll rule him now he's dead – even
against your will – with our hands. When
he was alive, he never listened to a word I said.   1070

A man of lower rank shows that his character is bad
if he does not obey the people who're in power.
Law and good order cannot prosper in a city where
there is no element of fear;
nor can an army have the proper discipline
if there is not the barrier of fear and of respect.
Even a man of great physique should realize
that something small can bring him down.
If someone has both fear and deference,
be sure that that will keep him safe;   1080
but where there's licence to be violent and do
just anything you want, know such a city will some time
lose favourable winds, and sink into the depths.
No! Let me see fear put in place where it's appropriate;
and let's not think that if we do all we desire
we will not pay the price in suffering.
Joy and grief alternate. This man was once
hot-tempered, violent; now I'm on top.
So I tell you you may not bury him;
if you do, you may fall into a grave yourself.   1090
I SAILOR: Menelaos, you've said some wise things;
      do not yourself outrage the dead.
TEUKROS: My friends, I'll never wonder if a man
      of lower birth goes wrong
      when the so-called nobility
      stray in their words so far from justice.
      Let's go back to the start; come, do you say

you brought Aias here, you found him as an ally?
Did he not sail himself, full master of his choice?
Why d'you think you're his overlord? Why should you   1100
have power over everyone he brought from Salamis?
You came as king of Sparta, not to lord it over us;
there is no way you have the legal power
to order him around, no more than he for you.   1105
Give orders to your subjects, spare your fancy words   1107
for lashing out at them. I will place Aias in a grave
whether you forbid it, or the other king.
It is his right; I do not fear your mouth.   1110
Aias did not come to this war to get
your wife back, like your hard-working subjects,
but because he'd sworn an oath to Tyndareus –
nothing to do with you; he had no time for nobodies.
So when you come back, bring more heralds
and the general; your noise will not divert
me from my purpose, while you stay the man you are.

1 SAILOR: I do not like such speeches at a time of suffering;
harsh words still sting when they are much deserved.

MENELAOS: The bowman has a high opinion of himself.   1120

TEUKROS: Yes; mine is a noble craft.

MENELAOS: How you would boast, if you could hold a
shield.

TEUKROS: Even without one I could beat you fully armed.

MENELAOS: You're fearfully courageous – in your words.

TEUKROS: When men are right, they can think mighty
thoughts.

MENELAOS: It would have been all right for him to kill me
and live happily?

TEUKROS: Kill you? A miracle – you're killed, but you are still
alive.

MENELAOS: He wanted me stone dead – a god saved me.

TEUKROS: Since the gods saved you, do not now oppose their
will.

MENELAOS: You think *I* would oppose the laws of
heaven?   1130

TEUKROS: Yes – if you're here to stop the dead from being
buried.

MENELAOS: When they're my enemies; it would not be right.

TEUKROS: Did Aias ever stand against you as your enemy?

MENELAOS: We hated each other, and you know it well.
TEUKROS: Because he found you'd cheated him by rigging
   votes.
MENELAOS: The judges ruled that he had lost – not me.
TEUKROS: You could do a good cover-up on any kind of
   crime.
MENELAOS: These words might end in pain for somebody.
TEUKROS: Not more pain than we will inflict ourselves.
MENELAOS: I'll say one thing to you; you cannot bury
   him.   1140
TEUKROS: Hear just one thing in answer; he'll be buried.
MENELAOS: I once saw a man of bold speech
   urging his crew to set sail in a storm,
   who lost his voice, when he was caught
   in the full blast; he hid under his cloak
   and let the crewmen walk all over him.
   So too you, and your violent tongue –
   perhaps a mighty storm could grow from a
   small cloud, and quench all your loud noise.
TEUKROS: I too once saw a man, a foolish man, who
   threw   1150
   his weight around when those near him
   were suffering. One day someone a bit like me
   saw him, and said something like this:
   'My good man, do not harm the dead;
   if you do, you will suffer for it.'
   That's how he chided the man who lacked sense.
   I see him now, and I think that he is
   nobody else but you. Is this a riddle?
MENELAOS: I am leaving; it would be shameful if people knew
   that I rebuked with words someone whom I can force.   1160
TEUKROS: Creep off! It would be the very depth of shame, if I
   listen to empty words from such a feeble man.

                                    [*Exit* MENELAOS, *right*]

1 SAILOR: This will be a strife-torn trial of strength;
            quick as you can, Teukros, seek out
            a hollow grave for Aias, where
            he'll lie for ever in a glorious
            but dark and musty tomb.

(*Enter* TEKMESSA *and* EURYSAKES, *left*)

TEUKROS: Yes; just at the right time, here come
   the wife of Aias and his son, to help
   with burying his miserable corpse.   1170
   Boy, you must come here, stand near,
   and touch the father who created you.
   Kneel as a suppliant, holding some locks
   of my hair, and of hers, and of your own –
   the offerings that give power to a suppliant.

(EURYSAKES *kneels beside the corpse;* TEKMESSA *behind it*)

   If any soldier tries to tear you forcibly away,
   may he fall to an evil death, and lie unburied,
   so his family's cut right down to its roots,
   just as I now cut off this lock of hair.
   Take it, my child, and treasure it;   1180
   let no one move you; kneel, and cling to him.

   Now you must not stand here like women,
   but like men, ready to help, till I return when I
   have made a tomb for him, though no one wants me to.

                               [*Exit* TEUKROS, *left*]

CHOROS 4

SAILORS (A1):   When will it end? When will
     the count of bruising years be full,
     which bring the endless suffering
     to me of making war
     on Troy's great plains – a sorrow   1190
     and a shame for all the Greeks?

  (A2):   If only he had gone
     up to the light of heaven or to Haides
     which receives us all, the man
     who taught the Greeks to league together

for this war that has created so much misery.
He has destroyed so many men.

(B1):   He did not give me the delight
         of festive garlands and   1200
         full cups of wine,
         nor the sweet music of the flute,
         nor the joy of a nightlong sleep;
         he has deprived me of the joys of love!
         I lie here, totally uncared for;
         my hair is always covered with
         the heavy dew – a souvenir
         of miserable Troy.   1210

(B2):   There was a time when warlike
         Aias could protect me from
         my nightmares and my enemies;
         but he is now the victim of a hostile
         god. Will I ever have joy again?
         If only I could travel where the woodland
         cape stands out, washed by the sea –
         the flat headland of Sounion,   1220
         so we could hail
         the sacred city, Athens.

FINALE

(*Enter* TEUKROS, *left*)

TEUKROS: I hurried back, because I saw the chief
    commander, Agamemnon, bearing down on you;
    I doubt if he will speak with much restraint.

(*Enter* AGAMEMNON, *right*)

AGAMEMNON: Hey, you! They tell me you have dared to let
      your mouth
    gape wide with insults to me, which have not been punished!
    Yes, it's you I mean; the captive woman's son.
    I am quite sure that if your mother was well-born,

you'd utter lofty words and strut around;   1230
you are a nobody, defending a dead nothing,
and you've still sworn we did not come here as
generals or admirals over the Greeks –
apparently you say Aias came as a chief himself!
Big words, aren't they, for us to hear from slaves?
This great man whose virtues you trumpet out aloud;
where did he go, where did he stand, where I was not?
Have we Greeks no one else but him?
We'll suffer for the day we summoned the
whole army to compete for Achilleus' weapons,   1240
if any result means Teukros denounces us,
and if you two would not agree, when you have lost,
to bear the verdict of a clear majority,
but alway try to get at us with hostile words,
or stab us in the back by treachery – because you did not
    win.
If people live like this, mankind
could not set up the rule of law,
if we must always push aside the men who've won
a fair contest, and put the underdogs in front.
This must be stopped! The broadest-shouldered   1250
men are not the most reliable;
in everything men of intelligence win out.
It only takes a tiny whip to make
a great big ox go straight along the road.
And I foresee the lash will come to cure
you quickly, if you do not get some sense.
This man is dead; he's just a shade, but you
are bold, and violent, and far too free of tongue.
Will you not get some sense? Remember who your mother
    was,
and bring another man here – someone free by birth –   1260
to state your case to us instead of you.
When you speak, I can hardly understand;
I'm not familiar with your foreign tongue.
1 SAILOR: I wish you both would use some sense;
    I cannot give better advice than this.
TEUKROS: When someone dies, how quickly people's
    gratitude flows right away, and is proved treacherous,
    Aias, if this man doesn't have the slightest memory

of you, not even a brief word, when you had risked
your life so many times in battle, working just   1270
for him. No; it's all vanished, flung aside.
You have just said so many mindless words;
have you forgotten utterly the time
when you were penned inside the camp?
You had been routed and reduced to nothing;
he came, and was the only one who saved you,
when fire burned round our ships' sterns and
the rowing benches, and Hektor leaped
over the trench towards the ships!
Who stopped that? Was he not the man, the one   1280
you say never set foot where you were not?
Don't you admit he served you rightly then?
Remember now when he confronted Hektor
one to one, not under orders but by right
of lottery – for his ballot was no sluggard,
made of sticky earth. No! It was bound to be
the first to leap out lightly from the helmet.
Here lies the man who did those things, and I
was at his side – the slave whose mother was barbarian.
You fool, what are you thinking when you talk like
    that?   1290
Have you forgotten your grandfather Pelops was
originally a barbarian from Phrygia?
That Atreus, your father, set before his brother
the most horrible of meals – his children's flesh?
Your mother was a Kretan girl whom her
own father caught screwing a slave, and ordered
to be thrown into the sea for fishfood.
That is your pedigree – and you pour scorn on mine?
I am the son of Telamon, who won
my mother as a bedmate when he proved the best   1300
in a whole army. By her birth she was
a princess, daughter of Laomedon; and Herakles
gave her to Telamon – a special gift, best of the spoils of
    war.
I am the noble child of two most noble parents;
how could I let shame fall on my brother,
who died wretchedly, and whom you're not ashamed
to say you want to cast away unburied!

Know this; that if you throw his body anywhere,
you'll have to throw us three out there to lie with him.
It's much more honourable if I die in sight   1310
of all, struggling to save my brother, than to get
that wife of yours back – or is she your brother's?
I don't care. Watch out – in your own interest, not mine.
If you harm me in any way, you'll come to wish
you'd been a coward rather than attacking me.

(*Enter* ODYSSEUS, *right*)

1 SAILOR: My lord Odysseus, you have come just in time,
if you are here to mediate and not to fight.
ODYSSEUS: What's happening, gentlemen? I heard from far
  away
the sons of Atreus shouting about this noble corpse.
AGAMEMNON: Yes, lord Odysseus; we have been most
  shamefully   1320
reviled by that man over there.
ODYSSEUS: What did he say? I would pardon a man
who is reviled if he replied in kind.
AGAMEMNON: I did insult him; he'd treated me shamefully.
ODYSSEUS: What did he do to harm you?
AGAMEMNON: He says he will not leave this corpse
unburied, but will defy me and bury it.
ODYSSEUS: Now; may a friend tell you the truth
and still be on your side?
AGAMEMNON: Of course; if not, I would be foolish,
  since   1330
I think you are my greatest friend of all the Greeks.
ODYSSEUS: Then listen. By the gods, don't be so hard
as to let him be ruthlessly cast out, unburied;
don't let violence conquer you, so you
hate him so much you trample on what's right.
To me as well he was the most hateful man in the
whole army, from the moment when I won Achilleus'
armour; but although he was like that to me
I never would show disrespect to him; I always said
that he was easily the best of all the Greeks   1340
who came to Troy – except Achilleus.
It would be wrong then if you paid him disrespect;

you would not any way hurt him – only the laws
set by the gods. It is not right to harm
a great man who is dead, not even if you hate him.

AGAMEMNON: So you, Odysseus, take his side against me?

ODYSSEUS: Yes, I do; I hated him, when it was good to hate.

AGAMEMNON: Should you not trample him in death as well?

ODYSSEUS: Do not take pleasure in rewards which are not
good.

AGAMEMNON: Kings find it hard to keep the path of
righteousness.   1350

ODYSSEUS: But they can still respect friends who give good
advice.

AGAMEMNON: Good men should always listen to their
overlords.

ODYSSEUS: Stop this; you'll be the winner, if you listen to
your friends.

AGAMEMNON: Remember just what kind of man you're
helping.

ODYSSEUS: Yes; he was my enemy, but he was noble.

AGAMEMNON: What will you do? Respect an enemy's dead
body?

ODYSSEUS: Yes; his greatness means more to me than our
enmity.

AGAMEMNON: People like you are always too impulsive.

ODYSSEUS: Many men can be your friends right now – and
later enemies.

AGAMEMNON: Do you approve of making friends like
that?   1360

ODYSSEUS: I don't approve of people who're inflexible.

AGAMEMNON: You'll make us both look like cowards today.

ODYSSEUS: No; men that all the Greeks will think did right.

AGAMEMNON: So you are telling me to let them bury him?

ODYSSEUS: I do; one day, I'll need a burial myself.

AGAMEMNON: It's all the same; everyone works just for
himself.

ODYSSEUS: And whom should I more rightly work for than
myself?

AGAMEMNON: People must say that you did this, not I.

ODYSSEUS: However it is done, you will have shown nobility.

AGAMEMNON: All right, but understand this well; I would
gladly   1370

give you this favour, or an even greater one.
As for this man, I hated him alive, and I still hate
him dead. Do what you like.

[*Exit* AGAMEMNON, *right*]

1 SAILOR: Odysseus, anyone who says you were not born
with wisdom, after what you have just done, would be a
fool.

ODYSSEUS: I tell you, Teukros, that from now on I will be
his friend as much as I was once his enemy.
I want to help you bury him, working
beside you, and do all those services for him
which we should give to the most excellent of men.   1380

TEUKROS: Most excellent Odysseus, I praise you in every way
for what you've said; you have relieved me from my fears.
You were his greatest enemy among the Greeks;
but you alone have stood here to defend him, and
did not dare to heap insults on his corpse,
like that most arrogant commander, who came here
when he and his brother determined they
would have his corpse defiled, cast out without a grave.
I call on Zeus, supreme lord of Olympos, and
the long-remembering Fury, and on Justice the fulfiller   1390
to destroy those vile men vilely, just as they
wanted to defile him and cast him out unworthily.

However, noble offspring of agèd Laertes, I'm
reluctant to let you touch him during the burial,
lest I do something this dead man would not accept.
In all else work with us; and if you want to bring
some other soldier, that's all right by me.
I will do all the rest; and you must know
that you have been a very noble man to us.

ODYSSEUS: Well, I wanted to; but if you would not like   1400
me to do it, I consent to your wish, and I will go.

[*Exit* ODYSSEUS, *right*]

TEUKROS: Enough; the time has stretched
too long. Some of you must hasten to

dig out a hollow grave; others bring
a cauldron set high on a tripod over fire,
to make the water for his ritual cleansing;
and yet another group must go back to
the tent, and bring his body-armour.
Boy, hold your father up, as much as you
have strength; touch him with love, and help   1410
me lift his body up; warm arteries
still ooze black blood.
Come, everyone who says he is a friend,
hurry, make haste, and work
for this man, excellent in every way.   1415
1 SAILOR: If people look, they can   1418
learn much; before he sees, no one
can prophesy the future.   1420

[*Exeunt left* TEUKROS, EURYSAKES *and* SAILORS
carrying the body of AIAS, *followed by* TEKMESSA]

ANTIGONE

Translated by Michael Ewans

THE ACTORS AND THEIR ROLES

ANTIGONE, daughter of Oidipous   Actor 2

ISMENE, her sister   Actor 3

COUNCILLORS OF THEBES   Choros

KREON, new ruler of Thebes   Actor 1

BODYGUARD   Silent Face, later Actor 2

GUARD   Actor 3

HAIMON, Kreon's son   Actor 2 or 3

TEIRESIAS, prophet   Actor 2

BOY   Silent Face

EURYDIKE, Kreon's Wife   Actor 3

SCENE I

(Enter ANTIGONE, *dragging* ISMENE *out from the* skene)

ANTIGONE: Sister! My dearest, closest sister Ismene,
   is there a single suffering from Oidipous which Zeus
   does not inflict upon us two who still survive?
   There is no suffering, disaster,
   shame or deprivation, which I have
   not seen in your misfortunes and in mine.
   What is this edict which they say
   the general has recently imposed on all the citizens?
   Do you know? Have you heard? Or is it hidden from you
      that
   our dear ones will soon suffer at the hands of enemies?   10
ISMENE: To me, Antigone, no word about those dear to us
   has come, pleasant or painful, since we two
   lost our two brothers on one day,
   when they struck each other down.
   And since the Argive army vanished
   earlier this night, I do not know whether my life
   is now more fortunate, or I have suffered more.
ANTIGONE: I knew it! And I brought you out,
   beyond the courtyard door, so you might hear alone.
ISMENE: What is it? Clearly some dark news is troubling
   you.   20
ANTIGONE: Has Kreon not decided that of our two brothers
   one
   deserves the honour of a grave, and one does not?
   They say he's buried Eteokles beneath the earth,
   according to our laws and customs; he'll receive
   full privileges down below among the dead,
   while as for Polyneikes, who died wretchedly, he has

apparently proclaimed to the townspeople that
no one may bury his body or cry laments for him;
he must be left unwept, unburied, a sweet treasure-trove
for birds who spot him to enjoy as food.   30
That's what they say the good Kreon has now
proclaimed for you and me – yes, I mean me – and he
is coming here to make his proclamation clear
to all who do not know it. He means business;
anyone who does these things will be sentenced, and
the people of the city will stone them to death.
That's what you're up against; you will soon show
if you are true-born, or disgrace your noble family.

ISMENE: My sister, this is terrible; but if it's true, what help
            could I
        give weaving or unweaving such a tangled skein?   40

ANTIGONE: Work with me, help me now.

ISMENE: What must I dare to do? What do you mean?

ANTIGONE: Help my hands lift the corpse for burial.

ISMENE: You're going to bury him, although the city is
            forbidden to?

ANTIGONE: Yes. He is my brother – yours as well, although
        you may not wish it; I will not be caught betraying him.

ISMENE: How are you so determined, when Kreon's
            opposed?

ANTIGONE: He has no right to keep me from my own.

ISMENE: No!
        Think, sister, how the father of us two
        died hated and despised, when his own search   50
        revealed his ghastly past, and he struck out
        both eyes with his own hand; then his mother –
        twice his, because she was his wife as well –
        destroyed her life by strangling in a woven noose.
        Third, our two wretched brothers on one day
        fought hand to hand and killed each other,
        bringing down upon themselves a common fate.
        Now we two girls are left alone – so think
        how terribly we'll perish, if we go against the law,
        defy our rulers' votes and powers.   60
        Consider this: we were born female,
        so we can't fight men – and we are ruled
        by people stronger than ourselves; we'll have

to bear in silence this command and others even worse.
So I will beg all those below the earth
to pardon me, since I am now compelled,
and will obey those in authority. There is no sense
in going further than we can.

ANTIGONE: I would not ask you; later, if you change your mind,
I would not welcome any help from you.   70
Be what you want to be, but I
will bury him. When I do that, death will be beautiful.
Dear to him, I will lie beside a dear one; I will be
a pure and holy criminal, for I must please
the dead below far longer than the people here.
I will lie there for ever; you, if you behave like this,
pay no respect to values which the gods revere.

ISMENE: That is not true – but I don't have
the strength to go against the other citizens.

ANTIGONE: That's your excuse; I'm leaving now,   80
to make a tomb for my own dearest brother.

ISMENE: You'll suffer for it; I am terrified.

ANTIGONE: Do not feel fear for me; just sort out your own life.

ISMENE: At least tell no one else what you
are doing. Keep it secret; so will I.

ANTIGONE: No, shout it out aloud! You will be even more my enemy
if you stay silent, and do not tell everyone.

ISMENE: Your heart is very warm for such chill deeds.

ANTIGONE: I know I'm pleasing those I am most bound to please.

ISMENE: If you can do it; your desire's impossible.   90

ANTIGONE: I'll do all that I can; then I will stop.

ISMENE: We should not even start to strive for what we
cannot do.

ANTIGONE: If that's your attitude, I'll hate you, and
you'll rightly lie beneath the hatred of the dead.
Let me, and my own "foolishness",
suffer this dreadful fate: I will not suffer anything
so much as if I do not die with true nobility.

[*Exit Antigone, right*]

ISMENE: Go, if you must. Know this, that you
are mad, but truly dear to all who love you.

[*Exit Ismene, into the* skene]

CHOROS I

(*Enter* COUNCILLORS, *left*)

COUNCILLORS (A1):   Ray of the sun, the very fairest   100
light that ever shone on Thebes
of seven gates,
you have shone out at last, eye of
the golden day, rising above
the streams of Dirke;
you have compelled the white-shield man
who came from Argos ready for the fray
to headlong flight.

I COUNCILLOR: Aroused against our land by angry claims   110
of Polyneikes, man of strife,
he was an eagle, crying out aloud,
when he flew over it,
covered in feathers white as snow
with many men at arms
and horse-tail helmet plumes.

COUNCILLORS (A2):   He hovered over our houses, his mouth
gaping with monstrous spears to rage
around our seven gates —
then went, before his jaws were sated   120
with our blood; so the torches of the god of fire
did not seize on our crown of towers.
Such a great clattering of War rose up
behind his back, too hard
for the great dragon's enemy to beat.

I COUNCILLOR: Zeus hates especially the boasts
of a big tongue, and when he sees
them drawing closer as a mighty stream

in all the over-confidence of ringing gold,   130
he lifts his thunderbolt and hurls
it on the one who rushed to cry
their victory from our highest battlements.

COUNCILLORS (B1):   Shaken down, he crashed to earth,
torch still in hand, the man who only recently
had raged against us
with blasts of hate,
possessed, and charging crazily.
It didn't work; the great War-god
dispensed to each his individual fate –
our mighty lead-horse, scattering them all.   140

I COUNCILLOR: At the gates our seven champions stood
      against
their seven, equal matched, and left their armour as
a victory offering to Zeus –
except the two unfortunates, born of one father
and one mother, who fought spear to spear
and have both gained their share in death.

COUNCILLORS (B2):   Victory has come in all her glory,
and answers back with joy to that of Thebes,
the city of the chariots;   150
forget the war,
and go to sing all night
in every temple of the gods.
Shaker of Thebes, Bakchos,
be leader of our dance!

I COUNCILLOR: The king is coming here,
Kreon, son of Menoikeus, our new ruler
because of new events sent by the gods.
What ideas is he turning in his mind;
why has he summoned each of us,   160
the city elders, to meet in special conference?

SCENE 2

(Enter KREON *left, attended by a* BODYGUARD)

KREON: Well, men, the gods have shaken up our city with
    gigantic waves
but now they've set it safely straight on course again.
I chose to send my messengers for you, selected from
all of our people, first because I know how constantly
you gave respect to Laios' power when he was king,
and then, when Oidipous was ruler of this city,
[my sister's husband, you were loyal too.]
After he died, you stayed true to their sons.
Now they have also perished, falling on one day   170
by a twin fate – they hit out, they were struck,
and were polluted by the stain of kindred murder.
I hold all power and the throne,
because I was the next of kin to those who've died.

It is not possible to know a man's whole character,
his mind and judgement, till he has
been tested in administration and in framing laws.
Now I believe that if the man who guides the city
as a whole does not cling firmly to the best advice,
but keeps his tongue locked tight because of fear,   180
that shows he is and always has been worthless.
If a man regards his friends or relatives
as more important than his native land, him I count as
    nothing.
May Zeus, who sees everything, know this;
I would not stand in silence if I saw destruction looming up
for people of this city in place of security; nor would
I ever make a man who was this country's enemy
my friend. I know our country is our saviour;
if she stays upright, and holds a steady course,
then we can make true friends.   190

These are the principles by which I'll make this city great.
And now I have proclaimed an edict, close related to them,
to our citizens about the sons of Oidipous;

Eteokles died fighting for this city, and
achieved surpassing merit in close combat; so
we will entomb him, and pay all the sacred offerings
which go below to the most excellent among the dead.
As for his kinsman – I mean Polyneikes, who was exiled and
came back intending to burn down from the citadel
his fathers' city and its native gods, taste kindred blood   200
and sell the rest of us as slaves:
it is proclaimed to Thebes that no one can
give him the grace of burial or sing laments for him;
his body must be left unburied, food for birds
and dogs to eat – mutilated in the sight of all.
That's what I want; people who harm us will
not ever get more honour from me than the just.
If anyone is well disposed towards this city,
I will honour him in death and life.   210

1 COUNCILLOR: Son of Menoikeus, this is what you want to
   do
about the man who hated and the one who helped this city.
You have the power to enforce any law you like
over the dead, and over us who still survive.
KREON: So now, look out and make sure what I've said –
1 COUNCILLOR: Order a younger man to take this task in
   hand.
KREON: I have soldiers already watching by the corpse.
1 COUNCILLOR: Then what else do you need from us?
KREON: Do not take sides with anyone who disobeys.
1 COUNCILLOR: No one could be so foolish as to fall in love
   with death.   220
KREON: Indeed, that is the penalty. But hopes of gain
have often brought men down.

(*Enter* GUARD, *right*)

GUARD: My lord, I cannot tell you I came out of breath
   through haste, and sped lightfooted here.
   I stopped quite often, paused for thought,
   and circled in my tracks to go straight back.
   I heard my soul say many times to me
   'fool, why go where you'll suffer punishment?'

You wretch, you've stopped again! And if Kreon discovers
    this
from someone else, will that not harm you too?'   230
I turned such thoughts around, and came reluctantly
and slow – so this short road became quite long.
Then finally the idea won of coming here
to you; and even if my news is worthless, I will still speak
    out.
I have come clasping firmly to one hope,
that I will suffer nothing which is not my destiny.
KREON: What is it that has made you terrified?
GUARD: I want to tell you first about myself; I did
not do this thing, nor did I see who did it,
and I should not justly come to any harm.   240
KREON: You've read me well, and put up fences right around
your business. Clearly you have some strange thing to say.
GUARD: Terrible news makes people very hesitant.
KREON: Won't you just tell me, and get out of here?
GUARD: I will. Someone has recently
buried the corpse – sprinkled dry dust upon
its flesh, performed the holy ritual, and gone.
KREON: What are you saying? Is there a man who'd dare to
    do this?
GUARD: I don't know. There was no pickaxe stroke, no earth
turned by a spade. The ground was hard and dry,   250
unbroken, not marked by the print
of wheels; the person who had done it left no trace.
And when the first man on the daylight shift shows what
had happened, it was like a miracle – and we were scared.
The body'd vanished from our sight – not buried in a tomb;
a light dust covered it, as if to ward pollution off.
There was no trace of wild beasts, or dogs,
coming near him or tearing him.

Then noisy curses flew between us;
guard blamed guard, and finally   260
it would have come to blows; no one was there to stop us.
It seemed that everyone had done the deed; no one
could be proved guilty, since we all claimed ignorance.
We were prepared to take a red-hot iron in our hands,
or walk through fire, and swear solemnly by the gods

that we had not done this, and weren't accomplices
with anyone who'd planned and done it.

At last, when all our searching got us nowhere,
someone spoke, and made us all bow down
our faces to the ground in fear; we could not see   270
how we could prove him wrong, or come out well
if we did what he said. His idea was that we must take
the deed to you at once, and not conceal it.
This won; the bad luck of the draw
condemned me to receive this privilege.
I'm here against my will, and I can see you don't want me;
nobody likes a messenger who brings bad news.
1 COUNCILLOR: My lord, for some time now I have been
    thinking
that perhaps the gods have done this deed.
KREON: Stop now, before your words make me brimful with
    rage;   280
don't show yourself a fool as well as old.
You are intolerable when you say the gods
would have the slightest care about this corpse.
Would they have covered him with earth because they
    honoured him
especially, as one who'd done great service – he who came to
    burn
their colonnaded temples and their precious offerings,
burn their land, and scatter to the winds their sacred laws?
Have you seen gods paying respect to wicked men?
It cannot be. Right from the start this city had a group
of dissidents who muttered secretly   290
against me, tossed their heads, and failed to keep their necks
under the yoke of justice, learn to love my rule.
It's absolutely obvious they bribed
these guards to do it. Money is the worst
invention humans ever made and used.
It sacks cities, and uproots men from their homes;
it throws good minds off course, corrupts them till
they turn to shameful crimes;
it's shown men how to practise villainy,   300
and be familiar with all kinds of godless work.
The people who took money to do this

have made sure soon or late they'll pay the penalty.
Now, as Zeus still remains my lord,
know this – and know it well, because I speak on oath;
if you do not find out the man who made
this grave, and bring him here into my sight,
then you will not simply be killed; I'll string you up alive,
until you have revealed to me just why
you did this outrage; afterwards, if you go thieving, you   310
will know where to gather booty; you'll have learned
not to love gains regardless of the source.
You'll see the loot from shameful actions usually
leads to destruction rather than to gain.

GUARD: May I say something, or just turn and go?

KREON: Do you not know your voice itself offends me?

GUARD: Does it bite at your ears – or in your soul?

KREON: Why do you want to know?

GUARD: The culprit hurts your soul – I only hurt your ears.

KREON: It's clear you've always been a babbler.   320

GUARD: That may be – but I never did this deed.

KREON: You did – and sold your soul for cash.

GUARD: Alas!
It's terrible when someone clever guesses – and guesses so
    wrong.

KREON: Play clever word-games all you like; but if you don't
bring me the culprits, you will come to realize
that gains from wickedness bring suffering.

[*Exeunt* KREON *and* BODYGUARD *into the* skene]

GUARD: Well – may he be found! Whether he
is caught or not – fortune will settle that –
there's no way you will see me coming back.
Beyond my hopes, beyond what I expected, I   330
am saved, and owe the gods great thanks.

[*Exit* GUARD, *right*]

CHOROS 2

COUNCILLORS (A1):   There are many wonders in this world –
and none is greater than Man;
he flies across the white-flecked sea
driven by stormy south winds, cleaving his path
beneath the crests of threatening waves –
and Earth, immortal, inexhaustible,
greatest of goddesses, he wears away
turning the soil with mules; his ploughs
go back and forwards year to year.   340

(A2):   He traps light-headed birds
and every tribe of savage animal
and creatures of the deep
in coils of woven nets –
this clever creature, Man; by his skill
he subdues wild hillside beasts –
puts yokes across the necks   350
of shaggy horses – and he tames
the powerful mountain bulls.

(B1):   He has learned language, thoughts
as swift as wind
and social feelings; he has learned how to escape
from sharp arrows of bitter frost
under clear skies, and darts of driving rain.
He's always ready – and he never tries to tackle
    anything
unless he is. Only from Death   360
will he not find release;
he has devised a cure even
for desperate diseases.

(B2):   There's something in his innovative skill
subtle beyond belief –
sometimes it leads him to disaster,
but at other times to good.
When he respects the laws of earth
and justice sworn to by the gods

he will stand high inside his city; there's no city for   370
a rash and wicked man.
Never may people share my hearth
or share my thoughts
who would do such a thing!

1 COUNCILLOR: Is this a portent from the gods?
          I know this girl. How could I
          deny she is Antigone?
          Oh pitiable child
          of pitiable Oidipous,   380
          what is this?
          Has someone arrested you
          for disobedience to the king's decrees
          and caught you acting crazily?

                    SCENE 3

(*Enter the* GUARD *right, dragging or pushing* ANTIGONE *as his prisoner*)

GUARD: This is the little bitch who did it; we caught her
   trying to bury him. Where is Kreon?

(*Enter* KREON *and* BODYGUARD *from the* skene)

1 COUNCILLOR: Just as he's needed, back he comes.
KREON: What is it? What chance must I match?
GUARD: Lord, men should never pledge their word on
      anything;
   for second thoughts can give the lie to first resolve.
   I could have sworn I'd never come back here   390
   after the deluge of your threats.
   A pleasure which is longed for, and then comes
   against all hope, is greater far than any other joy;
   and so I've come, although I perjure my sworn oath,
   bringing this girl, whom we caught making
   a grave. This time we did not cast the lots;
   the privilege belongs to me and no one else.
   Now, king, take her, do what you want with her –

question, interrogate; I am now justly
free, released from punishment.   400
KREON: You've brought her to me; how and where was she
   taken?
GUARD: She was burying him; that's all there is to know.
KREON: D'you understand what you are saying? Is it true?
GUARD: I saw this girl as she was burying the corpse
   which you've forbidden. Is that clear and plain enough?
KREON: How did you find and capture her?
GUARD: Something like this. When we got back
   with all those terrifying threats from you,
   we scraped away the dust which was spread
   on the corpse, and cleaned the moist, decaying flesh.   410
   Then we sat on the hill-top, well upwind,
   keeping our distance to avoid the smell;
   each man made sure the others kept awake
   with loud reminders of the fate in store
   if anyone was slack. That's how time passed
   until the sun's bright disc stood at its height
   and heat burned down. Then suddenly a whirlwind raised
   a storm of dust, a torment darkening the sky
   which covered the whole plain, polluting all
   the leaves upon the trees; the heavens were choked.   420
We shut our eyes, and suffered this disease the gods had sent.
A long time later, the storm passed:
   and then we saw this girl crying out bitterly –
   sharp sounds of grief, just like a bird which sees
   the bed inside her nest orphaned of young;
   when she saw that the corpse was bare again
   she groaned out loud, and raised a bitter curse
   against the people who had done it.
Straightway she brought dry dust by hand
   and from a beautifully engraved urn raised high   430
she poured a crown of three libations on the corpse.
When we saw this we all rushed there, and hunted
down our prey at once; but she was not disturbed.
We questioned her about what she was doing
   and had done; she did not deny a thing.
This gave me pleasure, and some pain as well;
   it is most sweet to have escaped oneself
from danger, but to bring someone you like

into misfortune's bitter. Still, all that to me
means less by far than saving my own skin.   440
KREON: You, with your face bowed down towards the
    ground,
d'you say, or d'you deny you did these things?
ANTIGONE: I say I did it; I do not deny what I have done.
KREON: (*to* GUARD) Now you can take yourself wherever you
    desire
free and released from this most heavy charge.

[*Exit* GUARD, *right*]

(*to* ANTIGONE) You will now tell me, not at length but in
    few words;
did you know I'd proclaimed no one may bury him?
ANTIGONE: I knew it; how could I not know it? It was
    publicly decreed.
KREON: But you still dared to go beyond these laws?
ANTIGONE: Yes! For me Zeus had not given these
    commands   450
and Justice, who lives with the gods beneath the earth,
never marked out such laws for mortal men;
nor did I think your edict is so strong
that it could override the unwritten
and everlasting laws made by the gods.
They are not just for yesterday and now; they live
for ever, and no one knows when they appeared.
How could I ever think of paying the due penalty before
the gods for breaking such great laws, because I was afraid
of one man's arrogant ideas? I knew that I will have   460
to die – how could I not? – even without your edicts;
if I die before my time, I will be better off.
When someone lives in utter misery like me,
how could death not be better?
So, for me to meet this fate
will bring no real pain. If I'd allowed
my mother's son to die and stay unburied, that
would have been painful; this is not.
And if right now you think I've been a fool, perhaps
the charge of folly truly lies with you, the judge.   470
1 COUNCILLOR: Look! The girl is savage as her father; faced

with suffering, she does not know how to give way.
KREON: Remember, over-stubborn people fall
  most often; and the toughest iron, tempered
  all round to greatest hardness by the fire,
  you'll see most often snapped to pieces.
  I know very bad-tempered horses have been tamed
  by tiny bridles; you cannot think big
  when you yourself are someone else's slave.
  This girl already knew how to be insolent   480
  when she transgressed the laws we had set down;
  and here's a second act of insolence, to boast
  about it and exult in what she's done.
  Truly I am the man no longer, she's the man,
  if she can win this victory without a punishment.
  Although she is my sister's child – if she were
  even closer to me than my family –
  she and her sister won't escape
  a most unpleasant death; for I accuse *her* of
  an equal share in planning for this burial.   490
  Bring her here now; I saw her recently
  inside the house, in frenzy, totally out of control.

                              [*Exit* BODYGUARD *into the* skene]

When people plan wrongdoing in the dark
the heart often convicts itself of secret crime.
I also hate it when someone is caught
and tries to make a deed of shame sound beautiful.
ANTIGONE: Do you want to do more than kill me?
KREON: No; that's all I want.
ANTIGONE: Then why do you delay? Nothing you say
  is pleasant to me, or would ever please me;   500
  and I'm sure you too hate every word of mine.
  What else could I have done which is
  more glorious than placing my dear brother
  in his grave? I know these men approve
  of what I've done; but fear has locked their tongues.
  Rulers have many privileges – one is that you can
  both do and say whatever you desire.
KREON: You are the only Theban who sees things this way.

ANTIGONE: These men see too; their mouths fawn on your
    will.
KREON: D'you feel no shame, if you think differently?   510
ANTIGONE: There is no shame in paying honour to your kin.
KREON: The man who died opposing him – was he not kin as
    well?
ANTIGONE: Yes, my mother's and my father's son.
KREON: Then why pay honours he will see as impious?
ANTIGONE: The dead man's corpse will not bear witness you
    are right.
KREON: He will, because you give the same respect to him as
    to our enemy.
ANTIGONE: It was his brother, not a slave that died.
KREON: – trying to conquer this our land, while he defended
    it.
ANTIGONE: I don't care; Haides wants these rites.
KREON: A wicked man should not receive the same care as a
    good.   520
ANTIGONE: Who knows if that's not right among the dead
    below?
KREON: An enemy never deserves love, even when he's dead.
ANTIGONE: I was not born to hate my relatives, but to give
    them my love.
KREON: If you want to give love, go to the underworld
    and love them there. No woman will rule over me while I'm
    alive.

(*Enter* BODYGUARD *from the* skene, *leading* ISMENE)

1 COUNCILLOR: Ismene has been brought outside
        pouring out tears of love for her sister;
        a cloud of grief casts shades
        of sorrow over her flushed face
        and drenches her fair cheeks.   530
KREON: You lurked snakelike inside the house
    and drank my life-blood secretly, so I was ignorant
    of nurturing two revolutionary, destructive girls!
    Now tell me; did you have a share
    in burying that man, or will you swear your innocence?
ISMENE: I did the deed – if she will let me – and
    I want to take my share of blame.

ANTIGONE: Justice will not allow you to do that, because
  you did not want to and I did not share my deed with you.
ISMENE: But now you are in trouble, I am not ashamed   540
  to sail with you across this sea of suffering.
ANTIGONE: Haides and those below know who buried him;
  I cannot love a friend who is a friend in words alone.
ISMENE: My sister, please do not reject me; let me
  die with you, and pay due honour to the dead.
ANTIGONE: You cannot share my death, and cannot claim
  work which you did not touch. My death will be enough.
ISMENE: How could I want to live, if I lose you?
ANTIGONE: Ask Kreon – you depend on him.
ISMENE: Why do you taunt me? It will not help you.   550
ANTIGONE: If I am mocking you, it hurts me too.
ISMENE: What else could I do now to help?
ANTIGONE: Save yourself. I won't be jealous if you can
  survive.
ISMENE: I'm desperate. Will you not let me share your fate?
ANTIGONE: No! You chose to live, while I chose death.
ISMENE: I spoke; I tried to stop you.
ANTIGONE: People up here approved of your ideas; the dead
  of mine.
ISMENE: But now we are both equally condemned.
ANTIGONE: Take courage. You are still alive – but my soul
  died
  some time ago, so I could help the dead.   560
KREON: I think that of these two girls one
  has just gone mad; the other always was.
ISMENE: Yes, my lord; when people suffer they
  cannot always stay sane.
KREON: You didn't, when you chose to join with her in
  wickedness.
ISMENE: Why should I want to live alone, without her?
KREON: This girl – don't speak of her. She is already dead.
ISMENE: Will you kill her, engaged to your own son?
KREON: Other women have furrows he can plough.
ISMENE: No one was ever bound so close as him to her.   570
KREON: I will not let my sons get worthless wives.
ISMENE: Poor, dearest Haimon, how your father wrongs you!
KREON: You and your bedroom talk are getting on my
  nerves.

ISMENE: Will you take her away from your own son?
KREON: For me, Haides himself will stop their wedding plans.
ISMENE: So it is certain she must die?
KREON: On that we are agreed. (*to* BODYGUARD) No more
    delay; take her
inside. From now on they must be
just women, not allowed to roam at large.
Even brave people try to run away, when they   580
see Haides coming near to end their lives.

[*Exit* BODYGUARD, *escorting* ANTIGONE *and* ISMENE
into the skene; *he then returns.* KREON *moves to the rear
perimeter of the* orchêstra]

CHOROS 3

COUNCILLORS (A1):   Blessèd are all who live without tasting
        misfortune.
    When a house is shaken by the gods, disaster
    never stops – creeping across the generations,
    like the surge of the salt sea
    driven by fierce winds from Thrakia
    across the darkness of the deep;
    it churns the black sand from the depths,   590
    and headlands, struck by bitter winds,
    cry out and groan.

(A2):   From long ago I've seen that in our royal house
    new sorrows fall upon the sorrows of the dead;
    no generation frees the next, but some god
    strikes them down, and there is no escape.
    In Oidipous' house the light was scattered
    faintly above the last roots of the family;   600
    but now the bloody knife
    of the infernal gods
    cuts it away with crazy speech
    and Furies in the mind.

(B1):   What human outrage, Zeus,
    could ever check your power?

– the power which neither all-ensnaring Sleep
nor the years' unrelenting months
can overcome; Time does not age you,
but you are the lord of all
Olympos' dazzling splendour.   610
Soon and for ever,
as in all past time, this law
will hold; no human being gains
great wealth without disaster.

(B2):   Hope wanders far and wide,
brings benefit to many – but
to others the false lure of empty needs;
it creeps up on someone who does not know,
until he's burned his foot on the hot fire.
A wise man said these famous words: 620
evil seems good when the god leads
someone to destruction; but the humble
man survives without disaster.

I COUNCILLOR: Here is Haimon, your last son.
Does he come in pain about
the death of his bride, his Antigone,
and very bitter for the marriage he has lost?   630

SCENE 4

(*Enter* HAIMON, *left.* KREON *moves back into the playing area
to encounter him*)

KREON: We will soon know, better than prophets.
Son, are you here in frenzied rage against your father
for my fixed decision that your bride must die?
Or are you on my side, whatever I may do?
HAIMON: Father, I'm yours; your good advice
sets out the path which I will follow.
I could not ever think a marriage matters
more to me than your fine leadership.
KREON: My son, hold this close to your heart,
that you must always stand behind
640

your father's will. All men pray they
will have obedient children in their homes,
to pay their father's enemies back their deserts,
and show their father's friends the same respect as he.
When a man fathers useless children,
what could you say but that he's sown himself
a crop of trouble, and his enemies will laugh at him?
My son, don't let desire for pleasure make
you lose your good sense for a woman; it's
a very cold embrace, if the partner in your house   650
is treacherous. Is there a greater wound
than having such a person in your family?
Spit her away as if she is an enemy, and let
the girl marry someone in Haides.
Since I caught her alone of the whole city
in open disobedience to me, I
will not be made a liar in the city;
I'll kill her. She can call on Zeus, the god
of kinship; but if I let anarchy prevail
among my relatives, I'll get it from others as well.   660

A man who proves his excellence at managing
his house always acts rightly in the city too.
I'm confident that such a man
will both rule well, and cheerfully be ruled,
and in the storm of battle he would stand
where he is set – a good and loyal comrade.
If someone goes beyond good discipline, attacks the law,
or thinks he can give orders to the rulers,
he cannot win my praise.
The person whom the city's set in charge must be obeyed 670
in small things as in great, just and less just.

Anarchy is the greatest of all evils.
It destroys cities, uproots homes –
and it has broken ranks of faithful allies
up in rout. Those who live in the right way
are usually preserved by their obedience.
So we must guard with care the order in our lives –
and never, no way let a woman conquer us.
Much better, if we must, to be defeated by a man;

no one could say we're weaker than the women. 680

I COUNCILLOR: Advancing age may have deprived us of our
      wits –
   but we think what you say is sensible and wise.

HAIMON: Father, the gods give wisdom to mankind,
   and it is far the best of all their gifts.
   I could not, and I would not, try to tell
   whether what you have said is right; 686
   but it is not your nature to anticipate 688
   all that people might say, or do – or criticize.
   Your eye is far too terrifying for the average citizen 690
   to say things that you do not want to hear;
   but I can hear the whispers in the dark.
   The city's weeping for this girl, saying
   that of all women she the least deserves to die
   so shamefully, when what she did was very glorious.
   When her dear brother fell upon the battlefield
   she would not let him stay unburied for
   the savage dogs and birds to eat;
   is she not worthy to be crowned with gold?
   These are the words that go in silent darkness round this
      town. 700
   My father, there is nothing in my life
   I value more than you and your success.
   What greater treasure could children acquire than
   their father's achievements – or a father than his son's?
   So do not wear one attitude unchanged,
   believing you, and no one else, are right.
   A man who thinks that he alone is wise
   and has no equal in his eloquence or mind –
   when opened out, they're found to be bereft of sense.
   It is not shameful for a man to learn, even 710
   if he is wise – and not stand too firm.
   Beside a stream in winter flood you see
   how trees that bend save every twig, while those
   that resist perish, root and branch.
   A ship's captain who holds the sheet
   tight-stretched, and never slackens it, capsizes and
   completes his voyage upside down.
   So stop being so angry, and allow yourself to change.
   If I, a younger man, may be allowed to say

what I think, it would be far better for   720
mankind if we were always born with wisdom;
since the scales often tilt against us,
it's good to learn from those who say the truth.

1 COUNCILLOR: My lord, if he's said something timely, you
      should learn
from him – and he from you; you have both spoken well.

KREON: D'you really think men at our age must
learn how to think from one so young?

HAIMON: Nothing that's wrong; and though I'm young,
you should look rather at what I've achieved.

KREON: Is it a fine achievement to support rebellion?   730

HAIMON: I would not ask you to support someone who has
      done wrong.

KREON: And is not that precisely the disease she's caught?

HAIMON: The people of this city as a whole say no.

KREON: The city's going to tell me what decisions I must
      make?

HAIMON: Can't you see that's a very immature remark?

KREON: Is anybody else but me supposed to rule this land?

HAIMON: There is no city if it's made up of one man.

KREON: Isn't the city usually thought to belong to the ruler?

HAIMON: You'd make a very good king – on a desert island.

KREON: It seems my son is fighting on the woman's side.   740

HAIMON: If you're the woman; it's for you I care.

KREON: Outrageous! Will you bandy with your father talk of
      rights?

HAIMON: Yes – you have made a terrible mistake about
      what's right.

KREON: How could I, paying due respect to my own powers?

HAIMON: You pay them no respect, trampling on the gods'
      dues.

KREON: You piece of scum, worth less than a woman!

HAIMON: You'd never catch me acting shamefully.

KREON: – but every word you say sticks up for her.

HAIMON: – and you, and me, and the gods of the
      underworld.

KREON: You'll never marry her while she is still alive.   750

HAIMON: So she must die. It will kill someone else.

KREON: Are you so bold you can make open threats?

HAIMON: Where is the threat? Just telling you what I think?

KREON: Your thoughts are empty, and you will regret them
     all.
HAIMON: If you were not my father, I would say you are a
     fool.
KREON: You are a woman's slave; do not try to sweet-talk
     me.
HAIMON: D'you want to speak, and then hear no reply?
KREON: If you think that, by heaven and all the gods, know
     this;
     I'll make you suffer for insulting me.

(*to* BODYGUARD) Bring out that filthy bitch; she'll die here,
     now,   760
     before his eyes – right at her bridegroom's side.
HAIMON: No – do not ever think it; she won't die
     right at my side – and you will never set
     eyes on my face again. If any of your friends still wants
     to listen, rant and rave to them.

                              [*Exit* HAIMON, *right*]

I COUNCILLOR: My lord, he's gone in anger and in haste;
     a young man's thoughts are dangerous when he is suffering.
KREON: Off he can go – to think and act beyond the bounds
     of sense;
     he will not save those two girls from their fate.
I COUNCILLOR: Do you intend to kill them both?   770
KREON: Not the one who didn't touch the body; you are
     right.
I COUNCILLOR: How do you plan to kill the other one?
KREON: I'll take her to a place where people never go,
     and hide her, still alive, in a rock cave,
     giving her just enough to eat, so that our city
     will avoid pollution and the anger of the gods.
     She only worships Haides: she can pray
     to him, and then perhaps she will be saved from death;
     or rather, she will learn – too late – that paying
     honours to the dead is very dangerous.   780

          [*Exeunt* KREON *and* BODYGUARD *into the* skene]

CHOROS 4

COUNCILLOR (A1):   Passion, unconquerable;
                Passion, destroyer of wealth;
                you spend your nights on watch beside
                a young girl's gentle cheeks;
                you roam across the sea,
                and by the wild men's huts;
                not one of the immortals can escape you,
                nor of us creatures who live just a day;
                the person who has you goes mad.   790

   (A2):   You warp good minds and turn
                them bad, so they are ruined;
                you stirred this strife inside
                a family; and the Desire
                which shines out from the eyes
                of an attractive bride conquers. It is
                enthroned in power beside
                the greatest divine laws; the love-goddess
                sports with her prey, unbeatable.   800

SCENE 5

(*Enter* ANTIGONE *from the* skene, *escorted by the*
BODYGUARD)

1 COUNCILLOR: I too am forced to go beyond
                the laws of loyalty, and I
                cannot restrain the streams of tears,
                seeing Antigone go to the bridal
                chamber where all rest in death.
ANTIGONE (B1):   Citizens of this, my fathers' land,
                you see me going on
                my last journey,
                seeing the sunlight one last time
                and never any more; Haides,   810
                who lays us all to rest,
                will drag me still alive towards

the shores of Acheron.
I've never heard the escort-song
for a new bride, and no one's sung
the morning-song for me after
my wedding night; I will be married to
the lord of death.

1 COUNCILLOR: So you will go famous and praised
to where the dead lie hidden.
Not stricken by a lingering disease,
not paying for a life of violence,   820
you alone have chosen to go down
to Haides while still living.

ANTIGONE (B2):   I've heard about the very miserable death
upon Mount Sipylos of Niobe,
who came here once from Lydia;
like clinging ivy, the stone grew
and overcame her.
People say that as she wastes away
rain and snow never leave her;   830
tears pour from underneath her eyebrows,
and fall down her neck. The god is taking me
to lie in a last bed like hers.

1 COUNCILLOR: She was divine, the daughter of a goddess;
we are human beings, mortal in our parentage.
Still, it's a great achievement for a woman if
you share the fate of one who was a demigod
both in your life and after you are dead.

ANTIGONE (C1):   You mock me!
By my fathers' gods, can you
not wait to insult me until I'm gone –   840
not throw this in my face?
This is my city, and you are
its richest men;
springs of the River Dirke,
sacred groves of Thebe,
I at least have you as witnesses
that I'm bereft of friends to weep for me;
look at the law which makes me go
into the rock-closed prison
of this strange new burial-place.
Poor me! Without a home among the living,   850

nor among the corpses, I will be
neither alive nor dead.   .

COUNCILLORS (A1):   You went to the limits of daring,
girl, and struck your foot against
the mighty throne of Justice up above.
You're paying for some of your father's suffering.

ANTIGONE (C2):   Now you touch upon
the bitterest of my thoughts,
my constant grief about my father, and
the miserable fate of us,   860
the famous house of Labdakos.
Think of the horror!
My own mother was ruined when she slept
in incest with the son
whom she herself had borne. He was
my father; I'm their wretched child!
I am accursed; I am not married; I must go
to share their house.
Oh brother, so ill-fated was
your marriage that in death   870
you have destroyed my life.

COUNCILLOR (A2):   Your reverence is a kind of piety,
but no one who has power can tolerate
defiance of that power; obstinate
and wilful, you've destroyed yourself.

ANTIGONE (C3):   Without a tear shed for me, without friend
or husband, I go in my misery
upon the road they have prepared for me.
This is my sorrow: I must never see again
the sacred sunlight;   880
not one friend will weep
or cry in grief for my fate.

(*Enter* KREON *from the* skene)

KREON: You know, no one would ever cease from pouring
out
songs and laments before they die, if they were allowed!
Take her away as fast as possible, and shroud her in
her vaulted cave-tomb, as I've ordered.
Leave her alone; then she can choose to die

or live entombed and treat it as her home.
We will not be defiled by anything to do with her;
but she will never live up here again.   890

ANTIGONE: Tomb; bridal chamber; everlasting prison
carved out of the rock; I go to you to find
my family – the many who have perished, whom
Persephone has welcomed to the company of the dead.
I am the last of you to go, and I'm by far the most
unfortunate, because I come before my natural span of life.
I nurture this one hope – that when I come
I will be welcome to my father, and to you,
mother; and specially to you, dear brother.
When you died, with my own hands   900
I washed you, dressed you, and I poured
the offerings upon your graves; Polyneikes, see
my recompense for tending your dead body.

But anyone with wisdom knows that I was right.
If I had been a mother, and it was my children,
or a husband had been mouldering in death,
I never would have done this in defiance of the citizens.
By what law am I right to say this?
If my husband were dead, I could have found another one,
and someone else's child, if I lost his;   910
but now my mother and my father rest
in Haides, I can't ever see another brother grow.
That is the law by which I gave the pride of place
to you; but, dearest brother, Kreon thought
this was terribly wrong, and I'd behaved outrageously.
So now I am his prisoner, and he'll take me away;
no wedding night, no bridal song – not any part
of all the joys of marriage and of raising children.
Yes, my fate is horrible; I'll go, bereft of friends,
while still alive into the vaults made for the dead.   920
What justice of the gods have I transgressed?
In this misery, why should I turn my eyes
to heaven? Which god could I call to help?
I've shown true piety, and now they say I'm impious.
If the gods are happy with my fate,
the suffering will teach me I've been wrong;

but if these men are wrong, I would not want
them suffering more than they unjustly do to me.

1 COUNCILLOR: The same gusts of the same
    winds still command her soul.   930

KREON: Her escort will
    be punished for their slackness.

ANTIGONE: Oh god, these words
    mean that my death is very near.

KREON: Let me advise you not to hope
    it will not happen.

ANTIGONE: Oh city of my fathers in this land
    of Thebe, gods who are my ancestors,
    I'm being taken; there's no more delay.
    Rulers of Thebes, look at me now;   940
    the last descendant of the royal house.
    See what is being done to me
    – and by what kind of men –
    because I showed true piety!

[*Exit* ANTIGONE, *dragged off by the* BODYGUARD, *right.*
KREON *retreats to the rear perimeter of the* orchêstra]

CHOROS 5

COUNCILLORS (A1):   Danaë was beautiful, but she was forced
    to leave the light of day for walls of bronze,
    and she was held fast in
    a chamber like the grave.
    Child, child! She too was noble, and she nurtured
    Zeus' precious, golden shower of seed.   950
    Destiny has fearful power;
    not wealth, nor war,
    nor city walls, nor black
    sea-beaten ships escape.

  (A2):   Lykourgos, hot-tempered king
    of the Edonians, was also bound;
    for his insults Dionysos walled him
    inside a rocky prison; there
    the terrible and ever-flowering strength

of madness drips away; he came to know   960
the god whom in his madness he'd abused.
He'd tried to stop the mainads
and the holy fire, and he annoyed
the Muses, who adore the music of the flute.

(B1):   Beside the Dark Rocks lie the shores of Bosporos
which joins the Twin Seas, and Thrakian
Salmydessos, where the god of War,   970
who lives nearby, once saw the fearful wound
which Phineus' second wife in frenzy dealt
to his two sons. She blinded them; their sightless eyes
cried out for vengeance, mutilated by the needle point
held in her bloody hands.

(B2):   Poor boys, they pined away, mourning
their cruel fate – children whose mother had   980
married disastrously. She once was a queen,
related to the ancient royal family of Athens;
but she'd grown up in distant caves
among her father Boreas' storms, to run
as fast as horses on the mountain-range.
A child of gods; but the eternal goddesses
of Destiny even caught her.

SCENE 6

(*Enter* TEIRESIAS *left, led by a* BOY)

TEIRESIAS: Leaders of Thebes, we've come together,
one seeing for two; the blind
can only walk with a guide's help.   990
KREON: Aged Teiresias, what's happened?
TEIRESIAS: I will tell you; listen to the prophet.
KREON: I have not yet ignored your thoughts.
TEIRESIAS: That's why you've steered this city right so far.
KREON: I've felt, and can bear witness to, your help.
TEIRESIAS: Then know that now you've gone right to the
sharpened edge of fate.
KREON: What do you mean? I fear what you will say.

TEIRESIAS: You'll realize when you hear the signs my skill
    has given me.
  As I went to the ancient throne I use for augury,
  the haven which I keep for every kind of bird,   1000
  I hear bird-noises new to me; they're crying out
  in furious rage, and making coarse, barbaric sounds.
  I realized they were tearing at each other, talons stained
  with blood; the flapping of their wings left me no doubt.
  I was afraid, and straightway tried to make burnt sacrifice
  upon an altar in full flame; but the fire-god
  would not burn up my offerings. A dank moisture
  seeped from the thigh-bones, trickled down onto
  the embers, smoked, and spluttered; gall
  was scattered to the air, and dripping thighs   1010
  lay bare of all the fat which had concealed them.
  That's what this boy told me about the failure of the rites,
  by which I asked for guidance – and received no sign.
  He leads me; I lead other men.
  The city is diseased because of your ideas;
  the birds and dogs are filling all our altars
  and our hearths with human flesh
  torn from that corpse, the wretched son of Oidipous.
  That's why the gods will not accept our prayers
  and sacrifices, or the flame from offerings of burned
    meat.   1020
  Birds' cries will not shriek out clear signs
  because they've feasted on a dead man's clotted blood.

  Now think, my son; all human beings
  make mistakes – but once we have,
  a man regains his wisdom, and is blessed,
  who cures the harm he's caused,
  and does not stay unmoved.
  Self-will can turn out to be foolishness.
  Pay the dead man his dues; do not stab one who has
  already perished; is it a sign of strength to kill him once
    again?   1030
  I'm on your side, and this is good advice. Learning from
  a good adviser's very pleasant, if what he says brings gain.
KREON: Reverend sir, you all shoot arrows at this man
    like archers at a target. I've been wounded in the past

by seercraft; many times people like you
have sold me and delivered me like merchandise.
Trade, make your profits how you like; in silver alloy
from Sardis, if that is what you fancy – or in gold
from India; you will not hide him in a tomb,
not even if the eagles of lord Zeus decide   1040
to seize his flesh and take it to their master's throne.
I don't fear that pollution, so
I won't permit his burial; for I am sure
that no mere mortal can pollute the gods.
The fall is very shameful, old Teiresias,
when very clever people express
shameful thoughts with eloquence for profit.

TEIRESIAS: Ah!
Does any human being know, does any think . . .

KREON: Think what? What gem of insight do you have for
us?

TEIRESIAS: . . . that wisdom is most powerful of all
possessions?   1050

KREON: Folly, I think, is the most harmful.

TEIRESIAS: That's the disease by which you are possessed.

KREON: I would not want to trade insults with you, prophet.

TEIRESIAS: You have already, when you said my prophecies
are lies.

KREON: All prophets have a love of money.

TEIRESIAS: All rulers make immoral gains.

KREON: Do you not realize you're saying this about your
king?

TEIRESIAS: I know; with my help, you have saved this city.

KREON: You are a clever prophet, but corrupt.

TEIRESIAS: You will stir me to utter secrets better left
alone.   1060

KREON: Stir them – unless you speak simply to make a profit.

TEIRESIAS: Is that really how I seem to you?

KREON: Just know that my resolve is not for sale.

TEIRESIAS: Then learn that you won't live
through very many circuits of the speeding sun,
before you will have given someone sprung from your own
loins
as corpse in payment for the corpses! You
have cast someone from up here down below,

outrageously confined a living soul inside a tomb;
and you have withheld from the underworld a corpse,   1070
who lacks his just deserts, his burial rites, his sacred dues.
You have no business with him now – nor have
the gods above, so you do violence to them.
Therefore you will be mutilated and destroyed
when you are caught by Furies sent by Haides and the gods,
so your own wicked deeds will catch you.
Well now, consider if I speak these words
because of bribery; wait very little time, and you will hear
an outcry from the men and women of your house.
In hatred of you the whole city is now stirred because   1080
the dogs have helped to bury his mangled remains –
and wild beasts, and winged birds, which have brought
    back
the stench of the pollution to the city's hearths.
You have provoked me; in my anger, I've become
an archer, aiming arrows at your heart.
Not one of them will miss; you won't escape the pain.

Boy, take me home; he can let loose
his temper against younger men.
He will learn to develop a much gentler tongue
and greater wisdom than he has just now.   1090

[*Exeunt* BOY *and* TEIRESIAS, *left*]

I COUNCILLOR: My lord, he's gone; and what he prophesied
    was terrible.
Once my hair was black; and all the time since it's
been grey, I know for certain, he has never
given us predictions which were lies.
KREON: I know that too; my mind's disturbed.
It would be frightful if I yield; but should I stand firm,
my anger may be caught in Ruin's net.
I COUNCILLOR: Son of Menoikeus, it is time you took some
    good advice.
KREON: What must I do? Tell me; I will obey.
I COUNCILLOR: First go and get the girl out of that chamber
    in the rock   1100
then raise a burial mound over the dead.

KREON: Is that what you advise? You think I must give way?

I COUNCILLOR: My lord, as fast as possible; Damages sent
    by
the gods are swift of foot, and cut down foolish men.

KREON: It's hard, but I abandon my cherished resolve,
    and I will do it; fighting against Necessity is bad.

I COUNCILLOR: Then go and do it; do not give the task to
    other men.

KREON: I'll go, just as I am; come, come, my men,
    both near and far, take pickaxes, and rush
    out to that hill which you can see.   1110
    Now that my judgement has been turned around,
    I put the girl in prison, and will go myself to set her free.
    I am afraid it may be best to reverence the laws
    established by the gods right through your life.

[*Exit* KREON, *right*]

CHOROS 6

COUNCILLORS (A1): Oh god of many names,
    delight of Theban Semele,
    offspring of Zeus the god
    of mighty thunder, guardian of
    glorious Italia, you are the ruler of
    Demeter's plain at Eleusis, where all   1120
    are welcome; Oh Bakchos!
    You live in Thebes, the mother-city of
    bakchantes, by the gentle stream
    of Ismenos, and on the soil in which
    the savage dragon's teeth were sown.

(A2): On the high ground above the Twin Peaks
    you've been seen, by fitful glare
    of smoky torches, where the nymphs
    of Korykis, your devotees, stream past,
    and the Kastalian spring.   1130
    The hills of Nysa, crowned with ivy, and
    the coastline green with many
    clustered vines send you to us;

choroses sing your praise
in chants of superhuman power
as you frequent the streets of Thebes.

(B1):   You hold this city first in honour,
        more than any other – you, and
        your mother whom the lightning struck;
        so now, when violent disease   1140
        holds our whole city and its people fast,
        come with your healing powers across the heights
        of Parnassos, or cross the groaning sea-strait!

(B2):   Oh leader of the dance
        of fiery stars, oh master
        of the voices in the night,
        son of Zeus, appear before us, king,
        and bring your bakchants who will dance   1150
        in frenzy all night long to honour you,
        giver of every good and ill, Iakchos!

                        SCENE 7

(*Enter* BODYGUARD, *right*)

BODYGUARD: Distinguished citizens of Thebes,
        no human life ever achieves a point
        of rest where one can simply praise or blame.
        From day to day Chance lifts up and casts down
        men who are doing well, or badly,
        and no one can foretell what is secure.   1160
        As I saw him, Kreon was enviable:
        he saved Thebes from our enemies,
        took the supreme power, and guided us;
        he had good health, and was the father of two noble sons.
        Now that has all been lost – for I believe
        that when a man will never enjoy anything again,
        he does not count as living, but is just an animated corpse.
        Heap up great riches, if you like, inside your house,
        live in the trappings of a tyrant; but if there's
        no joy, I would not give a man the shadow of   1170

a wisp of smoke for all the rest.

I COUNCILLOR: What's happened to our royal family? What
have you come to tell?

BODYGUARD: They're dead; the living caused their deaths.

I COUNCILLOR: Who's done the killing? Who is dead? Tell us.

BODYGUARD: Haimon is dead; kindred blood has been shed.

I COUNCILLOR: Did he die by his father's hand or by his
own?

BODYGUARD: He killed himself, in anger at his father for the
murder of his girl.

I COUNCILLOR: Prophet, your words were all too true.

BODYGUARD: That's what has happened; you must now plan
what to do.

(*Enter* EURYDIKE *from the* skene)

I COUNCILLOR: Look; I see unfortunate Eurydike, the
wife   1180
of Kreon. She's come from the house either because
she's heard about her son, or by mischance.

EURYDIKE: Men of this town, I heard some of what you've
said
as I was leaving, on my way to supplicate
the goddess Pallas with my prayers.
When I was just about to open up the doors,
the news of some disaster to my household
reached my ears; terror-struck, I fell back
fainting in the arms of my maidservants.
Now, tell the news again. I am   1190
not inexperienced in suffering; I'll listen.

BODYGUARD: Dear lady, I was there; I'll speak as an eye-
witness,
and I will not leave any of the truth unspoken.
Why should I try to treat you gently, if I'd soon
be proved a liar? Truth is always best.
I joined your husband as his guide, and led him out
to the high part of Thebes' plain, where Polyneikes'
body still lay without pity, torn by dogs.
We prayed first to Plouton and Hekate
not to let loose their anger, but be kind to us;   1200
then we washed the corpse with holy water, and

with fresh-cut branches burned up what was left of him.
We piled up a high burial mound, made of
his native soil, and went straight to the cave
where that poor girl was married on a bed of stone to Death.
But at a distance someone hears loud cries
from near that chamber for a bride
bereft of funeral gifts. He meets us, and tells lord Kreon.
Those incoherent cries of misery
surround him as he creeps up nearer; then he groans   1210
and says in bitter anguish: 'I am born
to misery! Am I a prophet? Am I creeping on
the most terrible path that I have ever walked?
My son's voice greets my ears. Rush on ahead,
my men: and when you reach the tomb,
pass through that gap in the great pile of rocks,
and go right to the inner chamber's mouth; find out
if I hear Haimon's voice, or if the gods deceive me.'
Such was the order Kreon gave in his despair:
we searched, and in the inmost part of the rock-tomb   1220
we saw her hanging by the neck,
slung by a noose of fine linen.
He clasped her round her waist, pressed tight,
pouring out grief because his bride was dead,
his father'd killed her, and his marriage was destroyed.
When Kreon saw him, he gave a dreadful cry,
and went inside, and croaked these words to them:
'You crazy girl, what have you done? What thoughts
possessed you? Were you driven mad by suffering?
My son, come out; I beg you, I implore you.'   1230
The boy looked at him with wild eyes,
spat in his face, made no reply, drew his
sharp dagger – but his father ran back out
in terror, so he missed. Then in his misery,
disgusted with himself, he strained at once
against the blade, and drove half of its length into his chest.
While still conscious, he clasped her in one last,
languishing embrace; and as he gasped for breath, he spurted
    out
a swiftly flowing stream of dripping blood on her pale cheek.
He lies there, corpse embracing corpse. Poor boy, he's   1240
got his wedding – in the halls of Haides.

He has proved to all mankind that lack of sense
is the worst evil which can fall on man.

[*Exit* EURYDIKE *into the* skene]

I COUNCILLOR: What do you think will happen? She's just
   turned
and gone back in, without a word of any kind.
BODYGUARD: I am surprised as well; but I feed on the hope
   that when she heard about the sufferings of her son,
   she did not want to show her grief out in the city, but went
      back
   inside to make the maids share her private laments.
   She's thoughtful and experienced; she would not act
      foolishly.   1250
I COUNCILLOR: I'm not so sure; to me that lengthy silence is
   as dangerous as lots of futile cries.
BODYGUARD: I will go into the house, and make sure she
   does not conceal inside a burning heart some strange,
   suppressed resolve; you give me good advice.
   There is great danger in so long a silence.

[*Exit* BODYGUARD *into the* skene]

FINALE

I COUNCILLOR: Here comes the king himself.
      His hands are carrying – if we
      may say this – a clear memorial not to
      anyone else's madness, but to his own folly.   1260

(*Enter* KREON *right, carrying the body of* HAIMON)

KREON (AI):   Oh,
      The folly of the darkness in my mind,
      stubborn and deadly!
      Look at us – the father who
      has killed, and his dead son.
      Lament for me, cursed with stupidity.
      My son, your life is ended – so young, so recently.

You've died, you've left us, not
through your own foolishness but mine.

I COUNCILLOR: You seem to see the truth – too late.   1270

KREON: Oh!
I know, I know! I'm miserable; I think a god
cast some stupendous weight down on
my head, drove me to paths of cruelty,
and overturned and trampled on my joy.
The suffering of humanity is very hard to bear.

(*Enter* BODYGUARD *from the* skene)

BODYGUARD: My lord, another burden lies in store for you.
You have one in your hands – but when you go
into your house you'll soon see yet more horror.   1280

KREON: What worse horror could follow this?

BODYGUARD: Your wife, true mother of this boy, is dead;
the miserable woman has just stabbed herself.

KREON   (A2):   Oh!
House of death, impossible to cleanse,
why are you ruining me?
You, messenger of horror,
monstrous grief; what are you saying?
I was already dead, and you have killed
me once again! Boy, what is this news?
Another bloody death?   1290
My wife is slain as well?

(*The* BODYGUARD *went into the* skene *during the last four
lines, and now returns with the body of* EURYDIKE)

I COUNCILLOR: It is no longer hidden; you can see.

KREON: Oh!
A second horror added to my suffering.
What destiny still waits for me?
I have just held my son's corpse in my hands,
and now I see another corpse confronting me.
Poor, wretched mother, and poor child.   1300

BODYGUARD: She struck herself with a sharp sword, and let
her eyes close into darkness, after she had wept
over the empty bed of her first son, already dead,

and then over Haimon's. With her last breath she called upon
the gods to bring misfortune on you, killer of her sons.

KREON (B1):   Ah! Ah!
    The terror paralyses me! Will one of you
    not cut me down with a sharp sword?
    I am a miserable wretch,
    and steeped in misery.

BODYGUARD: Yes – this dead woman put the blame on you
both for these deaths and those before.

KREON: How did she kill herself?

BODYGUARD: She struck below the liver, with her own hand,
as soon as she heard about Haimon's bitter death.

KREON: And I can never make the blame
for this pass on to anybody else but me.
I killed you! I'm a pitiable fool, and I killed you!
I did it; I can speak the truth.   1320
Take me as fast as possible, take me away –
I'm less than nothing; I do not exist.

I COUNCILLOR: That would be good – if anything can be
    good here.
With horror lying at our feet, least speech is best.

KREON (B2):   Come, come!
    Appear before me, radiant fate
    that brings me my last day,   1330
    my supreme bliss. Come, come!
    I do not want to ever see another day.

I COUNCILLOR: That is the future; others must determine it.
We must do something with what lies before us.

KREON: All that I want was summed up in that prayer.

I COUNCILLOR: Do not now pray for anything; no mortal
    man escapes
from a disaster which has been ordained.

KREON: Take this useless man away.
Against my will I killed both you, my son, and you,   1340
my wife. I'm wretched; I don't know
where I should go, where to find rest; all that
I touch is wrong, and an unbearable
fate has leaped onto my head.

[*Exit* KREON *into the* skene, *supported by the*
BODYGUARD]

1 COUNCILLOR: By far the most important need
               for happiness is wisdom; we must never deviate
               from reverence for the gods. Great words   1350
               spoken by men with too much pride
               are paid for with great blows,
               and in old age they learn they should be wise.

[*Exeunt* COUNCILLORS, *left. Attendants take the corpses
               of* HAIMON *and* EURYDIKE *into the* skene]

YOUNG WOMEN OF TRACHIS

Translated by Graham Ley

THE ACTORS AND THEIR ROLES

———————

DEIANEIRA, wife of Herakles	Actor 1
NURSE	Actor 3
HYLLOS, son of Herakles by Deianeira	Actor 2
YOUNG WOMEN OF TRACHIS	Choros
FIRST OLD MAN	Actor 2 or 3
CAPTIVE WOMEN, including IOLE	Silent Faces
LICHAS	Actor 3 or 2
SECOND OLD MAN	Actor 3
BEARERS	Silent Faces
HERAKLES	Actor 1

SCENE I

(Enter DEIANEIRA *from the* skene, *followed later by the* NURSE*)*

DEIANEIRA: There is an old saying that runs like this:
You cannot be sure that someone has had
a good or a bad life until he is dead.
Well, for my part, even with Haides not yet in sight, I am
certain that my life has been grim, a life to cry about.
While I was still at home in Pleuron, in the house
of my father Oineus, I faced the direst
prospect ever faced by a bride in Aitolia.
A river was my suitor, the river Acheloos, that is,
who came to ask my father for my hand in three shapes;   10
appearing, as you looked, as a sleek bull, or then
as a glistening snake in coils, or again as a bull-head
on a man's body, while streams of living water
poured down through the bush of his beard.
That's the kind of suitor I had to tolerate.
Poor thing. I wanted to die, prayed and prayed that I
would before I was put into bed with something like that.

A great deal later, and to my delight
Herakles came, the famous son of Alkmene and of Zeus.
He launched himself into battle with this creature, and in the
    contest
                                                            20
became my deliverer. I am not the one to give a blow
by blow account, because I wouldn't know how. Who
    could?
Whoever sat apart unmoved by what he saw then.
As for me – I sat there terrified, paralysed with the fear
that my beauty would in some way bring me to grief.

But Zeus, who presides over contests, gave us a happy result,
if this is happiness. I have my bed with Herakles, as his
    chosen bride;
but in it I breed fear on fear, always something new,
worrying on his account. Night after night takes up
the new load of worry and puts off the old, in succession.   30
Yes, we have had children together. But he has been
rather like a farmer who must take his plough to a distant
    field,
with one visit for sowing, and one again at harvest time.
His life has been just like that; back home and out,
constantly in service to someone or other, man that he is.

And now, when he is nearly at the end of his labours,
I feel these fears all the more sharply than before.
He killed the lord Iphitos; and since that time
we have lived here in Trachis, uprooted, in the house
of a close friend. Where Herakles has gone no one   40
knows. But he has left behind him, for me,
pain born of sorrow at his continuing absence.
I can almost feel sure that something has happened to him.
I'm not talking about a short space of time:
nearly fifteen months, and not a word about him.
Something dreadful has happened. That is the meaning
of the tablet he left behind with me, and I have often
prayed to the gods that it should not spell disaster.

NURSE: Deianeira, my lady. I have often seen you
in the past overwhelmed by floods of tears,   50
sobbing loudly when Herakles has left the house.
On this occasion, if it can be right for a slave to advise
the free, then I must tell you what you should do.
You have a good number of sons. Why don't you send
one of them now to look for your husband?
Hyllos is by far the most suitable, if he would like to be
    known
as having some concern for the success of his father.
There he is, running for all he is worth towards the house.
If in your view I have spoken to the point you now
have the chance to make good use of my advice, and of
    him.   60

(*Enter* HYLLOS *running, left*)

DEIANEIRA: My child, my boy. Good things may be said by those

who cannot boast about their family. This woman is a slave,
but her advice could have come from a free-born woman.

HYLLOS: What was it? Tell me, mother, if I am allowed to know.

DEIANEIRA: Your father has been away for a very long time. We don't know

where he is. You haven't asked. That's not to your credit.

HYLLOS: But I do know, if rumour is anything to go by.

DEIANEIRA: What have you heard? Where do they say he is?

HYLLOS: They say that for the full length of the last year
he was working in service for a woman in Lydia.   70

DEIANEIRA: If it has come to that, then rumour might say anything.

HYLLOS: But he is finished with that now, or that is what I heard.

DEIANEIRA: So what is the story now? Where is he? Alive, or dead?

HYLLOS: They say that he is attacking the land of Euboia,
the city ruled by Eurytos, or at least is about to do so.

DEIANEIRA: My son, did you realise that your father had left with

me a clear, written prophecy about that land?

HYLLOS: No. I know nothing of it. What does it say, mother?

DEIANEIRA: That your father is either reaching the end of his life,

or will take on this contest, complete it, and   80
for the rest of his life live in perpetual ease.
My son, you must go and help him. His life
is held in the balance. If he survives, then   83
we survive. If not, we all die together.   85

HYLLOS: Mother, I am on my way. If I had known what
these prophecies said, I would have been there already.
As things were, father's usual good luck did not allow us
to be too worried or too frightened in advance on his account.
But now that I do know, there is nothing I will not do

to find out how things stand with him, the complete
   truth.   90
DEIANEIRA: Go on, then, my son. A success story, even if
   you come to hear of it rather late, brings its own reward.

[*Exeunt* HYLLOS, *right, and* DEIANEIRA *and the* NURSE
                                       into the skene]

CHOROS I

(*Enter* YOUNG WOMEN, *left*)

YOUNG WOMEN (A1):   Helios, the sun, blazing child and
         destroyer
      of the sparkling night,
      who puts you to sleep in her turn,
      Helios, I call on you!
      Tell me where the son of Alkmene is,
      where he is living now! Tell me!
      You have the most powerful eye of all,
      you burn with a searing brightness.
      Where is he? At the straits of the Black Sea,   100
      or leaning against the twin continents?

   (A2):   I hear that Deianeira desires Herakles, thinks of him
      incessantly, Herakles who fought for her.
      Now like a wretched bird
      she never puts her desire to sleep.
      Her eyes are filled with tears.
      She is worn out by nursing her constant fears
      for him in an anxious, lonely bed.
      He is on the road. She hopes for nothing,   110
      but expects a grim, bad destiny.

   (B1):   You can see the waves passing you by
      and rushing over the wide sea,
      driven by the tireless
      south wind, or the north.
      Think of Herakles, of the race of Kadmos,
      like that. The labours of life,

like a Kretan sea, now whirl him back,
now uplift him. Some god keeps him
always out of disaster   120
away from the house of Haides.

(B2):   Deianeira, I shall oppose your complaints,
but offer comfort in your distress.
So I say you must not
let the good strength of hope
be worn down. The son of Kronos,
king and disposer of all, placed
pain in the path of all who must die.
Yet sorrow and joy come wheeling
round to all, like the stellar   130
circuits of the Plough.

(B3):   For mortals, neither grief,
nor wealth, nor the sparkling
night is stable, but all
disappear in an instant, and joy
or deprivation comes in turn to another.
Lady, my instruction; with this in mind
be firm in your hopes. For who has seen
Zeus to be so mindless of his children?   140

SCENE 2

(*Enter* DEIANEIRA *from the* skene)

DEIANEIRA: You are here because you know of my affliction,
or that's my guess. As for the heartache,
that is outside your experience, and I hope it remains so.
After all, young life is nurtured in its own special precinct
and neither the divine heat of the sun, nor the rain,
nor any of the winds can do it any damage.
Trouble-free, and delightful. Life grows like that,
until you find one day you are called a woman,
not a girl. Fear takes hold of you in the night,
for husband, for children. Part of your mind is theirs.   150
Someone who knew that, who could draw on her own

experience . . . she would understand what weighs me down.
I have had plenty to cry about in the past.
I'll tell you now what's new, what hasn't been the case
    before.
When Herakles my lord set out from our home
on this his last journey, he left in the house
an ancient writing-tablet, inscribed with ciphers.
He had gone off to face many combats in the past,
but he had never had the courage to decode it for me.
He went out in those days with success in mind, not death.   160
But this time, like a man with no future, he told me
which possessions I should take as his wife, told me
how he would share out their father's land amongst our
    children.
He gave precise indications of time: when he had been
away a year and three months, out of the country,
it was determined that at that time he would die,
or if he managed to survive that particular term,
he would live free from pain for the rest of his days.
The labours of Herakles, he declared, would terminate
in accordance with this prediction of his destiny,   170
decreed by the gods, as he had heard it spoken,
he said, by the ancient oak at Dodona, and its twin Doves.
The time has now come round, and is with us,
when the truth of this prophecy is bound to be fulfilled.
Sleep is sweet, my dear friends. But this is enough
to make me jump up in terror. Am I to remain
alone, lose the best man on earth? Is that the way it must be?
1 YOUNG WOMAN: Be careful what you say; don't tempt fate.
    I can see
a man coming. He has a wreath, as if he brings good news.

(*Enter* OLD MAN, *right*)

OLD MAN: Deianeira, my lady. I shall be the first with news
    that   180
will stop you worrying. The son of Alkmene is alive –
be sure of that – and is coming here in victory, with
spoils from the battle as offerings for the gods of our land.
DEIANEIRA: What was that you said, old man? What did I
    hear?

OLD MAN: The husband you have longed for is on his way
  back home, to your home, in full strength, victorious.

DEIANEIRA: How did you hear of this? From a citizen, or a
  foreigner?

OLD MAN: From Lichas the herald standing in the summer
  pasture,
  shouting to a crowd. I ran here, as soon as I had heard
  him speak, to be the first to bring you good news.   190
  My motive? If you're pleased with me, I might stand to gain.

DEIANEIRA: So why is Lichas not here himself, if his news is
  good?

OLD MAN: Lady, he's hardly master of his own movement.
  He's surrounded by everyone who lives in Malis
  in a circle of questions. He can't get away.
  Everyone has that one thing he really wants to know,
  and they won't let him go before they're fully satisfied.
  It's not what he wants, but it is what they want.
  He has no choice. You'll see him soon enough, plain as day.

DEIANEIRA: Zeus, for whom the meadows of Mount Oita are
  kept uncut,   200
  you have granted me joy in the fullness of time!
  Women, raise the cries of triumph! Inside our house,
  and outside our walls. This news was unhoped for;
  but now its star has risen, let us enjoy it.

(CHOROS 2)

YOUNG WOMEN: Cry out at the hearth!
  The house itself must shout in joy
  at the prospect of a marriage. Apollo
  and his arrows are our defenders:
  the men, too, must hail him in chorus.
  A paian! Unmarried, we shall   210
  sing out a paian together with them.
  Shout out the names of Artemis of Ortygia,
  deer-hunter, child of Leto, who carries torches in her
    hands,
  and her neighbours, the nymphs!
  The pipes master my mind.
  I shall not reject them. They lift me from the ground.

See, the ivy has –
Euoi! Euoi! –
sent me tumbling into the whirl of the dance
to Dionysos! Look at me, now!   220
Paian! Apollo!
Look, dear woman, look!
The truth is plain to see,
confronting you, with you now.

DEIANEIRA: Dear women, I do see. I have eyes, and that
group approaching has not escaped their vigilance.
I offer greetings to the herald, who comes before me
at long last, if he brings with him some joy to greet me.

(*Enter* LICHAS *and* SOLDIERS *escorting a group of* CAPTIVE
WOMEN (*including* IOLE), *right*)

LICHAS: Lady, your welcome matches my arrival, in good
   omen,
and fits itself to what has been achieved. A man's   230
worldly success must be rewarded with auspicious speech.
DEIANEIRA: My dear man, first of all tell me what I most
want to hear. Is Herakles alive? Shall I see him alive?
LICHAS: I left him alive, and in full strength;
flourishing in fact, and not weighed down by illness.
DEIANEIRA: Where is he? Abroad, or in his own land? Tell
me.
LICHAS: There is a promontory on Euboia, Kenaion, on
   which he is consecrating
an altar, setting ground aside to yield produce for Zeus.
DEIANEIRA: To fulfil his vows, or in response to some
   prophecy?
LICHAS: Vows, taken as he began the task of uprooting   240
the country of these women you now see before you.
DEIANEIRA: And they, by the gods, who are they? Whose are
they?
The state they are in deserves my pity, unless I am fooled.
LICHAS: Herakles chose them as a gift for the gods, and for
himself to keep, when he sacked the city of Eurytos.
DEIANEIRA: Was it the campaign against that city that kept
him

from me for such an unpredictable length of time?
LICHAS: No. For most of the time he was held against
his will, sold into slavery, as he himself says,
in Lydia. When Zeus is revealed as the enactor of what
        happens,   250
lady, then telling the story cannot be reprehensible.
He was sold to Omphale, the barbarian, and as
he himself says he served her for a full year.
That insult bit so deeply into him that he
swore an oath, binding himself to fulfil it, that
the day would come when he would enslave the man
who had brought this disgrace on him, with his wife and
        child.
No empty words, but when he was purified
he brought together an army and marched against
the city of Eurytos. For he claimed that Eurytos was   260
the single person responsible for his humiliation.
When Herakles came to stay at his home and hearthside
as a guest, an old friend, Eurytos heaped abuse on him
repeatedly, slander and malice combined, saying
that Herakles might have arrows that never missed their
        mark,
but compared to his own sons he was no match with a bow.
And again, the taunt: he was a slave, not free,
a broken man. When Herakles got drunk at dinner
Eurytos threw him out. So later, when Iphitos
came to the hill of Tiryns, on the track of some of his
        horses   270
that had strayed, with his eye on one thing
and his mind on another, in his rage at these insults
Herakles threw him down from the flat top of the tower.

This act provoked the anger of Olympian Zeus,
Lord and father of all, and he sent him away into
exile, sold as a slave. Herakles had killed Iphitos
treacherously, the only time he had done so. It was
intolerable. Had he taken revenge openly, then
Zeus would have pardoned a fairly won victory.
For the gods, like men, hate excessive violence.   280
Those who luxuriated in the arrogance of slander
are all of them now resident in the house of Haides,

and the city is enslaved. These women you see
were once prosperous; their life is now unenviable.
They have come to you. This was your husband's
instruction, and I have carried it out, faithful to him.
He will be here himself, be sure of that, once
he has completed holy sacrifice for the sack of the city
to Zeus, god of fathers. Of all you have heard,
in a long story fairly told, this is the best part.   290

1 YOUNG WOMAN: Lady, you now have clear reasons to
      rejoice. Some
are in front of you. What you have heard promises more.

DEIANEIRA: I would be completely justified in rejoicing at the
      news
of this great achievement of my husband. That is true.
I should be. My feelings must keep pace with events.
Nevertheless, anyone who considers things carefully
may well worry about success. It can end.
In fact, friends, as I look at these unfortunate women,
I am struck by a terrible pity. They are without homes,
and have lost their fathers. They are exiles in a foreign   300
land. They may perhaps have been the daughters of free
      men,
once. Now they are living the life of a slave.
Oh Zeus, who decides the issue of battles, may I
never see you coming at my children in this way,
not at any time. If you do, may I die first.
When I look at these women, these are my fears.

(She goes close to one of the younger captives – IOLE*)*

You are a girl, and bitterly unhappy. Who are you?
Unmarried, or a mother? To look at you, I would
think that was beyond your experience. A noble face.
Lichas, whose child is this girl? Tell me.   310
Who is her mother, and who is her father? Looking
at all these women here, I pitied her most of all;
she alone shows a keen sense of what has happened.

LICHAS: How should I know? Why do you ask me about it?
She's possibly from one of the leading families there.

DEIANEIRA: From the ruling family? Is she a child of Eurytos?

LICHAS: I have no idea. I didn't bother with many questions.

DEIANEIRA: But didn't you pick up her name from one of
those with her?

LICHAS: No. I certainly did not. I did my job in silence.

DEIANEIRA: Tell me yourself, poor girl, woman to woman.
It's   320
a really dreadful thing not to know who you are.

LICHAS: If she comes out with anything, I can assure you it
will be a complete breach of precedent. She has
not said a word the whole time. Not a whisper.
Just the pain of tears giving birth to more tears,
the poor girl, at the weight of this calamity, from
the moment she left her homeland to the winds. She
feels her loss badly. But we must have sympathy.

DEIANEIRA: Let's leave her alone, then. Let her go on into the
house
like that, as she prefers. As things stand, she has enough   330
sorrow to contend with. I should not wish to add
to her burden myself. In fact, let us all make a
move towards the palace. You have to get on
with your journey, and I have to organize things indoors.

OLD MAN: Just stay here a moment first, on your own,
without
these people. That way you'll discover who the new arrivals
are,
and find out things you should know, and haven't been told.
For I'm in possession of the full facts, in every respect.

DEIANEIRA: What is this? Why are you keeping me back?

OLD MAN: Stand still, and listen. After all, what I had   340
to say to you earlier was worth while. This will be too.

DEIANEIRA: Shall I call all of them back here again? Or
do you want to speak just to me and these women here?

OLD MAN: To you and these women. Nothing barred. Let
that lot go.

[*Exeunt* LICHAS, IOLE, SOLDIERS *and* CAPTIVE WOMEN
into the skene]

DEIANEIRA: Well, they have gone now. Proceed with your
story.

OLD MAN: Nothing of what this man just said was spoken
in accordance with the straight truth. Either he's lying now,

or he was dishonest in the report he gave before.
DEIANEIRA: What do you mean? Tell me precisely what you have
in mind. I don't understand what you said to me.   350
OLD MAN: I was there, along with many other potential witnesses,
and myself heard this man say that it was for the
sake of the girl you've seen that Herakles captured Eurytos
and the towering city of Oichalia. That the only god involved
in this campaign was Love, who used his magic on him.
Events in Lydia, hard labour as a slave for Omphale,
Iphitos hurled to his death: these had nothing to do with it.
Now he tells it another way, shoving Love out of the story.
Herakles tried to persuade the father to give him the girl,
to have illicit sex with her. When that failed   360
he prepared a petty grudge, and with that excuse
marched against her fatherland and sacked
the city. And now, as you can see, he is on his way
back home, sending her on in advance, not carelessly,
lady, nor as a slave. Don't look forward to that.
It's hardly likely, if he's all aflame with passion.
Mistress, it seemed the right course to reveal everything
to you, everything I happen to have heard from him.   370
A crowd of Trachinians heard all of this just the same
as I did, at the same time, with him in the middle,
enough to convict him. What I've said cannot
be pleasant to hear. I'm sorry. But it's the truth.
DEIANEIRA: Pleasant? I'm devastated. Where am I in all of this?
What kind of hidden trouble have I taken
under my roof? I can't bear it. Nameless, is she?
The man who brought her here swore to that.
A girl whose rank shines from her face, her whole body.
OLD MAN: As for her family; her father was Eurytos, and she   380
used to be called Iole. As for him; he was content
to say nothing of her parents. He didn't bother with questions.
1 YOUNG WOMAN: Bad men should die. If not all of them, then

at least those who disgrace themselves with treachery.

DEIANEIRA: Women, what should I do? The truth is that I
have been hit very hard by what I have heard.

1 YOUNG WOMAN: Go and find out from the man himself. If
you are

willing to press your questions, you may get clear answers.

DEIANEIRA: That is reasonable advice. I am on my way.

OLD MAN: Shall I wait here? Or what would you like me to
do?   390

(*Enter* LICHAS *from* skene)

DEIANEIRA: Stay there. Here is the man himself, making his
way

from the house of his own accord. No need for a summons.

LICHAS: What should I say to Herakles, lady, on arrival?
Tell me. As you can see, I'm starting on my journey.

DEIANEIRA: You took a long time in getting here, and now
you're

rushing off, before we've had time to renew our
conversation.

LICHAS: Well, if there's anything you want to ask, I'm still
here.

DEIANEIRA: Will you give me my due – the certainty of truth?

LICHAS: May Zeus be my witness, as far as I know it myself.

DEIANEIRA: Who, then, is the woman you brought here with
you?   400

LICHAS: A Euboian. I cannot tell you who her parents are.

OLD MAN: You there, look at me. Who do you think you're
talking to?

LICHAS: And what do you mean by asking me such a
question?

OLD MAN: Have the courage to answer me when I ask. If
you're wise.

LICHAS: I am speaking to Deianeira, a powerful woman,
daughter of Oineus, spouse of Herakles, and – unless
my eyes happen to be deceiving me – my mistress.

OLD MAN: That's exactly what I wanted to hear from you.
You say she is your mistress?

LICHAS: That's correct.

OLD MAN: Is that so? Then what punishment would you
   think correct   410
if you were found to be incorrect in your conduct to her?

LICHAS: What do you mean, incorrect? What game are you
   playing?

OLD MAN: Nothing. No game. You're the one who's doing
   that.

LICHAS: I'm going. I was a fool to listen to you so long.

OLD MAN: No, not before you give the answers to a few
   questions.

LICHAS: Ask away, then, anything you like. You're not the
   silent type.

OLD MAN: That prisoner-of-war, whom you escorted into the
   house:
you know who I mean?

LICHAS: I do. Why do you ask?

OLD MAN: You claim not to know who she is. But didn't you
   say that this woman was Iole, the daughter of Eurytos?   420

LICHAS: To whom? In what company? Who is your witness?
Who will come forward and say he heard that from me?

OLD MAN: A good many citizens. A great crowd of
   Trachinians
heard you say it, as you stood in the middle of them.

LICHAS: Yes.
They said they heard me. But it's one thing to say
what you think you heard, another to be satisfactorily exact.

OLD MAN: What they think they heard! Did you not declare
   on oath
that you were bringing her back as a spouse for Herakles?

LICHAS: As a spouse? I say that? By the gods,
   dear lady, tell me who on earth this stranger thinks he is. 430

OLD MAN: One who heard from you himself of a whole city
   destroyed by his passion for her. That no Lydian woman
was the cause of it, but his sudden love for the girl.

LICHAS: Mistress, this man should be encouraged to leave.
   There is
no sense in chattering with a man who is sick.

DEIANEIRA: By Zeus who hurls his lightning down on the
   heads
of the valleys of Mount Oita, do not lie to me!
You are not speaking to a woman of no character,

nor to one who is ignorant of what human beings are like,
that they do not take pleasure in the same things for ever. 440
Whoever takes his stand in the ring against Love, gets
to grips with him like a boxer, undoubtedly has no sense.
Love rules over any of the gods he chooses, and
over me. So why not over other women like me?
If my husband has been caught by this sickness
I should certainly be mad to find fault with him,
or with this woman, who cannot be held jointly responsible
for anything shameful, nor for any harm done to me.
That is not the case. But if you have learned to lie
from Herakles, then you have learned a disgraceful
    lesson.
                                                          450
If this is the result of self-education, you will
be seen to be worthless when you would like to be good.

Come, tell me the whole truth. For a free man
to be known as a liar is a disaster and a disgrace.
You cannot possibly hope to get away with it:
you were heard by a crowd, and they will tell me.
Are you afraid? Why be frightened unnecessarily,
when it is not knowing which would cause me pain?
What can be terrible in knowing? Do you think Herakles
has not bedded many other women? Don't I know?   460
And not one of them yet has had a bad word
from me, or been abused. Nor will this girl, even
if he is melted by the heat of his passion for her.
I pitied her as soon as I saw her, because
her beauty had destroyed her life. The poor girl.
A terrible fate to be the unwilling cause of the destruction
and enslavement of your fatherland. But let all
of that blow away with the wind. Prove worthless to anyone
else, but never tell me any lies. Those are my orders.

I YOUNG WOMAN: Be persuaded by good advice. This
    woman will see
                                                          470
that you don't regret it later, and you'll have my thanks.

LICHAS: Well, my dear mistress, since it is plain to me that
    you expect
people to be no more than human, and are reasonable,
I shall tell you the whole truth and conceal nothing.
Things are just as this man has described them.

At some point a terrible longing for this girl
shot through Herakles, and on her account he sacked
Oichalia, the city of her fathers, and destroyed it.
For his part – and this must be declared – he never
denied any of this, nor told me to conceal it.   480
But, mistress, I myself was afraid that I would
hurt your feelings if I told you what you have heard.
The fault was mine, if you count it as a fault.
But now, since you do know the full story,
for his sake and for your own, equally for both,
tolerate the woman, and keep firmly
to the words that you have used about her.
In every other struggle Herakles has been pre-eminent,
but he has been utterly defeated by his love for her.

DEIANEIRA: I already had it in mind to do what you say,   490
and will not take on a pointless fight with the gods,
succumbing to sickness myself. Let's go into the house,
and I can give you my instructions on what to say.
You must take gifts with you, an appropriate response
to the gifts you have brought. It would be wrong for you
to leave empty-handed, when you came in lavish company.

                   [*Exeunt* DEIANEIRA, LICHAS, *and* OLD MAN *into the*
                                                                 skene]

CHOROS 3

YOUNG WOMEN (A1):   Kyprian Aphrodite has great strength,
          and always
          carries away victory.
          I shall omit stories of the gods,
          and shall not tell of how she deceived Zeus son of
                  Kronos,   500
          or Haides, lord of darkness,
          or Poseidon the earthshaker.
          But instead, who were
          the strong contenders for the hand of this bride,
          who were those who came out to fight in dust and
                  blows
          to win the prize in this competition?

(A2): One of them was the strength of a river, four-footed
           phantom
       of a high-horned bull,
       Acheloos from Oiniadai, the other came from   510
       Dionysiac Thebes,
       shaking a curved bow, spears, and a club,
       son of Zeus. They came
       face to face in the middle, wanting a woman.
       In the middle, Kyprian Aphrodite alone with them,
           carrying
       the referee's staff, the bed's glad goddess.

(A3): And then, the clash of fists
           and arrows,
       mixed in with the horns of the bull,
       the ladder-climb of wrestlers, vicious   520
       blows from the forehead
       and straining groans from both.
       The girl sat on a distant bank,
       delicate and beautiful,
       waiting for her husband.
       I tell the story like a mere spectator.
       The bride looks pitiful as she is
       fought for and waits for the end.
       Then suddenly she is gone, taken from her mother,
       like a heifer out on her own.   530

SCENE 3

(*Enter* DEIANEIRA, *carrying a sealed casket, from the* skene)

DEIANEIRA: Friends, I have chosen the moment when our
       visitor
   is talking to his young prisoners inside the house, on the
   point of leaving, to come outside to speak to you in secret.
   To tell you what I have in mind to do, and to share
   my feelings with you, my misery and my grief.
   I have taken in a girl – no, not a girl any more, I'm sure,
   but a woman – like a ship's master takes on a cargo,
   a kind of trade that will drive me out of my mind.

And now the two of us wait under one bedcover
to share the same embrace. This is the reward that   540
Herakles, whom I have heard called a good and faithful
    man,
has sent me in return for all my housekeeping.
I do not have it in me to be angry with him:
he is ill, as he often is with this particular sickness.
But there again, what woman could live together with this
    girl
in the same house, sharing with her the same married life?
I can see for myself that her young life is advancing,
while mine is declining: men's eyes love to snatch at
the bloom of youth, but they walk away from age.
This is what I fear; that Herakles will be called   550
my husband, but will be the younger woman's man.
Yet, as I said, it is hardly right for a wife
with sense to get angry. But I shall tell you this,
friends; the distressing means I have found for release.

I have had, for a long time, a gift given me years ago
by a curious creature, which I kept hidden in a bronze jar.
It was from Nessos I received it, while a girl,
and it came from the death-blood flowing from his shaggy
    hide.
Nessos used to carry people across the deep-flowing
river Euenos, for a fee. No need for a ship with sails,   560
nor for the pulling-power of oars as transport; he used his
    arms.
He carried me too, on his shoulders, when I was
sent away by my father on my first journey with
Herakles, as his wife. When we were in mid-stream,
Nessos became aroused, and began to paw me. I screamed,
and the son of Zeus turned round immediately and
shot off a winged arrow. It hummed and sank into
Nessos's chest and lungs. As he died, the creature
said this to me: 'Daughter of old man Oineus,
if you'll listen to me you can have this advantage   570
from this crossing, since it's the last I shall make.
If you scrape off the blood as it clots around
this wound of mine, at the point where the poisonous
black bile taken from the serpent of Lerna has dyed it,

you will have a charm that will work on the mind
of Herakles, to make sure he'll never see another
woman whom he will love any more than you.'
My friends, I thought of this. It was in the house,
where I had kept it after his death, safely under lock and key.
I smeared this robe with it, applying it just as   580
he told me with his dying words. It's all prepared.
I wouldn't know how to do anything criminal,
and I hope I never learn; I hate those who do.
But if by any chance with this ointment I can
get the better of this girl, with spells cast on Herakles,
then the job is as good as done. Unless you think
I am doing something foolish; if you do, I'll stop.

I YOUNG WOMAN: As far as we're concerned your plan seems
      fine,
   if this kind of thing can be trusted to work.

DEIANEIRA: It can be trusted this far: it seems that it   590
   might work, but I have not as yet tried it.

I YOUNG WOMAN: You must try, and then you'll know.
      Unless you try,
   you cannot possibly be sure, whatever you believe.

(*Enter* LICHAS *from the* skene)

DEIANEIRA: Well, we'll know right away. I can see him
      standing
   there by the door. He'll be on his way very soon.
   One thing; please keep my secret. You'll never face shame
   if your actions, even shameful ones, are kept in the dark.

LICHAS: What's to be done? Instruct me, daughter of Oineus.
   I've already been far too slow about making a move.

DEIANEIRA: But, Lichas, that's exactly what I have had in
      hand,   600
   while you were inside talking to the foreign women.
   I should like you to take this long robe with you,
   as a gift from my own hand to that husband of mine.
   When you give it to him warn him that no other
   man should wrap himself in it before he does;
   that neither the light of the sun, nor any sacred
   precinct, nor the fire at any hearth should see it
   before he shows himself openly to the gods, standing

in full display, on a day set aside for the sacrifice of bulls.
For this was my vow; that if ever I saw him   610
safely back at home, or heard he was safe, then I
should rightly dress him in this robe, and display him
to the gods at sacrifice, a new man in new clothing.
You will carry a sign along with it, which he will
readily recognize, since it is the seal made by this ring.
Go now, and above all keep this law firmly in front
of you; no messenger should want to exceed his duty.
But, in addition, bear in mind that his gratitude
combined with mine will turn out double, not single.

LICHAS: I hold this office under Hermes, and I count
     myself   620
reliable. I shall not fail you in any particular.
I shall carry and deliver this casket just as it is,
and add to it the reassurance of your exact instructions.

DEIANEIRA: You can be on your way. You are fully informed
     about the state of affairs inside the house at present.

LICHAS: I am informed, and I shall declare that everything is
     secure.

DEIANEIRA: What's more, you have seen with your own eyes
     the welcome
that the foreign girl has had, how kindly I received her.

LICHAS: I did; and my heart was struck with joy at it.

DEIANEIRA: What else, then, might you have to tell him? I 630
     should be frightened if you mentioned my desire for him
     before I knew if he, for his part, felt desire for me.

[*Exeunt* LICHAS, *right, and* DEIANEIRA *into the* skene]

CHOROS 4

YOUNG WOMEN (AI):   You who live by the rocks, the
          harbour, and the hot springs,
     and by the cliffs of Mount Oita, by the
     enclosed Malian Gulf,
     and the headland sacred to the virgin-goddess of the
          golden arrows,
       where the Greeks hold famous gatherings at the Gates;

(A2):   the beautiful shout of the pipes will soon rise again
              for you,   640
        in an auspicious, resounding echo, like
        the divine music of the lyre.
        The son of Zeus and Alkmene is rushing home,
        carrying the spoils of complete prowess.

(B1):   We kept waiting for him,
        a man without a city, a man at sea,
        knowing nothing, for a full twelve
        months, while his own, dear wife   650
        wore out her heart with misery
        and with constant weeping.
        Now Ares stung to madness
        has given release from days of labour.

(B2):   Let him get here, let him come! No
        rest for the swinging oars of the ship he is in
        before he reaches this city,
        leaving the island altar
        where he is said to be sacrificing.
        May he come full of desire,   660
        infused with the covering
        ointment of persuasion, enticed by the beast.

SCENE 4

(*Enter* DEIANEIRA *from the* skene)

DEIANEIRA: Women, I am afraid that in everything I have
just been doing I may have gone too far.
1 YOUNG WOMAN: What is it, Deianeira, daughter of Oineus?
DEIANEIRA: I don't know. I'm desperate. I had fair hopes; but
what I have done may soon turn out to be a crime.
1 YOUNG WOMAN: You're not thinking about the gifts you
sent to Herakles?
DEIANEIRA: I am. So much so that my advice to anyone
would be 'don't be too keen if you're not really sure'.   670
1 YOUNG WOMAN: Explain to us, if you can, what has made
you frightened.

DEIANEIRA: Something has happened, women. The kind of thing
　　that if I tell you, you'll think it out of this world.
　　I was using a tuft from the fleece of a white sheep
　　to anoint the robe which Herakles will put on.
　　That tuft has disappeared, eaten down to nothing
　　of its own accord, not by anything in the house.
　　It crumbled away from the top of a stone. But I must
　　tell the story in full, if you're to follow what happened.
　　When the kentaur, the beast, was labouring with the sharp   680
　　barb stuck in his chest, he gave me precise instructions.
　　I neglected none of them, but had kept them all,
　　like writing on a bronze tablet that cannot be erased.
　　This is what he laid down, and this is what I did:
　　I was to keep the drug permanently in a dark corner,
　　away from contact with fire or with warm rays from the sun,
　　until the moment I should apply it by smearing it on.
　　And that's what I did, when action was called for.
　　I smeared the garment in secret, in a room in the house,
　　using a tuft of wool I'd pulled from one of our sheep,   690
　　then folded up the gift and placed it away out of
　　the sun's light in a deep box, the one that you saw.
　　But as I went back into the house I saw
　　something unspeakable, impossible to understand.
　　By chance I happened to have thrown the ball of wool   695
　　into the sunlight; as it began to get warm   697
　　it became unrecognizable, crumbling to dust on the ground.
　　To look at it now, it seems most like the sawdust
　　you would see falling as wood was cut.   700
　　That's what it's like. It's still there, on the ground,
　　and where it lies, a clotted foam is bubbling,
　　the kind that gathers when the rich juice of the violet
　　vintage is poured on the ground from the jars of Dionysos.
　　I feel wretched, and have no idea what I should do;
　　but I do see that I have done something dreadful.
　　What motive could the beast have had, as he was
　　dying, to show goodwill to me, the cause of his death?
　　No. He wanted to destroy the man who had shot
　　him, and so he used his magic on me. I have learned   710
　　that lesson far too late, when it is no longer of use.

I and no one else shall be the miserable means
of Herakles' destruction, unless I am mistaken.
For I know that the arrows that shot Nessos even did
harm to Cheiron, who is a god; they kill every wild
animal that they hit. That black poison, seeping
from the blood of his wounds, is bound to be lethal
to Herakles as well. How could it not? Or so I think.
In any case, I have made the decision, that if he
dies, I shall go with him in the same sweep.   720
For someone who prides herself on her good name,
it is unbearable to go on living with a bad reputation.

1 YOUNG WOMAN: Something dreadful may have happened.
    You're right
  to be afraid. But don't give up hoping before the end is
    known.
DEIANEIRA: There is no hope at all in disgraceful schemes
  of action, none which can give us any encouragement.
1 YOUNG WOMAN: Yet anger is less bitter when those who
    made the mistake
  did so unintentionally. You deserve to find that true.
DEIANEIRA: That's the kind of thing that can be said by
  someone not involved, who has no grief at home.   730

(*Enter* HYLLOS, *right*)

1 YOUNG WOMAN: No more talking now. You had better be
    silent, unless
  you want to say something about this to your son.
  He went off to look for his father, and here he is.
HYLLOS: Mother, I could wish I had found you one of three
  things: either no longer living, or alive but known as
  someone else's mother, or somehow changed, a
  better kind of person than the one you are now.
DEIANEIRA: What is it my son? What has made you hate me?
HYLLOS: The knowledge that today you have murdered
  your own husband, the man who was my father.   740
DEIANEIRA: Oh, my child, what have you just said?
HYLLOS: What is the case, and will be proved true. For who
  can make what has been done undone?
DEIANEIRA: What are you saying, my son? Who has
    denounced me

to you, told you I did something so ghastly?
HYLLOS: I had no need of informants. I saw my father's
disastrous condition with my very own eyes.
DEIANEIRA: Where did you find him? You were together?
HYLLOS: If you have to know, I should tell you everything.
When he had sacked the famous city of Eurytos he   750
took the trophies and first offerings of victory with him.
There is a headland, washed by the surf, on Euboia:
the heights of Kenaion. There he set up an altar
to Zeus the god of fathers, in a wooded precinct,
and it was there I first saw him, longing to do so.
As he was about to set the great sacrifice in
motion, our herald Lichas arrived from home,
bringing your gift with him, that deadly robe.
He put it on, just as you had instructed him.
He killed twelve perfect bulls, which he had   760
as his first choice of the spoils, but in all he brought
forward a hundred animals of different kinds.
Wretched man. At first when he made the prayers, he
was exhilarated, delighted with his beautiful outfit.
Then, when the flames began to crackle with
the oak sap and the blood of the ritual offerings,
the sweat stood out on his skin, and the cloth
began to stick to his ribs like glue, like the work
of a craftsman, to the whole of his body. Stabs
of pain convulsed his frame, and the deadly poison   770
began to eat into him, like the venom of a snake.
It was then he shouted for Lichas, unlucky
man, who was in no way responsible for your crime:
what was the scheme in bringing this robe?
Lichas had no idea. He said it was your gift,
and it came just as you sent it out. That was
his end. When Herakles heard him a searing
spasm took hold of his breathing, and he grabbed
Lichas by the foot, at the joint of the ankle,
and hurled him at a rock washed by the surf.   780
His white brains oozed out into his hair, and
mixed with blood as the centre of his skull smashed.
The whole crowd let out a shout, like a ritual
cry; one man sick, another dead and gone.
And no one dared to get close to Herakles.

The convulsions hurled him to the ground and up into
the air again, screaming, yelling. The rocks around boomed,
the mountain peaks of Lokroi, and the heights of Euboia.
Finally he tired of throwing himself on the ground
time and again, poor man, of screaming and wailing,   790
of reviling his luck in marriage with you, and your
viciousness, and his alliance with Oineus, through
which he had gained only the ruin of his life.
And then, turning his rolling eyes up and away from
the thick smoke of the sacrifice, he spotted me, weeping,
in a mass of people. He looked straight at me, and called:
'Son, come here. Don't run away from me in trouble,
not even if you have to face dying with me.
Lift me up, and get me out of here. Above all, put
me somewhere where no one alive will see me.   800
If you pity me, at least carry me out of this
country as fast as you can. Don't let me die here.'
Those were his commands. We laid him in the centre
of a boat, and brought him ashore here, but only
just, roaring and racked by spasms. You will see
him very soon. He may be alive, or he may now be dead.
You planned this, mother, and executed it against
my father. Now you are caught. May avenging Justice
and the Fury punish you for it. I exult in that,
if it is right. But it is right, and you have given me   810
that right, because you have killed the best man on
earth, the kind of man as you will never see again.

I YOUNG WOMAN: Why this silence? Why are you going?
   Don't you
realize that your silence argues for your accuser?

[*Exit* DEIANEIRA *into the* skene]

HYLLOS: Let her go. May a fair, following breeze
spring up to carry her far from my eyes.
Why should I cherish the name of mother
pointlessly, since she acts nothing like a mother?
No, let her go, and good riddance. May she
find such joy as she has given to my father.   820

[*Exit* HYLLOS *into the* skene]

CHOROS 5

YOUNG WOMEN (A1):   See how suddenly the word of the
   oracle
  has come to grips with us,
  the prophecy given long ago,
  which shouted out that the twelfth year in its full
   number
  of months should end, and bring completion of his
   labours
  to the true son of Zeus.
  A following breeze
  has made all of this certain.
  For how could a man who no longer
  sees the light, a dead man,
  still be a slave to labour?   830

 (A2):   For if the inexorable treachery of the kentaur
  is stinging his sides in a cloud of blood, and
  the poison is sticking fast to him,
  which Death gave birth to, and the shining serpent
   reared,
  then how can he live to see the light of another day,
  stuck to an apparition
  more deadly than
  the serpent of Lerna? The treacherous,
  mingling, murderous goads
  of black-haired Nessos
  boil up and torture him.   840

 (B1):   Saddened by what she saw approaching,
  the great threat rushing
  at her home in the new
  marriage, unshrinking she applied
  the poison herself, but it was the result
  of alien advice at a fatal meeting.
  What is left for her but despair
  and grief, the fresh dew
  of tears and more tears falling?

As it advances fate reveals treachery
and the enormity of disaster.   850

(B2):   A well-spring of tears has burst open,
a sickness pours over him, suffering greater
and more pitiful than
any that his enemies
inflicted on him in his glory.
Oh, black point of that spear prominent in battle!
You brought this bride
swiftly from steep
Oichalia. You won her!
But a silent attendant, Kyprian Aphrodite,   860
is revealed as the enactor of all of this.

SCENE 5

(*The* NURSE *cries out inside the* skene)

1 YOUNG WOMAN: Are my ears deceiving me, or do I hear
the sounds
of grief, starting up in the house? Just now.
1 YOUNG WOMAN: What should I say?
Yes, inside, all too clear. A cry of dreadful
grief from someone. Some new grief. In the house.

(*Enter the* NURSE *from the* skene)

1 YOUNG WOMAN: Look here.
An old woman is coming towards us, with something
to tell. Her forehead is creased, her face joyless.   870
NURSE: Children, it was the beginning of a heap of troubles
for us all, that gift that was sent to accompany Herakles.
1 YOUNG WOMAN: What do you mean, old woman?
Something new?
NURSE: Deianeira has trodden the last path of all
to be trodden, and hasn't moved a foot.
1 YOUNG WOMAN: Surely she is not dead?
NURSE: You have it all.
1 YOUNG WOMAN: Dead? The poor woman.

NURSE: I'll say it again; yes.
1 YOUNG WOMAN: The poor woman. Destroyed. How did
    she die?
NURSE: Cruelly, a cruel way to die.
1 YOUNG WOMAN: Tell me, woman,
    how she came to her end.   880
NURSE: It was a sharp sword that did away with her.

YOUNG WOMEN: What was the motive? Rage or sickness?
        The point of some vicious weapon
        took her away. Plot and execution,
        with death added to death,
        and on her own. The blow
        of the iron, and the groan.
        Are you sure? Did you see this violence?
NURSE: I saw it. How not? I was standing very close.
YOUNG WOMEN: Who did it? Tell us.   890
NURSE: She raised her own hand against herself. She did it.
YOUNG WOMEN: What was that?
NURSE: The truth.
YOUNG WOMEN: It was the bride who came with
        no ceremony. She gave birth
        to a great Fury for this house.
NURSE: That is too true. If you'd been close by and
    seen what Deianeira did, you'd have pitied her more.
1 YOUNG WOMAN: And could a woman's hand dare to do
        this?
NURSE: Yes. It was terrible. Listen, and be my witnesses.
    After she came through, on her own, into the house,   900
    she saw their son laying out a soft stretcher in
    the courtyard, preparing to return to his father.
    Then she hid herself where no man would see her.
    On her knees at the altars she lamented that they
    would soon be unattended; each long-familiar household
    object she touched, poor thing, made her cry.
    She wandered distracted throughout the house,
    and if she saw any of the servants she loved
    just the sight of them made her cry wretchedly,
    as she called on the powers that ruled her life.   910
    But all this came to an end. Suddenly I see   912
    her heading towards Herakles' bedroom. So

I keep myself in the shadows, out of sight.
Waited and watched. I saw Herakles' wife throwing the
bedclothes over Herakles' bed, and spreading them.
When she had finished that she jumped up
on the bed, and sat there in the middle of it.
She broke into floods of hot tears, and
said: 'This is my bed, and this my bridal room.   920
Farewell to you both, now and for ever. Never
again shall I be his partner in this bed.'
That was what she said. With tense fingers
she undid her dress, where the gold pin
rested in front of her breasts, and uncovered all
of her left side, and her left arm.
And then I ran for it, as fast as I could,
to tell her son what she was about to do.
But in the time it takes to get from here
to there and back she had stuck a two-edged   930
sword between liver and heart. That's what we saw.
He cried out, her son, when he saw her,
because he knew that his anger had brought her to it,
and he had learned from people in the house that
she was that creature's dupe. Learned too late.
After that the wretched boy wouldn't leave off
weeping and wailing, all over her, kissing
her on the mouth, and he got down next
to her, on the bed, lying side by side, crying
out that he had stupidly accused her of a crime,   940
that he was now an orphan, deprived of both
parents at one and the same time, alone for life.
That's how it all stands, in there. Enough to say
that if anyone counts ahead more than a day
or two he's stupid. For tomorrow doesn't exist until
you've seen the present day safely out to its end.

[*Exit the* NURSE *into the* skene]

CHOROS 6

YOUNG WOMEN (A1):   Which comes first? Grief for which?
    Which brings worse grief?
    Hard for me to judge, in sorrow.

(A2):   There is what we can see, here, at home;   950
    There is what we expect to see, waiting.
    Much the same; here and now, or soon to come.

(B1):   If only a breeze, a favouring gust of wind
    would blow around the hearth and whip me away from
        here,
    before I die of fright
    in one sudden look – just that –
    at the brave son of Zeus.
    He is on his way here, now, to the house,
    and the rumour is that there is no relief from his
        agony,   960
    and that what there is to see is unspeakable.

(B2):   Near and not far, the sorrow of which I sang like a
        sharp-voiced nightingale.
    A group of strangers, moving towards us, here.
    They must be carrying him, but . . .
    They are moving heavily,
    and yet noiselessly, like mourners.
    Ah, there he is! Carried, and silent.
    Can I judge? Which of these:
    is he dead, or asleep?   970

FINALE

(*Enter an* OLD MAN *with a group of men carrying* HERAKLES
on a stretcher, right, and HYLLOS *from the* skene)

HYLLOS: Oh, father, oh, I suffer for you, father, with you.
    What can I do? Can I think of anything to do?
OLD MAN: Be quiet, my child! You'll disturb

the wild pain that makes him savage.
He's alive, but flat out. Bite your lips,
and stay quiet.

HYLLOS: Alive, old man? Did you say
   that?

OLD MAN: You mustn't wake him, but let him sleep!
   Don't disturb that terrible   980
   sickness that has him
   in fits, my child.

HYLLOS: There is no limit
   to my misery, I am desperate to . . .

HERAKLES: Oh Zeus,
   where am I now? I am lying here
   worn down by pain without relief, and who
   are these people? The pain I am going through!
   This foul thing chews at my flesh. Ah!

OLD MAN: Couldn't you understand how much better
   it would be to keep quiet? You've
   shaken sleep from his   990
   brain and his eyes.

HYLLOS: But I don't know how
   I could bear to keep quiet looking at this horror.

HERAKLES: Altars based on Kenaion,
   which I wish I had never
   seen, I gave offerings.
   What favour have you
   earned for me in return? Oh, Zeus!
   You have given me ruin, and what ruin!
   This flower of madness
   that I can see, that no charm can heal.
   No spell-singer, no healer's   1000
   hands will charm away this
   abomination, except for Zeus.
   A marvel, but I would see it coming.

   (AI):   Ah!
   Leave me,
   leave me to
   my fate and my rest,
   to my suffering.
   Why do you touch me? Why turn me

over? You are killing me, killing me!
You've upset what little peace I had.
It's coming – aah! it's grabbed me again! Where are
    you,   1010
men of Greece, who have so little sense of justice? I
    purified
so much of the sea and all of the forests for you,
wearing myself out, and now when I am sick will
no one turn fire or a sword against me, to help me?
Ah!
Is no one willing to step up and strike
the head off this hateful body of mine?

OLD MAN: Boy, you are his son. This is a job that fits
    your strength better than mine. Give me a hand here,
    and help me to help him.

HYLLOS: Yes, I'll lend a hand.   1020
But there is nothing out here or inside that I can do
to give him a life in which pain is forgotten. That lies
    with Zeus.

HERAKLES (A2):   Ah!
My boy, where are you?
Here, here, help
me up, lift me!
Ah, oh god!
It's leaping, leaping on me
to destroy me, this
wild, untameable sickness!   1030
Oh, Pallas, it is tearing me apart again! Oh, my son,
have pity on your father. Draw a sword – you will not
    be
blamed – and stab me here, below the collar bone. Heal
    my
pain, the rage your godless mother gave me, whom I
would see fall just like this, as she killed me. Sweet
    Haides –   1040
ah –
brother of Zeus,
give me rest, rest, and
make death fly swiftly to end my agony.

1 YOUNG WOMAN: What has happened to our lord is
      appalling, my friends.
   I shudder to hear him. A great man, driven by disaster.
HERAKLES: I am a man of many heated labours, working
   with my hands, straining my back, a dreadful story.
   But nothing yet laid on me by the wife of Zeus
   or by Eurystheus, whom I hate, has ever matched
   this woven mesh of the Furies, which the daughter   1050
   of Oineus in her treachery has cast around my
   shoulders, and which is destroying me.
   Plastered on to my ribs it is eating my flesh
   to the bone, a living presence sucking out the air
   from my lungs. It has drained all the blood
   from me already, and my whole body is completely
   destroyed, chained to these unspeakable fetters.
   Something that no spear in battle, nor the ranks
   of earth-born giants, nor the violence of wild beasts,
   that neither Greece, nor barbarian territory, nor any   1060
   land I came to and cleared ever did to me
   a woman has done; a female, lacking a man's strength,
   without the stroke of a sword, alone, has put me down.

   My son, show yourself to be truly my son, and
   do not rate the name of mother above that of father.
   Go into the house and bring out your mother,
   and give her from your hands into mine. Then I will
   know for sure which tortured body distresses you more;
   mine or hers, disfigured by justice.
   Go on, my child. Find the courage, and the pity   1070
   for me, a spectacle of pity, a man moaning and
   crying like a girl, a sight that no one could
   say he had ever seen before. This man in this state,
   one who never groaned whatever had him in its grip.
   That was the man I was; now I'm found to be a woman.

   Come and stand here, close to your father.
   Look. See how it is with me, what is causing me
   this suffering. I'll lift the cloth, and show you.
   There, can you all see this miserable body,
   see the wretch, the pitiful creature I now am?   1080
   Ah,

It's burning, another spasm of agony, now, again,
stabbing through my side, a devouring sickness
like a grim wrestler who'll never let me rest.
    Lord Haides, take me!
    Zeus, strike me dead with a shaft of lighting!
Lord, and father, hurl it down at me like a weapon,
that bolt of lightning! The feast is beginning
again, the blossoming of pain, the assault.
Oh, my hands, my hands, my back, my chest, my   1090
dear arms! You are that body that once upon a time
subdued the lion that had its home in the valley of Nemea,
ravager of herdsmen, a savage, unapproachable
creature, and the serpent of Lerna, the uncouth
monstrous army of the kentaurs, men twinned with
the bodies of horses, violent, lawless, immensely strong,
and the beast of Erymanthos, and below the earth
the three-headed hound of Haides, unconquerable prodigy,
pup of the dreaded Echidna, and the snake that
guarded the golden apples at the end of the earth.   1100
Ten thousand other labours I tasted, and no one
ever raised the victor's trophy against my might.
But now my body is useless, my flesh hanging
in rags, a miserable ruin, sacked by an unseen doom,
I, who was known as the son of the best of women,
and said to be the child of Zeus of the stars above.
But you can be sure of this; even if I am
nothing, and cannot move, I shall get the better
of the woman who did this, even as I am. If she
would just come here, she will learn to spread a
    message: 1110
that alive or dead I took my revenge on those who deserved
    it.

1 YOUNG WOMAN: Suffering Greece, if you lose this man
I can see you will be in the grip of grief.

HYLLOS: Father, I know you are wasted by sickness. But you
have given me the chance to speak. Listen, and keep silent.
I ask no more of you than it is right for me to have.
Your anger is bitter, and bites deeply into your heart.
But hear me out. For in no other way can you know
how your desire for triumph and your resentment are
    mistaken.

HERAKLES: Say what you want to say, and then no more. I
  am   1120
sick, and I understand none of your subtle hints.

HYLLOS: I am going to speak of my mother, of how things
  are with her, and how she didn't intend to harm you.

HERAKLES: You scoundrel! Your mother has killed your
  father,
and you would mention her name again, in my hearing?

HYLLOS: But her condition is such that silence is
  inappropriate.

HERAKLES: You're right. What she has done to me deserves
  to be heard.

HYLLOS: You'll say the same about what she has done today.

HERAKLES: Out with it. But take care to appear a good man.

HYLLOS: Here it is. She is dead, just now dead.   1130

HERAKLES: Who killed her? A wonderful, if sinister,
  revelation.

HYLLOS: She did it herself. No one else was involved.

HERAKLES: A pity. Dead, before I could rightly get my hands
  on her.

HYLLOS: Even your anger would be tamed, if you knew it all.

HERAKLES: That's an ominous start. Tell me what you're
  thinking.

HYLLOS: Her intentions were good. The whole thing was a
  mistake.

HERAKLES: Good? To kill your father? How good are you?

HYLLOS: When she saw the bride you have indoors, she
  thought she was applying a love-charm. Mistakenly.

HERAKLES: Who makes spells of that strength in Trachis? 1140

HYLLOS: A long time ago the kentaur Nessos persuaded
  her to excite your passion with this particular charm.

HERAKLES: Oh, that is the end! I am dead and gone.
No more daylight for this poor wretch.
Oh, now I know the full depth of this disaster.
My child, your father is lost to you. Go and
call all your brothers and sisters. Bring them here.
And call poor Alkmene here, pointlessly partner
of Zeus. You must hear my last words, and
learn from me all that I know of the oracles.   1150

HYLLOS: But your mother isn't here. She has gone to
  the coast, to live at Tiryns as it happens,

taking some of your children with her, to look after.
If you ask, others are living in the city of Thebe.
But as many of us as are here, father, will do
what has to be done. We'll listen, and serve you faithfully.

HERAKLES: Hear what has to be done, then. You have reached
the point where you must show you're a man, and my son.
It was foretold to me a long time ago by my father
that I should not be killed by anything that breathed   1160
but by one who had died, and was in the house of Haides.
The beast, the kentaur, is that one, as was divinely
foretold, who – dead – has killed me, a living man.
I shall reveal new oracles in accord
with these, confirming what was said in the older ones.
I wrote them down when I visited the grove
of the Selloi, who live in the mountains and sleep
on the ground, listening to the many voices that come
from my father's oak. They told me that in this living
and present time now I should obtain release   1170
from my imposed labours. I hoped for good success.
But the meaning was only that I should die:
there is no further labour for the dead.
Since all of this has now come clear, my son,
you must now become my ally, and do your part.
Do not hold back until you have sharpened my tongue,
but give your consent and work with me, discovering
the best of laws, which is to obey your father.

HYLLOS: Yes, father, whatever you say. I will obey.
But I fear the point to which our words have led.   1180

HERAKLES: First of all, put your right hand in mine.

HYLLOS: Why are you insisting on a pledge of faith?

HERAKLES: Will you obey me? Quickly give me your hand.

HYLLOS: There it is. See? I shall not deny you anything.

HERAKLES: Now swear by the head of Zeus who gave me life.

HYLLOS: Swear to do what? That must be declared.

HERAKLES: Swear to carry out for me the task I shall describe.

HYLLOS: I do swear, with Zeus as witness of my oath.

HERAKLES: And pray that you suffer if you break your word.

HYLLOS: I shan't suffer. I'll do it. But I pray, none the less.   1190

HERAKLES: Do you know Mount Oita, sacred to highest
   Zeus?

HYLLOS: I know it. I've stood there at sacrifice, many times.

HERAKLES: With your own hands, and with those friends you
   choose, you must lift up my body and carry me there.
   You must cut a good quantity of wood from
   the deep-rooted oak, and chop many male wild olives.
   Pile the wood together, and throw on my body.
   Take a lighted torch of pine-wood, and set
   fire to it. No tears of mourning are to be shed;
   but do this, if you are my son, without tears and   1200
   without cries of grief. If you do not, I shall wait for you
   in the underworld, with a heavy curse.

HYLLOS: Father, what are you doing to me? What have you
   said?

HERAKLES: What has to be done. If you will not do it,
   find another father, and never again be called my son.

HYLLOS: Father, this is an awful thing you are telling me
   to do; to be your murderer, guilty of your blood.

HERAKLES: No, I am not. I am telling you to be my healer
   and the only physician for the pain I have.

HYLLOS: How can I heal your body by setting light to it? 1210

HERAKLES: If that frightens you, at least perform the rest.

HYLLOS: I shall not, at any rate, refuse to carry you out there.

HERAKLES: And the construction of the pyre, as I described
   it?

HYLLOS: To the extent that I do not touch it myself.
   I shall do the rest; you won't be hindered by me.

HERAKLES: Well, that will be enough. But add one small
   favour to these other, large ones you are giving me.

HYLLOS: Even if it were a large one, it would be granted.

HERAKLES: Then you know that girl, the daughter of
   Eurytos?

HYLLOS: As far as I can judge, you must mean Iole.   1220

HERAKLES: That's right. So this is my instruction to you.
   When I am dead, if you wish to be pious,
   mindful of the oaths sworn to your father, take
   this girl as your wife. Don't disobey your father.
   Let no man other than you yourself have her,
   never, since she has lain by my side. My boy,
   you must contract this marriage, you yourself.

Obey me. You have obeyed me in the larger things;
disobey me in the smaller, and you wipe out that favour.
HYLLOS: Oh, no. It cannot be good to be angry with a
sick   1230
man, but who could bear to see him thinking like this?
HERAKLES: You're talking like someone who won't do what I
say.
HYLLOS: But who would? The woman who alone shares in
responsibility for my mother's death, for the state that
you are in . . .? Who would make this choice, unless he was
ravaged by sickness? It's better for me to die,
father, than to live alongside my greatest enemies.
HERAKLES: The man, it seems, will show no respect to me
as I am dying. But you can be sure that the curse
of the gods awaits you if you disobey my instructions.   1240
HYLLOS: Ah, it seems you'll soon reveal how sick you are.
HERAKLES: I shall. You're rousing me and my sleeping agony.
HYLLOS: My life is worthless. I don't know what to do,
about anything.
HERAKLES: That is because you have chosen not to listen to
your father.
HYLLOS: But do I have to learn impiety then, father?
HERAKLES: It is not impiety, if what you do gladdens my
heart.
HYLLOS: So are you commanding me to do this? Absolutely?
HERAKLES: I am. I call the gods to witness on it.
HYLLOS: Then I shall not refuse, and will do it, showing
the gods that the decision is yours. I cannot appear   1250
to be a criminal through my obedience to you, father.
HERAKLES: That is the right conclusion. To this add your
favour,
quickly, my son, and place me on the pyre before
a spasm seizes me, or stings me to madness.
Quickly now, lift me up. Rest, the end
of all my troubles, and the end of this man. Finally.
HYLLOS: There is nothing to prevent this from execution,
father,
since that is your command, and it is compelling.

HERAKLES: Come on then, before you stir the
disease into life, stubborn soul; put   1260

a bit in your mouth that is set with
stones, and stifle that cry, to finish
the unwanted work with joy.

HYLLOS: Lift him, men. Grant me full
forgiveness for what has to be done,
and fully acknowledge the harshness
of the gods in what has been done.
They give life, and are renowned as
fathers, and then look on at sufferings like these.
No one can see into the future.   1270
But the present for us is pitiful,
shameful for them,
hardest of all for the man
who is facing his doom.

Young woman, do not stay behind at the house.
You have just seen a terrible death,
great pain and suffering in the strangest shape,
and there is nothing of this which is not Zeus.

[*Exeunt* OLD MAN, HYLLOS, HERAKLES, *bearers, and*
YOUNG WOMEN, *right*]

OIDIPOUS THE KING

Translated by Gregory McCart

THE ACTORS AND THEIR ROLES

PRIEST	Actor 2
CHILDREN	Silent Faces
OIDIPOUS	Actor 1
ATTENDANT	Silent Face
ELDERS OF THEBES	Choros
TEIRESIAS	Actor 2
KREON	Actor 3
IOKASTE	Actor 2
ATTENDANT	Silent Face
KORINTHIAN	Actor 3
ANTIGONE, ISMENE	Silent Faces
HERDSMAN	Actor 2
ATTENDANTS	Silent Faces
SERVANT	Actor 2

Preset an altar of Apollo, FC

The skene *represents the palace of* OIDIPOUS *and* IOKASTE,
king and queen of Thebes

SCENE I

(*Enter the* PRIEST, *left, with* CHILDREN *carrying suppliant
wands. Enter* OIDIPOUS *from the* skene, *with an* ATTENDANT)

OIDIPOUS: Oh children, new generation of old Kadmos,
why is it that you sit like this before me
with your suppliants' branches wreathed in wool?
The city's full of incense, full of groaning,
full of prayers to the Healer-god, Apollo.

Children, I'm right not taking someone's message.
I have come to listen for myself.
I am known far and wide as Oidipous.

Talk, sir. Your age makes you an obvious man
to speak on their behalf. How do you stand –   10
in fear or in affection? For I want
to help in any way. I'd be unfeeling
if I took no pity on this gathering.

PRIEST: Oidipous, governor of my land,
you see us at your altars – different ages;
these with scarce the strength to fly, and me,
weighed down with age. Yes, me, a priest of Zeus,
and this select band of unmarried youth.
The other people sit as suppliants in
the markets, near Athena's twin temples
and the oracular embers by Ismenos.   20

The city, as you yourself can see, is drowning,
tossing in the sea, and bursting to
the surface, close to a suffocating death.
Blighted are the fruits of fertile soil,
blighted are the cattle pastures, still-born
women's labours. In all this, the god of fever
swoops and plagues the city with a hideous
pestilence which empties Theban homes. Black
Haides fills with bellowing and groans.   30

Equal to the gods you're not, but I,
together with these children sitting round you,
judge you to be among the foremost men
in daily matters and in dealings with the gods.
For you came and loosed Thebes from the tribute which
we rendered to the cruel Sphinx's riddle.
This you did – knowing no more than we
nor under instruction, but, with god's aid,
you're known and praised for setting straight our lives.

Now, Oidipous, more powerful than anyone,   40
all these suppliants here are begging you
find some defence for us; either inspired
by god or known somehow from man.
For I see that experience in life
makes future planning more effectual.

Come, you exceptional man, and set the city straight.
Come, and think about it; Thebes now celebrates
you as its saviour for your earlier zeal.
Let's not remember of your rule that you
once set us straight only at last to fall.   50
Now set us straight again safe from collapse.
It augurs well that once before you gave
us happiness; now be like that again.
If you will rule Thebes, as you govern now,
better govern people and not empty space.
Towers and ships are nothing, if they're
destitute of people to inhabit them.

OIDIPOUS: Poor children, what you've come for, what you
       want,

is not unknown to me – I know. I see
too well you all are sick. But though you're sick,   60
your sickness does not equal my sickness.
Your pain is individual; it visits
each of you alone, whereas my soul
bemoans the city and myself and you.
You did not wake me up from a sound sleep.
You can be sure I've wept a host of tears
and wandered many pathways of my mind.

And on reflection, I could find one cure,
and acted on it. Kreon, my wife's brother,
Menoikeus' son, I've sent to the prophetic   70
shrine of Apollo to learn what I
must do or say to rescue this city.
Judging by the time he's been away,
it worries me what he is doing. He's been gone
beyond what's reasonable, more than expected.
When he comes, then I'd be in the wrong
if I did not do all the god reveals.

PRIEST: Well, that's appropriate – both what you've said
and what the children signal; Kreon's come.

OIDIPOUS: Lord Apollo, may our chances of   80
deliverance be bright as his appearance.

PRIEST: The news is sweet, I'm sure. He comes bedecked
with garlands made from berries and sweet bay.

(*Enter* KREON, *right*)

OIDIPOUS: Soon we'll know; he's close enough to hear.
Son of Menoikeus, Lord, my brother-in-law,
what message do you bring us from the god?

KREON: Auspicious. Ominous. I tell you, if
it turns out right, it turns out very well.

OIDIPOUS: What sort of comment's that? Is what you've said
supposed to make me confident or anxious?   90

KREON: If you want to hear with all these present,
I'm prepared to speak. Perhaps inside.

OIDIPOUS: Speak in public. For I feel these people's
suffering more than that of my own soul.

KREON: Then I will say what I heard from the god.

The Sun-god, Apollo, disclosed clearly to me, my lord,
we must expel pollution, festering in
this land, so that it does not grow incurable.

OIDIPOUS: How? By which purifying rite?

KREON: Banishment – or paying one death for   100
another. It's someone's blood which chills the city.

OIDIPOUS: Who is the man whose fate the god reveals?

KREON: Once, my lord, we had a leader; Laios,
before you steered the city on its course.

OIDIPOUS: Yes, I heard of him but never saw him.

KREON: He's dead and we are told that we
must act to punish whoever his killers are.

OIDIPOUS: And where on earth are they then? Where find
   tracks
of some old crime impossible to trace?

KREON: In Thebes, it said. 'There is no doubt you'll find   110
that which you seek; but what's forgotten's gone.'

OIDIPOUS: Is it at home or in the open or in
another land that Laios met his death?

KREON: He went, it's said, to visit Delphi's oracle.
But once he left, he never did come home.

OIDIPOUS: No messenger, no travelling friend, saw
anything? No one you could learn something useful from?

KREON: They're dead except for one who fled in terror.
He saw it but said nothing sure – bar one thing.

OIDIPOUS: What? One thing might lead us to learn much.   120
Even a paltry start gives us some hope.

KREON: Thieves, he said, met up with them and killed them –
not one man only but a host of them.

OIDIPOUS: How could a thief, without some financial
deal in Thebes, go on to be so reckless?

KREON: That seemed the case. With Laios dead, however,
and the disarray, no champion emerged.

OIDIPOUS: What stumbling block could stop investigation
when your king was felled in such a way?

KREON: The riddle-mongering Sphinx attracted our
   attention.   130
We ignored imponderables and watched our step.

OIDIPOUS: I'll start again and bring them all to light.
It's right of the Sun-god and of you
to turn attention to the dead man's case.

Naturally, you'll see me as an ally,
an avenger both for Thebes and for the god.
I'll scatter this foulness, not for the sake
of any distant relative, but for my own sake.
Laios' killer – whoever he is –
might want to raise that very hand to punish me.   140
So, in coming to his aid, I benefit.

[*Exit* KREON, *left*]

Now then, children, stand up quickly from where
you sit and take in hand your suppliants' branches.
Let someone bring the Theban people here.

[*Exit* ATTENDANT, *left*]

I'll make every effort. With god's help,
we'll show up prosperous or else we perish.

[*Exit* OIDIPOUS, *into the* skene]

PRIEST: Let us stand up, my children. We came here
for the very things this man has promised.
May the Sun-god who has sent these oracles
become the saviour who relieves our sickness.   150

[*Exit the* PRIEST, *left, with the* CHILDREN]

CHOROS I

(*Enter the* ELDERS OF THEBES, *left*)

ELDERS (A1):   Sweet word of god,
          you've come to radiant Thebes from gold-enriched
               Delphi,
          what for?
          I'm overstretched with fear.
          My heart's afraid.
          I cry to you, the Healer-god,
          in holy fear before you.

What's to happen now to me
– something new, or something known beforehand
as the seasons turn?
Oh tell me, golden child of hope,
immortal Voice.

(A2):   I call you first,
divine Athena, child of Zeus, your sister, Thebes'   160
protector,
Artemis, upon
her famous throne
in Athens' centre, and I beg
the sure marksman, Apollo,
show yourselves to me,
save me from death. If ruin reared before
above the town, you drove
the burning blight away. So now
again, please come.

(B1):   Oh, there's so many pains to bear.
I see the entire city sick. No weapon
comes to mind to ward off the attack.   170
The plantings in our fertile soil don't prosper.
Women cry in childbirth but there is no child.
You see lives, one by one, fly
like unerring birds,
who travel faster than relentless fire,
to the sunset shores of death.

(B2):   These countless deaths destroy the city.
Children lie collapsed upon the ground   180
and spread more death. It's callous, pitiful.
Young wives, what's more, and grey-haired mothers
    too,
flock to the altars' steps from everywhere. They moan
their sorry plight and cry out
begging pleas. Their prayers
and moans ring loud and clear. Because of these,
bright child of god, send fair relief.

(C1):   Ares, Slaughter-god of War, as if in battle,   190
         ringed by cries, confronts me
         with the burning plague.
         Grant that he turns his back
         and speeds away from Thebes
         and sets sail to the mighty Atlantic
         or toward the Black Sea's waters of unwelcome.
         What destruction's missed at night,
         the next day brings.
         Lord Father Zeus, who wields the power   200
         of the fiery lightning flash,
         lay waste this god beneath your thunderbolts.

(C2):   Apollo, god of light, I pray your arrows shower
         from the bowstring of twisted
         gold, the ruthless champions
         of our defence.
         I pray for Artemis'
         flaming torches lighting up the hills
         of foreign lands. I call Dionysos,
         the golden-crowned who shares a name   210
         with Thebes, flushed Bakchant,
         to whom the company of mainads
         cry, come with the blazing torch
         against this god dishonoured among gods.

SCENE 2

(*Enter* OIDIPOUS *from the* skene)

OIDIPOUS: You pray, but while you pray, take my advice;
         attend to me and what the sickness needs.
         You'll get relief and strength in this disaster.

         I'm the outsider in the story I will tell,
         outsider to what was done; and I'd not track   220
         the matter long if I did not feel bound.
         But as it is, at last, I've earned my civic rights
         and I proclaim to all you Thebans this;

Whoever of you knows the man who did
away with Laios, son of Labdakos,
I bid you give me a clear indication.
Let him not fear that by removing this
[charge from the city, he will bring sentence]
of death upon himself. He'll be unhurt
and suffer nothing more intolerable than exile.
If any knows of someone else, perhaps   230
a killer from abroad, do not be silent, for
I will reward him. He'll have thanks besides.

But even if you do keep silent, even if you
spurn my word in fear for self or friend,
then listen well to what I'll do.

I command that no one in this land,
in which I hold the power and the throne,
take in this murderer – whoever he is – or talk
to him or share with him in prayers to god
and sacrifices or in holy water.   240

I command that you all cast him from your homes –
we are defiled by him; the Pythian oracle
of god has just now spoken clearly to me.
This is the kind of ally that I am
both to the god and to this dead man.   245

I enjoin that you fulfil all this   252
– for me, and for the god, and for this land
of ours, so wasted, fruitless, lost to heaven.

Even if this matter was not god-inspired,
you could not rightly let it go uncleansed.
The man was noble, royal – and destroyed.
You had to investigate. Now as it is,
I happen to have the office he once had.
I have the same wife he had in my bed.   260
Our children even would have shared a common
parentage, if his had not miscarried.
As it is, chance struck his body down.

For these reasons, I will fight for him,
as if he were my father. I'll try everything
to seek and find the assassin of the child
of Labdakos, offspring of Polydoros,
old Kadmos and ancient Agenor.

I pray the gods for those who don't comply
that they send to them no fruits of the earth   270
or children for the women, but that they
devastate them with this plague and worse besides.

For the rest of you Thebans, who are happy with
this proclamation, may our ally, Natural Justice,
with all the gods be with you always.

I ELDER: I'll speak, lord, in compliance with your curse.
I did not kill him nor can I point out
who did. The Sun-god has consigned the search
and he's the one to say who did the crime.

OIDIPOUS: You're right, of course. But no one man can
     force
the gods to do what they don't wish to do.   280

I ELDER: I'd like to make a second point in this.

OIDIPOUS: And a third – don't miss the chance to speak.

I ELDER: I know that lord Teiresias is a seer
like our lord, the Sun-god, Apollo. Seek his
advice, my lord, to learn with utmost clarity.

OIDIPOUS: It's not been neglected. I have done it.
I have sent him messengers – twice now – on Kreon's
advice. It's surprising he's not here yet.

I ELDER: There's nothing else. The old rumours have died
     down.   290

OIDIPOUS: Like what? I will examine every story.

I ELDER: Laios was said to have been killed by travellers.

OIDIPOUS: I heard, but no one sees the man who saw it.

I ELDER: But if the man has any fear at all,
he'll not stand hearing curses such as these from you.

OIDIPOUS: Where there's no fear of doing, words won't
     frighten.

I ELDER: The man who will convict him is at hand.

They're bringing here the holy prophet who
alone of men has truth inbred in him.

(*Enter* TEIRESIAS *right, led by a* BOY)

OIDIPOUS: Teiresias, you know all kinds of things,   300
what's learnable, unnameable, earth-bound or divine.
And though you cannot see, you clearly know
how sick the city is. We find in you
alone, my lord, a leader and a saviour.

The god, Apollo – in case you haven't heard –
sent back this answer to our embassy;
release from our affliction would come only
if we discovered Laios' killers, and
killed them or sent them out from Thebes in exile.
Therefore do not begrudge us auguries from birds   310
or any other of your ways of prophecy.

Protect yourself and Thebes, protect me, and
protect us from infection from this corpse.
We are in your hands. The best thing you can do
is use what you have got, what you can do, to help.

TEIRESIAS: Oh. How awful to be wise and yet
not profit from that wisdom. And how well
I knew that, but suppressed it. For I should not have come.
OIDIPOUS: What's this? You were not eager to come here?
TEIRESIAS: Send me home. You bear your burden, I'll   320
bear mine. It's easier, believe me now.
OIDIPOUS: Holding back auspicious words is neither fair
nor friendly to the town which nurtures you.
TEIRESIAS: I see that in your case your statement's not
appropriate. And I won't make this same mistake –
OIDIPOUS: If you know, before the gods, don't turn
away – we're on our knees, all suppliants.
TEIRESIAS: You all don't understand. I won't disclose
my anguish so as not to expose yours.
OIDIPOUS: What are you saying? You know but will not
speak?   330
Have you considered this betrays us and ruins Thebes?

TEIRESIAS: I'll not distress you or myself. Why question
to no purpose? You'll not learn anything from me.

OIDIPOUS: Won't you – you utter coward – ever speak?
I mean you'd drive a rock to fury, really.
Must you be adamant, leave things so unresolved?

TEIRESIAS: You blame my temperament but you don't know
your own which lives with you. Still you find fault with me.

OIDIPOUS: Who could hear what you have said – insulting
words to Thebes – and not become angry?   340

TEIRESIAS: I cover up with silence . . . it will still come.

OIDIPOUS: If it will come, then mustn't you tell me?

TEIRESIAS: I'll speak no further. There it is. And you
can rage as fiercely as you wish.

OIDIPOUS: Oh yes, I will. I'll leave out nothing – I'm
so angry – that I know. It seems to me
that you helped cultivate the crime – you did it,
but not with your hands. If you could see,
I'd claim the crime was yours and yours alone.

TEIRESIAS: Is that so? Then I tell you; abide   350
by the decree you have announced, and from
this day, don't speak to these here or to me,
for you are this land's ungodly pollution.

OIDIPOUS: How can you come out with this so shamelessly?
What grounds do you think will give you leave?

TEIRESIAS: I have my leave. The truth's the strength I cherish.

OIDIPOUS: Who's taught you this? It's not come from your
craft.

TEIRESIAS: You did. You urged me speak against my will.

OIDIPOUS: Speak what? Well, speak again so I learn better.

TEIRESIAS: Don't you know already? Or do you test me?   360

OIDIPOUS: Not so as to say it's known. Tell me again.

TEIRESIAS: I say that Laios' murderer whom you seek is you.

OIDIPOUS: You'll regret that you've repeated this disgrace.

TEIRESIAS: Should I say more to make you angrier still?

OIDIPOUS: Whatever you like. Your words will not affect me.

TEIRESIAS: I say you're unaware that your love for
your partner is shameful; you don't see your misery.

OIDIPOUS: Do you think you can keep saying this and not
regret it?

TEIRESIAS: Yes, if there is any strength in truth.

OIDIPOUS: There is, but not in you. You have no strength   370 for you are blind in ear and mind and eye.

TEIRESIAS: You poor man, you cast in my face insults
which everybody will soon cast in yours.

OIDIPOUS: You're nursed in never-ending night. You can't
disable me or anyone who sees the light.

TEIRESIAS: It's not your fate to fall by me.
It's fitting that Apollo cares to make it happen.

OIDIPOUS: Kreon! Has this idea come from him?

TEIRESIAS: Your misery's not from Kreon – it's from yourself.

OIDIPOUS: Oh wealth and power and cleverness   380
beyond all cleverness, an emulated life,
how much envy is secured by you,
if on account of this pre-eminence, which Thebes
thrust, though unasked, into my hands, a gift,
if for this the loyal Kreon, my friend of old,
in secret conned me, wanted me thrown out,
concocted schemes with this here king-maker,
this crafty fakir who has eyes for profit
only, but in practising his craft is blind.

For, tell me, where are you a true seer?   390
How come when the bitch-sphinx sang her song
you uttered nothing to release these people?
For sure, the riddle was not for the first
man there to explain; prophetic power was needed.
You did not emerge with any knowledge
from some god or from the birds. No, I came,
knowing nothing, Oidipous, and stopped her,
with intelligence, not with bird-lore.
Me, whom you're trying to throw out, with thoughts
of standing close beside the throne of Kreon.   400

You will be sorry, sure, and he who's framed
the murderer's exile. If you didn't look
so old, you'd know through pain how rash you are.

I ELDER: My view is that the words of this man and
yours, Oidipous, compare – uttered in anger.
We don't need this; we need to look to how
we best discharge the god's oracular word.

TEIRESIAS: Authority is yours, but we are equal
in my right to answer and I claim it.

I'm not your servant; I'm the prophet-god, Apollo's.   410
Nor do I subscribe to Kreon's patronage.
I tell you, since you've taunted me with blindness,
you have sight but cannot see your misery,
not where you dwell, not with whom you live.
Do you know your parents? You don't even know
you're an affront to family in and on the earth.

The stroke of curses from your mother and father
will one day drive you out of Thebes in terror.
Now you see all right, but then darkness.
What harbour will there be for your howls then?   420
What part of Kithairon will not resound
when you understand that marriage, and the house,
no haven, you sailed into, on your 'lucky' voyage?

You've no idea of the scale of other ills
which will make you level with your children.
So throw your mud at Kreon and at what
my mouth has uttered. There is none alive
who will be rooted out so foully as you.

OIDIPOUS: Should I put up with hearing this from him?
No, be damned! Now, at once! Go back.   430
Go on, get away! Leave my house!

TEIRESIAS: I'd not have come if you had not called me.

OIDIPOUS: I didn't know you'd say such stupid things,
or there's no way I would have brought you to my home.

TEIRESIAS: I am precisely, from your point of view,
stupid, but from your parents', your begetters', smart.

OIDIPOUS: Who are they? Wait. Who then did beget me?

TEIRESIAS: This day begets your birth and your destruction.

OIDIPOUS: You talk in riddles, entirely in the dark.

TEIRESIAS: If so, aren't you the best to interpret them?   440

OIDIPOUS: You now throw in my face what makes me great.

TEIRESIAS: And this same lucky chance has brought you down.

OIDIPOUS: Well, if this city's saved, then I don't care.

TEIRESIAS: It's time to go. Here, boy, take me.

OIDIPOUS: Yes, take him. For here, you're in the way,
a pain; once gone, you won't distress me more.

TEIRESIAS: I'll say what I came to say, then go.
I don't fear your face. You can't destroy me.

I tell you this; this man you have been looking
for, among your threats and your decrees   450
about Laios's murder, he is here,
a resident stranger it seems, but soon
to be revealed as native Theban, a circumstance
without delight. For blind – though now he sees –
and poor – though now he's rich – he'll use a stick
to guide his steps into another land.
He'll be revealed a brother and a father
to his children in his house, husband
and son to her who gave him birth; wife-sharer
and the killer of his father. Go   460
inside, and work it out. And if you find me wrong,
say that I know nothing of prophecy.

[*Exit* TEIRESIAS *right, led by the* BOY. *Exit* OIDIPOUS
into the skene]

CHOROS 2

ELDERS (A1):   The voice of prophecy, the rock of Delphi,
                  sings;
               who is the man who's done with bloody hands
               horrific deeds,
               unspeakable?
               It's time for him to gear his feet to flee,
               to outrun horses swifter than a storm.
               The son of Zeus, Apollo, armed with fire and lightning
                  bolts,
               leaps down upon him,   470
               while the frightening goddesses of death, the Furies,
                  chase him
               and they never miss.

   (A2):   The word has just now come from Mount Parnassos,
               gleaming
           in the snow, to hound this unknown man.
           He roams the savage
           bushland, hides
           in caves and clambers over rocks, a man

alone, a man who's like a wandering bull,
with stumbling step on stumbling step, a man who
  shuns the
prophecies of Delphi's
shrine, the prophecies which hover round him still, for
  ever
while he stays alive.   480

(B1):   The wise interpreter of auguries has stirred me up no
          end,
no end, now. I do not know what to say.
Do I concur? Do I deny?
I do not understand what's past or what's predicted;
my heart flutters with anticipation.
I have never ever known, before or now,
of any lingering feud between
the house of Labdakos   490
and Oidipous, the son of Polybos.
No reason prompts me
to put to the test
the current estimation
of our king
in making a defence for Laios
and his unsolved death.

(B2):   It's true that Zeus is thoroughly aware – Apollo too –
          they know
what goes on earth. But there's no certain means
of judging with respect to mortals   500
whether this Teiresias has won more insight
than I have, though one person might perhaps
be wiser than another. But until
I know what's said is straight,
I'll never go along with those
accusing Oidipous. Time was when she
– the winged monstress –
came up against him. He
was tested, proven wise,
and welcomed into
Thebes. To my mind, he will never   510
stand accused of crime.

SCENE 3

(*Enter* KREON, *left*)

KREON: My fellow Thebans, I have learned the dreadful
charges Oidipous has laid against me,
so I've come. I'll not endure it. If he,
the way things are, thinks I have injured him
in what I've said or done, I've caused him harm,
then I have no desire to live much longer,
under the weight of rumour. Damage done
to me by this report is not so slight.   520
It's quite substantial; a traitor to
the city, called by you and friends a traitor!

I ELDER: Perhaps this insult was forced out by anger
rather than from any thoughtful purpose.

KREON: Was it not said that on my advice
the seer was persuaded to tell lies?

I ELDER: That's what was said – I do not know the
intention.

KREON: So, with clear eyes and with clear mind,
this accusation was declared against me?

I ELDER: I don't know. I don't see what the powerful are
doing.   530

(*Enter* OIDIPOUS *from the* skene)

But here's the man himself out from the palace.

OIDIPOUS: You, how can you come here? You have the face,
the effrontery, to come to my own house
and home? You blatant murderer of Laios,
you flagrant thief of my own royal crown!
Come, tell me before god, did you see me
a coward or a fool to plot against me?
Or maybe I'd not recognize your actions,
sneaking up on me, and learn of them and stop them?
Isn't this attempt of yours stupid,   540
an eager lunge for power without support
or allies, when success depends on wealth and friends?

KREON: You know what? You listen to my answer,

fairly. You learn first and then you judge.

OIDIPOUS: You're clever with your words but I'm no good
learning from you. I've found you hostile and perverse.

KREON: Listen to me and I'll explain this very thing.

OIDIPOUS: This very thing? Don't bother! Show you were
not at fault.

KREON: If you consider wilfulness is good
apart from sense, then you do not think straight.   550

OIDIPOUS: If you consider you can devastate
a kinsman without penalty, you don't think right.

KREON: I agree with that, correct. But tell
me what I've done or what you say I've done.

OIDIPOUS: Did you urge, or did you not urge, me
to send for that man, him, the holy seer?

KREON: And I am still of that opinion, yes.

OIDIPOUS: How long has it been since Laios was –

KREON: What's all this about? I do not follow.

OIDIPOUS: – was taken, unseen, by a murderous hand?   560

KREON: Many, many years have passed since then.

OIDIPOUS: But this prophet practised in those times?

KREON: He was as skilful then as now, and honoured.

OIDIPOUS: Do you recall at that time any talk of me?

KREON: No, nothing; not when I was standing round.

OIDIPOUS: Did you conduct no searches for the killer?

KREON: We did, of course, why not? We heard nothing.

OIDIPOUS: Well, why did this expert not speak up then?

KREON: I don't know; and when I don't, I keep quiet.

OIDIPOUS: You know so much and could tell what you do
understand.   570

KREON: Like what? I'll not refuse to speak of what I know.

OIDIPOUS: Like this; if he had not conferred with you,
he'd never have mentioned me as Laios' killer.

KREON: If he says so, you know yourself. But I've
learned just as much from you as you from me.

OIDIPOUS: Then learn this; I'll not be convicted of his
murder.

KREON: One moment. Are you not my sister's husband?

OIDIPOUS: Well, what you say can't be denied.

KREON: You rule with her, equal in governing Thebes?

OIDIPOUS: She gets whatever it is she wants from me.   580

KREON: And am I not an equal third with you two?

OIDIPOUS: Precisely; that's why you appear so vile a friend.
KREON: No, not if you reflect, as I have done.
Look first at this; do you think that anyone'd
choose to rule subject to terrors or
to easy sleep, with much the same authority?
It is not in my nature to desire
power more than doing powerful deeds,
as anyone who's prudent understands.
As it is, I get everything from you – no fears.   590
If I ruled, I'd be constrained in many things.
So how would sovereignty be sweeter for me
than this untroubled influence and power?

I am not yet so self-deceived as to
desire a good that's not to my advantage.
I'm popular now; everyone greets me.
If they need you, they talk to me at present;
their chances of success rest wholly there.
Why would I give up this and grasp for that?   599
I'm not in love with this sort of thinking.   601
I won't put up with anyone who is.
But test it, go to Delphi.
Find out the facts, if I reported clearly.

If not, if you catch me in some plot with
this prophet, do not capture and kill me on
one vote, but two, both yours and mine. Just don't
condemn me on the quiet without some proof.
It is not right to think good men, without
a reason, bad, or bad men good.   610
For it takes time to judge for sure, since Time   613
alone can make it clear a man is just,
while you can know a traitor in one day.
1 ELDER: That is well said. He's taken care, sir, not
to stumble. Hasty advice is not so sure.
OIDIPOUS: When someone plots, manoeuvres quickly,
    secretly,
then I must quickly plan my counter-attack.
If I stand still and wait, then he will do   620
what he will do and I'll have missed my chance.

KREON: What more do you want? To throw me out of
    Thebes?
OIDIPOUS: No, not at all. I'd like you dead, not fled.
KREON: So you will show that kind of malice towards me?
OIDIPOUS: You talk but won't comply; you can't be trusted.
KREON: I don't think you're sane.
OIDIPOUS: I am. I'm sane.
KREON: And I am just as sane.
OIDIPOUS: But you're a traitor.
KREON: And what if you misunderstand?
OIDIPOUS: I rule still.
KREON: You rule badly then.
OIDIPOUS: Oh Thebes, my city.
KREON: Not only yours. I share this city too.   630

(*Enter* IOKASTE *from the* skene)

I ELDER: Stop, my lords. I see Iokaste coming
    to you from the house and just in time.
    You must settle this dispute with her.
IOKASTE: What's this inconsiderate shouting match
    you've raised? Dear me! The city's sick. Aren't you
    ashamed to worry about your own concerns?
    Now you go on inside, and Kreon home.
    How can you make so much of such a little?
KREON: Your husband, Oidipous, dear sister, threatens
    me with dreadful things, in choosing one   640
    of two disasters; leave the city or die.
OIDIPOUS: That's right, Iokaste. I've caught him in the act,
    in a traitorous scheme, against my person.
KREON: Let no good come to me – curse me! – if I've
    done to you – on my death! – what you have charged.
IOKASTE: Before the gods, believe this, Oidipous.
    Above all, first, respect this oath to god,
    respect then me, and these who stand before you.

ELDERS (AI): Believe, agree, be sane,
    lord, I am begging you.
OIDIPOUS: What do you wish me yield to you?   650
ELDERS: Esteem this man; he's been no fool,
    and know his oath has made him strong.

OIDIPOUS: Do you know what you want?

I ELDER: Yes.

OIDIPOUS: Say it. Speak.

I ELDER: Do not cast off a friend who's made an oath,
     or hold his words unworthy on some unclear charge.

OIDIPOUS: Be sure of this, when you seek this, you seek
     my death or exile from this land.

ELDERS: Oh by the foremost god of all,   660
     the Sun, may I die, godless, friendless,
     the worst of deaths, if I have thoughts like these.
     The wasted earth consumes my heart,
     my soul's in grief, and to this existing pain
     is added pain from both of you.

OIDIPOUS: Then let him go, though I must surely die
     or be thrust out unhonoured from this land.   670
     I have compassion for this piteous plea of yours,
     not his. For where he goes, my hate will go.

KREON: Your hate's apparent, though you yield, as fierce
     as your excessive rage. It's right that natures
     such as yours become most painful to themselves.

OIDIPOUS: Will you leave me and go?

KREON: I'm on my way.
     You don't know me but these know I'm safe.

                              [*Exit* KREON, *left*]

ELDER (A2):   My lady, why delay
     in taking him indoors?

IOKASTE: When I have learned what happened here.   680

ELDERS: A dark suspicion rose, at first,
     a sense of wrong, in answer, raged.

IOKASTE: Was it from both of them?

I ELDER: Yes.

IOKASTE: What was said?

I ELDER: Enough, for me, enough, for one who cares
     for Thebes. So where it stopped, there let it stay.

OIDIPOUS: You see where you've come, although with good
               intention,
     you have restrained, you've dulled, my keen resolve.

ELDERS: Lord, I've said, and more than once,   690

you know I would appear as mad,
bereft of sense, if I cut you adrift –
for you it was who set my precious
city straight when it was floundering, at a loss.
Again, become our lucky guide.

IOKASTE: Before the gods, tell me, too, husband, why
you are so furious in this affair?
OIDIPOUS: I will, my wife. I prize you more than these.   700
It's Kreon – and the plots he's made against me.
IOKASTE: Tell me simply how the quarrel started.
OIDIPOUS: He says I stand to blame, that I killed Laios.
IOKASTE: He knows this himself or has someone told him?
OIDIPOUS: Ah, he sent the seer to do his dirty work,
so he can keep his own mouth out of trouble.
IOKASTE: Now you forget all that – all that you've said.
You listen and you'll learn from me that there
is no man born adept at prophecy.
I'll prove it to you by this brief example.   710

An oracle once came to Laios – not,
I'm sure, from god but from his acolytes –
that fate would have him killed by his own child
who would be born of Laios and of me.
But as we're told Laios instead was killed
one day by foreign thieves where three roads meet.
A child had been born, but three days later, Laios
had the feet of this child bound and pinned.
Someone tossed it in a mountain wilderness.
So there. Apollo didn't cause this boy   720
to be his father's killer. Laios didn't
bear the terror he feared from his son.
That's what the words of prophecy defined.

You turn your back on it. What god finds useful,
he himself can easily reveal.
OIDIPOUS: Iokaste, what I heard just now has caused
my heart to palpitate, my mind to race.
IOKASTE: What worry's made you turn and say this?
OIDIPOUS: This is what I thought you said; this Laios
was slaughtered near a place where three roads meet.   730

IOKASTE: That was the rumour and it's not died down.

OIDIPOUS: Where is this place where that happened?

IOKASTE: The area's called Phokis where the roadway
branches off to Delphi and to Daulis.

OIDIPOUS: What is the time that has elapsed since then?

IOKASTE: Not long before the time when you appeared
and took control, it was announced in Thebes.

OIDIPOUS: Oh Zeus, what do you plan to do to me?

IOKASTE: Why are you so concerned now, Oidipous?

OIDIPOUS: Don't ask me questions yet. Describe how this   740
Laios was built. And how young did he look?

IOKASTE: He had black hair, with streaks of grey in it.
His physique was pretty much like yours.

OIDIPOUS: Oh misery! It seems I've cursed myself
most dreadfully just now and did not know.

IOKASTE: What? I shudder now I look at you, my husband.

OIDIPOUS: I have a dreadful fear the prophet sees.
You'll unveil more if you tell me one thing.

IOKASTE: I'll answer what you ask, though still I shudder to.

OIDIPOUS: Did Laios travel with a few, or like   750
a chief, with many men as company?

IOKASTE: His comrades numbered five, including too the
courier. The only carriage bore Laios.

OIDIPOUS: Ah! That's the proof. Who was it then who
brought
the story of what happened back to you, Iokaste?

IOKASTE: Some household slave who escaped, and returned
alone.

OIDIPOUS: Is this man now employed still in the house?

IOKASTE: No, he's not. After he came back, he found
that you, with Laios dead, had taken power.
He pleaded with me forcefully – he clutched my hand –   760
to send him to the fields, the sheep pastures,
so far he couldn't even lay eyes on Thebes.
Well, I sent him. He deserved it. Such
a servant could have won a greater favour.

OIDIPOUS: I want him back here then immediately.

IOKASTE: That's easily done. But why d'you want him back?

OIDIPOUS: I am afraid, dear wife, that I have said
too much. And that is why I want to see him.

IOKASTE: So, then he'll come. For I deserve, I think,

to learn what so oppresses you, my husband.   770
OIDIPOUS: You will not be excluded, now I've come
so far in my anxiety. Who better
could I talk to in this circumstance than you?
My father is from Korinth, Polybos.
My mother Merope's a Dorian. I was
an important man in Korinth. Then something happened
to me, worthy of surprise, but not
perhaps of my disturbed reaction.

At a banquet, someone drank too much.
Intoxicated, he called me a bastard son.   780
This weighed on me. I scarcely kept myself
in check throughout that day. But on the next,
I went to my father and mother to question them.
The offence distressed them – and the drunk who hurled it.
They cheered me up but all the same the affair
kept grating on me, because the rumours spread.
Without my parents' knowing, I travelled to
Delphi. The Healer-god, Apollo, sent me off, however,
without respecting what I'd come for. Instead, he told
me clearly to my grief vile terrible things.   790
I was bound to mate with my own mother, expose
to the world a family not fit to see,
become the killer of the man who fathered me.

Well then, after hearing this, and guided
by the stars, I gave the land of Korinth
a wide berth, and found retreat where I'd
not see those shameful oracles fulfilled.
In my travels, I reached this country,
where, as you say, this ruler had been killed.

Iokaste, I will tell the truth. When I   800
came near a road which forked in three directions,
a courier and a man whom you've described,
who travelled in a colt-drawn carriage,
there met me. Well, the man in front and this older
man tried to get me off the road.
The carriage-driver shoved me. I got angry
and so I punched him. The older man

saw this. He watched me come beside the carriage
and then he cracked my skull with his forked club.

Well, he paid more than his due. Quick-smart, I hit   810
him with my staff in this hand, and out he rolled
from the carriage then and there, onto his back.

I killed the lot of them. But if there's some
connection between Laios and this stranger,
who is more miserable now than I?
Who is there more hated by the gods?
I cannot be received into the rooms
of citizens or strangers, can speak to no one.
I'm disbarred from homes. No one else but me
has laid these curses on myself.   820
I have defiled this dead man's bed with hands
which caused his death. Am I not wholly evil?
Am I not most unclean? If I must flee,
I cannot flee to see my family,
set foot on my home-soil, or I am doomed
to join my mother in marriage, kill my father,
Polybos, who gave me life and reared me.

Who would not judge my situation and rightly
say it's been caused by a savage daimon?
Never, never, awful reverence of the gods,   830
never let me see this day, but from
the living blot me out before I see
such a defilement fall upon me.
1 ELDER: This makes me tremble, sir. But till you learn
from that man who was there, you have some hope.
OIDIPOUS: The hope I've got relies entirely on
my waiting for this man, this herdsman.
IOKASTE: And once he has appeared then what's your
   purpose?
OIDIPOUS: I'll tell you. If we find his story coincides
with yours, then I've escaped a bad experience.   840
IOKASTE: And what's so special that you heard from me?
OIDIPOUS: Thieves, you said. That's who this herdsman
   spoke
of killing Laios. If he still claims it was

a group of men, then I did not kill him.
For one man's not the same as many men.
But if he clearly states it was a single traveller,
it's obvious the crime must point to me.

IOKASTE: Be clear; that's how his story was reported.
And he cannot claim this was not the case.
The city heard of it, not only me.
Even if he turns away from what he said before,   850
he cannot prove that Laios' death,
dear Oidipous, was as predicted. The Healer-god
plainly said a child of mine must cause his death.
Yet that poor wretch in no way killed Laios
since he himself had perished earlier.
So far as oracles are concerned, from now
on, I would not look one way or another.

OIDIPOUS: That's well thought out. But anyway, send
    someone
off to fetch this labourer. Don't let it slip.   860

IOKASTE: I'll do it straightaway. Let's go inside.
There's nothing I'd not do to please you.

[*Exeunt* OIDIPOUS *and* IOKASTE *into the* skene]

CHOROS 3

ELDERS (A1): May it be my destiny
            to live in holy purity
            in all my words and all my deeds
            as sanctioned by the laws on high
            created in the heavens above.
            Alone, Olympos fathered them;
            no race of mortals gave them birth.
            Nor will forgetfulness in time put them to sleep.   870
            The mighty god is in
            their midst and he never ages.

(A2): Wanton Violence breeds tyranny.
      And Wanton Violence, once stuffed inanely
      with so much that's out of time
      and out of place, climbs to the utmost

peak. It rushes up towards
the sheer and certain drop and finds
no place to set firmly its feet.
I pray the god; keep in your solid grip this city.   880
I will never cease
to hold the god my champion.

(B1):   If a man's contemptuous, and goes along
and acts and speaks without respect for what is right
and doesn't reverence statues of the gods,
then let a sorry fate destroy him
   – for his perverse pride – since he unjustly reaps
      rewards, does not respect what's godly,
lays hands in stupidity on what should not be
      violated.   890
If this were the case,
who can protect a life from the missiles of anger?
If behaviour such as this
is honourable,
then what's the point of
dancing holy dances?

(B2):   I'm never going reverently again to earth's
inviolate shrine at Delphi or to the Abaian
temple, or Olympia, unless   900
these oracles match up
for everyone to point
to them. Zeus, if it is accurate
to call you master,
lord of all, then do not let this matter slip by you or
      your
immortal endless governance.
The oracles concerning Laios fade;
they come to naught. There's no apparent
honour for
the god, Apollo.
Worship's dead and gone.   910

SCENE 4

(*Enter* IOKASTE *from the* skene, *with an* ATTENDANT)

IOKASTE: Citizens of Thebes, the thought occurred
to me to visit holy shrines with incense
and with olive-branches decked with wool.
Oidipous is very agitated
with all sorts of fears, not like a man
of sense who judges present issues by past ones.
If someone speaks of terrors, he concurs.

Since I have failed completely as adviser,
I've come, a suppliant, to the nearest shrine,
to you, Apollo, god of light, with prayer-offerings,   920
so that you might free us from pollution.
We all shudder when we see him panic-
stricken. He's the helmsman of our ship.

(*Enter the* KORINTHIAN, *right*)

KORINTHIAN: Sirs, I'd like to learn from you where
is the palace of King Oidipous.
Or, preferably, where he is, if you know.
1 ELDER: This is his home, sire, and he is inside.
This lady is the mother of his children.
KORINTHIAN: Then may the greatest happiness always
be hers, being the perfect wife to Oidipous.   930
IOKASTE: And to you too, sir. Your welcome words
make you deserving. Tell me what you've come
here for. What is it that you want to say?
KORINTHIAN: Good news, madam, for the palace and your
husband.
IOKASTE: Such as what? Who is it that you've come from?
KORINTHIAN: From Korinth. And the message I'll announce
will please you, without doubt; distress you too.
IOKASTE: What news can have such double impact?
KORINTHIAN: The people will make Oidipous king of
the land of Isthmia. That's what they're saying.   940
IOKASTE: How? Isn't old Polybos still ruler?

KORINTHIAN: Not so, for death now holds him in the grave.
IOKASTE: What's this you're saying? Oidipous' father's
    dead?
KORINTHIAN: If I'm not telling the truth, then I deserve to
    die.
IOKASTE: You there, go and tell the master this.
    Quickly.

[*Exit the* ATTENDANT *into the* skene]

    Oh you oracles of gods,
so there you are! This man whom Oidipous
long feared and fled from lest he kill him has died
a natural death and not through Oidipous.

(*Enter* OIDIPOUS *from the* skene, *leading* ANTIGONE *and*
ISMENE)

OIDIPOUS: Well, dear and loving wife, Iokaste,   950
    why did you send for me to come outside?
IOKASTE: Listen to this man. And then see to
    what point the oracles of god have come.
OIDIPOUS: Who is it? What's he got to say to me?
IOKASTE: He's from Korinth. He's announced your father,
    Polybos, no longer lives. He died.
OIDIPOUS: What's that you say, sir? You tell me yourself.
KORINTHIAN: The first thing that I'm clearly saying is: be
    assured that Polybos is dead and gone.
OIDIPOUS: By treachery? Or brought down by disease?   960
KORINTHIAN: A slight tip of the scales'll put the aged to rest.
OIDIPOUS: So he succumbed to illness then, it seems.
KORINTHIAN: Yes, and the measure of his many years.
OIDIPOUS: Ah! Why, my wife, would anyone
    consult the Pythian oracle, or tremble
    at the screeching birds above, on whose
    advice I was to kill my father? He
    lies dead in the earth and here am I, up here,
    not touched a spear. Unless he perished out
    of longing for me, then I'd be his killer.   970
    But Polybos has gathered up the prophecies
    and lies with them in Haides. They're worth nothing.

IOKASTE: Didn't I tell you this some time ago?
OIDIPOUS: You did. But I misled myself through fear.
IOKASTE: Don't take any bit of them to heart.
OIDIPOUS: How can I not fear my mother's bed?
IOKASTE: What should anybody fear? Chance rules
supreme. Does anyone have clear foresight?
Best live casually to the extent you can.
Don't be frightened of marrying your mother.   980
Many men sleep with their mothers in
their dreams. The man who treats those things as
unimportant lives a free and easy life.
OIDIPOUS: This would have been well said on your part if
my mother was not still alive. But since
she is – though you make sense – I must hold back.
IOKASTE: Still, your father's death's great comfort.
OIDIPOUS: I agree. But my fear's for the living parent.
KORINTHIAN: Who is the woman who makes you afraid?
OIDIPOUS: Merope, who lived as wife to Polybos.   990
KORINTHIAN: What is it about her that stirs your fear?
OIDIPOUS: A dreadful, god-inspired prophecy.
KORINTHIAN: Is it public? Or shouldn't other people know?
OIDIPOUS: Oh yes. The Prophet-god once said I'm doomed
to marry my own mother and to shed
with my own hands my father's blood.
Because of this, for ages Korinth has been far
from home to me, and I've been lucky. Still
it's nice to see one's parents face to face.
KORINTHIAN: You've exiled yourself from Korinth in fear of
this?   1000
OIDIPOUS: I didn't want to be my father's killer, sir.
KORINTHIAN: Why haven't I released you from this fear,
my lord, since I have come in friendship?
OIDIPOUS: If so, you'd get a fine reward from me.
KORINTHIAN: This is precisely why I came. So I
might do myself some good when you return to Korinth.
OIDIPOUS: No. Never. Not to meet my parents there.
KORINTHIAN: My boy, it's very clear you don't know what
you're doing.
OIDIPOUS: How so, old man? By god, you tell me then.
KORINTHIAN: These are the reasons you've refrained from
going home?   1010

OIDIPOUS: I'm frightened the Sun-god would prove them true.

KORINTHIAN: That you would be polluted through your parents?

OIDIPOUS: Just so, old fellow. It's my constant fear.

KORINTHIAN: Do you realize that your fears are unfounded?

OIDIPOUS: Of course not. Am I not a child born of these parents?

KORINTHIAN: Because Polybos was unrelated to you.

OIDIPOUS: What's that? Polybos didn't father me?

KORINTHIAN: No more than I did. Our relationship's the same.

OIDIPOUS: My father is the same as some stranger?

KORINTHIAN: That man did not father you, nor I.   1020

OIDIPOUS: Why is it that he used to call me son?

KORINTHIAN: You were a gift, you ought to know, from these hands.

OIDIPOUS: He loved me so much, yet I was given?

KORINTHIAN: He had no children. That's what won him over.

OIDIPOUS: You gave me to him. Was I bought or found?

KORINTHIAN: Found in the bush in Mount Kithairon's valleys.

OIDIPOUS: What were you doing wandering in that region?

KORINTHIAN: I was in charge of sheep there on the mountain pastures.

OIDIPOUS: You were a shepherd, roaming round for work?

KORINTHIAN: But at that time, my boy, I was your saviour.   1030

OIDIPOUS: How? What was wrong then when you picked me up?

KORINTHIAN: Your own ankles would testify to that.

OIDIPOUS: What? Why do you mention that old injury?

KORINTHIAN: I set you free. Your feet were pinned together.

OIDIPOUS: So since babyhood, I've had this awful defect.

KORINTHIAN: That's how you got the name which you still have.

OIDIPOUS: Tell, by god, who bound me? My father or mother?

KORINTHIAN: Don't know. The man who gave you knows this better than I do.

OIDIPOUS: You got me from someone else? You didn't find
me?

KORINTHIAN: No. Another shepherd gave you to me.   1040

OIDIPOUS: Who was it? Are you in position to reveal this?

KORINTHIAN: I think that he was named as one of Laios'
men.

OIDIPOUS: The man who was king of this land before?

KORINTHIAN: Yes, definitely. He was that man's herdsman.

OIDIPOUS: Is he still alive for me to see him?

KORINTHIAN: You people who live here would best know
that.

OIDIPOUS: Is there any of you present here
who knows the herdsman whom this man has mentioned,
who's seen him on the land or in the town?
Give me some sign. The time is ripe to find out.   1050

I ELDER: I think he's that same man out in the country
whom you tried to see before. But anyway,
Iokaste would be best to tell us this.

OIDIPOUS: Iokaste, do you know of him – the man
we've just now told to come here? Is he this man?

IOKASTE: Who cares if he is? Pay no attention. Don't
bother with what he said. Forget it.

OIDIPOUS: It wouldn't be right, now that I've clues like these,
not to bring my origins to light.

IOKASTE: Don't, before the gods, if you care for your life   1060
at all, pursue this. It's enough I suffer.

OIDIPOUS: Don't worry. Even if my mother, hers
and hers again, were slaves, your line is not affected.

IOKASTE: All the same, please listen to me. Don't do this.

OIDIPOUS: I'll not listen if it means I'll not learn the truth.

IOKASTE: I think for your good. I speak for the best.

OIDIPOUS: Your best is simply dragging out my agony.

IOKASTE: Unlucky man, may you not ever know who you
are.

OIDIPOUS: Will someone go and bring this herdsman to me?
Let the lady find her joy in her nobility.   1070

IOKASTE: Oh! Oh, you poor, poor man. This is all
I have to say to you. No more. Not ever.

[*Exit* IOKASTE *into the* skene, *followed by* ANTIGONE
and ISMENE]

1 ELDER: I am afraid – Iokaste's rushed out and
    she's most upset, Oidipous – I'm afraid .
    some evil will erupt out of her silence.

OIDIPOUS: Let whatever likes erupt! I want
    to learn my stock, even though it counts for little.
    Perhaps that woman – who thinks like some grand dame –
    is ashamed of my own undistinguished breed.

But I believe myself to be the child   1080
    of bounteous Fortune. I'll not be dishonoured.
    For she is my mother, and the months,
    my brothers, have defined my highs and lows.
    That's my ancestry. I cannot turn
    out otherwise; but I will know my kin.

CHOROS 4

ELDERS (AI):   If I can see the future,
            if I'm any sort of judge,
            then, by Olympos,
            you, Kithairon, by tomorrow night's full moon,
            will prove to be the birthplace of our Oidipous.   1090
            And he will glorify you
            as his nurse and mother.
            We will dance the holy dance
            to honour you since you have rendered to our king
            such service. Oh, Sun-god,
            we call on you,
            may these festivities prove pleasing to you.

(A2):   Who was it, child, who was it
            of the ancient race of nymphs
            who went with Pan,   1100
            your father in the mountains? Or did someone sleep
            with Apollo, the Prophet-god? He loves the open
            tablelands. Or was it
            Hermes, lord of Kyllene?
            Or was it Bakchos, god
            Dionysos, who roams the hill-tops, who received

you, a surprising gift,
from some nymph, with
her roving eyes, with whom he loves to sport.

SCENE 5

OIDIPOUS: Though I've had no dealings with him,
    Elders,
I would deduce, I think, I see the herdsman   1110
whom we have long sought out. For his great years
are similar in length to this man's here.
I also recognize those bringing him
are of my staff. Maybe you have the edge
on me in knowledge – you knew this herdsman earlier.

(*Enter the* HERDSMAN, *right, with* ATTENDANTS)

1 ELDER: I recognize him, surely – one of Laios'
men, a faithful shepherd, like any other.
OIDIPOUS: You, the man from Korinth, I ask you firstly,
is this the man you mean?
KORINTHIAN: The one you see.   1120
OIDIPOUS: Hey you, old man. Look here and answer what
I ask you. Were you one of Laios' men?
HERDSMAN: Yes, but I wasn't bought. I was reared in the
    household.
OIDIPOUS: What kind of work or livelihood preoccupied
    you?
HERDSMAN: I've been following flocks most of my life.
OIDIPOUS: Which places did you stay in specially?
HERDSMAN: Sometimes Kithairon, sometimes places near
    there.
OIDIPOUS: Do you know if you noticed this man there?
HERDSMAN: Doing what? No, which man do you mean?
OIDIPOUS: This man here. Or did you ever meet him
    then?   1130
HERDSMAN: Not that I can say straight off from memory.
KORINTHIAN: That's no surprise, my lord. He doesn't clearly
    recognize me. I'll remind him. I
am sure that he recalls when we looked after

flocks on Mount Kithairon – he had two
and I had one. [At that time, yes, I was]
associated with this man, from spring
to summer, six full months a year for three years.
Then in winter, I'd drive my flock into
sheepfolds, he'd drive his to Laios' stockyards.
Now am I saying what happened or not?   1140

HERDSMAN: You speak the truth – though it's so long ago.

KORINTHIAN: Come, say now, do you remember ever giving
me a child, an infant, for me to look after?

HERDSMAN: What's this? Why are you asking me this
question?

KORINTHIAN: This man, my friend, was that man who had
just been born.

HERDSMAN: Oh, you be damned. Why don't you shut up
now?

OIDIPOUS: Don't you chastise this man, sir. Your words
need to be chastised more than his words do.

HERDSMAN: Where, oh best of rulers, have I gone astray?

OIDIPOUS: You do not tell us of the child he asked
about.   1150

HERDSMAN: He speaks in ignorance. His effort's useless.

OIDIPOUS: If kindness cannot make you speak, you'll speak
in pain.

HERDSMAN: Before god, do not torture an old man.

OIDIPOUS: Someone, quickly, grab hold of his arms.

HERDSMAN: Please! What for? What more do you want to
know?

OIDIPOUS: Did you give this man the child he asked about?

HERDSMAN: I gave it! If only I'd died that very day.

OIDIPOUS: You still might die if you don't tell the truth.

HERDSMAN: I'm much more likely to die if I speak.

OIDIPOUS: This man's determined, so it seems, to waste
time.   1160

HERDSMAN: No, I've already said I gave it to him.

OIDIPOUS: Where'd it come from? Your household? Another
household?

HERDSMAN: No, not mine, certainly. It was handed to me.

OIDIPOUS: Which one of these people? Whose home was it?

HERDSMAN: Don't, before god, don't, my lord, ask more.

OIDIPOUS: You're dead, if I have to ask you this again.

HERDSMAN: All right, it was one of the children born in
     Laios' house.
OIDIPOUS: A slave? Or born of the same line as Laios?
HERDSMAN: Oh, I'm close to speaking of the horror.
OIDIPOUS: And I to hearing of it. But it must be heard.   1170
HERDSMAN: The child was called the son of Laios. The lady
     inside could say best, your wife, how things are.
OIDIPOUS: She gave it to you?
HERDSMAN: Yes, my lord.
OIDIPOUS: Why'd she do that?
HERDSMAN: So I'd put him away.
OIDIPOUS: My mother was so desperate?
HERDSMAN: To evade a dreadful oracle.
OIDIPOUS: Which said?
HERDSMAN: It said the child would kill his father.
OIDIPOUS: Then why'd you pass me over to this man?
HERDSMAN: Out of pity, lord, for I thought he'd carry
     you away to another place, his own. But he only
     saved you for the worst. If you are who   1180
     he says you are, you know your birth was cursed.
OIDIPOUS: Oh! Oh! It's all seen to have come true.
     Oh light of day! This last time let me look on you.
     Exposed; I shouldn't have been born. I made love
     to whom I shouldn't, killed whom I ought not.

> [*Exit* OIDIPOUS *into the* skene. *The* ATTENDANTS *follow*
>   *him. Exeunt the* KORINTHIAN *and the* HERDSMAN,
>   *right*]

CHOROS 5

ELDERS (A1):   Oh you mortal generations, I must count
     your life no life at all.
     For who of you is really happy,
     rather than appearing happy?   1190
     And appearing so soon falls away.
     You are my warning,
     you, your life, your daimon,
     oh poor Oidipous,
     so that I cannot call a human being blessed.

(A2):   This man hit the mark. He was superior, Zeus,
but in no way
had a happy life. He utterly
destroyed the riddling, taloned,
female Sphinx. He rose up like a tower
for my country   1200
against death. Since then
you're named my king, and have
been highly honoured through your rule in glorious
    Thebes.

(B1):   Who now is heard of
who is more afflicted,
more consumed by agonies and ruin,
whose normal life's reversed?
Poor Oidipous, famed Oidipous,
for you the same rich breeding ground
sufficed to serve you first as child
and then as bridegroom and as father.   1210
Oh, but how, how was your father's fertile ground
able to bear with you, poor man,
in silence
for so long?

(B2):   All-seeing Time
has found you unprepared
and sits in judgement on that mockery
of marriage which produced
offspring by its own offspring. Laios'
child, I wish, I wish I never
had laid eyes on you, because
I cry beyond all measure. Groans
flow unchecked from my mouth. And yet to tell the
    truth,   1220
you once restored me and then for
a while I
slept in peace.

FINALE

(*Enter a* SERVANT *from the* skene)

SERVANT: You've long been greatly honoured in this land.
You'll hear of things done now and see them, and
you'll feel such pain, if, true still to your race,
you turn in pity towards the house of Labdakos.
For I don't think the rivers Ister or Phasis
could wash this household clean. It hides such horror,
will bring into the light right now such horror,
done – not by chance – deliberately. Clearly,   1230
self-inflicted injury hurts most.
I ELDER: What we saw before did not stop short
from making us cry out in grief. You say there's more?
SERVANT: I'll tell you and you'll know in the fewest words
I can. Dear, noble Iokaste is dead.
I ELDER: Poor woman. Oh, what was the cause of death?
SERVANT: She turned against herself. The worst of what's
been done is out of sight. You didn't witness it.
But to the extent the memory stays with me,
you'll learn what she, in desperation, did.   1240

She raced into the hallway in a fit
of passion, and rushed straight towards her marriage-
bed, while tearing at her hair with both her hands.
Once inside, she slammed the doors behind her.
She calls out 'Laios' – though he's been long dead –
thinks back to that implanted seed, because
of which he died, left her a mother to
bear cursed offspring by his and her own son.
She bemoans the bed of her two-fold disaster –
a husband by her husband, children by her child.   1250

How she killed herself then I don't know exactly –
we could not see out her agony;
for Oidipous then dashed in shouting and
we watched him as he wandered round the place.
Up and down, demanding a sword, demanding
his wife, but not his wife, the twin maternal

seed-bed for his children and himself.
Some daimon led him in his fury –
none of us mere mortals standing by –
because he then screamed terribly and, as if guided,   1260
attacked the bedroom doors, and shoved them inwards,
bending back the bolts. He stumbled into the room.

There, hanging, we could see the woman, dangling
with the twisted rope around her neck.
He saw it and let out a dreadful bellow.
He loosened the hanging noose. And her poor body
lay upon the ground. The horror we saw then!

He unpinned and tore away the golden brooches
from the robes which she was dressed in,
raised them up and struck at his own eyeballs,   1270
yelling something like, 'You'll not look on the disgraceful
things I've done or have had done to me.
In darkness now you'll look on those I ought not
to have seen, and not know those I yearned to know.'

Intoning words like these, time and again
he raised his head and struck his eyes. The bloody
sockets wet his beard, each time, not by
discharging drop by drop, but gushing
each time in a black hailstorm of blood.

These disasters came from both, not one alone –   1280
mixed disasters for the woman and the man.
Their years of happiness before were truly
happy. But today, there's groaning, death,
delusion, shame, whatever evil can
be named on earth, not one of them is absent.

I ELDER: Has the poor man found some respite in his
     trouble?
SERVANT: He shouts for someone to open the door and show
   to all of Thebes a man who killed his father,
   and whose mother – I can't say the awful words.
   He wants to be cast out of here, and never   1290
   live in the house of curses which he's cursed.

He has no strength. He has no one to guide him.
His affliction is too much to bear.
And yet he'll show you, for the palace
doors are opening. Soon you'll behold such a sight
that even he who hates it must pity.

(*Enter* OIDIPOUS *from the* skene, *blinded*)

I ELDER: What dreadful suffering for anyone to see –
the most dreadful thing I ever have
encountered. You desperate man,
what madness has come over you? Which daimon   1300
has leaped such a mighty leap
into your luckless destiny?
Oh. Poor man, I cannot bear
to look on you, though there's so much to ask,
so much to learn, so much to make me look.
You've made me shudder.

OIDIPOUS: Ah! Ah! My catastrophe.
Where on earth do my poor steps carry me? How is it
that my voice flies round and round?   1310
Oh daimon, where did you leap?
I ELDER: To terror. We cannot listen, cannot look.

OIDIPOUS (A1): A cloud
of darkness isolates me – inescapable, unspeakable,
unstoppable, driven by cruel winds.
Oh!
Oh, how the stinging of the pins
and the memory of crimes combine within me.
I ELDER: No wonder, you are in such pain, that you
mourn evils twice as much, weep twice the tears.   1320

OIDIPOUS (A2): Friend,
you have stayed with me still, still steadfast, still
with patience looking after this blind man.
Oh!
You are not hidden from me, for I know for sure
the sound of your dear voice, although I am in darkness.

1 ELDER: How did you do such dreadful things, how dare
extinguish your own eyes? Which daimon drove you?

OIDIPOUS   (B1):   It was Apollo, friends, Apollo
          who brought to pass disasters, my disasters,   1330
          these my pains.
          But my own hand itself struck
          here, in my desperation.
          Why should I see
          when there is nothing sweet for me to see?
ELDERS: That's how it is, just as you say.

OIDIPOUS: What's there to see that I can
          love? What can I hear
          in conversation, friends, that is enjoyable?
          Lead me away from here, friends, quickly,   1340
          lead me away,
          a man destroyed,
          a man completely cursed,
          the man most hated, yes,
          of all men by the gods.
1 ELDER: Knowing how you stand is just as bad.
I can only wish I'd never known you.

OIDIPOUS   (B2):   Let him die, whoever he was, that shepherd
          who found me in the wild with shackled feet
          and snatched me away   1350
          from death and saved me – he
          did me no favour.
          For if I'd died,
          I'd not be the cause of this distress to me and mine.
ELDERS: I too wish it had been so.

OIDIPOUS: I would not then have come to be
          my father's killer, or be named
          by everyone as husband to the woman who bore me.
          Now I am god-forsaken, child of infected parents,   1360
          blood-relative to him who – unhappily – fathered me.
          If there's disaster that's beyond disaster,
          it's the destiny of Oidipous.

1 ELDER: I don't know how this was your best choice.
Better not to live than to live blind.

OIDIPOUS: Do not preach at me, do not advise me more,
that what's been done's not been done for the best.   1370
If I had sight, and went to Haides, I
don't know how I could cast eyes on my father,
or my unhappy mother, since I've done
such things to both that more than merits hanging.

How could the sight of my children delight
me when I looked on them, spawned as they were?
No, not with eyes of mine, no never, ever.

Not the city or its towers or the holy
statues of the gods – I, cherished as first
and foremost in the town, now wholly wretched,   1380
deprived myself of these. I made the edict.
Everyone must cast out the ungodly,
exposed by god as unholy and born of Laios.

How could I disclose this stain of mine
and yet look people here straight in the eye?
No, not at all. And if there was a way
to block the ears, to stop the hearing, I would not
have hesitated to imprison this body
so that I'd see and hear nothing. It's sweet
for thought to dwell beyond calamities.   1390

Oh, Kithairon, why'd you shelter me? Why not
take me and kill me then so that I'd never
expose to everyone how I was born?

Polybos! Oh, Korinth, claimed to be
the ancient homeland of my fathers, how
my childhood bloomed while sickness festered underneath.
For now I'm found foul and foully born.
Oh, three roadways and the hidden valley,
and the grove, the narrow intersection,
which drank my father's blood, my blood, poured   1400
by my hands, do you remember still

what I did in your sight, what more I then
went on to do in Thebes? Oh marriage, marriage,
first you gave me birth, and having spawned
me, then discharged this seed, producing brothers
to a father, children, blood-relations,
brides, wives, mothers, and all the most
disgraceful acts that can be done on earth.

But what's not good to do's not good to say.
Now quickly hide me away out of the sight   1410
of the gods, or kill me, or throw me in
the sea where you will never more lay eyes on me.
Come on, dare to touch an afflicted man.
Pluck up the courage, don't be frightened. No
one else but me can bear my infirmity.

1 ELDER: Here's Kreon come at the right time to advise
    and act on what you've asked for. He alone
    is left to guard this country in your place.

(*Enter* KREON, *left*)

OIDIPOUS: Oh, what can I say to him?
    How can I justify myself? It's turned   1420
    out that I was so wrong before about him.
KREON: Oidipous, I have not come to gloat
    or throw your earlier mistakes in your face.

(*To an* ATTENDANT) Though you've got no sense of shame
    for the human race, at least revere
    the Sun-god's nurturing light, and don't let this
    polluted man here be on show. The earth,
    the light, the holy rain, can't stand the sight of him.
    Come on quickly, take him off inside.
    It's only decent that just family   1430
    should see and hear about a family's troubles.
OIDIPOUS: Before god, since you've dashed aside my fears,
    and generously come to me, the worst of men,
    grant something. It's in your interest I ask, not mine.
KREON: What service are you keen to ask of me?
OIDIPOUS: Cast me out of Thebes as soon as possible
    to where I'll not meet up with anyone.

KREON: I already would have, you be sure,
   if I didn't want first to consult the god.
OIDIPOUS: But everything that he revealed leads to   1440
   my ruin, a father-killer, a debased man.
KREON: And so it was revealed. But all the same
   our need stands; to learn what's best to do.
OIDIPOUS: Will you consult the god about a man like me?
KREON: Now surely even you will put your faith in god.
OIDIPOUS: I lay this request on you, and will urge you;
   bury her in the palace as you yourself
   wish. It's right you do so for your own.

   Do not condemn me ever while I live
   to dwell here in the city of my fathers.
   Let me stay in the mountains, yes, Kithairon,   1450
   famous now for being mine, where, in
   their lifetime, my parents appointed me my grave.
   I'll die the way they wanted me to die.   1454

   Regarding my two boys, Kreon, you shouldn't   1459
   worry. They are men. No matter where   1460
   they are, they will not lack the means to live.

(*Enter* ANTIGONE *and* ISMENE *from the* skene.)

   But as for my two poor and pitiable girls,
   whose dining table was not ever set
   apart from me, who were inseparable
   from me, and always shared with me in everything,
   please care for them. And now especially let
   me touch them with my hands and cry my grief.
   Please, oh lord . . .
   Please, you worthy man. To lay my hands
   on them, I'd feel they were mine as when I could see.   1470
   What is that?
   Do I hear, before the gods, my dear
   ones crying? Has Kreon pitied me and sent
   to me my two most precious darling children?
   Am I right?
KREON: You are right. I'd already seen to it.
   I know they made you happy then, and do now.

OIDIPOUS: Bless you. You've let them come, so may
a better daimon care for you than cared for me.

Where are you, children? Here, come here towards   1480
my hands, the hands which are your brother's hands,
which made the once-bright eyes of him who is
your father see as they see now.
I became your father, children, but I didn't
know or realize who gave me birth.

I cry for you though I can't look on you.
I know the bitter days that lie ahead,
the life that people will cause you to lead.
What sort of friendly company will you keep?
What celebration won't you leave in tears,   1490
returning home instead of joining in?
And when you reach the point of being married,
who will have you? Who will run the risk,
my girls, that this disgrace will not prove equally
as damaging to your children as to mine?

Terrible things they'll say: 'Your father killed
his father, sowed his seed in that same womb
where he himself was sown, and then he fathered
you by her who'd given birth to him.'

They'll fling that in your face. So who'll marry you?   1500
No one, my girls. It's clear. You'll be wasted
like barren soil and you will never marry.

Son of Menoikeus, you alone are left
to be their father since we two, their parents,
both of us are lost. As father, don't see
poor, unmarried relatives go wandering.
Don't reduce them to my desperate straits.
Pity them. Young though they are, you see
they have lost everything except for you.
You're a good man. Take my hand. Agree.   1510

My girls, if you could only understand, I'd have
so much to say. I'd like you pray for this:

to live where time allows, and have a better
life than the man who fathered you.
KREON: Your weeping has gone far enough. Now go inside.
OIDIPOUS: I will, though without pleasure.
KREON: All things in their time.
OIDIPOUS: You do know my conditions?
KREON: I'll know them when you tell me.
OIDIPOUS: You must send me away.
KREON: That's for the god to give.
OIDIPOUS: But I'm hateful to the gods.
KREON: Maybe you'll get your wish.
OIDIPOUS: You agree, then?
KREON: I don't say what I don't mean.   1520
OIDIPOUS: Well now, take me inside.
KREON: Come on. Let go the girls.
OIDIPOUS: No, please, don't take my children.
KREON: Don't keep giving orders.
    Your lifetime has outlasted your authority.

[*Exit* OIDIPOUS *into the* skene, *followed by* KREON,
                    SERVANT, ANTIGONE *and* ISMENE]

1 ELDER: People of Thebes, look, this is Oidipous.
    He knew the famous riddles. He was a mighty king.
    He was the envy of everyone who saw how lucky he'd been.
    Now he's struck a wave of terrible ruin.
    While you're alive, you must keep looking to
    your final day, and don't be happy till
    you pass life's boundary without suffering grief.   1530

[*Exeunt* ELDERS, *left*]

NOTES

Aias

MICHAEL EWANS

The Actors and their Roles

The assignment proposed on p. 2 is bound to be controversial. I believe that to achieve the change of location in Scene 5, Sophokles must have used more than three actors in the Finale, so Aias can die in full view of the audience.[1] It makes great sense for his part to be assigned to an actor who has no role in the second half of the drama – except that played by his corpse, which is literally as well as metaphorically central right through to the end. The common assumption that Aias must have been played by the same actor as his half-brother Teukros is also worth questioning for another reason: Aias was, as every other character stresses, a unique figure, very different in physique and behaviour from Teukros the half-barbarian.[2]

This allows the other roles, including Odysseus and the challenging parts of Tekmessa and Teukros, to be allocated between the remaining two actors, with a supernumerary to play the cameo role of Agamemnon in the Finale. The conjectural allocation printed on p. 2 assigns the masculine roles to Actor 1 and the two female parts, together with Menelaos (the weakest of the three male parts), to Actor 3.

---

[1] See below on Scene 5. Both actual fifth-century practice, and Aristotle's discussion of the introduction first of one actor, and then of a second and third (*Poetics* 49a.15f.) imply that there were normally only three actors in Greek tragedy. The evidence is surveyed in Pickard-Cambridge 1988, 135–56; among the surviving dramas, only *Libation Bearers*, *Ai*, and *OKol* present difficulties with a maximum of three actors. However, the practice of normally having a maximum of three actors was not elevated into a 'rule' until Horace, *Art of Poetry* 192.

[2] *Pace* e.g. Ley 1988, 92.

The Production

This translation was first performed at King Edward Park, Newcastle, Australia in March 1997. The venue was a natural amphitheatre facing east, with sea views in the background. A sixteen-metre *orchêstra* circle was marked out, surrounded on two thirds of its circumference by an audience of up to 400 seated on sloping grass. Masks were not used. We placed the characters in a recent combat setting, where a multinational force besieged a foreign city (Kuwait under Iraqi occupation in 1991). The *skene* represented a modern army tent in desert camouflage, and the costumes used the ethnic differences between members of the western alliance to point up the antagonisms between the commanders from different independent *poleis* among Sophokles' Greeks. The Athenian spectators' viewpoint became an Australian one, so Aias and Teukros were Australian; Odysseus was French – echoing the distrust of France in Australasia because of the nuclear testing at Mururoa; and Agamemnon and Menelaos were portrayed as generals from southern states of the USA. This setting also effectively isolated Tekmessa, a lone Arabian princess surrounded by uniformed Caucasian males.

Scene 1

Sophokles delivers the first of four great *coups de théâtre* at once. Scene 1 establishes a diametric contrast between two intimate subscenes: Athena's playful challenges to her protégé Odysseus at 73ff., and her cruel toying at 94ff., in a hideous pretence of comradeship, with the man who has angered her. The dual image of Aias – at once exultant in his triumph, and covered in the blood and madness that make his subsequent shame and downfall inevitable – enables the goddess of wisdom to stress the fragility of human achievement at the conclusion. As a consequence the remainder of *Aias* is underpinned by the ideas of delusion and mutability in a way that could not have been achieved by a goddess who simply addresses the audience on her own.[3]

This opening scene presents a close interaction between three characters in total visual contrast: Odysseus in normal military costume and weapons, human and sane; Athena divine – in our production, pure in white; and Aias ghastly, mad, half-naked, covered in blood and

---

[3] As e.g. when Aphrodite opens Euripides' *Hippolytos*. In that drama, Artemis appears at the end, and speaks to Theseus and Hippolytos.

brandishing a whip.[4] Odysseus begins the scene hunting like a dog, and only briefly gains enough confidence to stand fully upright; Aias in our production was hunched over, deformed by his insanity; the goddess stands erect throughout, savouring her total possession of power.

Athena cannot have entered on the *mechane*, since it is not likely to have been used before 431 BC (Euripides' *Medeia*), and is not certainly attested before his *Bellerophon* (c. 425 BC). Several scholars and translators – perhaps fixated on the idea that divinities must appear aloft[5] – have claimed that Athena in this much earlier drama used the flat roof of the *skene* building as a 'theologeion', a speaking-place for gods.[6] However, the roof was occasionally used as an acting area, to represent the roof of the building that the *skene* itself represented;[7] how could Sophokles have expected his audience to realize that in *Aias* the *skene* roof is supposed to represent the thin air *above* the roof of Aias' tent?

---

[4] Tekmessa's narrative at 284 implies that Aias went out hastily, and did not dress or arm fully for his expedition. Certainly a powerful visual contrast is created if he begins the drama like this, as an image of his isolation and desolation, and then cleanses himself and resumes the full attire of his great days as a soldier when he has reconciled himself to death. This change must be made not for Scene 3 but for Scene 5; see line 655.

The whip is implied by the drama's ancient catalogue title, *Aias the Whip-Bearer*; librarians often chose subtitles which reflected an event in the first scene, so readers could check which Aias drama they had taken off the shelf without having to unfurl too much of a book-roll. Taplin (1978, 85) suggests that the sword, which Aias had taken out to kill the cattle (286), would be more appropriate; but (1) when Athena calls him out, Aias is torturing the animals with his whip (62ff. +240ff. +300); (2) the whip is a valuable prop for 110; and (3) bringing out Hektor's sword now blunts its dramatic impact at 645, when it becomes the focus of the action. Cf. Seale 1982, 177 n.10.

[5] This owes much to medieval Christian images of epiphany. From Homer onwards Greek gods normally appeared to mortals at ground level, whether disguised as human beings or presenting the full power of their immortal form. The *mechane* is the device of the last third of the fifth century, a time of increasing self-consciousness and scepticism when not all of the audience believed in the intervention of the Olympian gods in human affairs.

[6] E.g. Jebb 1907, 13, Seale 1982, 144–5, 176. *Contra* Pickard-Cambridge 1946, 48 and Ley 1988, 88–9. Cf. also Ewans 1995, 208 n. 23 against placing Apollo and Athena on the *skene* roof for the trial scene and Finale in *Eumenides*. The authors of this series do not believe that the *skene* roof was used in the fifth century as a 'theologeion'. This technical term dates from the Roman era, and all the relevant scenes in Euripides and Aristophanes would be much more effective using the *mechane* (pace Wiles 1997, 81).

[7] E.g. in Aischylos' *Agamemnon*, Aristophanes' *Wasps* and Euripides' *Orestes*.

There are also practical problems for Athena, when she summons Aias out from the building – leaning over the edge? – and for Aias, trying to respond to her when she comes out. And her final words are of key importance; the amount of power that would be gained by height above the back of the playing space could not compensate for the failure to place her where a character needs to be for such a speech; at the centre of the *orchêstra*.

By contrast, all the power of Scene 1 is liberated if Athena joins Odysseus on the level. Before a word is spoken, the first event in the drama is Odysseus' prowling, hunched-over search as he follows Aias' tracks; to 'milk' this effectively, he should make the long entry from the R *parodos*, then circle the perimeter almost to EFC before moving in towards the doors.[8] Athena interrupts him just before he reaches the tent.

Athena is at first invisible to Odysseus (15–16); but it is clear from the text that he can see her at the latest by 51ff. (and Aias sees her at once when he enters). I suspect that an Athenian audience would have had no problem with the convention that a human character cannot see a goddess until she wishes it. In our production, Odysseus always faced just to one side or other of Athena's position, never quite hearing the voice enough to place her properly.[9] Meanwhile Athena moves slowly but firmly towards the prominent position (BC) which she needs from 9ff., so her invisible but 'known' presence can become the anchor-point round which Odysseus frames his sinuous and excited narrative, searching her out, hoping that she may appear to him.

The first half of the scene explores the dynamics of the whole *orchêstra*; the *skene* door is forgotten as Odysseus circles round the goddess whom he cannot see, trying to persuade her of what he knows. He interacts more and more closely with her during the *stichomythia* – though still facing his mask always not quite towards her, to maintain her 'invisibility'. Athena takes up a position at or just behind C, so Odysseus will retreat towards the front perimeter in his terror, when

[8] Taplin 1978, 40. For an even more elaborate opening 'dumb-show' cf. the opening of *OKing* (with McCart's Notes, p. 269).

[9] A modern director might well fear that audiences will not respond to the convention of divine invisibility as fast as is necessary; our costume designer therefore cloaked Athena from head to foot in a shroud symbolic of the sky. She removed this suddenly at 51, to reveal her long white dress and golden sandals, hair and headband – making Odysseus cower on the ground, shielding his eyes from the fierceness of her appearance and gaze.

she reveals herself at 51.[10] Athena now commands the whole circle, and exhibits her power at once, advancing to C, and then circling around Odysseus, using striking gestures to illustrate the events of her narrative.

The physical dynamics of the scene change abruptly at 66, when the focus is deliberately brought back to the *skene* doors.[11] Athena advances confidently towards the *skene*, and calls out loud to Aias from C (perhaps raising and/or extending her hands to give the implicit ritual quality to her command). By having Aias disregard her first command, Sophokles builds suspense and terror before his entry; Odysseus retreats towards the front perimeter during the *stichomythia*, and Athena only manages to halt him with the reassurances of 85ff., after which she turns back towards the *skene* to resume her ritual address.

Aias pushes aside the opening of the tent and rushes out suddenly (see 303ff.). His first appearance demands a complex interpretation: the character's madness must be conveyed – in our production, by a manic laughter, a twisted stooping posture, and an almost childish glee in line 100; but under that must lie traces of his power and nobility, to show in one theatrical image the contrast between past and present, the 'mutability' that is the drama's underlying picture of human existence.

The subscene must bring out the contrast between Aias' delusion that the goddess is on his side, and the cruelty with which she plays with him.[12] And with Odysseus as well; she deliberately mentions him to Aias, and the actor playing Odysseus will cower back, as he faces Aias with only the protection of delusion between him and his savage enemy, half-naked, covered in blood, and brandishing his whip. In our production, Aias cracked the whip with manic energy at 110, pointed the stock threateningly at Athena at 112, and began to leave at the end of 113, restrained only momentarily by Athena's final words.

Properly enacted, this subscene has a shattering effect, on the audience as well as on Odysseus. Completely changing her tone after she has sent Aias indoors, Athena now forces Odysseus to recognize

[10] This is the moment when the goddess reveals for the first time the full force of her power. The only other feasible point for him first to see her is 36, which we found in rehearsal to be less effective.

[11] There has been no reference to the tent from 12 to 63.

[12] In our production this was established at once, by the irony with which Athena matched his exuberant tone at 'Well said.' She used this ironic tone again at 111.

the transitory nature of human existence. Aias was a model of heroic *arete* (119–20); and in one moment he has been destroyed – for reasons that are not yet known.

Aias' intense humiliation elicits an extraordinary response from Odysseus. In Greek ethics before Sokrates, it was normal and right to enjoy to the full an enemy's downfall;[13] instead, Odysseus here feels pity for Aias. The situation is so striking that it makes his reappearance in the Finale deeply expected, as well as completely surprising.

Athena concludes the scene; she dominates the *orchêstra* in her closing speech – beginning at C with arms outstretched, and then perhaps gliding backwards to BC for the closing peroration at 131ff. to the audience. No other surviving tragedy spells out so totally in its opening scene the tragic nature of human existence; and Athena's admonition against pride deliberately includes two fundamental components of *arete*: wealth and military ability (130). Even the qualities that Greeks most valued are worthless, in the absence of 'prudence' – *sophrosyne*.[14]

Choros 1

As the goddess leaves, followed at a distance by the humbled Odysseus, the *choros* is seen marching down the L *parodos* towards the *orchêstra*. Since this drama is concerned with a warrior's *arete*, away from his *polis* and not bound up with its fate, Sophokles chooses to make the *choros* represent his dependants.

Sophokles brings on a *choros* character with partial knowledge of the situation, not familiar with all that the audience knows from Scene 1, but seeking enlightenment.[15] This enables him to create a surprise at the end of Choros 1; the standard next move in this opening is for the principal character, whom the *choros* have called for in their lyrics, to emerge from the *skene* and deliver a substantial speech, which answers

[13] Adkins 1960, 154ff. Sophokles has been careful to remind us of this: 79. There is a partial precedent in Homer, when Odysseus restrains Eurykleia from the customary cry of victory after the slaughter of the suitors (Homer, *Odyssey* 22.407ff.), on the similar grounds that what has happened is the work of gods, not men. Odysseus' compassion for his fallen enemy is unparalleled for a male character in fifth-century literature and drama; but cf. Deianeira's response to Iole at *YWT* 463–5; NB also the tension that develops in *Phil*, because of Neoptolemos' growing compassion for the wounded hero.

[14] Cf. Winnington-Ingram 1980, 55–6.

[15] Cf. e.g. Aischylos, *Agamemnon*, Sophokles *Ant*.

their questions and moves the action forward.[16] Instead, a character appears who is totally contrasted with Aias in gender, ethnicity and size.

Choros 1 opens with an extended passage in *anapaests*, the marching beat characteristically used for the entry of the *choros*. In this sequence (to 171) the Sailors gradually explore and possess the whole *orchêstra*, moving from an expression of their dependence to a fear of the rumours they have heard, which leads naturally to a call for Aias to appear (164ff.).

He stays inside (like Klytaimestra after Aischylos, *Agamemnon* 83–104); so after a short pause the Sailors turn away again from the *skene*, and reflect on the situation in full lyrics (naturally therefore with more elaborate and expressive choreography). Now they accept that Aias might have done what the *daimon* Rumour says; and they speculate which god might have made him act crazily. They are of course right; their leader could not have done something so self-destructive without the intervention of a god. The audience, unlike the Sailors, knows which god, but Sophokles has deliberately withheld Athena's motives, and will not reveal them even to the audience until Scene 4.

At the end of A2, these reflections lead the Sailors back to a call for Aias to come out, which they elaborate in an *epode*, A3. But this comes to a sudden stop (the dancers should freeze on or after line 200). Will Aias answer their call?

Scene 2

Tekmessa and the Sailors (201–347) The suspense is broken with a surprise: a new and totally unexpected character enters, to begin what will become the second largest speaking part in the drama. By creating Tekmessa, Sophokles heightens Aias' isolation. Like him, the Sailors are Athenian and male, and as a *choros* cannot, by convention, deliver long speeches; Tekmessa is an individual, Aias' inferior in Athenian society; but she has borne his son and therefore has claims on him. She engages the audience's sympathy, and her power will completely alter the balance of the drama after Aias reappears, when she opposes his determination to die.

At this moment, Aias cannot move (206) – but Tekmessa can move and sing; and she does both, giving full lyric and dance exposition to

[16] Cf. e.g. Aischylos, *Agamemon*, Euripides, *Medeia*.

his downfall and her suffering. As a woman and a barbarian, she could express her grief without loss of dignity, where a Greek male could not;[17] and Sophokles exploits this by bestowing on her both total empathy with Aias,[18] and great insight into the situation. (This is shown at once with her prophetic choice of words at 217, 'he's been destroyed', and her realization at 244 that a *daimon* must have maddened him.)

Tekmessa begins in lyric agitation followed by a spoken, more reflective account of the same events and emotions – a sequence that was normally reserved for heroines who are about to die.[19] Tekmessa is dancing and singing Aias' actions and emotions, so Sophokles' dramatic technique here foreshadows *his* death.

The text of Tekmessa's lyrics is emotionally evocative, and it requires of the actress a volatile, dynamic and highly emotional sequence of choreography. After a relatively calm opening,[20] the Sailors react to Tekmessa's revelations with panic and despair. She is in total control of their mood, and they only venture an optimistic thought when she ends her dance by telling them Aias is sane again (and ominously calm).

The narrative expands Tekmessa's power. She presents her own concern for Aias, ruefully but feistily acknowledges the 'old, familiar song' (292) of male arrogance, and gives the audience an invaluable picture from inside the tent, and from a human perspective, of the divinely controlled events that we saw in Scene 1. Once again, but now in the more restrained media of speech and movement, Tekmessa must range over the playing space from 294, changing mood and tone widely as she enacts with her body the sequence of Aias' actions down to 310, where she should be seated on the ground, clenching her hair to embody his agony. Only then does the movement return to displaying her own feelings, as she shocks the Sailors, and the audience, with Aias' threat to torture her.[21]

[17] The shock is therefore all the greater when Aias does just this, later in the scene.

[18] Even though she was captured and given to Aias by force (212), she has long returned his love; she deliberately reminds him of this by the phrasing of 491.

[19] The closest parallels are Aischylos' Kassandra in *Agamemnon* Scene 6, and Antigone in *Ant* Scene 5.

[20] The original metre to 220 was *anapaests*, not full lyric.

[21] At Athens, slaves could be interrogated under torture. But Sophokles has already let us know that Aias regards Tekmessa more as his wife than his slave,

The last words of the speech prepare for Sophokles' next *coup de théâtre*. Tekmessa asks the Sailors to go inside the *skene*. Since actual entry by the *choros* character was rare in tragedy,[22] the Athenian audience would have expected something else to happen immediately. It does. Aias cries out;[23] and cries from inside the *skene* invariably led in tragedy to the entry either of the grieving character or (if the sounds are death-cries) of the murderer. Sophokles has deliberately stressed Aias' immobility (most recently at 323–4), to prepare for the fantastic surprise after 347; the *ekkyklêma* emerges, carrying Aias surrounded by dead sheep, sheepdogs and cattle (cf. 297).[24]

Aias and his *philoi*   Aias has progressively led us towards this horror – from the maddened Aias with his whip, through Tekmessa's dance and her vivid enacted narrative to this point where we see Aias himself, the fallen hero, immobile and surrounded by a 'wave of blood' (351).

Some scholars have denied that Sophokles used the *ekkyklêma* here;[25] but it was the only way in which tableaux could be exhibited from the darkness inside the *skene*, and the people involved could communicate with the characters in the open space represented by the *orchêstra*. And the formula of requests to 'open' and at the end 'close up' the *skene* doors is echoed in a comic scene where the *ekkyklêma* was certainly employed.[26] In our production, Aias' appearance made a powerful and effective impact on modern audiences that were totally unprepared for this, perhaps the most remote convention of a theatrical style 2,400 years old.

and this ruthlessness is designed to show how extreme his responses were when he regained his sanity.

[22] They do actually enter the *skene* at Euripides *Helen* 330ff., and cf. the fragments of his *Phaethon*, 245ff. A threatened entry is forestalled, as here, by an intervention on the *ekkyklêma* at Aischylos, *Agamemnon* 1350ff.

[23] A 'doglike yelping', according to one ancient commentator.

[24] This is the only known instance in which the *ekkyklêma* carries dead animals, as opposed to extras in the masks and costumes of murdered human beings. I have little doubt that Sophokles, who had no materials from which realistic replicas could be made, used recently slaughtered animals for the original tableau. (It only had to be exhibited once, and they could have been skinned and eaten later that day in the post-performance celebrations.) In our modern production, with ten performances spread over two weeks, we used taxidermists' forms for the sheep and bull heads, fresh fleeces moulded over polystyrene for the sheep bodies, and a stuffed Border Collie.

[25] Pickard-Cambridge 1946, 109–10, Stanford 1962, 107. *Contra* Seale 1980, 178.

[26] Aristophanes, *Acharnians* 411 and 479.

Although a tableau on the *ekkyklêma* supposedly represents people and bodies which are when it comes out inside the *skene* building, once the *ekkyklêma* has emerged the scene proceeds as if they were outside – a reasonable enough convention, given that in theatrical reality the actor and props *are* now outside.[27] Aias can get off the platform and interact with the Sailors on the assumption that he is outside the tent; indeed, he must do so, because his part is in lyrics from the outset; so he must soon abandon his immobility, and dance. However, once he gets back on the platform, just before the end of the scene, it is as if he were inside the *skene* again, and so can order Tekmessa to 'close up' the tent (593); stagehands must roll the *ekkyklêma* in during 594–5.

Like Tekmessa, Aias begins in lyrics. The shock for his Sailors of seeing their literally fallen hero is followed by the even more appalling shock that this noble man now bewails his fate, and immediately demands death (361). The male has been 'made female' (his own words later, 652), and once again (cf. 292–4), Sophokles plays ironically with his society's assumption of Greek male superiority; fifteen freeborn Athenian citizens are now facing Aias, but only his barbarian female slave stands up to him (371).

Aias' lyrics gradually expand, ignoring the muted, spoken responses in which Tekmessa and the Sailors attempt to restrain him, until in the C stanzas he launches into an extended monody, 'sung as Aias gains confidence and rises from his self-pitying state'.[28] In our production, he rose from the tableau at 394 and began to dance, then came to rest bowed to the earth, suiting the action to the words, at 426–7.[29] After that he comes forward, and delivers an extended, spoken meditation on his name and on his fate;[30] this becomes increasingly powerful as he begins to accept with his mind the situation that he has earlier made emotionally real through outcries and dance. The speech alternates at first between address to the individual Sailors and to his surroundings; then finally, in what is almost an interior monologue (in view of its

[27] Cf. Aischylos, *Agamemnon* Scene 7, with Notes in Ewans 1995, 154.
[28] Scott 1996, 76.
[29] *Contra* Seale 1982, 154–5.
[30] Names had great significance for the Greeks; cf. e.g. Introduction, p. xlvi on Antigone, p. lx on Deianeira, and Teiresias' comment in Euripides' *Bakchai* (367–8) on Pentheus' name, which sounds all too like the Greek word for grief. Aias plays at 430 on the similarity between his own name and the ritual cry of grief, 'aiai'. Since his name has invariably been Latinized to 'Ajax' and then mispronounced with a hard j, the point has for centuries been lost in translation.

importance, best delivered from the centre) 473–6, Aias reasons against living any longer. He is resolved to die (479–80), and turns to go inside.

Aias has totally ignored Tekmessa.[31] But while one of the Sailors briefly detains him, she comes forward decisively, confronts him before he is able to leave, and turns what he intended as a final monologue into the first half of an *agon*. It must have been a startling disruption of Athenian tragic convention; and Sophokles uses the focus which this gains for Tekmessa to deliver the only presentation to Aias of the drama's central theme of mutability. By the time this powerful appeal is finished, Tekmessa has created an alternative vision of male *arete*, opposing Aias' final statement at 473–80; for her, to abandon those who have cared for you, who depend on you, and have given to you is to forfeit your nobility.[32]

Though Tekmessa moves around Aias as she speaks, plangently trying to make an emotional impact on him, he must show his indifference almost throughout. This can be done simply by having him face away from her. And again Scene 2 moves on, in a virtually unprepared direction.[33]

Eurysakes (545–595) Aias now shows the volatility that has been impressed on us as a facet of his character since Tekmessa's narrative (mutability again): he is first harsh, then tender as he appreciates how Tekmessa has saved his son from possible death at his hands[34] – and almost at once the boy is before us, played by a mute child extra whom Tekmessa lifts into Aias' bloodstained arms. This is Sophokles' third *coup de théâtre* – one of the most powerful uses of children for emotional appeal in surviving Greek tragedy.[35]

[31] To help make this important aspect of the stage picture plausible, we let her sink in grief at the left front corner of the *ekkyklēma* after 392.

[32] Goldhill (1997, 130) notes the deliberate echo here of Homer, *Iliad* 6.454ff. It establishes Tekmessa firmly as being more Aias' wife than his mistress (cf. Winnington-Ingram 1980, 30 n. 57 and 32, n. 63); it also subconsciously prepared the Greek audience for the even more striking evocation of Hektor and Andromache when Eurysakes appears.

[33] 510–14 provide some partial anticipation.

[34] These moments echo the story, dramatized in Euripides' *Herakles*, that Herakles actually killed his sons (and wife), during a madness inflicted by Hera.

Eurysakes must be brought in from the left, not out of the *skene*; Ley 1988, 90.

[35] Cf. also e.g. O*King* (Finale); Euripides *Andromache, Trojan Women, Herakles*; and the exceptional use of speaking children in *Medeia*. Sophokles

Aias' long speech does not play well if he continues to hold Eurysakes, since it includes two addresses to his son, which themselves
demand distance from him, as well as a middle section (564ff.) directed
to the Sailors. We discovered that the most effective staging was for
Aias to place Eurysakes on the front of the *ekkyklêma* before 550,
among the slaughtered animals – and then move away to create some
space before embarking on the address to him (from BC).[36]

It has already been established that Tekmessa has far more insight
and foresight than the Sailors. Accordingly she should turn away in
deep distress (cf. 579–80), when 560ff. obviously – for her and for the
audience – present Aias' last will and testament. This distress subsequently motivates an essential move, which is signalled implicitly in the
text. Since the order to 'Close up!' (581) is effectively a repeat of 579,
and is itself repeated again at 593, Tekmessa must disobey Aias after
579. Instead of taking the child inside as ordered, she snatches Eurysakes from the *ekkyklêma*, and pulls him away before Aias moves back
towards it.

Aias clearly steps back on to the *ekkyklêma* before or during 585,
and the rest of the scene is a violent *crescendo*, in which the dialogue
fragments into *antilabe*. Aias stands on the *ekkyklêma*, leaning down
to browbeat a terrified Tekmessa, who pleads with him – perhaps
kneeling towards the final climax – from near one of its front corners
(Eurysakes is beside her, on the side nearer the audience). Then
suddenly the scene dissolves, as unseen stage-hands pull the *ekkyklêma*
into the *skene*, and Tekmessa – at last obeying Aias' repeated orders –
follows with Eurysakes, and closes the doors behind her.[37]

deliberately echoes for contrast the famous episode in Homer, *Iliad* 6. 466ff.
where Andromache lifts Hektor's child Astyanax up to him; Astyanax was
afraid, and cringed when he saw his father's plumed helmet (cf. Burian 1997,
194).

[36] Eurysakes is named ('big-shield') after Aias' legendary, gigantic shield (cf.
Homer, *Iliad* 7.219–223). But it is neither necessary nor desirable to introduce
that shield as a prop in this scene. So too Taplin 1978, 64.

Eurysakes is clearly old enough for Aias to assume he can understand the
speech. (In our production he responded to it, standing up bravely and smartly
during the sections that Aias addressed to him.) Presuming that Tekmessa's
native town was sacked early in the Trojan War, he is between six and eight
years old.

[37] A totally different staging for this scene is imagined by Seale 1980, 157–8.

Choros 2

In our production, the Sailors were so agitated by the argument that they rushed towards the doors – only to have them closed in their faces, after which they relapsed into the nostalgic opening of Choros 2. The power of these four stanzas lies in their simplicity, the ever-greater contrasts in the emotional pictures painted inside each stanza, and the total logic of the Sailors' conclusion: 'He's better dead' (633). Sophokles deliberately makes them express this now, for contrast with the opening of Scene 3.

Scene 3

This great speech has been the subject of much debate. Many scholars have treated Aias as if he were a real human being, and attempted to analyse in depth what state of mind might have led him to speak these words at this time.[38] Yet 'Aias' is no more (though also no less) than a theatrical character; Sophokles' interest, here as always, is in situation, in character-in-action. Aias clearly seeks to deceive the Sailors into letting him leave the tent with the sword.[39] He could not deceive the original audience, since an Athenian would have had to be both unintelligent in his or her response, and ignorant of one of the city's best-known legends, to believe that Aias means what he appears to say; nor Tekmessa, since Aias sends her indoors before speaking the highly ironic lines 690ff.; but we know that the Sailors certainly are deceived, since they launch at once, when he has gone, into a song of rejoicing.

So Aias reappears, still bloodstained (655) and carrying a new prop, Hektor's sword, which the actor will use at once, to illustrate 650–1. He speaks truth: at the outset he recognizes at last the cycle of mutability, which Athena, Odysseus and Tekmessa have all shown to be the way of Sophokles' world, and later he clothes it in powerful imagery (669ff.); but his claim that he has applied this insight to

[38] Cf. e.g. Reinhardt 1979, 23ff., Cohen 1978, 26, Winnington-Ingram 1980, 46ff. (including further bibliography at n. 107; also at Segal 1981, 433). It is improper to conjecture the thought-processes that Aias went through while inside the tent, before he re-emerged for this scene. By contrast Sophokles' reasons for having him re-emerge, and leave the camp with the sword, are fairly obvious; most of the rest of what he wants to show in this drama could not be dramatized if Aias committed suicide inside his tent. Sensible discussion in Taplin 1978, 128–31.

[39] Cf. e.g. Segal 1981, 113–14.

himself by changing his resolve to die is pure deception. He will indeed yield to mutability – but in quite another way: by changing from a mighty hero to a lifeless shade.[40] Sophokles gives the audience several indications of this. First, the surprise that Aias suddenly, after his total obduracy during and after Tekmessa's impassioned plea, uses the sword of war which is in his hand as his metaphor, when he claims to have been softened by her; then the irony of the proverb about the gifts of enemies, the strange reversal of yielding (normally to human beings) and reverence (normally for gods) in 666;[41] and finally the even stranger sequence (676ff.) in which he abandons the fundamental basis of *arete* – the duty to help your *philoi* and harm your enemies.

In performance the scene alternates between philosophical thoughts, for which Aias must stand still (e.g. 646–9, 664ff.), and sudden gusts of animation, for which movement – circling, to match the recurring idea of mutability – is needed (e.g. 650ff., 669ff.). In our production Aias stuck the sword decisively in the ground, suiting the action to the words at 659. This enabled him to play 666ff. unarmed, and therefore more vulnerable. He pulled it out and wielded it again at 678, when he returned to the centre to begin the closing portion of the speech.

The Sailors clearly retreat to the front perimeter to listen, when Aias – followed with oriental submissiveness by Tekmessa – appears at the end of Choros 2. For the last address, we moved them in a little towards Aias, during Tekmessa's exit move.[42] Then Aias pulls back, disengaging from them on 690, before turning to exit decisively at the end of the speech.

Choros 3

The Sailors in their naïve optimism sing a premature celebration of joy, which will be totally undermined in the next scene. It would be dangerous to conclude that such almost sick irony at his characters' expense was a special feature of Sophokles' style, since only seven out

---

[40] 'So Ajax's resolve to die is still firm, but out of pity he speaks of that coming death elliptically and in words of comfort, in one way a surface comfort which will "deceive" his [onstage] listeners gently until he has made his necessary death, but which will later bring a genuine consolation when the true meaning of his words are [sic] fully understood.' March 1991–3, 20. Cf. Moore 1977, esp. 56–7 and 59; Sicherl 1977, 88–9.

[41] Winnington-Ingram 1980, 49.

[42] This must begin at 684, because she is too intelligent to be allowed to hear 685ff. *Contra* Stanford 1963, 50.

of over ninety of his dramas survive; but he uses it in all four dramas collected in this volume.[43] Like the other examples, this ode is short; in performance it must be attacked with gusto, fast and vigorous.

Scene 4

The so-called 'messenger-speech' was frequently employed to convey in narrative events that could not realistically be represented on the Greek stage. In many tragedies the speech comes late in the action, and events are narrated which generate the final scene. The narrative prepares the way for the entry or re-entry of a principal character, who is then seen trying to come to terms with the catastrophe.[44] This character often brings a property – e.g. Haimon's body, or Pentheus' head in Euripides' *Bakchai* – or confirms in some other visually striking way (e.g. Oidipous' blindness) that the recently narrated disaster has happened, and has irrevocable consequences.

Here Sophokles uses extended narration for a different purpose.[45] By having a messenger bring Kalchas' prophecy to Aias' *philoi*, Sophokles virtually precludes himself from using narrative again later to convey the fact of Aias' suicide (as Aischylos had done in his lost drama *Phrygians*); he deliberately puzzled or challenged his audience, in preparation for the shock of the change of scene and Aias' suicide in their sight.

The Soldier's news injects Kalchas' knowledge into the middle of the plot, and like the 'deception-speech' in Scene 3 this is designed to provoke different reactions. Tekmessa and the Sailors try to fight even against what seems almost unavoidable;[46] but for the audience, the fact that Aias has gone out while Athena is still angry with him confirms the implications of that speech, that nothing can now prevent his death.[47]

[43] Cf. *Ant* Choros 6, *OKing* Choros 4, and *YWT* Choros 4.

[44] So e.g. in *Ant* (Scene 7) and *OKing* (Finale); Euripides, *Bakchai*. Cf. Introduction pp. xxxi–ii.

[45] Cf. *YWT* Scene 5.

[46] Greek tragedy depends on a world view in which people do not passively resign themselves to an overwhelming 'fate', but fight back against the prospect even of prophesied disaster. Cf. Introduction pp. lxix–lxx.

[47] It also adds a new dimension to their view of Athena. At the start of the drama, it seemed that Aias' madness and humiliation were sufficient punishment. Now we learn how long ago he first defied her, how totally he rejected her – and that she will only be satisfied by his death. Cf. how Aischylos'

Like the narratives in other surviving dramas, the Soldier's part draws heavily on an actor's resources – his ability to narrate, evoke a situation through enactment, and impersonate. He has at once to create an animated picture of the angry Greeks surrounding Teukros, leading back down to the gradual calming of the dispute by the Elders at the end of his opening speech (731-2).

The long speech at 748ff. is almost entirely imagined through the words of Kalchas. He has to be re-created first in action, then in indirect speech (752ff.), and finally, most vividly, in the extended direct speech relayed from 757. The Soldier must adopt an imposing delivery for 757–761 to characterize the prophet, because after that Kalchas' quoted direct speech does not have any distinctively prophetic elements until the end. The narrator must then achieve a relatively neutral tone at 761, in preparation for the need to characterize first Telamon, and then Aias' foolish remarks.[48]

The Sailors retreat to the opposite perimeter, EFL-EFC-EBR, when the Soldier runs in. He begins the narrative by a direct, close response to the speaker of 747, and should perhaps interact with other individuals by circling past them until 757ff., where the solemnity and importance of Kalchas' insight demand the use of the centre. Then he might again pick out individuals to whom to deliver portions of the story after 762, where the tone changes and the pace quickens. (Aias' own two reported comments play best if focused past the Sailors to the audience.)

The narrative leaves the Sailors speechless. After a short pause, one of them (BR) makes an instant decision, and steps back towards the *skene* to call Tekmessa out.

She enters quite altered in appearance – certainly wrapped in a long cloak, since she uses this later to shroud Aias' body; perhaps also with her hair unbound, to match the implication of the text that she comes out resentfully, dragged against her will from a deep sleep which has provided release from horror. She is alone – again isolated by her gender, and her special relationship to Aias; and the long cloak, covering her exotic barbarian costume, makes her look for the moment

---

Kassandra at first, in Troy, thought that Apollo's revenge against her was only that no one would believe her prophecies, and comes to realize in *Agamemnon* Scene 6 that he has brought her to Argos to be punished with death. Aias suspected the full truth as soon as he regained sanity (402ff.).

[48] 1010ff. should be used as guidance in creating Telamon's *persona*. The Soldier then needs to impersonate the younger, brasher Aias by reference to the voice and gestures developed by the actor playing the title role.

like any Greek woman in mourning – which is what she will soon become.

In contrast to the almost drugged tone of 788–9, she suddenly springs into action, rushing towards the Soldier on 791, presssing towards him again on 797 and 800, then rounding on the Sailors as soon as she understands the message. She must be central enough for 803 to be able to be addressed to the whole *choros*; then she wheels around, facing part of the group before a climactic moment of intro-spection 807–8 – played, of course, in Greek tragedy not inwardly but out, over the Sailors' heads to the audience. Then she is off; a sudden apostrophe from (BR) to her son inside the *skene*,[49] and in two lines she has left, running down the R *parodos*.

All the Sailors follow her.[50] In accordance with the convention of Athenian tragedy, the R *parodos* has until now signified the direction away from the tent towards the Trojan plain or the seashore, while the L *parodos* has indicated the direction towards the Greek camp. Aias exited right, so Tekmessa and all the Sailors must follow him, and split up after leaving into two subgroups, which then go different ways down the shore as Tekmessa has commanded.

Tekmessa wants a third group of Sailors to go and find Teukros. However, the whole *choros* almost certainly reassembles at once in Scene 5; so it is better for this instruction to be disregarded (or forgotten, as they split into groups during their exit R) rather than sending some of them offstage L, only to re-enter when Teukros comes. Then the Soldier, suddenly abandoned in their panic, can himself turn and go off left, towards the camp, to find Teukros.

Scene 5

From tent to seashore Sophokles now changes the location, and achieves another great *coup de théâtre* – an extended actor monologue

[49] *Pace* Seale 1982, 162. It is impractical, as well as over-literal, to bring Eurysakes on in this scene; she has servants to look after her child, she needs to leave at once, she cannot run with him, and he is clearly not with her when she discovers the body. The two lines referring to him (809, 944) should be played as apostrophes – like 340, where Eurysakes is certainly not present.

[50] McCart 1999, against e.g. Seale 1982, 162 and many translators. While just under/over half of the Sailors wait out of sight at the far end of the R *parodos*, Tekmessa and the rest of the Sailors must go round out of sight of the audience, and prepare to re-enter L in Scene 5.

in the centre of the drama,[51] leading to a climax of a kind that the tragedians normally avoided: an act of violence committed in (almost) full view of the audience. Aias' body then becomes the metaphorical focus for the rest of the drama.[52]

It should therefore be literally central in the *orchêstra* as well.[53] Most scholars believe that after the Sailors' exit, some bushes were pushed out from the *skene* on the *ekkyklêma*, and Aias committed suicide concealed behind these bushes;[54] but using the *ekkyklêma* here is implausible. In all the instances, both in tragedy and comedy, where the *ekkyklêma* was certainly or probably used, it had the same function – to roll out into the spectators' view a preset tableau which represents events that have taken place inside the *skene*. There is no known instance of its being used non-representationally, simply to deliver heavy props into the rearmost portion of the *orchêstra*.[55]

[51] Solo speeches after the first scene were rare, because they could only happen if the *choros* has temporarily left the *orchêstra*. Cf. Aischylos, *Eumenides* 235ff. (Orestes), and Euripides *Helene* 386ff. (Menelaos).

[52] Seale 1982, 167; Taplin 1978, 42.

[53] Golder 1992, 350–51: 'Sophocles puts not only the suicide, but the corpse itself centre stage.'

[54] E.g. Dale 1969, 120–21; Reinhardt 1979, 238–9, and – despite the quote in n. 53! – Golder 1992, 354–5 (cf. 1990, 24, 27, 33); 'the grave tableau – Ajax beside his upright sword – is now rolled out on the *ekkyklêma*' (no movement for Aias in the entire monologue?!). Also Arnott 1962, 132–7, and even Ley 1988, 92 and McCart 1999.

The main motive of these scholars has been to enable the actor who has played Aias to be replaced by a dummy or a mute extra; he would then be free to play one of the three speaking parts in the Finale. I have seen a production that did replace the actor with a dummy, and so destroyed all emotional involvement with the rest of the drama. I therefore prefer to believe that Sophokles obtained special permission to exceed the normal practice (not a rule – see above, p. 175) of using only three speaking actors. Aischylos had almost certainly done this for Pylades in *Libation Bearers*; Ewans 1995, 184–5.

Seale has an ingenious variant (1978, 166; cf. Stanford 1963, 174 and Wiles 1997, 164): he imagines a dummy on the *ekkyklêma* which is not pushed out to replace the live actor until after the suicide scene. It is absurd to suppose that such a substitution could/would not have been noticed in the Athenian theatre; and very doubtful whether it could have been tolerated, given that the corpse lies in full view, uncovered, from 865 to 913 and from 1002 to the end.

Macintosh 1994, 131 tries to save the situation; she would have an attendant bring the body out from the *skene*, covered by Tekmessa's rhetoric at 920, 'to the forefront of the stage [*sic*] to enable it to act as the focal point during the second part of the play'. At least she sees that Aias' corpse can't just lie on the *ekkyklêma* at the back of the performing space.

[55] *Pace* Dale 1969, 269–70, citing Aischylos, *Eumenides* (the image of

Aias' death does not take place inside the *skene*, but in the location now represented by the *orchêstra*, which is a lonely part of the seashore. Therefore his place of death could not be represented by the *ekkyklêma*; and to use it for this purpose would have been particularly confusing in *Aias*, since Sophokles has already used the *ekkyklêma* normally in Scene 2. Rolling it out again would have implied to the original audience that the *skene* is still in use, and represents a building; this would have made the rest of the drama impossible to understand.

Since the body now becomes central to the drama, it must lie at C, so other characters can stand behind or parallel to it while talking about it and tending it in the remainer of this drama. The focus now needs to be pulled forward from the *skene*, to communicate to the audience that the building will no longer be used.[56] This was the first role of the bushes, which are now set in the *orchêstra*, in a semicircle around the front of the centre point. (Their second role will be partially to conceal the body from the Sailors.)[57]

Athena), *Fishermen* (Danaë in the chest), and [Aischylos] *Prometheus Bound* (Prometheus' rock). For alternative stagings of all these scenes, which do not misuse the *ekkyklêma*, see Ewans 1995, 201, 1996, 222–3, and *ibid.* lviii–lix. In Aristophanes, *Peace* the *ekkyklêma* is used representationally, to portray the inside of the hole where Peace is buried.

[56] In both the other surviving dramas with scene-changes (Aeschylus' *Libation Bearers* and *Eumenides*), a prop is placed at C to pull the focus forward, during the part of the drama where the original audience was to imagine that there is no building where the *skene* stands. (Ewans 1995, 162–3, 175, 201). We felt that a modern audience would not automatically understand this ancient convention; so in our production of *Aias* stagehands rapidly demolished the tent between the Sailors' exit and Aias' re-entry.

Ley 1989 presents a very strong case (widely underestimated, and ignored e.g. by Wiles 1997, 161–2) for believing that *skenographia* – painted panels attached to the *skene*, and representing a small range of standard types of location – was introduced by Agatharchos (cf. Vitruvius *de Architectura* 158.20–8) towards the end of Aischylos' lifetime. The striking or placing of properties in the centre of the *orchêstra* to mark scene changes would then also have been accompanied by changes in these representative panels – in *Ai* from images of a tent to those of open (seaside) space.

[57] See 892. They were *not* needed to conceal the sword and Aias' body from the audience; this would have been impossible, as well as undesirable, given the steep rake of the *theatron* (so rightly Stanford 1963, 166). The suicide must have been visible for the actor Timotheos to have achieved a reputation for the realistic way in which he 'died' as Aias, giving the impression to the spectators that he had impaled himself on the sword (scholiast on 864); so rightly Seale 1982, 179. And Tekmessa *must* be visible to the audience – though not to one of the Sailors – at 891ff. (*pace* e.g. Moore 1957, 40).

The suicide of Aias   Aias' final monologue became a celebrated virtuoso piece.[58] It requires a change in his appearance. Aias has at last
cleansed both himself and the sword from the *miasma* of the animals'
blood, and he may even have changed from the near-nakednesss of his
night sortie to full ceremonial uniform. We see him in his final scene at
his best, an image of the noble warrior he once was to remind us of his
greatness; but also, uniquely, we see him alone; he has escaped from
the care of his *philoi* – and also from the obligations that he has to
them.[59] Alone, he can reach the peace that he sought in Scene 3.

Aias still carries the sword; he now plants it carefully in the soil, to
be the focal point for the beginning and end of the speech. Only after
this silent action does he stand back from the sword, look at it, and
then address the audience (816). He begins and ends near the sword,
which is his co-conspirator (823); but the sequence of prayers demands
a more expansive movement, ranging round the circle, with different
points of rest for the start of each of the separate invocations to Zeus,
Hermes, the Furies and the Sun-god.[60] He finally moves back to the
sword on 852.

The remaining lines need to be delivered in front of the point of the
sword, but still at a little distance from it (i.e. at L), to allow Aias to
turn in different directions for the invocations to the sunlight, to
Salamis and Athens, and to the plain of Troy (represented by the
orchêstra), without being crowded by proximity to the sword. He only
turns back to face the sword directly for the last line, after which he
immediately moves towards it and impales himself.[61]

---

[58] Later actors interpolated extra lines to prolong the speech in performance.
Lines 839–42 and 854–8 are omitted from this edition; they are obviously not
by Sophokles (cf. Lloyd-Jones and Wilson 1990 *ad loc.*).

[59] In our production he entered L. The conventions of the first part of *Ai* (L =
to rest of camp, R = to plain of Troy) have obviously ceased at the scene change,
and after some experiment we found that Scene 5 and the Finale only work in
performance if L still leads back 'home' – i.e., now, directly to Aias' tent, while
R leads out to the (mostly hostile) rest of the camp. So rightly Wiles 1997, 142.

[60] He should be still for 824–7/8, 831–4, 843ff. FC is a good location for
843–51.

[61] Celebrated actors like Timotheos, who gained a reputation for his playing
of the death scene, must have achieved this illusion realistically. Passing the
sword under the 'upstage' arm cannot be done realistically in a theatre in the
three-quarters round. Retractable prop swords were available in late antiquity
(see the ancient commentary *ad loc.*, Achilles Tatius 3.20, and Hesychios'
Lexicon, entry under *syspaston*); so I presume one could have been made in
Sophokles' time. Our own production used a complex underground hydraulic

The discovery of the body   This scene is very carefully structured. It opens with five chanted lines, presumably from a member or members of the first group of Sailors to re-enter, followed by brief snatches of free dialogue until the two groups are reunited. But then the AI stanza begins a complex, symmetrically repeated pattern of statement and response between Tekmessa and the Sailors, mixing lyrics and dialogue (879–924=925–973). As often in Greek tragedy, the moment of greatest pathos is delivered not in free verse but in carefully structured forms to create tension between order and the heights of emotion.

The Sailors re-enter in two straggling search-parties, one from each *parodos*; they all move slowly around the outside of the *orchêstra* circle towards EFC, miming weariness and exhaustion after a long search.[62] The audience, surrounding them from above, sees the corpse, and knows that both groups are visibly missing the object of their search; but the bushes front left, centre and right of Aias' corpse at C conceal it from the Sailors – who should look in all directions, including into the audience once they are in front of ERC and ELC. The Sailors were played by actors wearing masks, and therefore with limited peripheral vision; there was therefore not necessarily a comic effect when they fail to spot Aias.

The sailors cannot find Aias, but Tekmessa senses exactly where her lover has fallen. A Sailor formalizes his despair into an elaborate danced stanza (in our production, well away from Aias, at EFR); by contrast Tekmessa enters fast, and instinctively runs direct to the body.

Her screams draw the Sailors' attention to the centre; but at first they are concerned only with their own predicament (esp. 900ff.). None of them goes towards the body until 911–12; then Tekmessa refuses to let them near, covers the corpse – and alerts the audience that Teukros will be needed to move the drama into its final phase. Only after the A2 stanza, in which again perhaps a solo dancer acts out his lament for Aias, do the Sailors respond to Tekmessa's cries with some understanding of her suffering.[63]

Then the pattern is broken; the dialogue and chant after 950 are designed both to create an expectation that Agamemnon and Menelaos

system to meet the almost impossible expectations of audiences brought up on the cinema.

[62] Cf. the Furies at the opening of Aischylos, *Eumenides* Scene 2. Disunited entry or re-entry while searching was obviously a recurrent *choros* activity in tragedy, comedy and *satyr-drama*.

[63] But not enough; NB her fierce rebuke at 942, which another Sailor has to calm at 943.

will appear, and to plant the misleading suggestion that Odysseus might also come to rejoice. This triple threat gives the motivation for Tekmessa's great final speech. Here for the first time since her re-entry Tekmessa, who has been guarding the body closely – perhaps only retreating a little towards BC at 920 – needs a sequence of movements to bring out the pathos and nobility of her words. In our production she returned towards the body and knelt for 966–8; then stood, proudly addressing the Sailors with 970 (and 971, delivered specifically to the Sailor who sang 954ff.), before returning to Aias and kneeling for the last time on 'from me/he's gone', 972–3. She only moved away from the corpse as Teukros ran in; she then stood in shocked silence BL until he turns his attention to her at 984, and rouses her to run off and find Eurysakes.[64]

Teukros Teukros runs in, crying out in his despair, to begin the closing phase of the drama. On first seeing his brother's corpse, he is sunk into himself with shock; then he is suddenly animated by his fear for Eurysakes. Once Tekmessa has gone, he gathers himself for an extended speech over the body (992ff.), which Sophokles deliberately designed to belie in advance the taunts of the two sons of Atreus. In this emotionally wide-ranging speech we need to hear (in order) sincere emotion, grief, a touch of justified self-pity at 1005, a savage irony in his evocation of Telamon's anger, and an angry despair at 1026–7.[65]

Menelaos Sophokles has made Teukros remove Tekmessa's cloak from the body so the full horror of the dead Aias will be visible, uncovered, in the confrontations with Menelaos and Agamemnon. So now, while he is still laying the corpse on the ground, Menelaos enters[66] and gives a peremptory order. The Sailors should retreat into the FL sector in awe of this new figure (this also gives him a captive audience for his lecture at 1071ff.); but Teukros makes his resistance

[64] Seale 1982, 168 is simply wrong to send Tekmessa off immediately after her last speech. The imagery of 986–7 makes it certain that 984ff. are addressed to her.

[65] Lines 1026–7 are the last two before 1040 in this edition. We discovered in rehearsal that this has to be the moment where Teukros pulls Aias' corpse off the sword, and lays him on the ground behind it. Almost certainly the interpolated, obviously spurious lines 1028–39 were inserted to help cover this movement. But extra lines are not necessary, if Teukros grasps his brother's corpse angrily during the last sentence, and pulls it off the sword as soon as he has finished speaking 1027.

[66] Perhaps with a herald in attendance; see 1118.

totally evident, yielding ironically back, standing away from the corpse and from Menelaos (i.e. towards BL) when he gives his opponent the floor at 1050.

Menelaos takes up the invitation; he begins by talking to Teukros about Aias, and intensifies his attack at 1062–5; but at 1066ff. he is evidently fending off an aggresssive move by Teukros.[67] So this section must be delivered starting off near the corpse (BC), and ranging if desired round towards FC by 1060; this gives room for Menelaos to return and round on Teukros (BL) during the rest of the opening section. Then he can turn for 1071ff., just in front of the bushes at L, and begin his discourse on statesmanship by a close address to the Sailors.[68] However, this section returns from generalizations to specific meditation on Aias and his fate;[69] so by 1085 Menelaos must have circled to a point where he can face Teukros across the corpse (i.e., R) – and must go even nearer to him to give bite to the peremptory last two lines.

Teukros begins by deliberately ignoring Menelaos; he addresses his first four lines to the Sailors. Then at 1097 he turns back on Menelaos, wheeling around him in the first part of his speech, but then standing to defy him across the corpse (i.e. at R) by 1108–10.

The *stichomythia* after 1120 has to be carefully paced. This exchange of increasingly angry, sometimes highly ironic insults must be played face to face, with the two antagonists taking one or two steps towards each other on each line. They get closer and closer to each other, facing off just behind the corpse of Aias, until one of them weakens and turns away.[70] This happens at 1138, after which the confrontation between them can be finalized if each steps to one end of the body before delivering the symmetrical lines 1139 and 1140. Then the relative looseness, after this intense confrontation, of the two transparent

---

[67] The lame conclusion to this section, 1069–70, is very hard to play without enfeebling Menelaos. Even allowing for the anti-Spartan sentiments of an Athenian audience during the First Peloponnesian War, it is not desirable for either of the sons of Atreus to be totally caricatured, or there will be no real argument on what was to Sophokles an extremely serious issue (cf. *Ant*).

[68] We cast as Menelaos the actor who had played Kreon in *Ant* the previous year; with this casting the similarities to Kreon's rather longer discourses on the same subject became very obvious. *Ai* should therefore probably not be dated too far from *Ant* (438 BC).

[69] NB that even Menelaos is granted enough insight into the world of *Ai* to express the idea of mutability (1088ff.)

[70] Cf. Antigone and Kreon at *Ant* 508ff.

similes at 1142ff. and 1150ff. should be symbolized by free, expansive movements. Each speech begins with an address to the Sailors, which becomes more personalized until the speaker ends with a sudden three-line turn directly to his opponent.

Menelaos acknowledges defeat in the verbal combat (1159 should in performance provoke audience laughter), and departs to save face. Teukros' closing couplet is a good example of 'lines cast at a departing back'.[71] These need precise timing; Teukros must not deliver the lines so soon that the audience would expect Menelaos to turn round again, return and deliver a response – but not so long after Menelaos has started to stride away that his verbal defiance looks like cowardice.

Sophokles brings Tekmessa and Eurysakes back now, so Teukros can begin the rituals for Aias' burial before Agamemnon comes. The presence of Aias' wife and son mourning him symbolizes Teukros' determination to bury his brother, and becomes the backdrop for the Finale. It creates a decisive visual pressure for the right resolution, as the alternative to Aias' burial is now for all three of them to be massacred (1309).

Teukros meets them as they come in, receives Eurysakes from Tekmessa, and places him kneeling just behind Aias' head and shoulders – the R end of the corpse – on 1172. (Tekmessa should kneel behind the centre of the corpse, between BC and EBC).[72] Teukros must move a little away from Eurysakes for the address to him at 1176ff., which needs distance; at 1179 he mimes cutting off his own hair, then goes back and gives it into Eurysakes' left hand on 1180. A few moments of silent action follow 1181, since this is the only time Teukros has for miming cutting hair from Tekmessa, and from Eurysakes himself, as he foreshadowed at 1174. He adds the two locks to his own, which is already in Eurysakes' hand, addresses three brief lines to the Sailors, and exits.[73]

---

[71] Taplin 1977, 221–2.

[72] Her mask and costume were in Sophokles' original production now worn by a silent face, so one of the speaking actors was freed to reappear as Odysseus in the Finale.

[73] Eurysakes needs his right hand for holding on to Aias; but this pose can be quietly dropped during Choros 4, and resumed only in the closing sequence from 1402. Cutting all three locks off in audience view is more theatrically effective than having Eurysakes come in with two already in his hand (so Seale 1982, 171). But Teukros must not do it during 1172ff., interrupting the flow of the verse, as in Moore 1952, 52–3.

Choros 4

A simple but intense lament of desperate yearning.[74] Sophokles pours into four stanzas all the suffering of being stranded away from home on military service, to take us for a moment away from the confrontation with Agamemnon and Menelaos. The Choros ends with an unabashed patriotism. It is the Sailors' last lyric contribution to the drama; like the Young Women of Trachis, their characters do not have a perspective that would enable them to contribute adequately to the Finale.

Finale

Agamemnon Why did Teukros leave at the end of Scene 5? He does not bring back any implements for burial.[75] The exit seems to have been created solely to create pathos;[76] the corpse, woman and child are for a few minutes at the mercy of Agamemnon. (The Sailors are small protection: they have hardly lived up to Teukros' advice at 1182–3, and will show their cowardice overtly at 1264–5.)

Agamemnon is characterized as being more arrogant, forceful and colourful than his brother (he might bring a couple of soldiers with him to reinforce this, though it is not necessary); he is outrageously confident of the need for the interests of the stronger to be preserved.[77] In performance his more clipped and brutal speech needs at first to be focused directly against Teukros, who comically pretends for two lines that he does not realize Agamemnon is addressing him; see 1228. Agamemnon must at first be positioned so he can gesture effectively towards the corpse at C ('a dead nothing', 1231). After that (1235ff.) he can become more free-ranging, addressing his lines past Teukros to the Sailors and even to the audience. Only at 1257 does he need to be

---

[74] In the original Greek, in metres that emphasize its escapist mood; Scott 1996, 92.

[75] He requests the Sailors to get these at 1402ff., so the audience never sees them. In our modern-dress production he returned at 1223 with an army stretcher, which enabled the Sailors to carry the large actor playing Aias off in a dignified way at the end. Perhaps in Sophokles' own production Aias' gigantic shield, which is superfluous in Scene 2, was brought on here for this purpose?

[76] Taplin 1978, 149.

[77] Lines 1246ff. – probably one of the first texts to express this particularly extreme view of *arete*, which became increasingly more prominent in right-wing ideology at Athens. Cf. Introduction pp. xx–xxi.

back by the corpse, and near to Teukros (from whom he should
withdraw disdainfully on the last two lines).

Teukros starts his response slowly. But the two extended narratives
(1272ff.) generate a real impetus; and in the last portion of the speech,
using 1289 as a deft link back, he harnesses this energy to a crude and
vigorous counter-attack on Agamemnon's repeated charges that, as the
son of a barbarian princess, he is effectively a slave himself.[78] This
leads to the climax in which Teukros first turns away, ironically
affecting to have forgotten who was actually married to Helene – and
then rounds from a distance (1321) with extreme seriousness on
Agamemnon to deliver the final warning.

Odysseus   The impasse is resolved, by a superficially surprising, but
profoundly expected entry which at one stroke reveals the deep structure of the drama, and resolves the conflict. Odysseus returns, imbued
– despite the fears about him that Aias' *philoi* have expressed earlier –
with the same spirit of wisdom and reconciliation with his enemy that
he showed at the end of Scene 1.[79] He disregards the Sailor who speaks
to him as he enters, and walks straight to the middle of the two
quarrelling noblemen.[80] When Agamemnon replies, he draws him aside
(FL if, as in our production, Teukros is FR). Odysseus needs to play the
opening sequence relatively close to Agamemnon; but there is a strong
case for moving him back to BC by 1337, and then taking him back to
a relatively dominant position (e.g. FC to Agamemnon's FL) to play the
stichomythia, so that his dominant role is plain to the audience.
Agamemnon twice gets near to anger (1352, 1360); but Odysseus
presses the advantage when Agamemnon's 1362 evades 1361, and
implies that he is weakening; and while Agamemnon justifies giving
way by a cynical diagnosis that even his friend is acting selfishly (1366),
Odysseus has picked up with 1365 the import of his own insight in

[78] Teukros' rebuttal of this charge is central to the drama, as it backs Aias'
demand that Eurysakes – who is of exactly the same mixed parentage as
Teukros – should be treated as his heir (564ff.). So note how Teukros explicitly
includes Tekmessa and Eurysakes in his defiance of Agamemnon at 1309.

[79] Odysseus' surprising entry would have had even greater power if (like
Pylades' intervention in Aischylos' *Libation Bearers* Scene 6) it shocked the
original audience by being technically 'impossible' because all three of the
normal speaking actors are already in view, playing Aias, Teukros and
Agamemnon.

[80] Taplin 1980, 141 rightly contrasts this straight line with his circling entry
at the start of Scene 1. But Odysseus needs flexible movement, once he is in the
orchêstra, in both scenes; and at the end he goes off in a straight line both times.

Scene 1, and wins the exchange, trumping 1366 with the superb 1367.[81] Agamemnon should therefore be on his way while delivering 1368, pausing briefly to face Odysseus over the corpse for 1372–3 before a swift move to the R *parodos*.

Sophokles ends the scene by defining limits for Odysseus' great generosity; it cannot extend to helping to bury Aias, or his shade may be angry. Teukros sets this out in the last big speech of the drama, opening out from a straight tribute to Odysseus to an angry summary of exactly what Agamemnon and Menelaos have done; he builds on this, turning away from Odysseus for a powerful invocation to Zeus, the avenging Fury and Justice at 1389–93.[82] Then he turns back to Odysseus, and ends with a succinct two-line closure (1398–9). Odysseus responds with symmetrical brevity, inviting a crisp, militarily formal exit.

The Funeral Procession   Music now begins, ushering the drama into its final phase as Teukros moves to BC to supervise the funeral procession.

Lines 1403–9 have caused some scholars to assume that attendants enter at this point with the items mentioned;[83] others have imagined that the *choros* divides into three groups. Both ideas are wrong, because they pull focus from the intensity of Teukros' closing declamation. Once again (cf. Tekmessa's orders at 804ff.), the Sailors are to be imagined as dividing into groups *after* their exit from the playing space; and no extras are needed to carry Aias out, since it is right and proper that his Sailors themselves should do this. They take up positions by the corpse, while Teukros guides Eurysakes to help them lift Aias, at and after 1409; the rest of Teukros' chanted lines allow time for the body to be raised, and then Teukros and Eurysakes move to the head of the procession.

In modern performance, the closing three-line comment is best

[81] His sentiment is far from Christian ideals of selflessness; but it was vital in ancient Greek ethics to establish that any apparently harmful action was ultimately better for the doer, or the plea will fail. On this scene see Jones 1961, 186–91; cf. also Notes on *Ant* Scene 1, p. 205.

[82] The Athenian audience would recall that in the standard versions of the return from Troy Teukros' prayer was amply rewarded, with Menelaos' long and painful wanderings and Agamemnon's return home to death at the hands of Klytaimestra and Aigisthos. Cf. the prophecies of Polymestor at the end of Euripides, *Hekabe*.

[83] E.g. Seale 1982, 173.

delivered after the procession has begun, by one solo Sailor who remains briefly apart from the formation to deliver the final words, before joining the others as they march off slowly, followed by Tekmessa.

Antigone

MICHAEL EWANS

The Actors and their Roles

Though other doublings are possible, this is the most likely. The protagonist would have taken Kreon – the part with the most lines, the character most frequently in the playing space. Then his successive opponents will have been played by the second actor: Antigone, Haimon, Teiresias, Eurydike.[1] The smaller but still challenging roles of Ismene, the Guard, and the Bodyguard (when he reappears as a 'messenger' in Scene 7) go to the third actor.

The Production

This translation was first performed in the Drama Studio at the University of Newcastle, configured to provide a half size (ten-metre) *orchêstra* surrounded on three sides by an audience divided into six wedges of steeply raked seats. Masks were not used; the *skene* façade represented a boarded-up, partially war-damaged building, with one pair of double doors; the costumes were drawn from images of Sarajevo just after the siege of 1993–4 – a modern environment as fraught and battle-scarred as the ancient Thebes of Sophokles' imagination, and one to which extremism and socio-political violence are central. A Muslim society also provided a contemporary context in which Kreon's axiomatic assumption that adult male citizens are superior to females and youths, especially in political judgement, had as much initial plausibility as in ancient Athens.

Scene 1

I make no apology for the physicality of the first stage direction. Scene 1 is the first of three terrible scenes (cf. 3 and 4) in which the

---

[1] All these parts are women, boys or old men, and therefore easily played by a Greek actor with a light voice, specializing in character types other than the mature warrior/king. This doubling also assigns to the same actor the four characters who turn out to be absolutely opposed to Kreon.

relationships between *philoi* break down into hatred;[2] and Antigone's first speech establishes a pace, and an intense grip on the developing action, which are to become characteristic of this most closely focused of Sophokles' surviving tragedies.[3]

Antigone's energy, intensity and determination are placed in diametrical contrast with Ismene's caution, reluctance and hesitance about entering the playing space, because the *orchêstra* in all Greek tragedies – and perhaps most importantly in this one – represents the public arena, a world normally dominated by men.[4] The physical and dramatic contrasts that then develop could almost be set out in a table:

Antigone	*Ismene*
fast-paced	slower
extroverted	introverted
more angular	more flowing
harder	softer
imperious	plaintive
loves Polyneikes and death	loves Antigone and life

These antitheses tell only part of the truth. One of the greatest mistakes that can be made when producing this drama is to underplay Ismene – to see her as a fundamentally weak character, and 61ff. as a feeble or inadequate response. On the contrary, our decision as rehearsals progressed to strengthen Ismene's character both gave the right pathos to the end of this scene, and a power that is unachievable with a weak Ismene at the end of Scene 3. A mildly hostile reaction by

[2] Although Teiresias and Kreon are not *philoi* by blood-relationship, Kreon acknowledges (995) that Teiresias has always helped him in the past, so Scene 6 conforms to this pattern as well. And though Kreon and Eurydike do not meet, we discover that she committed suicide after cursing him (1304–5); the Finale therefore shows yet another breakdown in the relationship between *philoi* – this one destroying Kreon's entire family.

[3] The total playing time in the uncut première production of this translation was seventy-five minutes.

[4] Von Wilamowitz's contention (1923, 340) that Antigone comes from the R *parodos* and meets Ismene must be rejected; Ismene would not come out into the public arena of her own accord.

In our modern dress production costuming – bearing in mind that the scene is set before dawn – helped the actresses to communicate the contrast between the sisters. Antigone, who has already been up and about, and has heard about the edict, was fully dressed – in jeans, to symbolize her readiness to go out into the world of men; Ismene still in her nightdress, over which she has hastily pulled a shawl when summoned out by her sister.

Ismene to 38 will establish the right balance at once; Ismene is also a princess of the royal house, and Antigone has no grounds except her own conviction to assume that her view – which she has not yet even stated – of how the sisters should react to Kreon's decree is the only right and proper one for Ismene to hold.[5]

It is anachronistic to forget that in a world without handguns and automatic weapons women literally could not fight men, who were physically stronger, owned, and had been trained to use, daggers, swords and spears. Furthermore, the Greeks saw no nobility in suicide, and no eternal bliss to be acquired by martyrdom. The self-sacrificial determination that Antigone starts to exhibit at 72ff. would therefore have been far more eccentric for the ears of the Athenian audience than it must seem to modern spectators influenced by the Christian tradition.[6] In the late fifth century the ideas that 'might is right' and *dike* therefore consists primarily in yielding to the stronger were coming to the forefront of moral debate;[7] and it was highly abnormal to believe that suffering for a principle was to be preferred to yielding to expediency.[8]

---

[5] In view of some extraordinary miscastings (e.g. Gwen Taylor against Juliet Stevenson in Don Taylor's BBC adaptation) it must be added that the powerful emotional dynamics of their interaction in Scenes 1 and 3 will only work if Ismene and Antigone look as if they are sisters – and act as sisters who until now have been very closely bonded.

[6] On the relative value of life on earth and afterlife in Haides to the Greeks, the fundamental text is the chilling reply to Odysseus by Achilleus' shade in *Odyssey* 11. 489ff.: 'I would rather follow the plough as thrall to another/ man, one with no land allotted him and not much to live on/ than be a king over all the perished dead' (tr. Lattimore). No writer before Plato asserts any other view. Some mystical beliefs, which had attracted followers in Athens by the late fifth century, did claim that there would be particular blessings in the afterlife for their devotees; but Antigone recognizes in Scene 5 that she has no such hope.

[7] This is a central, amply documented feature of the period. Cf. Thoukydides (almost *passim*, but esp. 5.81ff.), Plato, *Gorgias* (*passim*, but esp. 358ff.) and *Republic* 336B–54B, Euripides, esp. *Hekabe, Andromache* and *Orestes*. Modern discussion begins with Adkins 1960, 195ff.

[8] This is precisely the point which, after the departure of Thrasymachos, the aggressive advocate of 'might is right', Sokrates is challenged by his friend Glaukon to prove in Plato's *Republic* (357Bff.). Glaukon requires Sokrates to prove that a real person is better off *in this world* to behave justly and passively, even if he has to suffer torture himself and see his family suffering atrocious torments (361E-62); and Sokrates fails during the remaining nine books of the *Republic*, since in the final analysis he has to appeal, with the Myth of Er (614ff.), to the minority belief in *post-mortem* rewards for wisdom and virtuous

Accordingly Ismene must be played as a person whose character and point of view are different from Antigone's, but who has an almost equal strength and intensity. The scene then becomes – after the opening moves, which should bring the two girls to the centre by line 20 – a sequence of two powerful speeches, one by each character, neither of which suceeds in persuading the other.

Then the emphatic stress on twos – the disastrous pairings in the house of Labdakos – in the first part of Ismene's speech (49–58) emphasizes the pathos of the conclusion.[9] Antigone's big speech at least gave some chance of reconciliation; Ismene's does not, and the extent of the breakdown is emphasized by Antigone's fierce response and the breakdown into a confrontational *stichomythia* (78ff.). The last two survivors of the royal family are torn apart, as Antigone tells the young woman who had been her 'dearest, closest sister Ismene' (1)[10] that 'if that's your attitude, I'll hate you, and/you'll justly lie beneath the hatred of the dead' (93–4 – lines almost as cold, addressed to a *philos*, as Kreon's to her in Scene 3).

The close affinity established between the sisters at the outset suggests using the degree of closeness of their body and hand contact as the theatrical means for communicating the through-line of the scene, the progressive sundering of their relationship. Antigone drags Ismene out; Ismene breaks away from her in her own first speech, but is then re-engaged by Antigone clasping her again, since she needs closeness for 18–19 ('I knew it! . . .') before embarking on 21ff.

Each of the two long speeches (21ff., 49ff.) needs to be a 'break-out'. They work well if the sister who is speaking first moves away

behaviour.

For a real-life example of astonishment that anyone should not accept that they must yield to superior force, but would prefer to die for a principle, see the 'Melian dialogue' in Thoukydides 5, esp. 111–13.

[9] The ancient Greek language had a set of distinct grammatical forms, the 'dual', to denote two people, as opposed either to one or to three or more. Antigone and Ismene use these forms for the 'natural but frustrated pairings' (Griffith *ad loc.*) of sisters and brothers; so do the Councillors (143–5); naturally, however, Kreon avoids them altogether (Knox 1964, 86). This translation renders all the duals in Scene 1 except line 61 by including the English word 'two'.

[10] The opening line has been the despair of translators. In the original it implies an even greater closeness and affinity between the sisters than in this translation (or indeed in any other known to me, except perhaps Hölderlin's notorious German rendering, '*Gemeinsamschwesterliches! o Ismenes Haupt!*' – discussed at Steiner 1984, 84–5).

from the other, leaving her at the centre of the circle, then circles the perimeter to achieve a dominant position (e.g. BC/EBC) towards the close, at the climax of the speech. Then their increasing separation will be emphasized if after 33ff. Antigone comes close, attempts to join hands with Ismene to link her into the deed she desires – and then fails, as Ismene first detaches herself in shock at 45, and then breaks away at 49 with a speech of no less emotional power than 21ff.

Then the disjunction becomes more extreme, starting with Antigone's almost brutal response at 69ff. For the vision of martyrdom (72ff.), Ismene must be forced to the periphery, so Antigone must dominate the *orchêstra* (i.e. from BC; not C, because she has been trapped there while Ismene circles her during her big speech).[11] She therefore needs a move to emphasize the coldness of 'I would not ask you'. The move must be to BC, because the rest of the scene needs to be played in the rear semicircle to make the two swift exits practicable.[12] Then the final *stichomythia* becomes a sequence of advances and retreats, increasingly strident vocally on both sides – as will all such dialogues be in this drama – as Ismene's fear for her sister comes more and more in conflict with Antigone's determination.

Antigone's final exit-lines are preceded by anger and sarcasm (93–5). This allows Ismene to hold the audience for a closing moment of pathos, with her expression of a true sisterly love that is now hopeless, while Antigone gradually goes out of sight down the *parodos*.[13] They came in close together; they leave totally separated. In one swift scene Sophokles has shown us a bleak world in which *philoi* are pulled apart, and the first of four family relationships has been (literally fatally) destroyed.

---

[11] For the technique of apparent *philoi* consecutively circling each other during long speeches before their relationship falls apart, cf. Scene 4.

[12] Note the sudden, shocking midline change of mood during 76, as Antigone turns from idealistic introspection to an attack on Ismene.

[13] Knox 1964, 81 (cf. also Blundell 1989, 121) translates the last line 'mad, but truly devoted to your *philoi*'. But Antigone's 'madness' *is* her extreme devotion, so Sophokles could not have put them in antithesis without making Ismene's closing line odd – and sententious. Though the language is ambiguous on a printed page, I believe the Greek audience could only have made sense of Ismene's words as they are translated here. This is also the better reading in performance, since it gives the actress a poignant closing moment; and it prepares the audience for Ismene's reappearance in Scene 3, maddened by the imminent death of the sister whom she still loves.

Choros 1

In Aischylos' *Persians* and *Suppliants*, and [Euripides] *Rhesos* the *choros* are the first characters to enter. In all other surviving dramas, there is a scene – usually for one actor, but sometimes, as here, for two or more – before their arrival. Since the characters who act Scene 1 normally depart before the *choros* enter, the playwright had three choices: the collective character played by the *choros* may be totally ignorant of what is known to the character/s in Scene 1 (e.g. Euripides, *Hippolytos*), partially aware (as in *Antigone*) or fully aware. This last option has the least potential for dramatic development, and it is therefore not surprising that it is rarely employed.[14]

Sophokles' decision to bring in the Councillors aware, like Ismene in Scene 1, of the lifting of the siege but unaware of Kreon's decree has many benefits. In Choros 1 they dance their joy at the city's deliverance. The lifting of the siege is real enough, and their heartfelt emotion is justifiable; but the audience, who already know about Kreon's decree and Antigone's defiance, are aware that these rejoicing Councillors will almost immediately be confronted with a difficult situation. The sheer power and beauty of this evocative victory-dance stand in stark contrast with what has preceded it: two very young women torn apart are succeeded by fifteen older men dancing in a united flow of emotion;[15] also with what follows, as we descend rapidly to the level of Kreon's political rhetoric and his inability to cope with opposition.

Choros 1 has an unusual structure: between each matching lyric *strophe* and *antistrophe* Sophokles inserted a non-matching stanza in *anapaests*, which metaphorically steps out of the action, and gives extra impetus to the narrative. I conjecture that they were each chanted by one Councillor, dancing apart from the others. The Argives are consis-

---

[14] Only in Euripides' *Herakles* and *Suppliants* among the surviving dramas.

[15] Although the character played by the *choros* is a group of grey-haired older men (see 1092–3), this does not mean that they doddered around ineffectually (cf. Ewans 1995, 130 on *Agamemnon*). Vigorous dancing was a central part of ancient Greek culture, and continued into middle and old age (as too in modern Greece; cf. Katzantzakis' *Zorba the Greek*). There is also good reason to believe that the *choroses* at the drama festival were played by young men, who marked by their participation the transition from boyhood to manhood (Tanner 1975). The Choroses in *Ant* contain some of the most vivid and evocative images in all surviving tragedy; I am certain that the young men who played the Councillors, though masked and costumed as older men, did full justice to that imagery with an uninhibited choreography.

tently imaged by singular for plural, so the 'white-shield man' of the first stanza, the eagle of the second and third, and the arrogant man who assailed the battlements and then fell (B1) can all be mimed by one dancer, temporarily isolated from the rest of the group.

The sequence of the Choros is steady and unbroken, from the wonderment of the release from siege, conveyed in the opening invocation to the Sun, through dances that evoke first the arrogant assault of the Argive army, then its defeat and their city's victory.[16] The continuity is deliberate; by leading us into this mood of victory, Sophokles achieves a greater contrast when Kreon appears.

Scene 2

Meeting his Councillors for the first time, Kreon's immediate concern is loyalty. These men, whom he himself has selected, have been loyal to the royal family; he is new to power, and holds it only by virtue of his sister's marriage to Oidipous; can he command their loyalty as well?[17]

This insecurity is the cause of Kreon's 'passionate obsession with power';[18] it later becomes the reason for his downfall. He is a cerebral man (159) who has thought out a way to make an immediate impact, to assert his authority and leadership ability. He will also turn out to have no understanding whatsoever of human emotion and passion – until they are forced from him in the Finale. His colloquies on statesmanship – which begin at once, 175ff. – have been much discussed; but rarely from the one point of view that matters in performance. What kind of an impact do they make on the Councillors? Is he

[16] In the Greek original, Sophokles used bright, upbeat aeolic/choriambic metres throughout.

[17] For reasons that soon become obvious, Kreon plays down the fact that his authority is itself dependent on a blood-relationship (*philia*). He uses a periphrasis, 'next of kin' in 174, and soon (187ff.) seeks to shade the word *philos* away from its primary sense, 'blood-relative' towards the other meaning '[electively chosen] friend'. Cf. Nussbaum 1986, 55 and Neuburg 1990, 71.

How would the banal and cursory reference to the well-known image of the ship of state have impressed members of the audience, especially those who knew Aischylos' Theban trilogy? Sophokles has already put *Seven against Thebes* into his audience's minds by echoing some of its imagery in Choros 1 (esp. 128ff.; cf. *Seven* 423ff.); anyone who had seen or read that drama recently would recall Eteokles' sustained, varied and effective use of this same image. A comparison between their rhetorical styles would not be to Kreon's advantage.

[18] Blundell 1989, 130.

going to achieve the unquestioning loyalty from them which his opening address shows that he needs?

Kreon's general principles, as enunciated at 175–190, are not convincing as a whole. First comes an admirable sentiment, which should please his Councillors: the ruler should 'cling firmly to the best advice' (later in the drama, Kreon will not); the final words evince an admirable patriotism; but in between (182–96) comes a firm statement of an absolute priority – loyalty to your native land, and to *philoi* selected on the basis of their patriotism alone, must in all circumstances take precedence over that to friends or relatives – which to fifth-century Athenian ears would sound autocratic, almost Spartan.[19]

If the principles themselves would have been puzzling for the Councillors, their reaction to the edict that follows is crystal clear. They will naturally show confidence and approval for the honour to be paid to Eteokles; but the decision to leave Polyneikes unburied and mutilated inspires their revulsion.[20] This should be shown in a physical reaction by some of the Council even while Kreon is speaking 202ff., since 211ff. are the sulkily deferential response of a man who disapproves, but knows that in his *polis* there is no right of free speech, because the new ruler has the power of arbitrary life and death. If anyone among the Councillors or the audience did not realize that Kreon both has this

[19] *Contra* Knox 1964, 37 citing Perikles at Thoukydides 2.60, and 1984, 37, citing Perikles' 'funeral speech' at 2.35–46, esp. 37, 43. However, Thoukydides' Perikles never places loyalty to the city against or above loyalty to close relatives, as Kreon does here.

[20] He describes it, quite casually, in language as brutally evocative as that used by Antigone herself; cf. 202–6 with 28–30. (cf. Seale 1982, 86). Pro-Kreon interpreters have produced real-life parallels (e.g. Thoukydides 1.139, Xenophon *Hellenika* 1.7.22) which are supposed to prove that the Athenians regarded it as acceptable to leave the bodies of traitors unburied (Oudemans and Lardinois 1987, 60ff., Sourvinou-Inwood 1989, 138–9; cf. Knox 1964, 84 and 1984, 40, Nussbaum 1986, 437). They do not; they only show that it was illegal to bury someone condemned for treason in Athenian territory; relatives who wanted to do so had (like Antigone) to use stealth.

However, the main issue, when preparing to perform Sophokles' *Ant*, is how the characters in this drama view Kreon's edict (198ff.) against burying Polyneikes *anywhere*, or even lamenting for him (so rightly Lesky 1964, 114–15). Not one of them approves of it. Antigone correctly notes at 504–5 that few are prepared to say so when the penalty is death; even so, by the end of Scene 6 Kreon's decree has caused such outrage that the list has grown quite long: Antigone, Ismene, Haimon, Teiresias and then at last some of the Councillors themselves.

power, and is prepared to use it, Kreon casually confirms the fact in his response to another Councillor at 221.[21]

Therefore it is vital to reject the critical tradition which suggests that (e.g.) 'of the validity and justice of Creon's opening statement there is no doubt. His initial speech is a definition of the Greek ideal of a just king.'[22] This might have been the view of some citizens in 343 BC, when Demosthenes quoted Kreon against Aischines as part of his attempt to bind an impoverished and defensive *polis* together in opposition to Philippos of Makedonia;[23] Athens in the early 430s was a very different city, the confident and wealthy leader of the Delian League, where a real (if limited-franchise) democracy was testing its powers for the first time in human history. Sophokles' audience is unlikely to have been impressed either by Kreon's repeated references to himself and his opinions or by his autocracy.[24]

Kreon's exposition has been passionate and harsh, in keeping with the assumed strength that he uses to disguise his insecurity. Given his many references to straight lines and to making matters straight,[25] it was an obvious, but effective device in our production to make Kreon always walk in straight lines until his resolve is broken at the end of Scene 6, for contrast with the flowing circles used by Antigone and Ismene, Haimon and Teiresias.[26]

Kreon may even (as in our production) be about to leave by the L *parodos* when a new character sidles in by the R *parodos*, interrupts, and re-enacts by stop-start movements during his opening speech the hesitancy that he felt on the way here. Kreon's ability to create fear has

[21] This fast *stichomythia* plays best with a different speaker for each line.

[22] Taylor 1986, xlvii. Cf. also e.g. Calder 1968, 394, Burton 1980, 66, Oudemans and Lardinois 1987, 161 and 193, Sourvinou-Inwood 1989, 135 and 142.

[23] *On the False Embassy* 246–7.

[24] Cf. Winnington-Ingram 1980, 123–5.

[25] Nussbaum 1986, 58. NB also the single-period build of the verbal rhetoric through 198–206; Griffith on 192ff. and 198ff.

[26] Predictably, given their overall reading of the drama, Oudemans and Lardinois (1987, 199) imagine the movements of both central figures as 'rectilineal' in contrast to the circling, hesitant Guard. In performance, however, giving Antigone straight lines like Kreon would be false to a vital aspect of Sophokles' drama: she is not suppressing her womanhood, but focusing it totally onto the burial of Polyneikes (cf. 900ff., and see Segal 1964). Foley (1996, 65) correctly dissociates Antigone's 'unflagging, even obsessive devotion to principle' – obvious in the text – from her 'flexible moral style', which must be brought out in performance.

already been implied by the Councillors' response in the *stichomythia*.[27] It is confirmed now, since the Guard is genuinely terrified of him, and his part in the scene is shaped in ABAC form: first terror, then a gradual loss of his reluctance, after the direct order at 243, leading to an increasingly deep involvement in the narrative as it unfolds; then terror again, when Kreon rounds upon him at 304ff.; then the extraordinary surprise at the end (315ff.), when the Guard – born survivor though he is[28] – dares to play word-games with the ruler, and wins.

Kreon's 243 can only be played as a direct, snap order; 248 as utter, horrified disbelief; and the big speech at 280ff. is pure paranoia, starting with sophistry, passing into conspiracy theory, and ending with sadistic threats (304ff.).[29] Naturally, the Councillors wilt under this avalanche of threats. We used Kreon's fury at 280ff. to drive them from their normal, fairly powerful first distribution in an arc from EFL to EFR (the best position for listening to an opening speech by a leading character) up into a cowed huddle at BL.

This clears the performance area for Kreon's speech, which provides a good example of how directors of Greek tragedy must be alert to the different addressees implied by subsections of a long speech, who often include all the other characters present, the gods, and the audience.[30] First he harangues the Councillors on the subject of religion (282ff.), then addresses almost as an aside to his Bodyguard the remarks about dissidents (289ff.), before rounding on the Councillors again with the outburst at 293–4. After turning back to the Bodyguard for the discourse on money, he must return suspiciously to the Council at 302–3. He then achieved a position of full authority (just B of C) to invoke Zeus at 304ff. before turning back to attack the Guard (who is of course somewhere between CR and BR).

Kreon cannot be played as a fundamentally good ruler, responsive to the deep needs of his *polis*, who gradually descends into folly. Harsh though it is for both actor and audience, Kreon must begin

---

[27] Kreon is of course attended by at least one Bodyguard, like Aigisthos in *Agamemnon*, Lykos in *Herakles*, and other new and autocratic rulers. Attendants (plural) are implied at 932. However, in the half-size playing space of our production one was enough. This large, menacing, silent and trigger-happy figure played a crucial part in establishing visually the brute force that is at the heart of Kreon's regime; and his transformation at the end, when he returned to deliver the narrative in Scene 7, was also highly effective.

[28] Cf. 297ff., 388–400, 434ff. Griffith on 223ff.

[29] Cf. Vickers 1973, 531.

[30] Cf. also the Notes on 450ff. and 891ff.

to rant and rave in his very first scene, as soon as he finds out that
his edict has been disobeyed. He shows himself at once as someone
who cannot brook dissent; will invent the most paranoid expla-
nations[31] when confronted with that dissent; and thinks nothing of
threatening to use torture and murder to repress it. The only development later is that when he finds out who the culprit is, he actually
does torture her to death (and very nearly her sister as well) – even
though Antigone is a member of the royal family and he is responsible
for her welfare.

There is nothing in Kreon remotely like the gradual descent of
Oidipous from the beneficent king of the opening scene to the moment
where he has the old Herdsman tortured (*Oidipous the King* 1152ff.).
Though few classical scholars agree with him, Vickers was right: 'it is
not as if Kreon suddenly loses his charity and good temper [towards
the end of Scene 3]. From the beginning he has been harsh and brutal,
and as the play goes on he gets worse.'[32]

The idea that particularly inflames Kreon is the Guard's belief that
the burial was almost miraculous (249ff.), leading to speculation by
one of the Councillors that the deed was the work of the gods. The
main point of this is to allow Kreon to work himself into a rage,
showing as he does so that for him even the gods hold the same moral
values as Kreon.[33] Unfortunately the interpretation of this aspect of the
scene has been misdirected by a scholastic debate about the two burials
of Polyneikes.[34] It is absolutely obvious from the Guard's narratives in
Scenes 2 and 3 that Antigone did indeed go out and bury Polyneikes,
as she said she would, after Scene 1 – and then, naturally, stayed

[31] The audience *knows* they are paranoid, because Scene 1 has shown us who
did bury Polyneikes – and why. Hence the gender irony which Sophokles inserts
at 248 – a chilling assumption in retrospect, given the misogyny that Kreon will
show later.

[32] 1973, 534.

[33] Kreon's fundamental supposition – that the gods of Thebes would not
favour a native son who returned to attack his own *polis* with a foreign army –
is correct. Unfortunately for him, the Greek gods uphold some other values as
well, to which he has attached no importance, including the right of *philoi* to
bury their *philoi*. And like the gods of the *Iliad* (24.23ff.), the gods of *Ant*
ultimately place these larger values, and the horror of *miasma*, above their own
personal loyalties to particular *poleis*.

[34] There have been theories that one of the burials was performed by the
gods alone, or by Ismene (starting with Drachmann 1908). This nonsense should
have been stopped altogether by Kitto 1956, 140–45. But it wasn't; see
bibliography at Seale 1982, 110.

nearby to make sure that her work was not undermined. When it was, during the many hours that are to be imagined as passing during Choros 2, she seized the first opportunity to give Polyneikes proper burial again. Sophokles had a good reason for having her do this: he wants to show us Kreon first reacting to the news that his decree has been defied before he knows who did it, and then reacting in Scene 3 to the almost incredible fact that the person who defied him is one of his nieces.[35]

The gods did not perform either of the burials; but the Guard's narrative emphasizes that the first burial was 'like a miracle' (254) – the light sprinkling of dust, and the fact that this alone was enough to dissuade the wild beasts and dogs; Antigone's sudden appearance as a captive is itself 'a portent from the gods' (375); and there was definitely something miraculous about the second burial. Antigone was able to accomplish it at high noon because suddenly, out of nowhere, a whirlwind rose which enabled her to come back and get near enough to the body to cover it with dust again and pour libations. The superstitious Councillor was wrong to think the gods did the deed themselves; but any Greek hearing this narrative would rightly think that the gods approved of it, and twice helped Antigone to bury her brother.[36] Only later will the bleakness and cruelty of Sophokles'

[35] Cf. Kitto 1956, 152 and 156–7 and Gellie 1972, 38–9.

[36] Kitto *ibid.*; Winnington-Ingram 1980, 125. Cf. Ewans 1995, 161 and 164–70 on the ways in which Aischylos in *Libation Bearers* dramatized the idea that 'gods help those who help themselves' in the context of giving proper funeral offerings to a dead relative. The light dust that is sufficient to prevent pollution would also bring to an Athenian's memory the ways in which, towards the end of the *Iliad*, the gods prevented Achilleus' outrages to Hektor's body from disfiguring it until Priam is able to come and retrieve it for burial (23.184ff.). The Homeric poems were a central part of the school curriculum for educated Athenians; illiterate members of the audience would also know them, since their city hosted annual competitive recitals of Homer at the Panathenaic Festival.

The idea that sudden changes of weather manifest the gods' approval or disapproval of human beings is also fundamental in fifth-century thought. Cf. e.g. Aischylos, *Agamemnon* – both the change of wind at Aulis (184ff.), and the giant storm that scattered the returning fleet after the Greeks destroyed the altars and temples of the gods in Troy (338ff. + 649ff.). Another striking example is the rainstorm that saved Kroisos from being burned to death by Kyros, in the *Histories* written by Sophokles' friend Herodotos (1.87; like the dust storm in *Ant*, this rain came out of clear blue skies). Cf. also the thunder that calls Oidipous to his end in *OKol*, 1456ff.

universe be revealed, when Antigone realizes in her last moments that despite that fact, no god will intervene to save her from death (921ff.).

Choros 2

The Councillors use the daring of the unknown person who buried Polyneikes as the springboard for a short but complex and far-ranging meditation on the larger theme that this implies: the extraordinary nature and achievements of human beings. Sophokles will use the choral odes in this way again in Choroses 3, 4 and 5; it is characteristic of all his surviving work, but nowhere employed more finely than in Antigone.[37]

'Wonders' is not adequate to Greek *deinos* in 332. The word constantly has the overtones of 'strange', 'awe-inspiring', even 'terrible'; and it was normally used, before this Choros, of the gods and of natural phenomena.[38] Here, for the first time in western culture, the human becomes the most remarkable, strange and terrible creature in this world; a thought that at once puts the focus of the drama back onto human actions and human thoughts, after the divine and miraculous elements which intruded against Kreon's will in the last scene.

Choros 2 flows smoothly and naturally, with ever-increasing power. It evokes in the first two stanzas mankind's daring, skilful conquest of our physical environment, and then passes onto intellectual and social achivements. A1 and A2 both end without climax, easing the dance on into the next stanza; by contrast B1 ends with a sober warning that we are not (like the gods) immortal, woven into its praise of the then rapidly developing science of medicine, and B2 reaches its climax in a contrast of heights and depths: first the image of the man standing high inside his city, then the powerful rejection of the 'rash and wicked man'.

Some commentators have rushed to conclude that the Councillors have someone particular in mind;[39] but it is simply impossible for the

[37] Note that the opening and closing odes do not have this breadth; at start and finish of the tragedy, the Councillors focus more narrowly on the situation that confronts them.

[38] But NB Aischylos, *Libation Bearers* Choros 3; Sophokles' opening words echo those of that Choros, where the subject is monsters, first literally, and then metaphorically, referring to murderously wicked women. Cf. also Rehm 1992, chapter 7.

[39] E.g. Kreon (Kitto 1956, 157); *contra* Burton 1980, 98 and Gardiner 1987, 87. Cf. McCart's Notes, p. 288, for similar reactions to O*King* Choros 3.

audience to tell what side the Council will take in the contest between Antigone and Kreon, for that contest has not yet been begun. At this point the Councillors can only be understood as simply speculating in general, returning their thoughts to where the ode began, but now exploring the dangerous side of human nature. They believe that obedience to divine and to man-made laws goes together. They will soon be undeceived.[40]

Like Choros 1, this ode is sharply terminated by the arrival of new characters, forcing the drama back from generalizations to real human beings. It is therefore tempting to make (deliberately misleading) theatre sense of B2 in immediate retrospect: first, assigning the stanza to the self-righteous, pro-Kreon Councillor who will later speak 471–2, and then having the Guard bring Antigone into the *orchêstra* just after the stanza is completed. Then the visual sequence of the culprit Antigone appearing immediately after the last lines implies that *she* is in some way rash or wicked – and the wonderment in the words of the more sympathetic Councillor who declaims 376ff. will reinforce this false impression by contrast.[41] By the end of a performance, if anyone still remembers 368–71, (or, for that matter, 473ff. in the next scene) the lines turn out to fit not Antigone but Kreon; but by then much more will have been said about him (by Haimon, Teiresias, and Kreon himself in the Finale), which puts the same point far more precisely.

Scene 3

This scene contains the only confrontation between Antigone and Kreon, and climaxes with the second and last appearance of Ismene; it can and should be one of the most powerful and appalling scenes in Greek tragedy. Making it work in the theatre begins from one crucial decision: where is Antigone placed throughout the many lines before she speaks?

Since she is brought in from the right, normal blocking for a confrontation would place her in the BR sector, so Kreon can come out

[40] Segal 1981, 152–7 traces the ironic tensions between the vision presented in this ode and the picture of man's relationship with nature implied by the drama as a whole. Cf. also Segal 1964 *passim*, Aylen 1985, 127–34, and Scott 1996, 40.

[41] The amazement is partly due to the gender contrast (the Councillors, naturally, expected any great and rash action to be done by a man); partly to Antigone's royal parentage.

from the *skene* and become her antagonist BL.[42] But this positioning gives equality to the two characters; and much of the power of the drama lies in the fact that they are not equal. In outward appearance they are totally unequal; Kreon is male, a mature warlord, armed himself and with an armed bodyguard; Antigone is a young, unmarried woman, alone and a prisoner on a capital charge. Yet when she finally speaks, she becomes far the more powerful. How can this contrast between inner and outer strength be brought out, in theatre terms?

Our solution seemed very radical at first in rehearsal, but solved this problem, and provided several additional benefits. On arriving at the perimeter the Guard, who had been forcing Antigone along the *parodos* at a half-trot, one hand at the scruff of her neck and the other on her belt, hurled her forward so that she stumbled, fell, and came to rest prone in the exact centre of the *orchêstra*.[43]

The resulting position, apart from making Antigone the centre of attention during the following narrative, precisely conveys the required power relationships. Antigone is at the centre, so she will have the fullest power when she finally gets up to speak the 'unwritten laws' speech; but her inferior status is fully pointed up by her prone position, and the fact that she, as the only female, is a flash of colour in a scene otherwise occupied by males, most of whom are armed.[44]

This positioning also makes more sense of 442ff. Why *is* Antigone bowing her face towards the ground? (I would expect a standing Antigone to look Kreon full in the face from the moment he turns to

[42] That is how the scene was performed in my first experience of *Ant* in performance, a student production at Oxford. Antigone was unable to move, since two guards held her, hands tied behind her back to their crossed spears. Similar blocking has been frequent in professional stagings. However, the effect in performance is most detrimental, and I cannot now believe that Sophokles conceived the scene in this way.

[43] If you think this action too violent for Sophoklean tragedy, bear in mind that Sophokles undoubtedly enacted the following scenes in the *orchêstra*: the forcible abduction of Antigone at 938ff.; the suicide of Aias; the torture of the Theban Shepherd in *OKing*, and the kidnapping of Antigone in *OKol*.

[44] In our production it was also evident from her face and costume when she stood that the Guards had manhandled Antigone and beaten her up when they caught her. Too many productions play the Guard as a 'nice guy', the likeable ordinary man caught in a situation way beyond his depth (cf. Waldock 1951, 114 on his 'honest compunction' and self-disgust). I see him as a smarmy, sophistic and totally amoral survivalist (NB 440; cf. Nussbaum 1986, 53); I was therefore not prepared to let him get away with the rank hypocrisy of what Griffith calls 'a note of sympathy, even affection' for Antigone at 438–9.

her.) And why the lethargic, almost drugged tone of her first two responses?[45] If she is on the ground, hurt, gradually rousing herself for the contest of wills and words, then everything makes sense. Antigone began the play believing, like any teenage idealist, that in a good cause 'death will be beautiful' (72); Scene 3 is immensely more powerful if she begins it by suffering, realizing that the reality of defying an edict in a police state is degradation and physical pain; and then overcomes that pain to recover her full resolve and deliver the 'unwritten laws' speech.

The Guard   Every character who comes back in this drama returns changed. Everyone else is changed for the worse – Antigone, Ismene, the Bodyguard, and Kreon; Haimon and Eurydike return as corpses. It is therefore vital to mark the change for the better in the Guard by giving him the fullest freedom of movement in this scene, to contrast his garrulous joy in 388ff. with his hesitant, halting steps in Scene 2.[46] Outrageously but in his case correctly, he trusts that since he has justice on his side he will be free. So, if he has thrown Antigone to the centre, he can then move firmly around the perimeter, to approach Kreon from FL; after that the Guard can and should move back towards R round the whole *orchêstra* circle to illuminate his narrative.[47] By 423 he needs to be in a position where he can easily point to Antigone as part of the acting out of the narrative (e.g. BR); but he needs to work round again, passing in front of her, to a position where he can finish his report to Kreon and also be glared at by Antigone on 438. This position is just up-*orchêstra* from CL, and he must reach it by the end of 436.

When the Guard has been dismissed, he circles jauntily round in front of Antigone, and marches off out of the drama.[48]

[45] Griffith *ad loc.* hears 'impatience and contempt' in the Greek text of 448. However, performing her first two replies on this reading would validate the reactions of the Councillor and of Kreon after 470 – which is not desirable.

[46] This is another good practical reason for having him lose physical contact with Antigone as soon as possible, instead of being stuck beside her, still holding her as his prisoner.

[47] In performance Seale's suggestion (1982, 90) that 404–5 are impertinent was fully justified. Then, given that Polyneikes' sister is lying at C, we found it irresistible – if outrageous – for the Guard to mime 409–10 over her body, and then retreat quickly towards FC on 411–12 – as if going upwind from her (so practical, so unconcerned with ethical issues, as Griffith rightly notes *ad loc.*) – before resuming his story.

[48] 'Antigone *stays* to fulfil her destiny. This is the noble acceptance of death against the vulgar preservation of life.' Seale 1982, 91 (his emphasis).

Antigone The great speech of absolute defiance at 450ff. only works if it is seen not as a static declamation but as a volatile sequence designed not only to attack Kreon but also to attempt to convert the Councillors;[49] it also contains moments of introversion. So she rises up, motivated by his incredulity, and by doing so immediately converts the centre from a position of weakness to one of strength. Kreon stopped at BC, in astonishment at the prone girl before him, when he came in; this move now gives her enough power to drive Kreon off the centreline towards BL with the strength of the opening lines, directly addressed to him as she walks straight back towards BC (450–5). This blocking shows how a small young woman can over-power a large and armed mature man, by the sheer power of her vision and of her words.[50]

After such a move Antigone can turn to face forward, and show her absolute mastery of the playing space by advancing down the most powerful line in it, from BC towards C, over the next two, visionary lines 456–7; she remains facing forward (apart, perhaps, from a disdainful nod or gesture towards Kreon at the start of 460) until the centre of 460.

Here, however, the scene works best if she confronts the Council, again with a sharp turn towards Kreon on 'even without your edicts', facing back to them (the Councillors are still BL) for all except the meditative 'so, for me to meet this fate . . .', and turning finally to face Kreon, and move a few steps towards him, in the last two lines.

Kreon's response at 473ff. is furious, and becomes filled in retro-spect, especially after Scene 4, with bitter irony; the audience comes to realize that he is just as he imagines her to be (wrongly, since she never yields).[51] He begins by responding favourably to the Councillor's remark, and circles between the Councillors and Antigone (who will of course not deign to face him), trying to convince them of what he is

[49] Sophokles reinforces the utter isolation of Antigone by making the most hostile, pro-Kreon member of the group comment at 471 about her speech.

[50] Only after blocking it this way – and indeed well into the run of performances – did we realize that some of the most famous lines in Greek tragedy were being delivered by an actress facing away from almost all of the audience. In the Greek theatre shape, once you gain confidence at working in the 3/4 round, letting actors face away from part or all of the audience while speaking – difficult to do at all in the proscenium arch theatre – becomes quite normal; and in performance even this extreme effect worked (the sounding board of the *skene* façade makes sure that her words can be heard).

[51] Knox 1964, 62.

saying, and also provoke Antigone into submission. But the speech is outrageous; by what right can he regard a princess of the royal blood (or indeed any freeborn Theban) as his slave?[52] If that were not bad enough, an almost paranoiac fear of being beaten by a woman now invades his judgement;[53] finally he implicates Ismene in a capital offence on no evidence whatever, and orders her to be brought out for interrogation.[54] Then he ends by taunting Antigone, trying to provoke a response.

Like every meeting between relatives in this drama, this chilling confrontation, between a niece and an uncle who simply wants her dead, ends in a furious *stichomythia*. Evenly matched placing is possible here – but again undesirable; it is worth starting with Antigone in a more powerful position (e.g. EBC to Kreon's CL) to make him struggle to make his points; some of them have some cogency,[55] but her youthful idealism carries the day, right down to the marvellous line 523 ('I was not born to hate my relatives, but to give them my love') – on which of course she must break out of their increasingly intense, head-on confrontation and move away from him, to deliver its universal force out to the audience. This forces Kreon to chase after her to deliver the truly horrible pair of closing lines in which he tries to counter that force, and reassert his power.

[52] Line 479 puts him very far down the way towards the totally anti-democratic, tyrannical stance that he overtly adopts at 733ff. Cf. Cropp 1997, 157 n. 39, and Griffith *ad loc*.

[53] Kreon gives full expression to 'the uneasiness and ambivalence which the Greek male in the fifth century seems to have harboured towards the mature woman' (Segal 1981, 192).

At 487 it was impossible to stay close to the original; the line literally means 'even closer than Zeus, guardian of the courtyard' (i.e. of the household, Kreon's sacred, blood-related family itself). This is gross impiety (cf. Vickers 1973, 533); it is no accident that precisely the members of his immediate family, Haimon and Eurydike, come to hate him for what he has done, and destroy him. Cf. Knox 1984, 42.

[54] I presume Sophokles lets Kreon go this far, with no spoken resistance, so the audience agree with Antigone that (at least most of) the Council would approve of her if fear had not 'locked their tongues' (504–5, 509).

[55] As Blundell correctly notes (1989, 114; cf. Winnington-Ingram 1980, 132), animosity between *philoi* who had been murderers and victims continued beyond the grave; Kreon is probably therefore right to say at 516 that Eteokles' shade will resent her equal treatment of Polyneikes. But this point would only carry if any of the audience had time to think about it, while listening to this furious shouting match!

Ismene Sophokles now takes the tension of an already excruciating scene to breaking-point; the Bodyguard brings Ismene out into the embers of this exhausting *agôn*, and plunges her into the middle of the unremitting mutual hatred between Antigone and Kreon.[56]

Unusually, there is an entrance announcement, chanted in the original by one member of the *choros*; normally such stanzas were reserved for characters entering by one of the *parodoi*, to cover the time between their first coming into view of some of the spectators and entering the *orchêstra*, which actors coming out of the *skene* did at once.

The main reason why Sophokles wrote this five-line chant was to establish Ismene's mood; tears on a mask would not be visible when a character entered, even from the front rows. It also has the advantage of giving the audience a moment's break, and allowing the actors to regroup for the final and most pathos-filled part of the scene; Antigone resolutely faces out into the spectators, away from both Ismene and Kreon, while Kreon has time to break away from his last, furious riposte to Antigone, wheel round, and go up to menace Ismene in her turn.[57]

The wonderful surprise of this subscene, and the source of its pathos, is that although threatened with death by Kreon and his Bodyguard, Ismene only cares about what Antigone thinks of her. So any production must have her move hesitantly towards Antigone, who rounds on her, rejects her firmly,[58] and so precipitates another *stichomythia* of increasing intensity.[59] Antigone's absolute rejection of Ismene in 543–4 demands she turn and move away from her sister; this forces Ismene to follow – in our production, for a few lines actually kneeling in her desperate supplication. Antigone can turn back to respond to some of the subsequent appeals; but she must turn away from Ismene again, totally isolating her, at 558–9.

[56] The use of the third actor here, to cap a scene between two, is to my mind even finer than O*King* 631ff.

[57] The extreme violence of Kreon's verbal assault on Ismene led me to incorporate into our production an image of torture which has haunted me since first encountering Peter Weiss's documentary play *The Investigation*, culled from the Frankfurt trials of Auschwitz personnel (1966, 95ff. esp. 106). Our modern-dress Kreon rounded on Ismene, drew his pistol and placed it sadistically against her temple as he began 531. This then brings out visually the power of Ismene's astonishing decision to implicate herself, ignore him and move instead towards Antigone.

[58] But not harshly; NB 551 (*pace* Blundell 1989, 112).

[59] Note how it begins with two lines each, and Ismene reduces this to one when she attempts a direct emotional appeal.

After Antigone ends the argument with this couplet, Ismene has accepted Antigone's determination, and the scene's exploration of the past is complete. Kreon changes the focus with a sarcastic comment addressed to the Bodyguard or the Councillors. This allows Sophokles suddenly to invent[60] an even greater bond between Antigone and Kreon than that of niece and uncle: she is betrothed to his own son, and (570) emotionally very close to him. This new development generates most of the remainder of the drama: can Kreon kill Antigone without destroying his own family?

Here once again, as in Scene 1, directors have to choose between a plaintive, relatively deferential Ismene and a fuller response to his challenge. In performance a strong Ismene gives the scene balance, and the power needed to drive to a conclusion. So Ismene should round firmly on Kreon with 563–4. She is a princess, caught between two hostile characters, fighting for her sister's life and for her own; then her courage in responding to Kreon's brutal taunts[61] will lead to a powerful emotional impact when even she is stopped by the appalling sarcasm of 'on that we are agreed', and the two sisters are forced back into the *skene*.[62]

[60] See Introduction p. xlvii, and Notes to Scene 4, below.

[61] His fear of women has come out already (484ff.); but Kreon goes much further with 569 – a shocking devaluation of women even in a culture where women were regarded as inferior, and men gave away their daughters, in the words of the Athenian marriage ceremony, 'for the ploughing of legitimate children' (see Griffith *ad loc.*, and cf. Vickers 1973, 534).

This line is always softened in translation, presumably to make Kreon sound less coarse and brutal; 'there are other fields for him to plough', Fagles 1984, 89; cf. e.g. Segal 1981, 165, 173, and 181 and Nussbaum 1986, 57; Kitto (1994, 21), translating in 1951, was even more euphemistic. For Kreon, women are just cunts. Discussing lovers' true feelings is 'bedroom talk' (573), which gets on his nerves. The sequence conveys a deep loathing of sexuality and of sexual love.

[62] Line 572 has often been assigned to Antigone, 576 to a Councillor. Even more implausibly, Dawe 1979 gave 574 and 576 to Antigone (so too Gardiner 1987, 89). All such reassignments must be resisted, because they wreck the power of the confrontation in the theatre by pulling focus away from the contest between Ismene and Kreon. There are also good scholarly reasons for the attribution printed here; see Mastronarde 1979, 95–6, Lloyd-Jones and Wilson 1990, 127–8, and Griffith *ad loc.*

Choros 3

The Councillors have just seen the last surviving descendants of Labdakos herded inside to await their execution at the pleasure of a sadistic tyrant. Choros 3 therefore opens as a dark, subdued meditation on disaster in families, which is specifically linked in the second stanza to the impending extinction of the royal house of Thebes.

Many scholars have believed that Sophokles – or at least his Council, which is not the same – asserts here that a family curse is destroying the house of Labdakos. Easterling refuted that view in a closely argued interpretation of the ode,[63] and this translation has been careful to avoid importing ideas that are not present in the original Greek. In marvellous imagery which needs a strong choreographic response, the Councillors evoke the cumulative force of inescapable disaster across generations (not analysing who is or was responsible for it); they then apply this to what they have just seen. However the Councillor who sings A2, like the speaker of 471–2 (perhaps they should be the same person) sees the action from a more limited perspective than Sophokles expects from the audience. We heard little, if any 'crazy speech' from Antigone in Scene 3; and no one with 'Furies in the mind' – if that means, as it probably does for the Councillors, acting tempestuously and thoughtlessly – could have argued against her judge with such clarity and courage, while knowing that she is under sentence of death.[64] In the next three scenes, the course of the action will force the Councillors one by one to abandon this wrong perspective on the action.

The emotional pattern of the B stanzas is clear: power and light invade the dance in the first half of each stanza, before the closing return to the idea of disaster from A1, which closes both stanzas in the Greek as in this English version. But what is their relevance? The

[63] 1978, 141–8, esp. 142. However Burton 1980, esp. 105 and 111, Winnington-Ingram 1980, 143 and Mogyoródi 1996 attempt to reassert the presence of the curse.

[64] Easterling 1978, 156; Burton 1980, 110. However, in a literal sense of the words, Antigone might well have had Furies in her mind. In Greek belief, the Furies of a dead man or woman rose from his or her spilled blood and called upon the nearest surviving male relative to avenge the death, and on the nearest surviving female to care for the body. Their invasion of that relative's mind simply gives them strong motivation; it does not normally cause insanity. (Orestes in Aischylos' *Libation Bearers* is in a unique position, obliged to avenge his father's death upon his mother.)

Councillors offer in B1 the old popular belief, explicitly opposed by the wiser Elders of Aischylos' *Agamemnon* 750ff., that great wealth automatically leads to disaster; and once again (cf. Choros 2), though there is no explicit reference to any one character, some commentators have felt that B2 contains much that will subsequently apply to Kreon.[65]

I doubt whether Sophokles intended to affect his spectators in this way. Kreon's impending downfall is not caused by his wealth, nor by empty hopes, but by gross misjudgement, coupled with an obstinate and blind confidence that he alone is right. Of the whole two stanzas, only the last three lines of B2 could conceivably be applied to him. The second half of the ode – again, if the choreography is sufficiently evocative – gives us a picture in general terms of the appalling vulnerability of human beings. But the traditional ideas in the Choroses are in sharp contrast with 'the action and the "modern" dialectic of the characters'[66] in the scenes of *Antigone*, and I would prefer to stress the essential irrelevance of the B stanzas to the unfolding action.[67] The Councillors are clutching at straws, trying to use popular beliefs to interpret the events that they are witnessing. This is consistent with their overall role; from Antigone's return as a prisoner in Scene 3 until the end of the Teiresias scene, they are quite simply out of their depth.

Sophokles suggests this by one particular piece of stagecraft. It is clear from 626ff. that Kreon has remained outside the *skene* during this ode; and the presence of a solo actor during a *choros* is a striking, though not unparalleled, breach of Greek theatre convention.[68] The effect in performance is not for the ode to take on special reference to him; on the contrary, his distracting, 'upstaging' presence pulls the audience's focus away from concentrating on the Councillors' analysis of the situation. Since that analysis is itself neither correct nor fully focused, Sophokles may have left Kreon in sight to achieve just that.

Contemporary audiences do not know the conventions of Greek drama, and Sophokles' unusual procedure will not now be appreciated

[65] E.g. Gellie 1972, 42; Winnington-Ingram 1980, 170–72.

[66] Easterling 1978, 155. As she notes, the contrast between Choros 3 and Scene 4 is one of the most striking examples.

[67] Cf. Scott 1996, 45. He claims that the less tight metrical construction of the B stanzas in the original Greek symbolized the arbitrariness of the Councillors' implicit assumption that Zeus' judgement is the cause of Antigone's suffering.

[68] The effect is normally reserved for characters who deliberately take root in the place represented by the *orchêstra* – e.g. Sophokles' *Elektra*, and his *Oidipous* when he reaches Kolonos.

without some device to highlight it. In our modern-dress production Kreon sat down at a table preset just outside the *orchêstra* EBR, helped himself to a glass of raki and smoked a cigarette. This brought out his absolute indifference to the starting-point of the song, the fact that his decision to condemn the two girls to death will finally extinguish the house of Labdakos.

Scene 4

The relationship between father and son was the most crucial of all the *philos* relationships that bound Greeks together. Without sons, a man had no one to tend him in his old age, and could not pass on his name and lineage. The earliest Greek narrative, the *Iliad*, reaches its climax and its catharsis in the mutual lamentation of Priam, who has lost his son, and Achilleus, who will never see his father again; one of the two main focuses of the *Odyssey* is the relationship between Odysseus and Telemachos; and the theme recurs in much subsequent poetry and drama.[69]

Its introduction in *Antigone* is surprising, unexpected – and creates the central scene. In previous versions of the myth, Haimon had been killed years earlier, by the Sphinx;[70] now we have suddenly learned from Ismene (568) that in this drama he is alive, and engaged to Antigone. Almost before the audience has had a chance to absorb the innovation, here he is; and the Councillor's announcement puts the issue precisely; both his suggestion that Haimon might be 'very bitter', and Kreon's talk of 'frenzied rage' evoke the (entirely reasonable) fear that passion for Antigone might be swaying Haimon's judgement.[71]

His opening words reveal that Haimon knows his father all too well,

[69] Homer, *Iliad* 24.467ff.; *Odyssey, passim*. NB esp. Klytaimestra's choice of image for the climax of her rhetoric at Aischylos, *Agamemnon* 898, and Oidipous' diatribe in *OKol* (1362ff.) against the sons who have obliged his daughters to perform the son's duty of looking after him in old age.

[70] Fragment of the epic poem *Oidipodeia*, cited and discussed in the Introduction p. xlvii n.96.

[71] As Griffith notes *ad loc.*, father and son only rarely meet each other in public in Greek tragedy; and sons were of course not expected to shame their fathers by confronting them and arguing with them in public. However, Ismene introduced Haimon's love for Antigone at 570, because the audience needs to know before he arrives that this was not just a politically expedient, arranged marriage. Then they will at first be anxious about his opening reaction, and then reassured by it – but they are also prepared for the tremendous explosion when he fails to persuade his father.

and is aware that any such show of emotion will have a disastrous effect.[72] His task must be to demonstrate by reasoning that the decision to execute Antigone is not a good example of 'fine leadership'.[73]

Haimon's first four lines at first seem to reassure Kreon; but they invite him to explain himself – and this puts his father on the defensive. Kreon has to launch out into a long speech justifying his advice, and so precipitates the longest formal *agôn* in this drama: one long speech for each protagonist, each with a formal two-line comment from the Councillors, precipitating a *stichomythia* of rapidly gathering emotion in which all the tension between them is brought out, climaxing in two closing speeches, each of four lines.[74]

Scenes like this will not work as virtually static diatribes; and attempting to block them with simply a few steps by the speaker towards, and away from, the listener looks very ineffective. The shape of the *orchêstra* led us to another solution. Noting that in this scene each speaker keeps changing tack, trying to find new arguments which will persuade the other character, we ended up placing the silent figure at the centre of the circle, while the speaker moved around, going from point to point around the listener, stopping and then starting again when he thought of a new argument. Kreon still moved in straight lines; but Haimon, since he is in Kreon's view on the woman's side, and in anyone's view is less rigid than his father, circled in curved movements like Antigone and Ismene.

A silent, rocklike posture for Haimon perfectly expresses the ineffectiveness of Kreon's homily. After beginning with a clichéd decoration of the theme of the virtue of obedient children, Kreon starts at 648ff. to reveal once more (cf. 569ff.) his fundamental fear of women, and indeed of passion of any kind. Vickers was rightly revolted by 653: 'Antigone is reduced to the status of an orange pip, or some irritating piece of food stuck in one's teeth. No other character in Greek tragedy

[72] In our production the Councillors sat down, relieved, as Haimon completed his first couplet, so clearing the playing area for the two principal characters. Their failure to support Antigone or Ismene in Scene 3 has now marginalized them.

[73] Cf. Angas 1995. Actors and directors must decide to what extent, if any, Haimon should show the audience the effort he is making to be restrained.

[74] Griffith *ad loc.* rightly notes how this 'rigid formalism . . . contributes to the current of pent-up emotions that pervades the scene' – especially since the two long speeches are forty-one and forty-two lines long (they would be exactly equal in length if, as some scholars suspect, a line has been lost between 690 and 691).

has this consistent cold unfeelingness. Iago, or the Doctor in *Woyzeck*, are the only parallels that I can think of.'[75]

Now Kreon gives concrete form to the most disturbing feature of the theory of political morality that he outlined in Scene 2: here he explicitly places loyalty to the *polis* above his own obligations to Antigone, above the rights, guaranteed by Zeus himself, that she has as his kinswoman.[76]

But the situation has changed since Scene 2; and Kreon's position has also – under pressure – become more explicit on the subject of leadership. Although the lines follow a fully democratic sketch of the ideal citizen,[77] 667ff. amount to 'obey me or else'. In themselves, Kreon's thoughts on the danger of anarchy (672ff.), like his opening ideas about obedient children, would be unexceptionable to most Athenians.[78] However, placed as they are between an undemocratic insistence on obedience to the ruler in all things, just or unjust (667–72), and the closing return at 676ff. to the misogyny of 648ff., they do not have the intended effect – except on one dull-witted Councillor.

The tragedy of this scene is that even Haimon's tactful and subtle approach cannot work on Kreon. Avoiding the trap of mentioning his own deep love for Antigone, he takes an almost equal risk by telling his father that public opinion is against him. This has the useful side-effect of putting the Councillors, quite rightly, out on a limb in their continued support for Kreon, and fear of defending Antigone. This is the only surviving Greek tragedy where 'a chorus composed of "representatives of the people" is shown up as not being representative of the people'.[79]

Public opinion should be important to any responsible leader; but not Kreon. By 700 Haimon has got nowhere; Kreon remains silent; so he tries a different tack, arguing from Kreon's own self-interest – a

---

[75] 1973, 535. I would add John Claggart, in the Forster/ Britten opera based on Melville's *Billy Budd*. Note however that none of these three characters is ever forced by higher powers, like Kreon, to acknowledge his error.

[76] Blundell 1989, 120–22; as she notes, Kreon has already disregarded the possible anger of Zeus, in his capacity as god of the household, in 486ff. There is great, nicely understated irony when these lines are followed by 661ff.; Kreon is not managing his household well at all.

[77] Lines '668–70', translated here in Seidler's transposition as 663–6.

[78] On anarchy, cf. e.g. Athens' patron goddess herself at Aischylos, *Eumenides* 696ff.; on fathers and sons, Griffith *ad loc.* compares YWT 1174–80.

[79] Vickers 1973, 83.

consideration that was normally decisive in Greek ethics before Sokrates. But even the passionate entreaty of 701ff. doesn't work,[80] so in conclusion he attempts a sequence of maxims on the virtues of being able to yield.

Unfortunately, the speech has begun and ended with the idea of wisdom; and Kreon is intelligent enough to see Haimon's (correct) implication that he, Kreon, is being unwise. So he rounds on the Councillor who dares to suggest there is something in what Haimon has said, and when Haimon deflects his father's anger (which he now knows, despite 718, he has failed to check) back onto its proper target, a furious *stichomythia* propels the scene to its climax. Haimon brings out to the full Kreon's arrogant tyranny and the wrongness of his actions;[81] but the argument is broken off (like that against Ismene, at 577) with Kreon's brutal reassertion that Antigone will die (750).

Now there is no longer any point in Haimon's hiding his love for her. At this point the furious tempo should be stilled for a moment (in our production Haimon turned away, and addressed 751 away from Kreon, out into the L segment of the audience), to give a point of rest before driving to the climax at 758ff. Here the Bodyguard must actually start towards the *skene* doors on 760–61, to convey the real prospect that we might see Antigone killed in public, before our eyes;[82] he only stops, puzzled, as the king's son blurts out his terrible final lines, blinded by rage and emotion, and pushes past his father to the *parodos*.

Kreon is shaken for the first time, and a Councillor manages to save Ismene's life;[83] meanwhile he decides on a method of killing Antigone which is different from the public stoning proposed in his original edict (36). Kitto speculated that this is because after what we have heard in

[80] In our production Kreon at several points between here and the end of the speech had his back totally turned to Haimon.

[81] NB esp. 739 and 745ff.

[82] Scholars tend to assume that an act as violent as murder could not be enacted in sight of the audience in Greek tragedy; but how can we be sure that the Athenian audience would be certain of that, at a climax this drastic, in the hands of the dramatist whose Aias had committed suicide in mid-*orchêstra*? In our production Kreon seized and brandished his own handgun on 759; he hates Antigone so much that he intends to execute her himself. It is easy to imagine Sophokles' Kreon drawing his sword or dagger at the same moment and with the same intent.

[83] This is just. But Ismene has told us her life will be meaningless without Antigone, and Antigone regards herself in Scene 5 as the last descendant of the royal house (940); so if any spectator were to think about Ismene after this (which is unlikely), they might well feel she would be better off dead.

Scene 4 the people of Thebes might not cooperate in publicly stoning
Antigone to death.[84] This could occur to some of the audience; but
Kreon gives his own reason: he does not want the *miasma* of her death
to fall on the city. By this invention, Sophokles positions himself for
Kreon's inconsistent rejection of belief in any kind of pollution, at the
height of his folly in the Teiresias scene (1039ff.); also for Antigone's
characteristic decision to hang herself at once after being entombed,
rather than sit quietly in limbo, eating for a day or so in the dark and
then waiting to die by starvation.

Kreon and his Bodyguard should leave at the end of this scene.
There is no dramatic point in having Kreon remain to pull focus from
Choros 4 (as there is for Choroses 3 and 5);[85] and there is great damage
in having him present for the start of Scene 5, to pull focus from
Antigone's dance of death and the interaction between her and the
Councillors.[86]

Choros 4

Since both Kreon's position and Haimon's are now irrevocable, Sophokles moves as fast as possible towards Antigone's death. Choros 4
contains only two stanzas, flowing straight on into the lyric opening of
Scene 5; but these two stanzas go right to the heart of the situation.
Sexual Passion ('Erôs') makes males accept the power of femininity,
not attempting to subjugate erotic power, but acknowledging its
supremacy. This force, which Kreon loathes and dismisses, is at the
heart of the imminent destruction of his household.[87] For the Greeks –
quite rightly – Passion could be a dangerous force, able to destroy
human beings, and make fools even of gods.[88] Sophokles now brings
out the hidden force that plunged Haimon towards his deeply disturbed
exit.

[84] 1956, 166ff. Cf. Seale 1982, 98, and Knox 1964, 72.

[85] The text does not support the view that Choros 4 is designed to 'mitigate
[Kreon's] anger at his son by reminding him that such youthful folly is nothing
new' (Griffith *ad loc.*).

[86] *Contra* Kitto 1956, 146ff. and 167ff., Winnington-Ingram 1980, 137, and
Bain 1981, 28. If Kreon leaves, he returns unannounced at 883; but there are
parallels for this – e.g. Klytaimestra's entrance in Scene 3 of Aischylos, *Agamemnon*, Oidipous' for Scene 2 of *OKing*, and Theseus' in the Finale of *OKol*.

[87] Kitto 1956, 163, 167 and 176ff.; Winnington-Ingram 1980, 97.

[88] Humans: Euripides, *Hippolytos, Medeia* (esp. Choros 3); gods: Homer,
Odyssey 8.267ff.

The choreography must reflect the subject-matter: sinuous and powerful, in designed contrast with what happens next. Antigone, the virgin bride of Haides, has awakened Passion in Haimon; but she herself will never be sexually fulfilled; so on her appearance their dance changes at once, and becomes an expression of sympathy.[89]

Scene 5

Like Aischylos at the climax of *Agamemnon* (Scene 6, the Kassandra scene), Sophokles now has *choros* characters who are older, and male, surrounding a young female who knows she is about to die without ever fulfilling the goal of Greek womanhood – marriage, and childbearing. He treats the situation in the same way as Aischylos, first with solo-actor lyrics in which Antigone dances to express the intensity of her emotion, and then with speech, in which she can reason through and come to terms with her death.

Aischylos' Elders become gradually more sympathetic, as a group, to Kassandra. Sophokles deliberately withholds that comfort from Antigone, and leaves some of the Councillors hostile to her to heighten the pathos of her isolation in this, her final scene before execution.[90] She never knows – as the audience does, from Haimon (693ff.) – that the ordinary people of Thebes support what she has done; and though some of the Councillors at least feel sorry for her (801ff.), other voices express thoughts that only increase her feeling of isolation (834ff., 853ff.; cf. 929–30). Sophokles manipulates the Councillors very carefully; if they were less complacent (or scared of Kreon), they should have been fully converted by the Haimon scene; but Sophokles needs to present Antigone isolated, confronting almost fully hostile *choros*-characters of the opposite gender, to gain full audience sympathy for her plight; so he allows them at the end of Scene 4 only to intercede for Ismene, and holds their full conversion back until the end of the Teiresias scene. In our production the Councillors danced in and from

---

[89] The language of Choros 4 recalls that of a wedding celebration; Seaford 1987, 108. Winnington-Ingram 1980, 96 brings out the continuity of the bridal theme from stanza A2 through into Scene 5. Cf. Griffith on 806–16, with references, for the parallels between Greek wedding and funeral rites which Sophokles plays on in this sequence.

[90] Elsewhere in surviving tragedy only in Euripides' *Bakchai* does a principal character go to his or her death, like Antigone, in the face of a hostile *choros* character of the opposite gender – and Pentheus is so deluded that he does not realize what is going to happen to him.

positions along the rear perimeter of the *orchêstra*, forming a backdrop to the solo actor's role in the *kommos*.

Antigone's dance of death is accompanied by sung words of vivid power, which bring out directly, in the very first stanza, the full pathos for a Greek *parthenos* of a virgin death – and the particularly revolting prospect of being buried alive.[91] The Councillors (embarrassed, and therefore tactless) twice try to praise her; but she is naturally hypersensitive, so the first attempt leads her to compare herself with Niobe (who like her died neither from disease nor violence), and the second, reminding her that she is not a demigod like Niobe, provokes a furious reaction, in which Antigone proclaims her isolation from all human comforters (846), and then touches on the outrage of Kreon's law, which is to become the closing theme of her final speech, before ending in self-pity.

Once again echoing the pattern of Aischylos' Elders in *Agamemnon* (1141ff.), the Councillors are disturbed by the intensity of her emotion, and now (853) meet her in full song – probably, in the original, in unison to contrast with the chanted individual responses earlier in her dance. They criticize her (853ff.), and will not even allow her to pity herself (since she has no pity from them). Their final comment (856) leads her to dance out the horror of the royal house, desperately trying to arouse some sympathy in them, even expressing the humiliation of having to go back to share her parents' house in Haides. But she fails to move the Councillors; so she ignores the final accusation, and concentrates in the last stanza on the pathos of her utter isolation.[92]

Although she has stopped lamenting, Kreon comes out to bring a halt to all this, orders the Bodyguard to take her away as fast as possible – and then allows Antigone to deliver an extended final monologue! This is unrealistic, and therefore goes against the normal convention of spoken dialogue scenes in tragedy; but – perhaps because this section is framed between the preceding lyric section of the scene and the chanted conclusion at 929ff. – Sophokles may have felt that the drama is at this point near to the convention that in sung passages time may 'stand still', and resume wherever the dramatist wishes.[93] And he needed to employ that convention because Antigone must linger in our minds, for she will not be named again after she has been

[91] Winnington-Ingram 1980, 139–40. On the imprisonment of women (cf. Choros 5), see Seaford 1990.

[92] In the original Greek it is marked off by a change of metre, to trochaics.

[93] Cf. Bain 1981, 24–9.

dragged away; yet her execution and its effects overshadow the whole of the rest of the drama, and the great speech at 891ff. allows the actress to achieve this.[94]

Antigone first advances towards the R *parodos*, because it is being gradually more strongly established, as the drama unfolds, as the way that leads to death; and that is where she will soon be taken to the tomb. But she cannot play the whole speech facing that way. She should wheel round after reaching BR, facing forward, to play 895ff. to an imaginary family in front of her (i.e. towards FR), perhaps even kneeling for the intimate address to Polyneikes at 899ff.

Lines 905ff., her final public self-justification, must be begun as an argument directed at the Councillors, with Antigone advancing towards them. In our production they were at this point huddled BL; that gave Antigone an effective turn away from them at 908, wheeling forward so as to arrive FC by 913 – from where she can first address the next lines to the imaginary Polyneikes at FR, and then turn to look directly up the centreline at Kreon (who obviously must be BC for this part of the scene) on 916. If she advances towards him during the next few lines, that allows her to reach C and turn to face forward, taking command of the *orchêstra* from Kreon, to give the fullest power to the passionate appeal to the audience, against Kreon's idea of justice, at 921.

Here we reach the climactic theatrical expression of the grim world-view which Sophokles presents in this drama.[95] Antigone has indeed transgressed no 'justice of the gods' – on the contrary, she has obeyed their 'unwritten laws', and showed true piety by burying her brother; but the heavens do not save her. In the dénouement of this drama, there is none of the *dike* which makes ultimate sense, in Aischylos, of human affairs and our place in the universe.[96]

[94] There has been futile, depressing scholarly debate since 1821 over whether Sophokles wrote 904–913/920. The lines were quoted as genuine by Aristotle (*Rhetoric* 1417a32–3), less than a century after Sophokles' death. Antigone's argument that her natural bond with her brother Polyneikes has primacy is utterly intelligible and actable, especially given the stress earlier in this scene on Antigone's death before the ritual of marriage fulfilled her as a woman; the problems are only real for scholars in the study.

The lines are discussed, and the text defended, by Knox 1964, 106ff., Lloyd-Jones and Wilson 1990, 138, Neuburg 1990 (particularly thorough and convincing), Foley 1996, 54 and Griffith *ad loc.* Cf. also Cropp 1997.

[95] Cf. Winnington-Ingram 1980, 148–9.

[96] Ewans 1995, xxvii–xxxiv. The contrast with Aischylos' Kassandra is

Antigone's modest, final prayer at 927–8 – her last defiance of Kreon – is followed by a sudden resumption of music; the chant at 929ff. is the signal that her last moments have come. Once again a Councillor insists wrongly[97] that Antigone is frenzied; then Kreon's order starts the Bodyguard off on his way to take her.[98] The cold cruelty of the double negative in 935–6 seals Antigone's fate; she utters a last appeal to her fatherland and its gods; and as she is seized and dragged off (939ff.), Sophokles chooses to make Antigone address her last words directly to the Councillors, laying the utter injustice of her death, the extinction of the house of Labdakos at Kreon's hand, before their eyes as witnesses who have failed her.

The use of chant makes this section seem like a miniature Finale (which, for Antigone, it is); but the way in which Choros 5 begins as an address to Antigone demands continuity. So in our production, the Councillors were so disturbed by Antigone's brutal abduction that they rushed to gather at the BR perimeter, and watched her being taken away, then moved at once back into the body of the *orchêstra* to segue into the start of Choros 5.

Choros 5

The Councillors perform their last wide-ranging lyric meditation on the action: a dark song, with 'a dense, choking atmosphere'.[99] It flows inexorably on to the violence at the climax of B1 and from there to the grim picture of human limits at the close.

The springboard is a consolation addressed to Antigone, as she recedes into the distance; the Councillors' theme is imprisonment, and they try to think of people who were imprisoned but later freed – Danaë, who accepted a god's desire (but needed a miracle to free her from persecution by her father Akrisios), and Lykourgos, who in his madness defied a god;[100] but then in the second strophic pair the sense

---

helpful; she had broken a promise to a god, and comes to realize that her punishment is death. Antigone has done nothing to offend any god; on the contrary, she has upheld their laws. Cf. Introduction pp. xxii and xxiv.

[97] *Pace* Winnington-Ingram 1980, 146.

[98] The sequence only makes theatre sense if blocked so the Bodyguard has quite a way to go before he can manhandle her out of the playing space; from EBC near the doors to Antigone at (e.g.) FL.

[99] Nussbaum 1986, 77.

[100] Some commentators (e.g. Kitto 1956, 173, Winnington-Ingram 1980, 103–4) think the Councillors – or Sophokles through their choice of subject –

swerves away from the main theme.[101] Kleopatra (the unnamed queen who had been Phineus' first wife) was probably imprisoned, and the concluding lines refer obliquely to this; but the main image is of the bloody violence that his second wife dealt to Kleopatra's innocent sons. The reference is obscure to us (Sophokles wrote two dramas about Phineus, both lost); but this stanza obviously anticipates the violence that will break out at the end of *Antigone*.[102]

The Councillors refer twice (at the end of A1 and B2) to the power of Destiny. It does indeed have fearful power in Sophokles; but in this drama, as in the stories of Danaë, Lykourgos and Kleopatra, human destiny is forged by human actions.[103] Now we are about to be told that the actions of one human, Kreon, have so disturbed the order of nature that they will destroy him. And the Councillors' passive consent and fatalism have done much to assist him. Kreon should therefore remain in sight once more – silent, brooding and indifferent – while the Councillors try to come to terms with the consequences of his action.[104]

Scene 6

Teiresias, the legendary prophet of Thebes, appears both in *Antigone* and *Oidipous the King*. There is a striking contrast between his sudden, unannounced entry and abrupt opening dialogue with Kreon here and the long build-up in *Oidipous* Scene 2 before he begins to prophesy. That is needed because what Teiresias has to say to Oidipous is so unbelievable that without preparation we would not expect him to be believed. And even after Oidipous' gracious acknowledgement of his

---

want the audience to think of Kreon; but Kreon, unlike the great victims of Dionysos, never goes mad; he is merely (extremely) foolish. Only slightly more plausibly, Winnington-Ingram 1980, 101 likens Kreon to Akrisios. Griffith, in a fine discussion *ad loc.* of this Choros as a whole, is rightly more cautious, and alert to the way in which Sophoklean allusions to myth can impact subtly and obliquely on the action, rather than being intended to make the audience take them as direct comments on the situation of one or both of the protagonists.

[101] In the Greek original, the metre changed, ominously, to the logaoedic and trochaic combination used for Choros 3, and for Antigone's brooding stanzas towards the end of the *kommos* in Scene 5.

[102] Cf. Burton 1980, 131

[103] Cf. McCart on *OKing* 1457, with references; below, p. 300.

[104] *Pace* Seale 1982, 101. NB that while the Councillors announce Teiresias for Scene 6, Kreon is not announced; contrast e.g. 386.

ability, the king's reactions, when he is told the truth, are disbelief and anger.

By contrast, what Teiresias discloses to Kreon is all too credible, and eventually terrifies even this arrogant man who – as the prophet rightly tells him at once – has gone 'right to the sharpened edge of fate'. Sophokles introduces Teiresias to do what no one of lesser authority could do; to break Kreon's resolve. The opening exchange takes him to a dominant position (surely, c); and Kreon is, for the first time in the drama, alone during this confrontation.[105] Teiresias launches into an extended speech of great theatrical power. The omens tell him that the gods are disturbed by Polyneikes' unburied corpse, and the pollution created by his act is literally spreading to the city – but can be cured, if Kreon yields.

For reasons that are hinted at but not explained (1034–5), Sophokles makes Kreon revive against the prophet the accusations of corruption which were his first response to news he did not want to hear, in Scene 2. He has learned nothing since then; and he goes even further, briefly embracing at 1040ff. the idea that the gods are unaffected by human actions. That is not true in this drama.[106]

Paranoia again, then; and in his last confrontational *stichomythia*, continually accusing Teiresias of corruption, Kreon breaks down the prophet's restraint and is then devastated, reduced to silence by the terrible prophecy that he evokes.

Teiresias may be blind, but he should not be motionless. He walks with the aid of his boy, but does not need to be played as totally dependent on him; and he can sense where Kreon is by his voice. So a sequence of moves can be created in which Teiresias alternates between standing still, being guided by the boy, and throwing off that guidance – as in the last speech, where in our production he broke away from the boy at 1064, leaving him at the centre, and drove Kreon in front of him to the edge of the circle, advancing to match the power of his rhetoric until he brought Kreon to his knees. Then 1077 can be accompanied by a brusque gesture, which brings the boy fast to lead

[105] He now lacks the support of his Bodyguard, who has left to entomb Antigone. Kreon's human power is useless against Teiresias' divine power, and it would therefore be superfluous for its physical representative to be present in this scene. The prophet cows the Councillors into total silence (in our production they prostrated themselves in reverence for him); this further isolates Kreon.

[106] Nor in general Greek belief, even in the later fifth century. But the idea that *miasma* is not effective was part of the progressive 'new thought' of the times. Cf. e.g. Euripides, *Herakles* 1232, *Orestes* 73ff.

him back to C for the final peroration (1080–87). Their progress to the exit should be stopped at the edge of the circle, so the last two lines can be delivered back at Kreon, almost as an afterthought. Then Teiresias urges the boy back onto the exit route, down the *parodos*.[107]

At last Kreon crumbles. In Griffith's view, this shows that 'despite his outbursts of temper he is at bottom a sensible and well-meaning leader'.[108] This is too kind. The greatest test of leadership is the ability to recognize and accept good advice regardless of the source. A 'sensible leader' would not have needed a prophet of awesome authority to tell him truths that he could not accept in the mouths of his niece or his son – and would therefore not have caused three deaths. Sympathy is generated for Kreon in the Finale not because the audience sees his underlying merits, but because it sees a man, who has made horrendous misjudgements through defensive arrogance and inadequate understanding, acknowledging too late how great his folly has been.

In performance, his fall should be reflected now in his first indecisive, circling steps, as the Councillors finally find voice and one by one bring pressure on him.[109] Then he calls impulsively to his men[110] – and rushes off, after voicing two 'pre-exit', mouth-of-*parodos* lines to express how much he has learned in so short a time.

Teiresias implied (1067ff.) and one of the Councillors bluntly and explicitly told him (1100) that he must free Antigone first. If he does so, she might be saved and Teiresias' prophecies proved false – for the first time ever. The audience must regard this as a real possibility.[111]

---

[107] The received text of 1080–83 is puzzling, since it suggests that 'all the cities' are angry with Kreon for failing to bury their sons. This might refer to the legend that Theseus of Athens had to intervene to force Kreon to bury the Argive dead, which was told in the epic poem *Thebais*, and later dramatized in Euripides' *Suppliants*. However, that wider focus is not appropriate in *Ant*, where the clear implication is that only one body on either side was left unburied: that of Polyneikes. Since the text is corrupt and disputed, I have emended the translation to reflect this.

[108] On 988ff.; cf. on 1091ff.

[109] Griffith *ad loc.* rightly notes the irregularity of the line-distribution in this dialogue (431122). This demands an equally random, uncertain movement pattern in the staging. Alternating the Councillors' lines between speakers far apart from each other, making Kreon turn to face them successively, helps to achieve the right effect.

[110] The gesture is so fleeting that we do not need to flood the playing space with extras; the audience will imagine that they join Kreon out of sight, after he has left.

[111] Line 1092ff.; cf. 1023ff. Seale 1982, 103 rightly develops the contrast

But what will Kreon order his men to do first, when they gather on the hill that overlooks Thebes?

Choros 6

The Councillors called on Bakchos (Dionysos) to lead their dances of celebration in Choros 1; they recalled the legend of his defeat of Lykourgos in Choros 5; now they devote all four stanzas of this Choros to invoking him in a powerful prayer, to implore his help.[112] But Dionysos will not give them what they need. He is the god of the power rising in the sap of young plants and the blood of young animals – and human beings;[113] and the narrative in Scene 7 will reveal that two young people have created the catastrophe by their headstrong and swift reactions to Kreon's entombment of Antigone.

Dionysos was also the god of 'ekstasis', of escape from normal reality – especially when it threatens to become intolerable. Sophokles deliberately placed this upbeat, escapist dance immediately before the dénouement to create a total contrast at the end. Just after the final, culminating cry of Dionysos' name as a god of renewal, 'Iakchos!', the Bodyguard enters, dishevelled and haggard, to bring the news of two deaths.

The intended effect is achieved only if the dance is choreographed as a steadily flowing, solemn but increasingly ecstatic dance with a pounding beat, evoking the power of the ritual worship of Dionysos, and abruptly brought to a halt at the climax.[114]

Scene 7

The events on the hills and in the cave are brought before the audience in a gripping narrative. This gains very greatly in impact if it is spoken by a person who has already been established for the audience as an

with OKing Scene 3, where the king, because he has already fulfilled the prophecy Apollo gave to Laios, cannot profit from Teiresias' words and avoid disaster.

[112] For a fine analysis of this ode – wide-ranging and fascinating, though far removed from performance considerations – cf. Segal 1981, 204–6.

[113] Dodds 1960, xii.

[114] Sophokles intensifies the impact of the catastrophe by preceding it with a contrasting, upbeat Choros in four of his seven surviving dramas: Cf. Ai Choros 3, YWT Choros 4 and OKing Choros 4. In performance the effect is – or ought to be – almost sickening.

admirer of Kreon; the faithful Bodyguard who without question was
prepared to intimidate, manhandle and murder at Kreon's orders. He
now returns, dishevelled and dirty from burying the body and breaking
into the cave-tomb; the visible descent from his crisp military appearance in previous scenes prefigures both the horrors he has to relate and
the similar, even worse downfall of Kreon when he appears for the
Finale. And this visual content matches the burden of his opening
address; as we reach the climax of *Antigone*, Sophokles sounds one of
the recurrent themes of his tragedies: the suddenness of mutability in
human affairs.[115]

  Though the fact that he has sons presupposes that Kreon has a wife,
there has been no reason to suppose that she will be a character in this
drama. Eurydike's hesitant, totally unexpected entry transforms the
scene. Before she comes, the Councillors have simply been told the bare
facts. Having the story told to them alone would not be remotely as
effective as bringing on a member of the royal household, closely
related to all the protagonists. Eurydike's presence, and the fact that
the Bodyguard warms to her and will not protect her by omission or
euphemism, gives a reason for a detailed narrative of all the events –
and a silent listener on whom it will have an intensely personal impact.

  After his initial, deferential hesitation, the story begins confidently at
1196, and the confidence should continue, with vigour and clarity,
right through the account of the burial of Polyneikes (to 1205), to
contrast the Bodyguard's ignorance with the audience's realization that
Kreon has reversed the order of the advice that he was given at
1100–1.[116]

  As the scene changes to the bridal tomb (1206ff.), and the focus
narrows down from the group's vision of events to Kreon's, the
narrator needs to take a slower pace; he must also throw himself fully
into Kreon's anguished role, when he quotes his direct and desperate

[115] Cf. esp. YWT 129–35, Ai 131–2, OKing 1168–7; Jones 1961, esp. 175.
The sudden reversal is more important here than the fact (stressed by Winnington-Ingram 1980, 112) that the Bodyguard is too simple in his perception, when
he ascribes to blind Chance a downfall that we know from Teiresias is the
inevitable consequence of Kreon's obstinacy.
[116] This is a crucial point; but it has been played down by some commentators
(e.g. Waldock 1951, 129ff.; Griffith on 1196–8), and completely denied by
Gardiner 1987, 94–5. Kreon's failure to anticipate Antigone's, and Haimon's,
probable reactions to her entombment is his final mistake, the last of a long
series of misjudgements of the actions and motives of every other character in
the drama; cf. Foley 1996, 60–61.

speech at 1211ff., and speed up the tempo again at 1226ff., ready for
a final return to a slower pace at 1231.

The reactions of the silent Eurydike are crucial to the success of this
scene. In our production, she showed increasing concern from 1206 to
1220; then the news of the death of Antigone caused her to break
away, shocked and nauseated, almost to the front of the *orchêstra*.
This forced the Bodyguard to come forward in turn (1226), to try to
re-engage her; he should be able to look at her directly by 1228–9,
because the narrative is about to reach its climax, and because of the
irony that Eurydike too (like Antigone, who was played by the same
actor in Sophokles' original production) is about to behave – from a
'rational', 'mature male' perspective – like a 'crazy girl . . . driven mad
by suffering' (1228–9), and take her own life.[117] In our production
Eurydike only managed to face the narrator again at 1231; she endured
his words face on until the middle of 1235, where she lowered her
head into her hands, and remained folded in upon herself until
1240–41.

Here Sophokles brings to its appalling climax the complex interplay
of perverted marriage/death imagery which began in Scene 5. In the
cave, which is both her bridal and her burial chamber (1205ff.), Kreon
has – as promised, 654 – given Antigone a wedding in Haides; Haimon,
whose name means blood, now drips blood in place of semen onto her
dead cheek (1239). A girl's cheeks were an erotic zone for the Greeks,
as Sophokles deliberately reminded his audience at 783–4; so the union
of Haimon and Antigone is now consummated in death. This breaks
Eurydike. During the last two lines, she suddenly moves, and decisively
crosses almost the whole *orchêstra* to push through the double doors.

Worry, hope and caution; the blocking after her exit is tentative and
uncertain for both the Councillors and the Bodyguard, until his sudden
resolve at 1253.

Finale

Sophokles does not wait for the Bodyguard to return, or give the
choros even a stanza – let alone a full ode – before driving the drama
on to its last tableau; Kreon walks on, carrying his son's body.[118] From

---

[117] Segal 1981, 195 draws out some structural parallels between the two
women.

[118] The text is clear on this point (1257–8), so there is no question of Kreon
walking beside a bier carried by attendants (Jebb 1891, 223; cf. Griffith *ad loc.*).

1290 to the end the Finale traps Kreon in the upper third of the playing space between two bloodstained corpses whose deaths he has caused – the first Haimon's, which he brings in himself and places at c to lament over it; the second Eurydike's, which the Bodyguard brings out and places at BC.[119] Here Sophokles' strategy of isolating Kreon from what should be his own *oikos* achieves its climactic effect. After Eurydike's suicide in its inner depths (1293), even the house into which Kreon must go to rest is a place of death, hostile to him. Director and actor need to create a close emotional interaction first with the one corpse, then with both, as Kreon cries out in anguish to the Councillors and to the Bodyguard; only in the B2 stanza does he lift his eyes up beyond the visible characters and the bodies.

The emotional position of a man who has caused his own son's death, and recognizes the full extent of his folly, is extreme; Sophokles therefore symbolized the fact that Kreon is at last forced now to acknowledge the power of human feelings by having him break four times into lyric.[120] However, in the Finale Kreon's overwhelming emotion is sternly counterpointed by the Councillors, who sheet the responsibility firmly home to him at the start of the scene, and three times rebuke him for continuing to lament. The Bodyguard's narrative of Eurydike's death is charged with her bitter anger against Kreon;[121] and Kreon rightly calls for someone to take him away when at 1317ff. he acknowledges his full responsibility.

But he remains, characteristically, excessive in his emotion right to the end – note how the Councillors insist, in their three speeches from 1322, on the need for silent acceptance of what has happened; and he leaves the playing space with his dignity shattered, near to collapse,

The physical feat is itself an important part of the effect. Kreon literally bears responsibility, at last.

[119] This scene does not absolutely require the *ekkyklêma*. It is arguably more effective without; when Kreon refuses to believe the Bodyguard, he simply goes inside again, and carries out the body of Eurydike.

[120] His metre in the original Greek was the dochmiac, the most violent lyric metre.

[121] There is a puzzle here. In the only surviving version of the death of Kreon's first son (Euripides, *Phoinikian Women* 834–1017) Kreon is blameless, indeed actually tried to prevent his son Menoikeus from sacrificing himself for the city's sake. In Aischylos, *Seven against Thebes* 473 Kreon's son was called Megareus, and did not die, since he defended Thebes successfully at the third gate. Sophokles is probably alluding to a version of the story that we don't know (or perhaps inventing one that the original audience, like us, would have found provocatively oblique).

unable to find rest anywhere. He has been completely broken by his own folly and lack of insight (both have been stressed repeatedly throughout the Finale); and the *choros* characters gain wisdom now the protagonist has lost it;[122] the last words that the Councillors chant as they leave, far from being (as sometimes in Euripides) a loose generalization, precisely stress what little the audience can learn for their future conduct from this drama (as opposed to being enlightened as to how tragic events happen in human life). Sophokles' gods may not have saved the young woman who supported their laws; and the Councillors' insight hardly does justice to Antigone's devotion to her *philoi* or to her inspired determination;[123] but the mature man who lacked wisdom has been destroyed in just one day.

[122] Cf. e.g. Aischylos, *Seven against Thebes*, 677ff.
[123] Cf. Scott 1996, 64–5.

Young Women of Trachis

GRAHAM LEY

Myth and Subject

Young Women of Trachis, alone among the surviving tragedies of
Sophokles, takes its title from the *choros*, and for a modern audience
at least this obscures its subject. It is, in the first instance, a tragedy of
adultery, and its pre-eminent subject is the Greek folk-hero Herakles.[1]
In our concern for the savage eroticism of infidelity and its consequences, prominent in the first part of the drama, we may fail to notice
how resolutely the theme of death as the end of the labours of Herakles
engages the full action of the tragedy. Indeed death – or dying – in
agony is dramatically so dominant in the Finale that it has provoked a
critical debate about Sophokles' intentions. Those critics who wish for
some relief have expected or hoped to find a clear reference to the
apotheosis of Herakles, but this may be a misguided search.[2] The
ancient wisdom with which Deianeira opens the script holds little
comfort for mortals, and there is none for any of the characters
contained within the drama.

Herakles is a unique figure in the Athenian theatre, because his gross
proportions fit themselves to comedy and *satyr-drama* as well as to
tragedy.[3] In Euripides' *Alkestis* (a serious drama, but performed in the
place normally reserved for a *satyr-drama*) this dual presence is at its
most suggestive, because his lust for life, intruding into a scene of
mourning and loss in the form of gluttony and drunkenness, becomes
the means to challenge death and wrestle a life from its clutches. His
almost recklessly vigorous character also has purely tragic implications.
For Euripides in *The Madness of Herakles*, it is the capacity for
violence that can be perverted by a goddess and produce a destructive
and pitiful insanity. In Sophokles, his brute male strength is led into an
effeminating torture and tragic ending by the capacity for predatory,
violent lust.

[1] 'The Mythical Life of Heracles' in Kirk 1974, 176–212 provides a good
introduction to the hero.

[2] Cf. n. 54 below.

[3] There is an extended discussion in Galinsky 1972; cf. Silk 1985, 19 who
feels that the figure of Herakles 'dislocates' the structure of the two tragedies in
which he appears. Herakles is not known to have been a character in any other
tragedy apart from the two that survive.

Modern appreciations of *Young Women of Trachis* begin effectively with Easterling's sensitive questioning of the views of Kitto.[4] Easterling offered an holistic view of the thematic range of the tragedy, and her awareness of the significance of the bestial in the curiously archaic mythology of the action was amplified and almost enshrined by Segal, for whom *Young Women of Trachis* was exemplary: 'The antithesis between man's civilizing power and the brutish violence that he both opposes and admits, between his ordered creations of house and city and the primordial forces both within and without, is sharper here than in any other Sophoclean play.'[5] Seaford's is perhaps the most subtle of more recent contributions: he has demonstrated the ways in which tragedy explored the uncertainties awakened in and by the rituals of marriage in Athenian and Greek society.[6] The perception that sexuality is dangerous, and that gender may be unstable, readily involves a contemporary audience with this drama. The death-agony of Herakles, and the patriarchal enormities of his energy, become extremely powerful in performance in the Finale when Herakles assumes – with the procession, the robe, and the 'unveiling' – some of the characteristics of the bride.

Dramatic Style

Studies of performance bring to the fore qualities that may remain latent in literary criticism. Following the tenor of this series, which concentrates on the practicability of the script for and in performance, these Notes pay close attention to the evidence for the disposition of performers in the playing space. To introduce them, I refer here to a number of features that affect the question of what we might expect from a Greek tragedy. The first is that in this medium action is interaction, and consequently deceit can engineer the tension quite sufficiently throughout extended scenes, as it does, for example, in Scene 2 of this tragedy. For modern audiences, accustomed to the dominant contemporary mode of physical theatre, this may require an adjustment. Physicality is treated differently, so a physical state – one of virtual paralysis apart from the use of voice and hands – can occupy the thematic and theatrical centre of the Finale.

A second feature, or quality, is that of narrative provided by a

---

[4] Easterling 1968, qualifying Kitto 1966 (cf. Kitto 1961).
[5] Segal 1981, 60.
[6] Seaford 1986 and 1987.

character. Sophokles offers us an unusual vision of this dramatic mode in Scene 1, in which as an audience we gradually inscribe a character (that of Deianeira – daughter, girl, prize, bride, wife, mother, pessimist and mortal) onto a mask in the course of what is virtually an autobiographical soliloquy. Narratives may also contain impersonation of another character, as part of the recalling of events. Deaineira, Hyllos, and the Nurse (Scenes 3, 4 and 5 respectively) all use this resource, and it is often introduced climactically, as with Hyllos and the Nurse. A narrative of this kind is a performance piece, but our attention may be called to the reactions of its auditors in the drama as much as to the speaking performer; this is notably true of the effect on Deianeira of Hyllos' savage account of the delivery of the poisoned robe to Herakles.[7]

Perhaps the most important introductory task still is to provide some guidance on what to expect of the *choros*. In relation to their songs in this tragedy, I should probably draw attention to what might be described as a state of suspended judgement on the part of a group of given status – of reactive feelings suspended in a certain state that does not permit the acceleration of the dramatic action. The verbal composition that accompanies the lyric metres of song, with its strong, associative potential, is a perfect dramaturgical instrument for this. Dramatic lyric is about surprise and (often mistaken) anticipation, and accomplishes a combined intellectual and emotional stasis, in which the collective character played by the *choros* absorbs the situation of the individual with which it is involved or concerned. Yet this suspension or stasis is dynamic, for all the complex reasons that the state of tension within a sequence of actions is dynamic. Choral songs take their place in a dramaturgy constructed and developed to highlight decisions, decisive words or actions, and to register the reflective and emotional impact of those decisions. So individual songs in this tragedy carry the qualities of a triumphal hymn to the gods (Choros 2), a song of victory for an athlete (Choros 3), and a lament (Choros 5). These qualities, and the path of the Young Women's uncertain relationship with Deianeira, will receive commentary below.

These Notes include insights gained during a workshop that took place in the Drama Department at the University of Exeter in the early months of 1997, using an *orchêstra* twelve metres in diameter and a *choros* with five members.

[7] See the Notes to Scene 4 below, pp. 256ff.

The Actors and their Roles

The most probable distribution of roles for the original production at Athens would have had the leading actor playing first the role of Deianeira, and then that of Herakles. A second actor would have taken Hyllos, and a third actor the Nurse and the Old Man. If the second actor took precedence over the third, then he will have played Lichas, and the third will have played the Old Man; but the alternative is practically possible. The role of Iole is non-speaking, and my suggestion is that it may have been played by a young actor in training (see Notes to Scene 2, below).

The combination of two principal roles for a leading performer presents the kind of virtuoso (and potentially prizewinning) challenge found elsewhere, in *Aias* (Aias and Teukros[x]) and Euripides' *Hippolytos* (Phaidra and Theseus). During the same period, an alternative mode of composition would offer a role to be sustained throughout the drama, and this kind of challenge to the leading performer is found in *Antigone* (Kreon) and *Oidipous the King* (Oidipous), and in Euripides' *Medeia* (Medeia). Singing is regularly an additional demand on the performer, and the role of Herakles is realized in this way as well as in the delivery of verse lines. Plainly, Greek actors could not only portray male or female roles, but could alternate them within the same production. In this respect, as perhaps in others, the idea of the 'virtuoso' performance may be helpful to our understanding of the quality of Greek tragic acting.

Scene 1

Deianeira appears from the *skene*, which represents her home, and addresses the audience, whom she does not directly acknowledge. Because of the initial absence of dialogue, it is not apparent whether the Nurse is with her from the beginning, but the Nurse plainly responds to the last part of Deianeira's complaint (36–48).[9] In that

---

[x] Following the traditional distribution; but see *contra* Ewans, p. 175 above.

[9] Kamerbeek 1959, 39 seems in favour of the Nurse's constant presence; those undecided include Easterling 1982, 71 and Davies 1991, xxxviii. Seale 1982, 183 follows Kamerbeek in his main text, but suggests an alternative in his notes (212 n. 4): 'It is possible that she is not present for most of Deianeira's speech and enters later, in time for her own speech.' I offer below my own reasons for keeping back the Nurse's entrance.

final section of her speech, Deianeira turns our attention to the most
recent absence of her husband Herakles, and the Nurse's intervention
(49–60) specifically responds to 40–41. In our workshop, 40–43 were
directed to the Nurse, who then has time to gather the resolve to
intervene.

Hyllos is seen running towards the house; he arrives from the L
parodos, that is from 'the downtown district of the place in which the
action is located'.[10] The contrast with his subsequent departure establishes the lateral axis of the playing space. Once instructed, Hyllos will
leave at R (90), and when he returns it will be as a changed man. The
passage from boyhood to manhood, from dependence on the mother
to an irrevocable inscription into paternalist values, which is a recurrent concern of Athenian tragedy, can be marked in the use of space.[11]

After her intervention the Nurse does not participate in the exchange
between Deianeira and Hyllos, and a central focus is clearly required
for these two. Hyllos leaves R, and 86 must be easier to deliver if some
movement in that direction is apparent at that moment. The Nurse
enters the *skene* at the end of the scene, to reappear only at a climax of
the drama (868). There is no firm indication of whether Deianeira
remains in the playing space or not; but for some consideration of this
question, see the Notes to Scene 2.

Deianeira's soliloquy has no clear parallel in the surviving plays of
either Aischylos or Sophokles, although the Watchman in *Agamemnon*
reflects briefly on his own situation, and that of the house on top of
which he is set. Deianeira's soliloquy is extended and strikingly self-
reflective; this second feature distinguishes it from introductions by a
god or by someone totally dependent on the actions of principals, like
the Nurse in Euripides' *Medeia*. It also lacks reference to current
actions, or to a visible tableau, which are the characteristics of otherwise comparable soliloquies, such as those by Andromache in Euripides' *Andromache* and Iolaos in Euripides' *Children of Herakles*.[12] The

[10] See Note on the Translations and Notes, p. lxxvii.

[11] For a provocative psychological thesis on the rite of passage in tragedy, see
Slater 1992.

[12] The problem of defining this kind of open address, which occurs most
distinctly in the introductions to tragedies, has not been satisfactorily resolved.
Unfortunately, Bain 1977 confined his attention to more direct forms of
'audience address' in comedy. Heiden 1989 considers the audience as 'sympathetic outsiders', in a phrase that captures some of the quality of this kind of
performance; but the convention is subtle and culturally specific, and to date

narrative is selective, and ominous; it conjoins domesticity with monstrosity, physicality, and male violence.[13] The fight for possession of Deianeira later becomes the subject of the song in Choros 3, at a moment when another young and silent woman has been fully introduced to the action. Deianeira defines herself in relation to her successive *kyrioi*, her father and Herakles. The confidence that might come from Herakles' strength and the fact that his father is Zeus is dissipated by his long absence, by the mention of the murder of Iphitos (which might well involve blood-guilt) and of the written tablet, which is left unexplained, but which seems to contain an ominous prophecy. Deianeira starts with 'beginnings', and leads herself inexorably through the recapitulation of successive worries to the sense of an approaching 'ending' for Herakles. Beauty and apparent security both bring fear, and accompanying isolation and sorrow.

There is nothing in the script, which lacks all points of reference except to the *skene*, to encourage a particular interpretation of how this soliloquy was performed. I see no reason for introducing the Nurse as a conversant immediately, because her interjection then becomes delayed and obvious, rather than (as it seems, 52–3) courageous in some part. In our workshop Deianeira came aside from the *skene* to look out at R hopelessly, turned to address the audience with her first lines, and progressed diagonally across the *orchêstra* to EFL at 17. The performer then moved to FC, across to a position at EFR at 30, and back to C by 35, when reference to the *skene* and the setting is paramount. The Nurse may be introduced at any moment before this, but it is better if she *hears*, rather than is *told*, 38–42; the audience should not be given a first impression that the Nurse is ignorant of the situation. Consequently, I would place her EBC just off the central line until 43, when she comes forward to join Deianeira at C. If she stands to the right of Deianeira, she can see Hyllos approaching at L. Deianeira may plausibly move a little towards Hyllos initially, bringing him back towards the Nurse at C, who would then stand aside. There is nothing in the subsequent dialogue which detracts from their fullest attention to each other, until Hyllos starts to leave.

eludes our close understanding. For a further attempt at definition see Wiles 1997, 211–19.

[13] This conjunction and contrast is particularly studied by Segal 1981.

Choros 1

The *choros* arrives singing, or arrives and then starts to sing.[14] The arrival in the playing space of a large body of people, uniform in appearance (as vase-paintings seem to show), is a physically impressive as well as a 'dramatic' event, and it will be motivated. The Young Women arrive by the L *parodos*, since it is as members of the surrounding locality that they have heard (102) of Deianeira's anxiety over Herakles' latest, long absence. That Deianeira has been expressing those anxieties in public in Scene 1 is at least an indication to the audience of relatively public behaviour over a period of time, which conforms with the supportive reaction of the *choros* (102–11, and 141–2).

Sophokles' choice of the character of young women native to Trachis for the *choros* contrasts their relative security and inexperience with that of the married exile. Masks are important and significant (in a literal sense) here. The age of the Nurse, the middle age or maturity of Deianeira, and the immaturity of the hopeful and piously trusting group are presented to us in a telling 'set'. It must also be certain that the mask of Iole subsequently created a strong association with those of the *choros*, one which is then tragically belied by revelations about her identity.[15]

The appeal to a god for knowledge is combined in A1 with the idea of succession, to which the song returns in its optimism in B1–3.[16] The desire for knowledge is paramount in Choros 1 of *Oidipous the King*, and Helios the sun is invoked in Choros 1 of *Antigone*, where the song closes with a vision of dancing continuing into the night. The song here alternates its concern for Herakles (A1, B1) and for Deianeira (A2, B2 and B3). The waves of the sea, and the stars, are adduced to lend conviction to the idea of flux in the affairs of humans, but the final

[14] Seale 1982, 184 (following Pickard-Cambridge 1988, 242–3) assumes that this *choros* arrived in silence, and then started to sing. This assumption is based on the absence of any preliminary *anapaests*, a metre that is usually taken to indicate progress or directional movement.

[15] Gardiner 1987, 120 in her consideration of the question of 'whether the distinction between women and maidens was immediately obvious to the audience', strangely fails to mention masks. Seale 1982, 184 and 188 is distinctly more alert, and rightly contrasts the *choros* with the captives as well as with Deianeira.

[16] Hoey 1972 expands on this opening appeal of the Young Women to the sun to examine the full implications of its symbolism in the song.

emphasis rests merely on the assertion that current deprivation and distress will yield to a joyful outcome. Hope offers human beings a sense of continuity even within flux, and Zeus is the guarantor of what hope promises, because he is the father of Herakles. The wordly and natural wisdom of the Young Women, for all its suggestive insights, is actually facile, and open to far less optimistic interpretations and constructions than those which they themselves offer.[17]

I should expect a choreography that presents the formal wisdom, balance, and optimism of the song and the youth of its singers, and which for those reasons has the quality of a presentation rather than that of a significant intervention. The sententiousness is marked – cf. B2 and B3 generally, but especially 122–8; this is bound to register for an audience introduced to Deianeira as we have been. A *choros* may through characterization by gender, age, and status be significantly hostile to or supportive of a leading figure. Deianeira's isolation is intensified by what we see and hear in this first song, but that effect is achieved with considerable subtlety.[18]

Scene 2

Scene 2 is extremely long, taking in a short, celebratory *paian* from the *choros*, and moving Deianeira from a position of ignorant isolation to one of tragic knowledge. This movement is achieved, in the physical aspect of performance, by the addition of a bewildering group of figures, whose status, knowledge and experience are only gradually made clear through conflict and investigation.

[17] Cf. Scott 1996, 99. Winnington-Ingram 1980, 330–31 in his discussion of this song rightly notes that 'if the alternations of nature are a just analogy and prove that sorrow is transitory, the same must also be true of joy', and questions 'whether the analogy of natural process is not fallacious when applied to human life' (331). *Contra* Easterling 1982, 85 who writes of 'the authority of the great lines describing the cycle of joy and sorrow: it is only the Chorus' diagnosis of Heracles' situation that is to prove wrong, not their insight into the working of the universe'.

[18] Burton 1980, 42 seems to miss this important constituent of the drama when he refers to 'the sympathy, common sense, and understanding of the young women'. By contrast, Gardiner 1987, 123 chooses to emphasize a lack of 'familiarity' and an 'absence of intimacy between Deianeira and the chorus'. Her later summary (128) of their relations during the tragedy establishes the tension: 'The chorus are young, Deianeira is not; they are natives, she is a foreigner; they are maidens, she is married and the mother of a grown son; they are confident, she is pessimistic and fearful.'

There is no particular reason for Deianeira to remain in the playing
space at the close of Scene 1; the Nurse plainly leaves, and Deianeira is
not greeted by the *choros* nor addressed until well into the song (B2,
122). The Young Women have not been summoned by her, nor are we
given any reason to suppose she was expecting them. Her opening
words (141–2) do not constitute a reply to the address from 122 to
124. She says she is 'guessing' at the motive for their arrival, and seems
instead to be speaking, in what immediately follows, to their appearance and not to their words. It is not a matter of any great importance,
nor of any certainty, but I am inclined to have her reappear from the
skene after the *choros* has closed its song and turned to face the *skene*
at 138.[19]

Deaianeira will start from the *skene* and progress towards the
Young Women, and by the end of her speech she has joined them,
accepting their sympathy. In the workshop we divided the *choros*, and
kept them facing the *skene*, in small groups at FR and FL. As she
addresses them, and tells them what she knows about this last
absence, they might well gradually sit down on the ground. At 178
one of the Young Women jumps up as she sees the Old Man
approaching in some haste at R. The Old Man would come right up
to Deianeira in his enthusiasm, but after the short initial exchange at
C he is ignored by the script until his interjection at 335. Deianeira
can be involved by the Young Women in their premature celebrations
at 205–24, which start explicitly as a *paian* and then modulate into
an ecstatic dance. In our workshop, the figures of Deianeira and the
Old Man were surrounded by a 'whirling' (219) choreography, which
broke open and then back as the procession of figures became visible
at 225, approaching along the *parodos* at R.[20]

[19] Burton 1980, 44 imagines Deianeira as reappearing halfway through the
song, although he is worried by the lack of parallels in Greek tragedy; Taplin
1977, 248 and 263 believes she remains throughout, and is followed in this by
Seale 1982, 184–5 and Gardiner 1987, 122–3. Easterling 1982, 84 inclines
towards the idea that Deianeira is not present; Kamerbeek 1959, 48 and Davies
1991, 76 are undecided. The fact that the Young Women address Deianeira
does not prove she is present; principals who have not yet appeared from the
skene are addressed in their absence during Choros 1 of e.g. Aischylos, *Agamemnon*, Sophokles, *Ai*.

[20] Kamerbeek 1959, 70–71 would have one part of the *choros* dancing while
the other sings, with these roles changing at 216, and in addition considers that
women from inside the house joined them, following Deianeira's instruction at
202–3. Both of these suggestions can be acknowledged as possibilities; but I see

Deianeira's account of the contents of the tablet is of what Herakles told her was in it, and it seems probable from the text that she is presented as unable to read, like Iphigeneia in Euripides' *Iphigeneia at Tauris*.[21] Her dependence on what she is told by men is emphatic in this scene, and it is interesting in this respect that the Old Man chooses not to mention the group of women that Lichas has with him, let alone their identity. For his part, Lichas both conceals and distorts the truth, and his performance should presumably offer an assertive authority that cannot quite bear itself with total confidence.[22]

The disposition of performers in the rest of this scene can be deduced with some accuracy from a number of clear indicators in its central part. At 329ff., Deianeira encourges Lichas and the group of captive women to move towards the *skene*; she herself is detained by the Old Man at 335, while Lichas and the group keep moving. Deianeira then asks if she should call them back (342); she does not, and at 345 Lichas has entered the *skene* with the captives, leaving the Old Man, Deianeira and the Young Women in the *orchêstra* at some distance from the *skene*.[23]

no reason for the playwright to involve another group of extras, or a subsidiary *choros*, at this point.

[21] Deianeira can repeat some of the import of the tablet (76–85), and worry over it (43–8); this places her in a similar position to Euripides' Iphigeneia, who can repeat the contents of her letter to Orestes *verbatim*, although it was written down for her by a prisoner (*IT* 582ff.). The 'ciphers' (157) are probably Sophokles' attempt to indicate the strangeness of writing in heroic times, but it is also fairly clear from this passage as a whole that Deianeira has no independent access to their meaning.

[22] Both Winnington-Ingram 1980, 332–3 and Davies 1984, 480–83 usefully concentrate on the degree of Sophokles' invention in this speech. But Lichas' tortuous exposition should be an interesting sign of deceit for an attentive audience, and a challenge for the performer (cf. the Old Man in *El* 680ff.). There is a sensitive, critical discussion by Easterling 1968, 61–2 and 65; the extended analysis by Heiden 1989, 53–64 is arguably more tortuous even than the original.

[23] The language in this extended passage clearly details a gradual, progressive movement of Lichas and the captives from a position in the *orchêstra* towards and into the *skene*; I have given a full analysis in Ley 1994, 32–6. Failure to accept the spatial implications of orchestral performance can lead to unnecessary puzzlement, for example Davies 1991, 118, on 336: 'after this categorical exclusion of the captives, it is decidedly odd that Deianeira should still be asking at 342–3 whether she is to call them back.' Seale is caught between his unfortunate adherence to a raised stage (1982, 212 n. 22) and his intuitive sense of a theatrical dynamic for the scene: 'Deianeira is surrounded by younger

Before he leaves at 329 to enter the *skene*, Lichas must be with
Deianeira, probably at C, and Iole at least must be close to them to be
questioned unsuccessfully. The group including her will have been
introduced from R to a position FR, and the *choros* must be displaced
after their celebratory song, probably to a grouping between EBL and
ELC, symmetrically balancing the captive women at FR. Deianeira is
then placed between two groups of younger women, almost certainly
contrasted with each other in their costumes (or at least in the state of
them), and providing a clear image of the contrast between 'those who
have experienced suffering and those who have found joy', as Seale
expresses it.[24]

The Old Man must give way to Lichas for the exchange between
Lichas and Deianeira, perhaps moving to EBL. Humiliating speeches
can result in the withdrawal of a female character into the *skene*;[25] so
while Lichas gives his account, ranging from C to EFC and across to
the group of captives at FR by 283, Deianeira might well withdraw
towards the *skene* from C to BC, within view of the Young Women
and perhaps the Old Man. She resumes the initiative at 293, turning to
include the captive group gesturally in an aside to the Young Women
(298), but showing diffidence initially. The captive women are at first
pitiful objects to look at, but her confidence appears to grow to the
extent that she can finally address Iole in person. So Lichas might well
hold to C, avoiding questions from 310 to 320, while Deianeira
approaches Iole, who stands at the front of the group of captives at
RC. He might then come to stand between Deianeira and Iole at 322,
in order to put an end to an awkward moment. The Old Man,
fascinated by this exchange, has moved unnoticed to a position near to
or among the *choros* at ELC.

The Old Man intervenes suddenly at 335, coming from ELC to
Deianeira near the centre, while Lichas and the group of captives move
towards the *skene* from R. The *choros* will then come forward gradually, and gather round the developing incident. In our workshop
Deianeira remained at C, while the Old Man moved away to EFR, since
his declarations are awkward for him.

These two are joined again by Lichas after 390, and the subsequent

women; more specifically she is physically placed between two distinct representative groups' (190; cf. 192, quoted in the main text).
[24] Seale 1982, 192; he also believes that the captives may be 'dressed as
slaves' (see n. 27 below).
[25] Cf. Scene 4, and *Ant* Scene 7.

exchanges have a clear rhythm of confrontation and evasion. That Deianeira withdraws at some point after 402 is relatively certain, because the force of her speech at 436 demands a starting-point off the centre; but the movement may be minor. It is also likely that Lichas, in fear, moves forward away from C, and perhaps speaks from EFR or EFC at 472.

This is a scene that relishes the disposition of a full complement of three actors, with a large group of extras in addition to the *choros* in the *orchêstra* at some distance from the *skene*.[26] It is redolent of deceit and innocence, as full of silence as it is of loquacity, of apprehension and emotional turmoil. The masks of the silent group of women captives (young and older?) may have contrasted, in a portrayal of fixed grief, with those of the *choros*. Whether that of Iole had the standard open mouth suggesting she might speak is an intriguing question. Although we may casually categorize the role of Iole as one for an 'extra', it is demanding – consider the interrogation by Deianeira (307–30) – and might well be suitable for a young actor in training.[27]

Choros 3

This song has, inevitably, one central concern – the decisive power of Aphrodite.[28] It is relatively short in the circumstances, consisting of a

[26] The three-actor exchange is discussed by Reinhardt 1979, 41–5 who contrasted it in particular to Scene 5 in *OKing*; one notable similarity in performance is the threat of obstruction or physical violence between visible characters. The intricate section after the reappearance of Lichas operates with two sets of dialogue (between Deianera and Lichas, then the Messenger and Lichas) concluded by an extended protest from Deianeira. Sophokles uses couplets, single lines, shared lines (*antilabe*), and two sets of three lines (405–7, and 431–3) in the exchanges, in a formal pattern which is balanced but also flexible.

[27] Seale 1982, 188 envisages the group of captives in 'masks of mourning' and possibly 'dressed as slaves'. How Iole may have been distinguished from the others is less obvious: Seale suggests a 'special mask', thinking of her 'distinctive beauty' in particular, and a costume that established her 'superior status and nobility' (188–9). This leaves rather less than I would like to the performer, and to spatial disposition. (However, Seale does hint at this later, when he writes (193) of 'a stance of proud composure'). Mastronarde 1979, 76–7 explores the significance and implications of the silence of Iole.

[28] For Burton 1980, 55 this is a 'lyrical ballad' and a form of 'choral lyric narrative', terms that echo those of Reinhardt 1979, 242. Easterling 1982, 133–4 rightly draws attention to the specific qualities of the 'epinikian' (victory)

single group of three stanzas; but it is dramatically relentless, declining to divert attention from Deianeira. The song is, in effect, a lyric realization of Deianeira's opening summary of the symbolic violence of the combat for her hand, and insistently intertwines the human relationship of Herakles and Deianeira with the 'natural' and bestial world. Since the final image compares Deianeira with a heifer, it does not seem inconsonant for her suitor Acheloos, a river, to appear as a bull.

The Young Women are timid about possible impieties in A1, in a standard form of introductory refusal leading to an emphatic subject. The scene is imagined, rather than witnessed, and the Young Women suffer their own vision of a marriage, presented as little more than a triumphant physical union, with the girl as a prize for combat in a forlorn substitution for cattle. One of the final implications of the song is that to be a spectator, or to tell a tale or sing the song, is nothing compared to the pathos of experience, in which the silence of Deianeira prefigures the silence of Iole.[29]

Scene 3

The intuitive quality of Choros 3 initiates the Young Women into a stronger role of support, in which they may be treated as confidantes. After the crowded Scene 2, Deianeira comes from the *skene* – and presumably well away from its doors – to share a secret scheme. Prominent in this revelation of secret actions is the casket containing the robe. How exactly this casket should be handled poses some problems. An attending slave is clearly a possibility, and yet the quality of both this scene and the next, and of the narratives of Deianeira's preparation of the robe, almost requires the casket to be seen in her hands.[30] In the workshop we found that the best solution was to have Deianeira appear carrying the casket, followed by a slave, to whom she hands it at some point before 554. On the reappearance of Lichas from

ode in a sensitive and adroit summary: as she notes, Aphrodite not Herakles is the victorious athlete, in a contest in which, ironically, she is also the referee.

[29] In the Greek text of line 526 I accept the reading 'thater' (spectator) for 'mater' (mother), which is singularly inappropriate in the context.

[30] At 578–81 Deianeira says she removed the ointment from its place of hiding, and smeared the robe with it herself (compare her second account, 684–92). Seale 1982, 198ff. has Deianeira 'carrying a casket in her hands'; Easterling 1982, 139 envisages a 'servant'; Davies 1991, xxxviii has Deianeira 'carrying the *peplos* [robe]' (!).

the *skene*, Deianeira takes the casket from her slave at 600, holding it until 613, when she hands it to Lichas and is free to show both the seal and her ring to him. We also had Lichas accompanied by a soldier, to whom he hands the casket at 623.[31]

There are no explicit indications within Deianeira's speech (531-87) of particular movements. If the *choros* as a whole is a confidante, and there are fifteen of them, it seems appropriate to place them in small groups, FR and FL, which Deianeira approaches and addresses. She is then in a position to spot Lichas at the *skene* doors (594-5), and he will come forward dutifully to C. Like Hyllos, he can finally move towards R, and it is surely correct to assume that Deianeira's final words are spoken as he leaves, rather than to him.[32]

Deianeira's sexual and emotional despair has driven her back into a past of violent sexuality, providing her not just with the magic she needs but with the kind of archaic prophecy (from Nessos, 569-77) he wants to counteract the insistent threat to her marriage. That the robe and the ointment must not be shown to two of the most sacred sources, the sun and the hearthfire (606-7), is as ominous as the poisonous origin of the charm in a mixture of blood and venom (572-4). Her hesitation marks Deianeira as both human and desperate, and prepares for her fear and revulsion in Scene 4. The moment of sacrifice she envisages as appropriate to the decisive display of the robe may suggest, in its mention of bulls (608-9), a disturbing parallel to the equation of animal with human in Choros 3. The robe was intended as a final celebration of Herakles' return from danger (610-13), but the seal from the signet-ring conveys, in return for deception, deception rather than trust.[33]

[31] I suggest this detailed compromise because in the workshop it became quite apparent that to have Deianeira holding the casket throughout her long speech 531-87 was both impractical and inappropriate. This forms a correction to my conclusion in Ley 1994, 36, and confirms the feelings expressed to me by Professor Easterling when that article was in proof.

[32] So Easterling 1982, 151. Cf. the end of *Ant* Scene 1, with Ewans' Notes p. 207.

[33] This is also the function of Phaidra's seal on the tablet she leaves for Theseus to find after her suicide in Euripides' *Hippolytos*; but, in Phaidra's case, revenge rather than the restoration of love is the motive. Seaford 1994, 390-91 has a short but excellent discussion of the ritual significance of the robe in *YWT*.

Choros 4

The drama has reached a climax of expectation, and this song gathers together almost every component of favourable anticipation for the last time, before the *peripeteia* begins. A1 opens the possibility of celebration to all members of the local communities, inland and on the coast, and to the south, and A2 and B1 reassert the conviction of the Young Women that hardship and labour will be crowned in success. The names of the gods combine in the conviction of achievement, and the violence of war (the god Ares) is understood unequivocally as the final escape from labour. In the Young Women's philosophy, the cyclical pattern applies both to the extent of Herakles' absence and to Deianeira's concomitant distress (B1). That Herakles is sacrificing (B2) is seen to be the appropriate, ritual consequence of victory, and the prelude to the domestic and communal celebration that they anticipate.

The song concludes with a final wish for the efficacy of both persuasion and desire. The Greek text here is unreliable, but reference to the ointment and its source is plausible, if not certain. The fragility of optimism, and the excitement of premature celebration, are both carefully controlled constituents of dramaturgy in tragic, choral song.[34]

Scene 4

Scene 4 explicitly recalls Scene 3 in its mode of presentation, with the variation that total secrecy is not now the immediate issue, and the corollary that the magical property is fatefully absent. The comparable relation of the exchange between Deianeira and the *choros* to the *skene* is interesting.

In Scene 3 Deianeira has brought an object out and away from the *skene*, in which Lichas still remains, and the nature and purpose of the object engage a narrative that refers to Iole and, historically, to the violent proximity of the *kentaur* Nessos. In Scene 4 Deianeira's narrative envisages the house represented by the *skene* in detail, and in material and spatial terms, as a domestic interior stained by poison.

---

[34] Cf. *Ai* Choros 3, *Ant* Choros 6 and *OKing* Choros 4, with the Notes by Ewans and McCart pp. 188, 237 above and 293 below. Burton 1980, 59: 'Lyric thus crystallizes the irony inherent in such situations, establishing a deluded emotion just before the revelation of the truth.' Kirkwood 1958, 199–201 places a consideration of these particular songs in the broader context of what he terms Sophokles' 'contrastive' technique.

The confidential exchange with the Young Women is interrupted, and confirmed in its worst expectations, by the arrival of Hyllos from a distance. His heavy narrative overwhelms the relationship between Deianeira and the Young Women, driving Deianeira back into the now threatening *skene*. In Scene 3 the reappearance of Lichas from the *skene* was briefly and easily integrated into the plan of action, as he left carrying both hope and desire out and away from the home. At a crucial moment, the playwright chooses to deploy parallel resources and a comparable structure to display the tragic contrast between intention and effect. It is a relatively simple case of thoroughly assured artistry in the theatre.

The opening dialogue (663–71) offers us a contrast with Deianeira's continuous exposition in Scene 3, and it must be tempting to assign a slightly different pattern of performance. Since Deianeira does not now have the same need to conceal what she says from a figure (Lichas) who was then restless in the *skene*, I would allow her to speak initially from close to the *skene* doors. The indications at 678–9 are of a launch into the full narrative, and perhaps at this time the *choros* may follow her away from the *skene*. In the workshop I was tempted to group the Young Women behind Deianeira (now C); they then come forward individually during the narrative, to surround her R/BC/L.

The arrival of Hyllos at R must be followed by his assumption of the dominant narrative role, as a prelude to Deianeira's silent and final entry into the *skene*. To allow her to occupy a position BC by the time he arrives seems appropriate, and so Deianeira's exchange with members of the *choros*, perhaps a pair, might see those three figures moving towards the *skene* (719–33). With Deianeira somewhere near the *skene*, Hyllos (at C) may after 750 direct his speech away from her towards the rest of the Young Women, who have moved to ELC and ERC; but his opening condemnations should be delivered to her face.

The vigour and violence of his narration are a vehicle for perform-ance, and an immediate audience of young women and the wife of the central, agonized figure provides the most effective sounding-board for the cruelty of the events. The speech is, from that point of view, a gross disruption of optimism and the domestic scene, and the more that the performer engages with its vision the greater our sense of the later misery and dejection of Hyllos.[35] Any disposition within the playing

[35] Heiden 1989, 108–19 provides a long analysis of this scene, but his conception of 'rhetoric' does not seem to include the performance of narrative; Seale 1982, 201 confines himself to noting the 'long and graphic description' by

space must permit the narrator the greatest histrionic freedoms. What we tiresomely have come to call 'the messenger-speech' is all too clearly the most enhanced form of some specific performance skills in the Greek theatre. Panoramic vision and an intense sequence of (often) fatal action are climactically released into our understanding of the stillness of other, listening characters.

It seems to be the case that Hyllos follows Deianeira into the *skene*, as he can be later found by the Nurse inside the building (927–8).[36] Deianeira's departure is an instance of a device regularly deployed by Sophokles, even in the small group of the surviving tragedies. Iokaste in *Oidipous the King* (Scene 4) and Eurydike in *Antigone* (Scene 7) both fatally enter the *skene* in this manner, Eurydike silently and Iokaste after a short, impassioned exchange with Oidipous.[37] In this drama, we should be warned by what Deianeira has said at 719–22. The final lines of Hyllos (815–20), with perhaps a pause after them, allow his entry into the *skene* to follow after a reasonable interval.

Choros 5

The Young Women's optimism is now shattered, although they are still conscious (813–14) of the innocent intentions of Deianeira. This keeps their contribution distinct: Hyllos may condemn her, and the audience may have forebodings of her self-destruction, but the Young Women

Hyllos. In the comparable speech from *Ant* Scene 7, direct quotation from the victim also occupies the climactic position in the narrative and the performance. The emphasis in narrative on the pathos of the father–son relationship prepares for the Finale of the tragedy, in which Hyllos will suffer just as he has here inflicted suffering. Cf. Ewans, p. 225 above on the exchange between Haimon and Kreon in *Ant*: 'The relationship between father and son was the most crucial of all the *philos*-relationships that bound Greeks together.'

[36] In the Nurse's narrative of events in Scene 5, Deianeira first sees Hyllos laying out a stretcher for Herakles in the central courtyard (900–902). Most Greek houses had a division between men's and women's quarters, and there is no problem in assuming that Hyllos is separated from Deianeira after this moment. In Euripides' *Alkestis*, Herakles feasts in one section of the house while the rest is gripped by mourning.

[37] Seale 1982, 201–2; cf. Ewans' Notes on *Ant* Scene 7, pp. 238–9 above. Easterling 1982, 173 independently observes that the repeated references to Deianeira's departure (813 to 819) would suggest a slow movement by Deianeira into the *skene*.

in Choros 5 do not allow us to presume too much.[38] The pace of their adjustment to a sequence of revelations is the controlling theatrical means in the subsequent transitional section, which includes Choros 5, Scene 5, and Choros 6 before the arrival of Herakles. Our own theatrical sense is doubtless more impatient, and if there are no obvious remedies for this in performance or reading, we do need to allow ourselves a metaphor of something close to cinematic slow motion.

Revelations are sudden, in contrast to the beguiling constancies of hope or optimism, and it is the force of the sudden revelations about Herakles that preoccupies the singers. Two kinds of ominous probability are displayed in A1 and A2: the resolution of a prophetic enigma in A1, and the deadly history of the specific venom in A2.[39] But probability is not certainty, and the suspense maintained in B1 and B2 is dramaturgically essential, as is the full acceptance of grief and suffering. These are the tonal qualities that must at this moment prepare for but not anticipate Scene 5, and it is of additional significance that the cyclical convictions of the *choros* finally give way to the tragic potential of Aphrodite. For the following, inexorable sequence, the faith in Zeus as father and preserver of Herakles is displaced temporarily by Aphrodite's decisive influence.[40] This tragic function of the goddess occupies a similar – instrumental and climactic – position in *Antigone*, from which the drama distracts us by the appeals of its characters to other gods, Olympian and of the underworld.[41]

---

[38] As Gardiner 1987, 127 observes: 'The stasimon (821ff.) is concerned with Heracles' fate; they speak [sic] of Deianeira only in the second *strophe*, and then return to Heracles: their stream of tears (851) is not for her.'

[39] Several commentators have noted the inconsistencies in the information we receive as an audience about the oracle: at 44–5 and 164–5 Deianeira mentions an absence of fifteen months, while in B1 of Choros 4 it is twelve months. Here the *choros* sings of twelve years, which may readily be thought to be an appropriate length for a full cycle of twelve Labours (cf. Easterling 1982, 176). The most blunt comment is probably that of Burton 1980, 65, that 'the inconsistency in the time-references must simply be accepted'; Davies 1991, 268–9 offers some thoughts on how the variations might be considered dramatically purposeful.

[40] This tragic potential was not explicitly acknowledged by the Young Women in Choros 3, where Aphrodite presides over a happy outcome, although the victorious tenor of the song is clearly belied by circumstances. For Lichas (250), as for the sceptical Hyllos at the end of the tragedy (1264–78), Zeus is ultimately responsible. For a full and perceptive discussion of the authority of Zeus in relation to Aphrodite, see Winnington-Ingram 1980, 86–90.

[41] *Ant* Choros 4 insists on the power of Eros just after Haimon has quarrelled

Scene 5

In this scene the *choros* is once again visited by a figure from the *skene* with a disclosure to make. It is a gruelling and yet fascinating scene, which concludes with another gruesome and emotive narrative. The concentration of Choros 5, in (B1) and (B2), on grief and suffering is followed by cries of lamentation from the *skene*. It seems evident from 869ff. that the Young Women do not immediately draw close to the *skene*, but remain at an apprehensive distance; the 'old woman' (Nurse) approaches them, and in 870 there is a description that must presumably have corresponded to her mask. It is just possible that the mask has been changed from Scene 1, while the costume remains the same.[42] If apprehension, rather than curiosity, is the reaction, then the Young Women might initially draw back in small groups, which then gather around her.

The text of the following section (871–95) has been variously debated and suspected as spurious by scholars.[43] The emended Oxford text offers: (1) a spoken exchange between the Nurse and *choros* members, which includes *antilabe* (876, 877, and 879); (2) the *choros* changing to song, and so probably dance, from 880 to 895; (3) the Nurse continuing to interject with spoken lines (881, 889, and 891). The sung passage suggests agitation after the news that Deianeira died by a sword-thrust, which subsides only when the suicide has been confirmed. The final, spoken question from a *choros* member (898)

with his father Kreon, and the final result is attempted parricide and then suicide by Haimon. The fullest discussion is again by Winnington-Ingram 1980, 92–8; cf. also Ewans' Notes, pp. 228–9 above.

[42] A change of mask within a tragedy is guaranteed for the supposedly mourning Helen in Euripides' *Helene*, and in my view probable for the self-blinded Oidipous in *OKing* (Ley 1991, 17–19; but on Oidipous see *contra* McCart below, p. 298 n.92). It might have been considered expensive to change the Nurse's mask, but it might also be effective; a manifestly 'joyless' visage would not exactly suit the Nurse in her attempt to counteract Deianeira's inactive fatalism in Scene 1.

[43] It would be difficult, if not impossible, to summarize the textual debates and problems effectively here: the clearest and most recent account is that by Davies 1991, 207–8. One guiding principle is that the Nurse probably speaks throughout, and I have followed that in the translation. A supplement at 881 (details in Davies 1991, 209), specifying the weapon used, presents this sequence: the fact of death, the method of death, and then the fact of suicide. This has an emotional logic which would be convincing and relatively clear in performance.

then prompts the Nurse's narrative. In the introductory exchange (871ff.), the announcement that Deianeira is dead is first made obscurely (871–2, 874–5) and then clarified repeatedly (876–7), before attention turns to the means of death.

Granted the uncertainties, interpretation for performance is open to many possibilities.[44] In the workshop we allowed questions from separate *choros* members as the Nurse approaches and becomes surrounded (863–79), and then unified the Young Women vocally in the song (880–95), retaining that unison for the short, lyric interjections at 890 and 892. This marked the contrast between speech and song simply and strongly, but many other variations would be possible.

For the Nurse's narrative, the most attractive option is to permit the Young Women to draw back, in groups or individually, to the perimeter of the *orchêstra*. The Nurse must refer to the *skene*, and her narrative should be easily associated with it. In the workshop her attention was divided between the place which was the scene of what she has just witnessed, and her immediate audience. It is also plausible that the Nurse partially enacts the roles of both Deianeira (whom she quotes, 920–22) and Hyllos. This skill is obviously always available to the actor-narrator in tragedy, and the status of the Nurse might perhaps be understood to permit her a greater degree of liberty than would be appropriate for either Deianeira or Hyllos.[45]

There is no particular significance to the Nurse's departure, which could be into the *skene* or out the L *parodos*; in performance it may well have been covered by the beginning of Choros 6.

[44] Cf. e.g. Burton 1980, 74–7, Easterling 1982, 182–3, and Gardiner 1987, 127–8.

[45] It is difficult to defend this assertion with any great confidence: both Deianeira in Scene 3 and Hyllos in Scene 4 impersonate by quoting directly (Nessos and Herakles, respectively). Both are also extremely agitated. But the status of the Nurse, and her immediate audience of the Young Women on their own, might argue for a greater freedom. Cf. Ewans' Notes to *Ant* Scene 7 (especially 1206–31), and McCart on the *OKing* Finale (esp. 1223–96) on impersonation in narrative at climactic moments in Sophoklean tragedy; pp. 238–9 and 297–8.

Reinhardt's strictures (1979, 34–63) against the narrative style of this tragedy, which he believed must indicate an early date for it, pass over the exciting possibilities that dramatic narrative offers for performance.

Choros 6

This is the final song from the Young Women and, apart from two short comments (1044–5, 1112–13), their final contribution to the drama.[46] This relative silence, after the arrival of Herakles, underlines how far they have been involved with the situation of Deianeira, in many respects emotionally. The playwright has no role for young singing female characters once the (at first, sung) physical agony of the male hero Herakles becomes the principal theatrical focus – not even in the revelation of the true quality of Deianeira's intentions; that is given to Hyllos.

This song decisively accomplishes the end of their involvement. The scale of grief has increased gradually in intensity with Deianeira's death, and the effect of A1 and A2 – each almost as short and formally balanced as a refrain – is to provide an unequivocal conclusion to optimism.[47] The degree of resignation finds expression in B1, where the image of the 'favouring wind', turned to harsh effect by Hyllos at 815, offers the Young Women a glimpse of escape from what they are constrained to witness. That they believe the vision of Herakles will be 'unspeakable' is perhaps an introduction to (and retrospectively an explanation of) their subsequent silence. Unlike even the animal ferocity of the marriage of Deianeira and Herakles, this prospect does not encourage either narrative or song.

What the *choros* members did in the last third of the tragedy – their dispositions and reactions – is hidden from us by their silence. However, the fact that the Young Women would wish to leave, but cannot (B1), provides us with the clearest indication we have of their reactions during the Finale. They give no interpretation of the approaching group, because the silence of that group might signify either sleep or death (B2).

[46] Burton 1980, 79 comments that 'overwhelmed as they are' by Deianeira's death and the sight of Herakles the *choros* 'take no part in the anapaests or the lyrics which open the final scene'. Gardiner 1987, 132 notes that the 'relation between the *choros* and Heracles appears to be entirely one-sided. Heracles is always in their thoughts and words, yet when he is at last physically present they do not speak to him, nor he to them.'

[47] The repetitions, and the pattern of the balanced, three-line introductory stanzas indicate 'a lament in ritual form' (Burton 1980, 77; cf. Easterling 1982, 193–4). Compare Aischylos' *Persians* 694–6 and 700–702, where the *choros* of Elders is awestruck at the appearance of the Shade of Dareios, their former king, on his tomb.

Finale

In view of the Young Women's apprehensions, and their desire to escape, it seems plausible to have them withdraw to BL as the cortège approaches at R. Hyllos speaks first. The Nurse's narrative had placed him in the *skene*, where he was preparing a bed for his father. So it seems almost certain that he must appear at the *skene* doors, and join the procession as it is arriving.

Lines 971–1003 are composed in *anapaests*, the regular metre in tragedy for progressive movement.[48] In principle this seems completely appropriate, yet it would mean that Herakles' first lines (983–7, admittedly an outcry, and 973–1003) were spoken or chanted while he is still being carried in on the stretcher.[49] If the *anapaests* have these implications, then the progress of the group into and in the *orchêstra* is slow.

Herakles is the mythical embodiment of male vigour and strength, and his paralysis is a formidable theatrical image in itself. If the Old Man restrains Hyllos (albeit ineffectively), this may be BC near the doors of the *skene*, while Herakles is carried past them and brought slowly to a position at C. It is possibly significant in this connection that there is no acknowledgement from Herakles at this time of the presence of his son. He is surrounded by his stretcher-bearers, who are Euboians ('strangers' to the *choros*, 963); they certainly remain for the duration of the Finale, since Hyllos instructs them to carry Herakles out at 1264.[50]

Herakles sings his agony in *strophe* (A1: 1004–17) and *antistrophe* (A2: 1023–43). In A1, he asks to be left in peace to sleep (1004–6), and then exclaims against the interference of someone (who must be the Old Man) attempting to move him on his stretcher (1007–9). Subsequently, in between *strophe* and *antistrophe*, the Old Man invites

[48] 'An anapaestic passage, marking the arrival of the procession': Easterling 1982, 196. *Anapaests* are the metre used for the final lines of this tragedy (1259–78), when Herakles is taken out to the pyre on Mount Oita, and all leave the *orchêstra*.

[49] This initial outcry is balanced by Herakles' final command to himself to 'stifle that cry' at 1262, also in *anapaests*.

[50] The visual recall of the arrival of the captives brought by Lichas is paramount, and must release perceptions in the audience of an ironic contrast. For an introductory discussion, Seale 1982, 203–4; Seaford (1986 and 1987) examines the influence of wedding ritual on the structure of the play, and Herakles' final role as a substitute 'bride'.

Hyllos to lend him a hand, and it seems that Herakles is 'lifted' up, probably propped up, in some way (1025). Only now does Herakles recognize his son, and from this moment onwards the demands placed on Hyllos are insistent.[51] In this respect, the change between the appeal in A1 to 'men of Greece' (1011), whom Herakles believes to be under obligation to him, and the appeal to Hyllos in A2 to put an end to his misery must be significant.

If spoken partly raised, partly lying as it must be, the speech 1046–111 is a *tour de force* of acting by any standards; of breathing, voice-control, and physical expression without the use of locomotion. Herakles, particularly in this state, must be an awesome, pathetic, and terrifying figure, by whom all are appalled. The obvious if unwilling exception has to be his son, who is drawn to Herakles at 1076, as Herakles lifts the cloth that covers him.[52] Hands and forearms are throughout essential to this extraordinary performance, and symbolic of Herakles' lost strength. Gestures to the *skene*, which contains Deianeira, must surely be made at 1066–7 ('Give her from your hands into mine') and 1070, and again at 1076. They are also likely to be used in the invocation of Hades and Zeus at 1085–6, and at 1090ff. Herakles conducts a review of his devastated body.

Hands are all that Herakles now has, but they would by implication be enough to kill Deianeira (1133), were that act necessary. The revelation that occurs at 1114–42 leads abruptly to resignation (1143–50), and the performer might well choose to calm his gestures, in preparation for the clasp of hands between Hyllos and his father (1181–92). This symbolic tableau binds Hyllos by oath to his father's wishes, and the emphasis on hands remains firmly implied in the actions Hyllos must subsequently perform (1193).[53]

[51] On the significance of this movement, Seale 1982, 207, citing Winnington-Ingram 1969, 46. Sorum 1978 offers a sensitive treatment of Hyllos in the close of the tragedy.

[52] Pragmatically, I doubt whether the question of exactly what was revealed to the audience can be answered with any confidence: for suggestions, Seale 1982, 205–6, citing Slater 1976, 64. Seaford 1986, 56–7 connects this raising of the robe with part of the wedding ritual, so rendering Herakles into the third tragic bride of this drama.

[53] Herakles won Deianeira with his hands and strength, and he killed both Iphitos and Lichas in anger with his hands. Hands and voice are clearly the principal resources for the actor in this Finale, and in their significance and symbolism should remind us of the relatively inadequate connotations of our standard term 'gesture' when applied to Greek tragedy.

If Herakles in his agony and rage is terrifying, so is the knowledge that Hyllos and the Young Women carry with them until the full revelation to Herakles of Deianeira's intentions. The scene demands that the Old Man and the bearers withdraw, probably to EBR or ERC, while the Young Women remain at EBL. If we accept the implications of 1076 ('Come and stand here . . .'), then until that moment Hyllos himself will have hesitated to draw close to his father: a position behind Herakles at BC, reacting out of sight until this point, is a convincing choice. Hyllos' relative lack of movement, and the misery of his dreadful knowledge of the true situation, would probably be apparent to the audience in his reaction to the homicidal instructions of his father at 1066 and 1070. His approach to his father at 1076 would be reluctant, and temporary, but Herakles' lapse into silence at 1111 gives him the opportunity to take the intiative. He would not now, I believe stand above his father, but would come to his side, perhaps at RC, with some possible support from the presence of the Old Man at EBR.

This position is a suitable one for the reaction, after the central swearing of the oath, to the instructions to burn his father alive.[54] Hyllos must attempt to find some refuge when faced by this repugnant task, although neither the Old Man nor the Young Women are remotely adequate – as the script shows by their silence. I feel that he would attempt to appeal to each, without conviction, and that the playing-space behind his father's body at least offers some kind of asylum. If he is there when the instruction to marry Iole is given (1221–9), then even that space in its proximity to the *skene* and to Iole

---

[54] On the question whether Herakles' death on the pyre should be linked to the apotheosis he receives in other versions of the myth there is no obvious conclusion, except that any such understanding would have to lie in the audience, since there is nothing explicit in the tragedy. Winnington-Ingram (1980, 215 n. 33) rightly draws attention to the similar ending of *El*, in which there is no mention of the pursuit of Orestes by the Furies – and none should be supplied from other versions. Cf. Silk and Stern 255; Ewans 1996b, 453–4.

Hoey 1977, 272 insists that there is some (indirect) allusion to an apotheosis; cf. Holt 1989. Segal 1981, 99–101 goes further (100): 'It is hard to see how Sophokles could lay such emphasis on the pyre if he had not intended us to think of its purpose, the apotheosis.' Rather more satisfying is the perception that sees Mount Oita as the continuation and fulfilment of the sacrifice to Zeus begun on Mount Kenaion: this is one of the substantial themes of Segal 1977, 99–158 (=1995, 26–68, esp. 53–5).

becomes distinctly threatening to him.[55] All that would then remain would be an escape at R or L. If these are blocked by performers (bearers, Young Women), then Herakles' condition and paternal authority will have effectively enclosed his son. At this point, somewhere in the final exchange (perhaps 1249, or even 1257–8), Hyllos may come forward in resignation to his father's side.

The bearers are commanded to lift at 1264; they may have come to Herakles' side during 1259–63, since the Finale from 1259 is once again in *anapaests*. If Hyllos remains to the right of Herakles, as the cortège leaves at R he can address the Young Women at BL, calling on them to leave.[56] The *skene* is left to our view as an audience, its closed doors concealing the dead body of one woman and wife, and the living body of another, silent one.

[55] The language suggests marriage rather than the role of a concubine: Segal 1994 (also 1995, 86ff. with 237, n. 59), against McKinnon 1971.

[56] There is no consensus on whether the last four lines are spoken by Hyllos, or by the *choros* to themselves. Burton 1980, 81–2 suggests that Iole might have appeared, to accommodate the reference to her at 1222; yet if she was present, Herakles would hardly need to refer to her in the way he does at 1219. So the reference to 'Young Woman' at 1275 must be to the *choros*; Easterling 1982, 231–3 carefully argues for the ascription of the lines to Hyllos.

Uncertainty also surrounds the exit of the *choros*. Do the Young Women cross the *orchêstra*, joining the final procession out by the R *parodos*; or do they choose to go back to their homes by the L *parodos*, providing a contrast to the men's departure to the right?

Oidipous the King

GREGORY McCART

The Production; the Actors and their Masks

The premiere production of this translation took place on 22 March 1996 in the Bridge Street Quarry, Toowoomba, Queensland, Australia. Three actors in masks played the eight individual characters.[1] Following Sophokles' probable distribution of the roles, the first actor played Oidipous, the second actor played the Priest, Teiresias, Iokaste, the Herdsman and the Servant, and the third actor played Kreon and the Korinthian.[2] Silent masks were used for Antigone, Ismene and the Attendants. The production used a single, masked Speaker for the Elders;[3] the dancers representing the Elders, and the supplementary *choros* of children, were presented with faces painted, for the most part, white. The performance took place on a circle of sand twenty metres in diameter in front of two monuments of rock and earth representing the doors of the palace. The seating conformed to the configuration of the Theatre of Dionysos in Athens (three-quarter circle) although the *theatron* was minuscule in comparative size, seating 350. Musical accompaniment was provided for the choral dances and

---

[1] The second actor was female – a deliberate departure from ancient Greek theatrical practice, to test the possibilities of the mask in allowing for cross-gender performance. Spectators canvassed after the production said that they had no difficulty in accepting the masked female actor in her one female and four male roles. (Note that all but one of the second actor's male roles are old men, implying that Sophokles used a specialist with a light voice to play women and old men, as in *Ant.*)

For a critical view of gender politics and tragedy, and comment on cross-gendered acting in ancient Greece, see Case 1985. For a discussion of the way ancient Greek tragedians employed multiple role-playing in composing tragedy, see Damen 1989.

[2] Some scholars (e.g. Pickard-Cambridge 1968, 141) reverse the roles of the second and third actors. With the exception of Teiresias who might be played by either actor, the other allocations cannot be altered – unless the Servant makes an ungainly and distracting exit after Oidipous' entrance at 1296 in order to return as Kreon; see below on the Finale.

[3] This is only one way in which the Choroses might have been performed during the classical period. Ewans 1995, xxii–xxv presents counter-arguments in favour of distributing lines among all the individual members of the *choros*.

on occasion during the scenes by a didjeridoo player and by clapsticks.[4] The performances took place at sunset.[5]

Choreography

Since we know so little about the choreography used in tragedy – a great loss, given its importance in the performance – modern productions must invent their own. Our production employed an Aboriginal – to be more precise, a Murri – choreographer from the Kumilaroi tribe in southern Queensland.[6] A second Murri choreographer provided training in Murri movement and orchestrated choral responses during the scenes. In ancient Greece the dance was imitative.[7] So too is the dance in Murri culture, which has a history of tens of thousands of years. In both cultures the dance is grounded in spiritual evocation. The choreography was also grounded in a clear articulation of the meaning of the odes and the emotional states of the Elders as implied by the text. This was then translated into gestures, movements and postures derived from Murri dance. The *choros* of *Oidipous the King* represents male Theban Elders. Their gender, however, is not critical to the action as it is in some other tragedies (e.g. Aischylos, *Agamemnon*; Sophokles, *Aias*; Euripides, *Medeia*). In our production, the *choros* included male and female dancers representing the people of Thebes. This had some consequences for the choreography (see below on Choros 1).

The setting

This drama requires entrances from the palace and from inside and outside Thebes, provided by the doors of the *skene*, the L *parodos* and the R *parodos* respectively. It also requires 'altars' (15), one of which is a shrine to Apollo (919–20; cf. 80–81). In our production, the shrine

---

[4] The didjeridoo is a wind instrument consisting of a one- to two-metre tree limb hollowed out naturally by white ants or artificially, with a mouthpiece of beeswax. Clapsticks are resonant wooden sticks held in the hands.

[5] Ashby (1991b) concludes that a warm temperature and spectator comfort were paramount in determining the siting of theatres in ancient Greece. Similar environmental factors affected the production in Toowoomba.

[6] I am indebted to Sharmon Parsons for information on Murri culture recorded in these notes.

[7] Pickard-Cambridge 1968, 248–9; Rehm 1992, 54.

to Apollo was set two metres in front of the centre of the *orchêstra*, while two other shrines were set EFR and EFL.[8]

Preliminary action

Significant action commences in this drama before a word is spoken, although how this action might have been staged has been a matter for long debate. Who was represented in the action has also been contentious. The possibilities for staging include the suggestion that Oidipous and the Priest address the spectators as if they were the suppliants.[9] But this makes nonsense of Oidipous' first reference to their suppliant branches (3) and his later command to them to pick them up (143). It has also been suggested that the *choros* of Theban Elders entered as the suppliants before the drama started.[10] This is against normal Greek practice, and also demands a theatrically awkward transition from suppliants to Theban people in full view of the spectators. The only possible option is to use a supplementary *choros* of suppliants.

In determining who actually comprises this supplementary *choros*, there is considerable dispute over the precise meaning of lines 16–17 in the Greek text.[11] Is there more than one Priest? If so, the others are ignored by both Oidipous and by the one Priest who speaks. Do the phrases 'these with scarce the strength to fly' – a reference perhaps to their parlous health rather than, as is usually assumed, to their age – and 'this select band of unmarried youth' refer to the same or different groups of young people? The numerous references in the scene to children ('*tekna*', a generic word for 'children', in 1, and '*paides*', more

---

[8] Ashby (1991a) is of the opinion that altars in Greek theatres sat on the periphery of the *orchêstra*, where they were both visible and important without constituting a major obstacle to performance. Our experience accorded with this view to some degree (cf. also Ewans 1996a, xxxviii and xlv on Aischylos' *Seven* and *Suppliants*). We found however that, although the periphery was suitable for the two lesser-used shrines, a position two metres in front of the centre of the *orchêstra* – eight metres in from the periphery – was the best site for the main shrine of Apollo. Here it was prominent, but still allowed the actors to use C as the principal focus point, and was not an obstacle in performance. On the contrary, it provided an excellent point of reference for some of the choreography. Cf. Wiles 1997, 78ff. for theoretical considerations in favour of central altars.

[9] Calder 1959, 125 (although he does allow for two attendants to the Priest, 129); Arnott 1989, 21–2.

[10] Walton 1984, 119.

[11] Recently, Arnott 1989, 148; Hogan 1991, 22; Rehm 1992, 110.

specifically 'boys' or 'girls', at 32, 58, 142, and 147) suggest, against
the one use of the disputed word '*êitheôn*', 'unmarried youth' (18),
that supernumeraries representing prepubescent children accompany a
single Priest. The adults, as the Priest informs Oidipous, are elsewhere,
gathered at Athena's twin temples and the shrine of Ismenos (20–21).

Each suppliant carries a branch of olive entwined with tufts of
wool.[12] They are costumed in the white garb of suppliants. The
supplementary *choros* enter from the L *parodos*, that is, from the city
of Thebes, and proceed to the shrine of Apollo at FC. They then gather
around the shrine, facing the doors of the *skene*, representing the
palace of the house of Labdakos, kneel in the manner of suppliants,
and lay their suppliant branches on or near the altar.[13]

Scene 1

The first actor, in the mask and costume of Oidipous, traverses the ten-
metre distance from the *skene* to the centre of the *orchêstra*.[14] The
visual and acoustic properties of the Theatre of Dionysos, no less than
those of the later theatre at Epidauros, promote a preference for using
the centre of the *orchêstra* as much as possible, since the actor is most
prominent here, both visually and vocally. This preference was used as
a principal guide in blocking moves. In our production, the chant
ceased before Oidipous addresses the suppliants.

Oidipous describes Thebes as full of incense, groaning and prayers
to the Healer-god Apollo.[15] The first actor introduces himself as the
renowned Oidipous, who has chosen to come himself from the palace
to listen to them rather than send some emissary. He singles out the
Priest and invites him to speak on behalf of the suppliants. The
invitation takes five lines, long enough for the first actor to vacate the
centre of the *orchêstra* and for the second actor to move to it. Dawe
notes Sophokles' ability to convey both primary and secondary mean-

---

[12] Cf. line 3, with the scholiast's comment.

[13] In our production, the supplementary *choros* began to chant a summons
to Oidipous, begging him to come to them. The chant was in the language of
the Kumilaroi tribe: '*Njaia Njummi Oidipous*' ('I see Oidipous') and '*Njaia
Winunji Oidipous*' ('I hear Oidipous').

[14] The significance of entrances and exits in the 'spatialization of the tragic
event' is explored by Brault 1989.

[15] On the conventions of defining location in tragedy, cf. Arnott 1989, ch. 5.
On those governing identification of speakers, cf. Manton 1982.

ings in one phrase.[16] Here the Greek words 'pro tônde' (10) convey the meanings of 'in front of' and 'on behalf of' the others. The first indicates the Priest's position on the orchêstra, while the second indicates his seniority. This opening sequence, with the two short, sympathetic speeches of Oidipous framing the long narrative by the Priest, powerfully describes the present crisis and Oidipous' past success. Oidipous' response is to comfort the children with a speech which is 'marked by a certain amplitude in the deployment of antithesis and repetition',[17] and to announce that his one action to date has been to send Kreon to Delphi to seek the advice of the god Apollo.

Kreon's arrival is the first of three in the drama which have been long awaited, but take place right on cue. (The other two are the arrivals of Teiresias in Scene 2 and of the Herdsman in Scene 5.) These instant arrivals 'as expected' do not appear to be circumstantial in performance, because characters are basically functions of the plot,[18] and these entrances help to tell the story in a direct and well-paced manner. The third actor, wearing the mask of Kreon and 'bedecked with garlands made from berries and sweet bay', makes the long entrance down the R parodos. The Suppliants gesture or run towards him (they 'signal' his arrival at 79), while the first and second actors exchange seven lines of dialogue (78–84) concluding with a statement from Oidipous that Kreon is now close enough to hear – which means the third actor must by 85 be well inside the orchêstra.

Oidipous' integrity is again demonstrated in his rejection of Kreon's offer to receive the news from Delphi inside the palace and his insistence on the suppliants' hearing it as well. The subsequent exchange between Kreon and Oidipous also reflects favourably on Oidipous with respect, in particular, to his unfaltering commitment to investigating the murder of Laios[19] and releasing Thebes from the ravages of the plague. However, there are disturbing elements. Given that the ancient Athenian spectators knew the basic elements of the legend,[20] Oidipous' question – 'who is the man whose fate the god

[16] Dawe 1982, ad loc.

[17] Dawe 1982, ad loc. Oidipous is, after all, talking to children.

[18] Aristotle, Poetics 50a15ff.; but see Vince (1997) for a critical evaluation of Aristotle's preference for promoting text over performance. On arbitrary entrances, cf. Arnott 1989, 185.

[19] For a fanciful discourse which sees this drama as an example of the detective story, cf. Belton 1991. For a more sober discussion, cf. Knox 1957.

[20] There is however debate as to how relevant this was in the reception of

reveals?' (102) – might have sounded ironic. The sequence also includes the first of the alternations during the drama between singular and plural usage when reference is made to Laios' killer(s). Here Kreon speaks of 'thieves' while Oidipous, in the next line (124), speaks in the singular. The same usage occurs later in this scene (139, 141) and again in Scene 2 when, in an exchange about the manner of Laios' death, a Theban Elder speaks of travellers, but Oidipous responds in the singular (292–3). In his earlier address in Scene 2, Oidipous also confines himself to the singular (224, 227, 238, 266).

The issue of one or many killers becomes critical in Scene 3. Here the slippage is part of the inexplicable which abounds in the drama, teasing the spectator.[21] It is also disturbing that Oidipous immediately suspects, like the misguided Kreon in *Antigone* (289ff.), that bribery is at the root of Laios' death (124–5). In performance the first actor is given an almost irresistible opportunity to combine gesture – raising the hand that he identifies later (811) as having struck down Laios – with location on the *orchêstra* (C), when he delivers the additional ironic lines: 'Laios' killer – whoever he is – / might want to raise that very hand to punish me' (139–40).

These ironies and slippages do not, however, undermine the depiction of Oidipous as a caring and intelligent ruler. This is reinforced by his turning to the children for the third time at 142 as Kreon exits along the L *parodos*,[22] asking them to take up their branches as a sign that their supplication has been successful.[23] He prepares for the entrance of the *choros* of Theban Elders by commanding that someone other than the children bring the people 'here' (144). Presumably, this other person is an attendant. The time-lapse between the command and the need for it to be executed is very short (six lines), as with a similar incident later in the drama (three and a half lines) when Iokaste sends an attendant to fetch Oidipous (945–6), requiring rapid exits on

tragedy; cf. Ewans 1995, xxviiff. against Taplin 1978, 162–5 and Hogan 1991, 19.

[21] This 'heightens the irony of unconscious personal reference' (Hogan 1991, 28). Cf. Rehm (1992, 110) and Ahl (1991, ch. 10).

[22] *Pace* Calder 1959. In Scene 1, Kreon enters along the R *parodos* because he has arrived from Delphi. In Scene 3, he enters from the L *parodos*, because his first lines would be nonsense if he lived in the palace and not the city. He therefore must exit along the L *parodos* towards the end of Scene 1.

[23] To have left them there would have implied lack of success; Jebb 1902, 11 compares Euripides, *Suppliants* 259 and 359.

both occasions.[24] The supplementary *choros* of Suppliants follows the Priest out by the L *parodos*, passing the *choros* of Theban Elders as they enter.[25]

Choros I

The mood of the first Choros is anxiety, emanating directly from the central concerns of the first scene, namely the plague in Thebes and the oracle from Delphi. In A1 the Elders crave to know whether this message from the prophet-god Apollo will turn out to be good or bad for Thebes. Throughout the ode, as in all odes in the drama, the appeals are in the first person singular; this makes them all the more personal and moving. The metre used in the Greek for A1 and A2 is the solemn dactyl, and incorporates a falling rhythm suggesting melancholy.[26] In A2 they call on the powerful trinity of gods – Athena, Artemis and Apollo – to come and save them from death as they had in the past.

In our production, the choreography for the first *strophe* and *antistrophe* was based on the impassioned plea to the Sun-god for help. During A1 the *choros* entered to the sound of didjeridoo and clapsticks, swaying from side to side with hands open in a supplicatory gesture. In A2 they moved into and away from the shrine of Apollo FC mimicking the motion of a flying eagle, as the Sun-god's totem. The movements were gender-specific, in keeping with the conventions of Murri dance. The men's vigorous stomping contrasted with the more gentle side-to-side motion of the women as they supplicated the god in traditional Murri patterns.

In B1 the Elders develop the Priest's account of the plague from the previous scene (25–30). The metre used in the Greek for B1 and B2 is basically trochaic but with a number of substitutions, making the

[24] These can be accomplished without a necessary silence, *pace* Poe 1992, 129. They contribute to the pace of the story-telling.

[25] It is interesting to speculate on whether the conventions applying to entrances by actors by either *parodos* applied to the *choros*, which usually had one entrance and one exit only in the entire performance. In our production, the *choros* entered by both *parodoi* for choreographical reasons. An entrance by an entire *choros* from the L *parodos* could be rather cramped, especially considering that in this drama the supplementary *choros* was making its exit simultaneously by the same path. Using both *parodoi* also allowed for harmonious balance in initiating the first dance.

[26] For additional detail on metre, see Jebb 1902, lxiii–xcv, and Dale 1969.

rhythm 'logaoedic', that is, closer to prose, perhaps suggesting recitative. In B2 they relate how the corpses of children lie rotting in the street, causing infection to spread, and how women wail at the altars. For their sakes, the Elders beg Athena to send relief.

Our choreography attempted to capture the melancholy and the mourning, with the focus on the cry of childbirth and the infertility of the soil. Each woman danced in small circles, time and again raising her right hand, bringing it to her heart and thrusting it down sharply to the ground, representing shedding tears, heartache, uterine contractions, and stillbirth. Each man stamped the earth and gathered soil in one hand after the other and let it flow in sweeping gestures to the ground, signifying both the infertility of the land and efforts to dry the tears of the women.

In C1 the Elders compare the ravages of the plague with the ravages of war. They implore Zeus to turn destruction onto the god of war himself. In C2 they pray again to Apollo and Artemis and make a special plea to Dionysos whose cult in Greece began in Thebes. The metre used in the Greek for C1 and C2 is trochaic but with rising rhythms indicating agitation, which concludes with a cessation of movement as Oidipous enters to address the Elders.

Our choreography represented a communal invocation to Murri spirits corresponding to the Greek gods. The *choros* mimicked the motion of various animals – the eagle, the kangaroo, the goanna, the emu and the Rainbow Serpent. These are known as totems in Murri culture. *Mimesis* allows the spirit of the animal to enter and strengthen the dancer. The dance closed with the *choros* around the shrine of Apollo and a mimicry of the Rainbow Serpent drinking the water and then showering the barren earth with life-giving rain. The *choros* then lay still upon the ground until aroused by the rapid rhythm of the clapsticks as they announced the re-entry of Oidipous. As he made his way to the centre of the *orchêstra*, the *choros* 'bowed out' in a conventional Murri way of vacating the dancing area with head bowed, arms opening out and closing, and stepping gently from side to side. This could be seen in performance as an acknowledgement of the authority of Oidipous.

Choros 1 calls on the fire of the gods to destroy the fire of fever: the Sun-god (A2), Zeus with his lightning flash (C1), and the torches of Artemis and Dionysos (C2) against the 'burning blight' (A2) and the 'burning plague' (C1). The number of gods named – Apollo, Athena, Artemis, Ares, Zeus and Dionysos – and the number of times they are named set Thebes' desperate straits firmly in a religious and spiritual framework. The Elders continually recall this framework throughout the drama.[27] Our choreography with its circling patterns, mimetic gestures and focus on the shrine of Apollo FC captured the anguish of the Thebans and powerfully evoked the spirits of the earth and sky.

Scene 2

The Theban people, represented by the Elders, now witness a scene that commences in confidence and concludes in confusion. The first actor returns to the centre of the *orchêstra* and presents a very different Oidipous from the caring but perplexed – though eventually resolute – leader of Scene 1. Here he promises 'relief and strength' (218) and goes on to outline his strategy for achieving this end.[28] The series of commands and curses which constitute this strategy also constitute an ever-intensifying dramatic impact. Oidipous' plea to the people to come forward with information about Laios' killer is followed by the curses of immediate ostracism and eventual exile on the killer.[29] The subsequent encomium for Laios is followed by the curse of infection from the plague 'and worse besides' (272) on those who do not comply with the commands now promulgated.

[27] Burton 1980, 138–85.

[28] Dawe 1982, *ad loc.*, transposes sections of this speech to make it more 'logical', and closer to the actual legal practice of Sophokles' time (cf. also Hogan 1991, 33–4). However, in performance it makes perfect sense, and magnificent theatre – with the exception of six interpolated lines (246–251):

> My curse on the perpetrator, one
> alone, in hiding, or with others, is:
> eke out your wretched life as badly as you've lived.
> I further pray that even if this person's
> intimate in my house, and I know,
> then I will suffer what I've just now prayed for.

The passage seems to confuse the killer with the informant, and indulges in an irony that is simply too heavy-handed. Cf. Lloyd-Jones and Wilson 1990, 86.

For an examination of Sophokles' possible use of Athenian legal procedures in O*King*, cf. Lewis 1988.

[29] There has been long debate on the interpretation of lines 227–9 and 236–41. On the former, I follow Lloyd-Jones and Wilson 1990, 85 who believe that a line is missing after 227. I translate their suggestion as the bracketed line 227a. For a defence of the manuscript reading, cf., for example, Henry 1969, 125. On the second set of disputed lines, I defer to Jebb's construing and translate Oidipous' prohibition of social intercourse to apply to the Theban people, not to the unknown murderer. *Contra* Tanner 1966.

In this address the ironies of Scene 1 are succeeded by even crueller ironies. Oidipous suggests that the killer might be from abroad (231); he himself arrived in Thebes from Korinth. He identifies himself with Laios through his royal office, his marriage to Iokaste, and the fact that his children and those of Laios – had they not 'miscarried' (262) – would have been related. He promises to fight for Laios 'as if he were my father' (265), and this leads him to pay tribute to the royal Theban lineage to which he, though he does not yet know it, belongs.[30] The threads of irony and of the inexplicable which have been woven into the drama before Teiresias' entry become a much more obvious and contrasting pattern in the subsequent contest between Oidipous and the prophet.

This contest is presented in the sequence 300–462; it has caused both scholars and actors some difficulty because of apparent contradictions and inexplicable misunderstanding on the part of Oidipous. Though it is true that in performance the pace, the vigour and the passion of the scene – both men, so an Elder tells us (405), speak in anger – give spectators little time to dwell on any apparent inconsistencies, it is essential that the actors know clearly what they are saying and why at each turn.

On three occasions Oidipous explodes in anger against Teiresias and on each occasion the reasons for his doing so appear at first glance slight. Closer examination however reveals an impossible dilemma which thwarts Oidipous because he does not have sufficient or correct

[30] The Theban royal house included many characters who featured prominently in the legends of ancient Greece. Kadmos was renowned for introducing the alphabet to Greece. The lives of his children were an extreme mixture of the auspicious and the inauspicious: Semele bore the god Dionysos to Zeus and perished as a consequence, Agaüe was sent mad by Dionysos and decapitated her own son Pentheus, Ino took her children with her to a watery death, and Autonoë's son, Aktaion, was torn to pieces by his own hounds because he glimpsed the goddess Artemis bathing. The male line produced a number of Theban rulers: Kadmos' only son Polydoros, Labdakos whose name derives from the crooked letter of the alphabet, lambda, Laios whose name means 'left' and by implication 'sinister', and Oidipous whose name derives from words which mean 'swollen-foot' and 'knower'. For elaborations on the implications of this naming, cf. Vernant 1981, 96–7 (rpt. E. Segal 1983), Pucci 1992, 66–78. On Thebes as both locale and 'common-place', that is, a cluster of ideas, themes and problems, cf. Zeitlin 1986, 343–78. Edmunds believes the Oidipous story, through the homology of incest and autochthony, was linked, as a version of the Kadmos story, to ancient Greek religion; 1981, 236–8.

knowledge.[31] On the first occasion (334) Oidipous is incensed[32] that Teiresias, despite his moral responsibilities towards Thebes, refuses to fulfil his duty by revealing what he knows so that Thebes can heal. This outburst is as brief as it is sudden, for Oidipous apologizes immediately (335).

The second occasion occurs soon afterwards (345–9) and is prompted by Teiresias' rejection of Oidipous' attempt at reconciliation. This time, Oidipous charges the prophet with being an accessory in the death of Laios. The unexpectedness of this accusation is partly mitigated; it is made in anger (344, 346, 405, 523), and Oidipous can see no other possible explanation for the prophet's stubborn uncooperativeness.[33] But for Teiresias it is insufferable, and prompts the angry counter-accusation that Oidipous himself is the murderer of Laios. Finally, beside himself with passion, Oidipous dismisses the prophet – rather than punish him – out of respect for his age and fragility (402–3).

Oidipous clearly understands one thing Teiresias is telling him: that he killed Laios. But the rest is a puzzle: that his marriage is shameful, that he does not know who his parents are, and that he will be made equal with his children. Furthermore, in his parting address, Teiresias adds to the litany of horror a series of riddling assertions.[34] Some scholars believe that Oidipous should exit before this final address because he could hardly fail to understand what the prophet is saying.[35] Such an exit would result in the ludicrous stage action of having the

[31] Cf. the detailed analysis by Vickers 1973, 502–25.

[32] Dawe 1982 notes *ad loc.* that 'this sudden outburst is phrased in language of abnormal vehemence'.

[33] Cf. the similar reaction by Kreon to Teiresias at *Ant* 1037–8. Accusations of conspiracy abounded among political leaders at the time Sophokles composed this tragedy, and there are varying views on the political connotations of Oidipous' speech; Francis (1992) compares Oidipous' behaviour with that of a Persian king while Rigsby (1976) discusses Oidipous' use of the word 'magos' (387) as equivalent to accusing Teiresias of being a political conspirator. Easterling (1997) warns against a limited socio-political model in the interpretation of tragedy, and addresses examples of the ways in which tragedians created fictive worlds which had a number of resonances for audiences then and later.

[34] Havelock (1984, 188–90) suggests that the constant repetitions and recapitulations of essential events in the life of Oidipous throughout the drama reflect the processes of oral composition. It is teasing to speculate that they might also reflect oral processes in rehearsal and in learning lines and moves.

[35] Cf., for example, Hogan 1991, 43; Segal 1993, 108–9.

blind Teiresias' final command – 'Go / inside and work it out' 460–1 –
uttered to the empty air.[36] But there is no need for Oidipous to exit,
since he is completely unable to make sense of Teiresias' gnomic
utterances.[37] During the sequence, both declare their credentials: Teiresias, as the servant of the Prophet-god Apollo, has his reputation for
unerring prophecy while Oidipous, after initially calling Teiresias a
leader and saviour, reviews this in the light of Teiresias' failure and
Oidipous' success in solving the riddle of the Sphinx.

And so the contest becomes one between two individuals who trust
absolutely in their power to know. Oidipous cannot accept that
Teiresias' knowledge comes from his craft (357), for this would be to
accept its infallibility. The fact that Oidipous' knowledge is based on
false premises is the fundamental given that determines the ultimate
outcome of the drama.[38] Here he can only conclude that a conspiracy
between the seer and Kreon is the explanation for Teiresias' otherwise
inexplicable accusation that he is the murderer of Laios. It also means
that punishing Kreon with death or exile will liberate Thebes from the
plague.

On Teiresias' entrance, Oidipous recalled the oracle that Kreon
brought from Apollo (305–9). After their dispute degenerates into
personal insult, Teiresias claims that it is none other than Apollo who
will bring Oidipous down (377). Then Oidipous makes his own connections: Teiresias–Apollo–Delphi–Kreon, and Kreon's delayed return
from Delphi. For him, these connections confirm conspiracy and
explain Laios' death; Laios was, and Oidipous is, primed to be a
victim in the plot to snatch the throne. At this point (380ff.), Sophokles makes use of the *agôn* or formal debate: Oidipous is the pros-
ecutor, Teiresias the defendant, and both their speeches follow a
ring-cycle pattern.

The significance of the speeches prompted both actors, in our
production, to assume in turn pre-eminent focus near the centre of the
orchêstra, although the savagery of Oidipous' attack on the prophet in
the second half of his speech drove the first actor to vacate the centre
earlier than would normally be expected (which would be during the
four-line choral intervention between the addresses at 404–7) and to
circle the besieged Teiresias where he stood BR. Oidipous asserts that

[36] Bain 1977, 74. *Contra* Knox 1980, 325–6.
[37] So rightly Taplin 1978, 44; Scodel 1984, 64; Gould 1988, 150–53.
[38] Vernant 1983, 191–2: 'Oedipus does not hear the secret discourse which is
established, without his knowing it, at the heart of his own discourse.'

his eminence has made Kreon envious; he questions Teiresias, challenging his claim to authentic prophetic powers, and concludes with threats. In reply, Teiresias asserts his own authority and contrasts it with Oidipous' ignorance. He questions Oidipous about where, as a blind man, he will ever find safe harbour and finishes with predictions of his disgrace.[39] The impasse concludes with riddling bickering over Oidipous' parentage.[40]

The contest here between the 'seeing' and 'unseeing' masks of Oidipous and Teiresias makes for a blocking different from any other in this drama. Prominence in performance on the *orchêstra* is normally achieved by a dynamic mutuality between the masked actors and members of the *choros* engaged in the contest.[41] However, when one mask is blind that character's movements can only be driven by what is apparently heard and not by what is seen. This places the character to significant extent at the mercy of the 'seeing' mask.[42] In our production the second actor restricted the space used by Teiresias to the area defined by BR and C, while the first actor made use of the entire *orchêstra* during the sequence.

This allowed Oidipous to give vent to his passion through constant motion. Like waves battering a rock, Oidipous approached, retreated from and circled the blind man. He used his sight as a weapon to attack. The blindness of Teiresias condemned that character to follow the sounds of Oidipous' rage and enjoined a stillness that ultimately signified his uncompromised authority. The *choros* responded throughout the scene with restricted moves and gestures evoking trepidation – unwilling witnesses to the apparent and terrifying truncation of the one avenue that might lead to Thebes' recovery from its sickness.[43]

[39] Kithairon is first mentioned at 421. Its circumstantial role in the life of Oidipous is explored extensively in the last 500 lines of the drama (at 1026, 1089, 1127, 1135, 1391, and 1451).

[40] Riddling use of language and repetition in Sophokles present problems for the translator. The triple use of the word for 'beget' at 436–8 is one example of riddling repetition preserved in this translation, while the use of the one word to mean 'purpose', 'advice', and 'intention' at 524–7 is impossible to capture in English. On repetition in Sophokles, cf. Easterling 1973.

[41] Pickard 1893; Ley and Ewans 1985. Beer (1990) works hard to find staging correspondences to the three generations of the Sphinx's riddle; but his considerations are blighted by his presumption of a low platform stage (117), and by the fact that his analysis is ultimately irrevelant to performance.

[42] Cf. Ewans' Notes on *Ant* Scene 6, above, pp. 234ff.

[43] Gardiner (1987, 107) is of the opinion that *OKing* is Sophokles' 'most

Choros 2

The concerns of this Choros derive from Oidipous' proclamation of ostracism and exile against Laios' killer at the start of the scene and, in particular, from the furious contest the Elders have just witnessed between Oidipous and Teiresias. In A1 the Elders narrate an imaginary flight by the panic-stricken murderer of Laios. In both A1 and A2 the language is precise and descriptive; in the original Greek the trochaic metre, logaoedic rhythm and varying line lengths reflect the contrast between the scurrying mortal and the implacable vengeance of Apollo and the Furies. In A2 the Elders picture this man running away like a terrified bull over rocks and through the wild seeking somewhere to hide. At the start of the ode in our production, the *choros* again moved near the shrine of Apollo and implored him with repetitive waves of supplicatory upper torso gestures to hound the killer. They followed this action with repeated sequences of fists beating on the earth in consternation over the argument, alternating with arms raised in questioning the accusation of Teiresias.

In B1 the Elders are dumbfounded by Teiresias' terrible accusation, as they know of no possible grounds on which it could be true.[44] Both B1 and B2 commence with the passionate choriambic metre in the Greek, before continuing with the animated ionic metre. In B2 the Elders judge the issue in favour of Oidipous but in doing so, they foreshadow the much more serious doubts that Iokaste later raises about the efficacy and trustworthiness of the oracles. For the first time in the drama, the innocence of Oidipous is linked directly to the fallibility of prophecy. At the start of this strophic pair the *choros* in our production broke from near the shrine with a distinctive Australian Aboriginal movement called descriptively 'shake-a-leg' and reminded themselves, in the depths of their distress, of their totems, mimicking the eagle and the serpent. The dance intensified in energy, with hands beating the chest and thrusting forwards and backwards as if exorcizing unwanted thoughts and fears. Then it closed with pairs of dancers imitating physically the conflict between Oidipous and Teiresias until Kreon entered and interrupted the action.

static' drama since no action occurs until the suicide and self-mutilation. This judgement acutely undervalues the theatrical power of scenes like this one.

[44] Cf. Rehm (1992, ch. 7) for Sophokles' use of the word *deinos* here and throughout the tragedy.

Scene 3

There are three parts to this, the longest scene in *Oidipous the King*:

(1) the dispute between Oidipous and Kreon (513–648), which takes heroic conflict to even greater heights than in the previous scene as Oidipous turns his aggressive attack onto Kreon as co-conspirator;

(2) the *kommos* sung and danced by Oidipous, Kreon, Iokaste and the Elders, which is the turning point in the scene;

(3) the exchange between Iokaste and Oidipous over the uselessness of oracles and the circumstances of Laios' death and Oidipous' arrival in Thebes. This leads Oidipous to turn his investigation onto himself for the first time.

Oidipous and Kreon The third actor enters down the L *parodos*, and proceeds to C; from this dominant position he presents Kreon as a man of complete integrity, from the opening complaint about Oidipous' charge against him to his final confident assertion of the support of the Theban people for him (677). In contrast, Oidipous is presented, for much of this sequence, as a man of anger and spite. The initial exchange between Kreon and an Elder finds the latter trying futilely to ameliorate the situation. Oidipous' entrance from the palace is explosive – it is covered by one line only (531).[45] This suggests that he begins to speak the moment he steps onto the *orchêstra*. The enmity between the two contestants prompted in our production full use of the vast spaces of the *orchêstra*. The first actor took up a position just right of EBC. His first words drove the third actor to just left of EFC, leaving the two antagonists separated by the entire diameter of the *orchêstra*. As Oidipous' spiteful attack and Kreon's outraged defence continued, the combatants moved in counterpointed blocking along lines defined by EBR/ERC/BLC/L (Oidipous) and EFL/ELC/RF/R (Kreon). The *choros* huddled in groups stretching from EBL to EFR. This blocking effectively isolated Oidipous from the Elders and gave their positional support to

---

[45] Although it is normal in tragedy for a character's entrance to be narrated or at least noted, Lloyd-Jones and Wilson (1992) accept Rose's deletion of 531 (1943, 5) as an unnecessary clarification by an actor or editor. However, if it is cut there is no time for the first actor to make an entrance, without severely distracting from the exchange between Kreon and the Elder. Perhaps therefore, if Sophokles did not compose this line, an actor found it necessary to add it for effective performance.

Kreon, whose need to exploit this support proves critical in the *kommos*.

On his entrance, Oidipous pours scorn on Kreon's alleged attempts to wrest the throne from Laios and from himself. He uses the same words for 'power' and 'wealth' (541–2) as he did in his condemnation of Kreon and Teiresias in the previous scene (380). A series of bitter, punning responses to the accused's pleas for a fair hearing follows; then Oidipous begins a line of questioning designed to show up an inconsistency in Teiresias' behaviour. This sharp interrogation of Kreon demonstrates Oidipous' intelligence at work[46] and is grounded in the apparent anomaly that, if Teiresias knew all along that Oidipous was the killer of Laios, why did he not speak up earlier? Kreon cannot provide an explanation (569), but Oidipous believes he can: only a conspiracy between the two could have led to the outlandish accusation (572–3). In reply, Kreon argues soundly against the desirability of being an absolute ruler when all the benefits of influence and peace of mind can be had without the pressures and distress of pre-eminent power;[47] he then refers to his excellent relations with the people of Thebes gathered around him. Oidipous however has gone too far in his fury and, despite an Elder's intervention in support of Kreon, dismisses the argument out of hand without any attempt to answer it. Here Sophokles breaks the tragic convention that a clear explication of one position in a debate normally requires a response of similar length. Oidipous' reply is a contemptuous four-line refusal, promoting action over argument (618–21). This shows Oidipous in a poor light, which is only made worse by the following heated exchange in *stichomythia*, in which Oidipous demands Kreon's death rather than exile. The exchange ends in a shouting match of half-lines, which brings Iokaste suddenly from the palace.

Iokaste, Kreon and Oidipous   During the Oidipous–Kreon contest in our production, the third actor at no time lost touch with the *choros* in the front half of the *orchêstra*, while the first actor was isolated for much of the time in the back half. The anger in the scene intimated a

[46] Vickers (1973, 500–501) details the evidence for Oidipous' effective use of his intelligence throughout the drama.

[47] The translation follows Lloyd-Jones and Wilson's suggestion (1990, 93) that, on the grounds of irrelevance and awkwardness, lines 600 ('Thinking properly does not beget an evil mind') and 611–12 ('For I consider that to cast away a good friend / is the same as casting away one's own life, which he loves most') have been interpolated.

possible physical engagement before a scandalized member of the *choros* stepped between the two men and announced Iokaste's timely arrival. The entrance of the second actor[48] (in her third role in as many scenes) provided an opportunity to present the implacable forces in momentary balance as Oidipous and Kreon confronted each other along the LC/RC line with Iokaste completing the triangle at BC. The dialogue sequence closes with a terrible curse which Kreon lays upon himself (644–5); this oath of innocence provokes vigorous support from Iokaste and from the Elders, who are now emboldened to intercede more actively on Kreon's behalf.

The excitement of the performance now reaches new heights, as the actors and the members of the *choros* sing and dance their reactions to the dramatic turn of events in a *kommos*. Lines 649–65 and 678–96 were originally sung in strict responsion (lines 666–77, which separate the *strophe* from the *antistrophe*, are spoken by Oidipous). In the Greek text the iambic metre of speech gives way to a mixture of iambic, trochaic, cretic, bacchius and dochmiac metres: the first and second actors speak in the normal iambics, while the *choros* sings the other metres. This cocktail of metres, and particularly the use of the dochmiac (the most agitated Greek dance metre), and the alternation between sung and spoken verse, reflect the intensity of the drama at this point.

The alternation between song and speech, between dance and blocked movement, also enhances the volatility of this subscene in performance, and aptly conveys the explosive nature of, and the terrible consequences spelled out in, the argument. Iokaste's plea to Oidipous to believe Kreon's oath out of respect for the god, for herself and for the people of Thebes is taken up by the Elders; they succeed in persuading their ruler to change his mind. As two hemi-choroses, grouped ELF/FL and ERC/FR in our production, begged Oidipous in waves of supplicatory movement, Iokaste and Kreon held their ground C and RC respectively. Only the distraught Oidipous[49] was on the move, exploring the consequences of the choral plea in question after question, and eventually isolating himself EFC, where he capitulated.

---

[48] Sophokles' use here of a female character to quell the tempers of two bitterly arguing relatives is a similar dramatic ploy to that used in *Ant* Scene 3 when Ismene enters to quell the fury of Kreon and Antigone.

[49] Gardiner's argument (1987, 102, n. 31) that there is insufficient evidence in the text to support the view that Oidipous is emotionally agitated at this point cannot possibly be sustained in performance.

Oidipous seems to be the only character who clearly understands the consequences: if Kreon is not guilty of conspiracy with Teiresias, then Teiresias must be right in judging Oidipous to be the killer of Laios. This means, as he says, that, in accordance with his curse, he 'must surely die / or be thrust out unhonoured from this land' (669–70). The first half of the *kommos* spells the end of Oidipous' first defence against realizing the truth – the idea that a conspiracy between Kreon and Teiresias was responsible for the death of Laios and for plots against himself.

Oidipous and Iokaste   The results are mixed. Before the responding A2 part of the lyric system begins, Kreon departs – relieved, though incensed at Oidipous' undiminished hatred. Oidipous himself is distressed and at a loss. The Elders seem unaware of the consequences of their successful intercession and they reiterate their loyalty to, and dependence on, Oidipous. And Iokaste wants to know more: how did the conflict start? In naming the seer as the source of his information, Oidipous prompts a response from Iokaste that leads to another twist in the plot, and turns the investigation onto Oidipous himself.

A chance comment in Iokaste's speech rejecting the authority of oracles provokes the scene's final sequence (726ff.) which belongs, with the exception of one important intervention by an Elder, to the first and second actors. The Elders' role is to watch and listen – in some trepidation, as their present reactions must imply and the following Choros confirms. We found in performance that there is ample opportunity here for the *choros* to respond quite energetically to the unfolding narrative. As Oidipous' anxiety about his situation and Iokaste's contempt for oracles intensified, the *choros* in our production divided in two: one hemi-*choros* skirted around the action towards EBC, distancing themselves from the contest, while the other hemi-*choros* remained gathered at the perimeter between FR/ERC. Both actions provided telling comment on the drama for the spectators. The actors had the *orchêstra* almost to themselves, and the emotional nature of the exchanges and the narrative suggested a blocking that made extensive use of it.

Following Oidipous' slighting reference to the seer as the mouthpiece for Kreon, Iokaste debunks prophets as sources of reliable knowledge on the basis of her own experience with the prophecy given to Laios, namely that he would be killed by his own son. That prophecy proved incorrect, she discloses, as Laios had the child exposed and he himself was killed by thieves. Her casual reference, during this diatribe, to a place 'where three roads meet' as the site of Laios' murder[50] surprises Oidipous and prompts an enquiry during which, in effect, the 'conspiracy plot' is replaced by the 'victim plot'.[51] Again Oidipous asks the precise questions that expose a truth. He uncovers the incontrovertible clues: the place, the time, the description of Laios, and the number of his travelling companions. These all point towards the inescapable conclusion that he was the man whom Oidipous killed. One additional piece of evidence is needed, as an Elder crucially points out (834–5): the word of the lone survivor and witness, the Herdsman. Confirmation by him that Laios was killed by a number of men will, it is hoped, abort the coincidence.

The exchange between Oidipous and Iokaste (698–770) grows in frenzy as Oidipous explores the implications of that death where three roads meet and comes closer and closer to identifying himself as Laios' killer. Iokaste does not know the import of Oidipous' questions but is profoundly disturbed by his manner and his anxiety (746). This suggests in performance extensive use of movement, as if the characters are unable to contain themselves physically as well as emotionally. The importance of Iokaste's story about the death of her child suggests that the actor should be at C, with Oidipous within conversational range. As others have noted,[52] Iokaste's mention of the three roads prompts a movement from the first actor to register its significance for Oidipous. Given the size of the performance space, this movement must be emphatic – e.g. a decisive break away.

While Iokaste relates the terrible story of the callous death of her child, Oidipous is preoccupied, apparently disturbed by Iokaste's narrative but, for spectators aware of the legend, actually for an entirely different reason. As Oidipous pursues his interrogation, a pattern of agitated moves by both characters, crossing the centre towards ELC and ERC, reflects their anguish. The fear of making some terrifying discovery is powerfully conveyed if the actors rarely confront each other, but turn constantly away – as if Oidipous seeks to avoid the emerging truth, and Iokaste cannot bear to look on her distressed companion. When the interrogation intensifies and Oidipous concen-

---

[50] We know from the single fragment of Aischylos' version of the Oidipous story that he placed the junction of three roads near Potniai, which effectively put the drama in the domain of the Erinyes or Furies; Jebb 1902, xviii–xix. Sophokles' relocation of the junction to Phokis is significant; it sets the action in the domain of Apollo.

[51] Vernant 1983, 189–209.

[52] Taplin 1978, 65; Halliwell 1986, 188.

trates on the details of Laios' manner of travelling (748ff.), it makes for effective blocking if the first actor occupies the centre of the *orchêstra* – steadfast in his focus on the truth – while the second actor traverses the front perimeter as if trying to escape the insistent and disturbing questions.[53]

Oidipous agrees to reveal to Iokaste what it is that has caused his present distress; he does this by a long narrative (771ff.) in which he describes rumours in Korinth of his illegitimacy, his journey to the Delphic oracle, his flight to Thebes, and his violent encounter with travellers near Daulis. The narrative is beautifully crafted. The geographical references provide it with a particular linear impetus, which drives inexorably towards the terrible meditation on the consequences of the possible coincidence that one of the men killed by Oidipous where the three roads meet might well have been Laios; Oidipous seems to have cursed himself. The agitation of Oidipous in recounting this frightening story was represented in our production by the first actor pacing out the geography of Oidipous' journey on the *orchêstra*, using an Elder's staff, and re-enacting the violent encounter at the junction.[54] In doing so, the first actor traversed an extensive area from BC to ELC across C to FRC and back again to BC. The impact was that the narrative became geographically specific, the restless anxiety of the narrator was clearly conveyed, and the critical importance of the Herdsman's report was brought into sudden and terrifying clarity.[55]

Iokaste, although disturbed by the account and its possible consequences, is adamant that the Herdsman's report mentioned a number of thieves. She dismisses oracles out of hand because the one relating to the manner of Laios' death was clearly – to her knowledge – unfulfilled. In making this impassioned defence of Iokaste's position and attempt at relieving Oidipous of his concerns, the second actor, in our production, completed almost an entire circuit of the *orchêstra* from CL, encircling the haunted figure of Oidipous at centre. The scene ended with Oidipous, only slightly mollified, moving to her (FL), and insisting on seeing the Herdsman. Iokaste's promise to please him in any way accompanied the offer of her hand and demonstrated a

[53] Cf. Ewans' blocking in *Ant* Scene 3 where Antigone is thrust to the centre while other characters in the scene move around her, above, pp. 216ff.

[54] Halliwell (1986) notes the theatrical potential of the recurring images of crossroads in the drama.

[55] The spectators at this point do not know for certain that Oidipous is doomed (*pace* Arthur 1980). The issue of impending but not-yet-determined *moira* remains; indeed, it becomes more critical.

moment of intimacy between them.[56] They then departed, hands joined in a formal gesture of mutual support and union.

Close examination of this scene uncovers some puzzling questions. Why doesn't Oidipous make the connection between the child with pinned feet and his own crippling injury? Why does he not find it a strange coincidence that Laios was told he would be killed by his son and that he himself was told that he would kill his father? What was the precise sequence of events regarding the death of Laios, the destruction of the Sphinx, Oidipous' ascent to the throne and the Herdsman's plea for release? Since in contemporary Athens there was considerable scepticism about oracles, what would the spectators' attitude have been towards believing, or not believing, that a prophecy from Delphi would come true?

Answers have been suggested to these questions: Oidipous does not know how or when he received his injury (1035), many common themes ran through oracles, a probable sequence of events can be articulated, oracles often came true in real life,[57] – and Sophokles' plot, when it is complete, clearly vindicates the prophecy given to Laios. It is important for the actors to work through these questions and answers in order to play the sequence with conviction. For spectators, however, the questions do not arise with the clarity that reflection bestows or rehearsal demands.[58] Instead they provide additional contributions towards the notion that coincidence and the inexplicable combine, as the drama unfolds, as powerful elements in the story of the life of this man.

The scene concludes with both encouraging and disturbing expectations. The Herdsman needs only to confirm that many men killed Laios and his companions for Oidipous to be released from his fears. But if that is so, Iokaste must be right about the oracles. This occupies the minds of the Elders in the following ode.

---

[56] Reinhardt 1979, 119–20 rightly attributes Iokaste's vehemence and confidence to her determination to defend Oidipous against his own argument. The charge of levity in her behaviour, deriving from Schlegel (1846, 102), is improper.

[57] Cf. Herodotos *passim*. Oracles were also at times flexible: in 7.141, Herodotos records that, after hearing dismaying words from the prophetess at Delphi concerning the coming war with Xerxes, the Athenians went to the oracle a second time with 'branches of olive in their hands and in the guise of suppliants'. They then received a less menacing response. Thoukydides' more jaundiced view is expressed in 2.54. Cf. Bushnell 1988 *passim*, but esp. 67–88.

[58] Arnott 1989, 149.

Choros 3

This ode has generated a great deal of critical discussion,[59] much of it too linguistic or literary to be relevant to performance. It is agreed that the Elders are thunderstruck by Iokaste's repudiation of the efficacy of oracles but, in articulating their concerns, the Elders do not specify any individual as, for example, they specify Oidipous in Choros 5. In their meditation on the *daimôn Hybris* (Wanton Violence), the Elders address the generic issue of a pervasive godlessness in which Iokaste, in particular, appears embroiled.

A1 is a prayer; in contrast to the brazenness of Iokaste, the Elders bow their heads to the eternal laws from Mount Olympos. In A2 *Hybris* is imaged as making a headlong dash towards great heights with little forethought for the perilous fall in store. The Elders pray that god may keep the city in his 'solid grip' – a term from wrestling. The impression that the Elders have Oidipous in mind here[60] does not sit well with their loyalty to, and confidence in, him (e.g. 501–7, 690–95). They are contrasting their own piety with its opposite. Throughout the first strophic pair, while the Elders reflected on what had just eventuated, the choral movement in our production was based on the flight of the eagle as a divine totem blessed with clear vision.

B1 continues the reflection begun in A2. The Elders curse the ungodly, and make their point specific by calling attention to their own holy dance as possible only in a culture of reverence.[61] In B2 they call on Zeus – 'if it is accurate/ to call you master' – to reassert the integrity of the oracles before worship disappears entirely. If the oracles do not have integrity, then fulfilling Delphi's word to find the killer of Laios will not save Thebes. Our choreography made use of two pools of water ER and EL. Hemi-*choroses* grouped around these shrines and made as if to scoop up water and cleanse themselves in undulating movements in preparation for whatever might come. Then during the last verse, the *choros* 'bowed out' in waves of movement drifting towards the back of the *orchêstra*. They lunged forward in a vigorous women's movement, shaking their arms, exorcising the frightening

---

[59] E.g. Winnington-Ingram 1980, 179–204; Scodel 1982; Sidwell, 1992; Segal 1993, 119–20.

[60] Jebb 1902; *ad loc.* Against similar attempts to refer Sophokles' choral imagery too specifically to the principal characters cf. Ewans' Notes on *Ant* Choroses 2, 3 and 5; pp. 215, 223 and 233 n. 100 above.

[61] Taplin (1986, 169) rightly rejects the view that this is a reference to dancing as a metatheatrical device, akin to a comic *parabasis*.

things that they had just heard and the insolence and contemptuousness of mortals who do not revere the gods. The *choros* swayed their upper torsos in a negative response to the thought of never again going to the temples.

Scene 4

Circumstance abounds in Sophokles' version of the Oidipous story, and nowhere more obviously than in Scene 4. Polybos happens to die, and news of his death is brought by none other than the Korinthian who received the baby from Laios' Herdsman. And this Herdsman himself turns out to be none other than Laios' travelling companion who escaped death at the hands of Oidipous where the three roads meet. For the ancient Greeks, circumstance was an instrument of the gods;[62] in this scene and Scene 5 the spectators witness that instrument in operation in a way that makes apparent mockery of human knowledge.

Scene 4 has four parts, three of them of equal length:

911–49 (39 lines): Iokaste's prayer to Apollo and the Korinthian's report of the death of Polybos;

950–88 (39 lines): the apparent vindication of Iokaste's repudiation of oracles and the consequent joyful relief for both her and Oidipous;

989–1046 (58 lines): the startling news from the Korinthian that Polybos was not the father of Oidipous and the revelation of the circumstances of Oidipous' arrival in Korinth;

1047–85 (39 lines): the contrasting responses from Oidipous and Iokaste.

Though Iokaste has repudiated belief in oracles, she demonstrates here her continued reverence for the gods, in particular for Apollo, the god whose influence is never far away throughout this drama. The second actor enters from the *skene*, in company with a supernumerary as attendant, who carries the incense and suppliant's branch (912–13). The blocking of the end of the previous Choros left the Elders fanned across EB so that their responses to what will be revealed in this climactic scene would provide a powerful visual background for the

---

[62] Reinhardt 1979, 121: 'it is the *daimon* cutting across the action'; Taplin 1986, 151, Kovacs 1993, 67. For a discussion of human action in the context of *moira* cf. Ewans 1996b, especially 443–5 on O*King*.

spectators and also complete the circle of the *theatron*,[63] entrapping the main players and the action.

The shrine at FC had been identified as Apollo's during the first scene, and this is where Iokaste conducts her silent supplication[64] before addressing the Elders, gathered behind her,[65] on her failure to quell Oidipous' fears. She prays that Apollo will release Thebes from pollution. Her prayer will be answered very shortly, but in a way that is utterly unexpected.[66] The previous scene prepared the spectators to anticipate that the third actor in the mask of the Herdsman would enter from out of town along the R *parodos*. This expectation is thwarted however, as the new mask at this entrance is that of the Korinthian with news of the death of Polybos.[67] An excited and triumphant Iokaste summons Oidipous, and again publicly proclaims her contempt for the oracles.

[63] Davidson (1986) suggests that during scenes the arrangement of the *choros* in a 'basically circular fashion' was 'at least a not infrequent occurrence' (45). See now also Wiles 1997, esp. 93–7. It is certainly true that the circular performing space tends to shape choral dance and positioning in circular or part-circular patterns; and note how the Newcastle production of *Ant* used a parallel effect, moving the *choros* to a partially circular pattern on the perimeter EBL-EBR to become a visual background to Antigone in Scene 5.

[64] An alternative, arguably more natural blocking in terms of Greek tragic conventions, would be to have Iokaste going to the centre and conducting her ritual during lines 911–18. The pace of our production, however, prompted us to 'take breath' at this point and have Iokaste perform her ritual in dumb show.

[65] Even the most naturalistic acting conventions do not require characters always to look at the character(s) they address. To do so would make for very predictable and uninteresting blocking. With masked acting on a circular performing area with spectators almost surrounding the action, there is even less need. Here, there is no difficulty for the second actor to address the Elders grouped behind her by facing out to the *theatron*.

[66] The suppliant's branches remain in full view for the remainder of the drama, a visual reminder to the spectators, as Kitto noted (1961, 139), of the terrible answer the god makes to her petition. Cf. also Mikalson 1989, 83 and 87.

[67] Hamilton's study (1978) of announced entrances in tragedy concludes that 'a character whose entrance directly followed a choral stasimon was not announced unless he was part of a tableau . . . All other entrances . . . would be marked by an announcement, unless they were to be surprising' (72, see also 75). This unannounced entrance of the Korinthian is a typical example of the latter case, and the only example in *OKing*. This strengthens its circumstantial nature.

A vase illustration from Syracuse, dated to 375–350 BC,[68] most likely represents a particularly dramatic moment in this scene. A figure in rustic garb on the left of the illustration stands with his left hand in open gesture, appearing to be relaying information to a dark-bearded character whose right hand is raised in apparent reflection to his face. To his right, a female character raises her left hand (concealed by her cloak) to her left cheek, as if in horror.[69] To her right again, there appears to be an attendant. Beside the central figure, two girls are standing. Trendall conjectures that this illustration depicts the moment when the Korinthian informs Oidipous that the baby rescued from Mount Kithairon was from the house of Laios. Oidipous is puzzled but Iokaste, who now perceives what happened to the child she and Laios sought to kill, is horror-stricken. The two children appear to represent Antigone and Ismene.

The existence of this illustration prompted the introduction of two silent masks representing the girls into this scene in our production. Their entrance with Oidipous holding their hands demonstrated the close bond between father and daughters (to which Oidipous refers in the final agonized moments of the tragedy 1462–5), while the constant presence of the silent masks throughout this revelatory scene conveyed a sense of vulnerability and impending doom.[70] The silent mask in performance is a powerful tool, especially in conveying helplessness associated with suffering in silence.

The sequence that follows Oidipous' entrance is the most light-hearted in the drama – short-lived as it is. Oidipous' reaction to the Korinthian's news is precisely the same as that of Iokaste: relief from anguish and contempt for the oracles. Their shared joy prompted the actors in our production to clasp each other's hands in triumph and sweep from the back of the *orchêstra* to FC, as if seeking an intimacy away from the prying eyes and eavesdropping ears of the other characters. The front area of the *orchêstra* is the most appropriate part for the enactment of intimacy, for it is here that the actors are most comprehensively embraced by the spectators. The dismissive suggestion from Iokaste regarding men dreaming of sleeping with their mothers

[68] Trendall and Webster 1971, 66, 69. Cf. Green (1991) for a discussion of the use of vase paintings in relation to stage formations in general.

[69] The masked actor must discover corporal signs to express emotion usually conveyed by facial expression. The vase illustration here is an example. Shisler encountered difficulty in describing action by masked actors that conveyed emotion; 1945, esp. 391–3.

[70] Cf. Sifakis (1979) on general issues concerning children in tragedy.

and her radical views on chance ruling everything[71] promoted in performance a sensual and flirting delivery by the second actor, almost in contempt of any threatened doom, which contrasted with the more restrained and careful language and manner of Oidipous. The actors' interactions reflected a long-standing intimate relationship.

The Korinthian has been listening from a slight distance (*not* out of earshot) to the dialogue between Oidipous and Iokaste, and he intervenes at 989 to tell Oidipous the truth about his rescue as a baby – motivated, as it emerges, by concern about what reward he will receive for his journey (1005–6).

Lines 1000–1046 represent the longest passage of *stichomythia* in the drama. The effect of *stichomythia* in the performance of this sequence is to delay crucial information until it cannot but be spoken.[72] The release of information is circuitous: the Korinthian promises to release Oidipous from his fear at lines 1002–3, but does not actually tell Oidipous that Polybos was not his father until 1016; and his information is not complete until 1044.[73]

The same effect occurs – even more dramatically, but with different motivation – in Scene 5, with the exchange between Oidipous and the Herdsman (1146–76). The Herdsman is terrified about relaying what he knows and employs delaying tactics as much as possible, whereas the Korinthian now appears to be enjoying spinning out his yarn even though it makes Oidipous impatient (1009). The investigatory nature of the plot development driven by the character of Oidipous means

[71] The word *tychê* occurs frequently in O*King*, suggesting the interplay of human accident and divine purpose. Cf. Pucci 1992, chs. 1 and 2. Pucci also explores the riddling implications of Iokaste's argument about incestuous dreaming, at 94–104.

[72] Arnott (1989, 101–3) surmised that the convention of *stichomythia* might have been adopted so that spectators would know, through expectation, which mask was speaking. However, the fact that some stichomythic passages incorporate two-line as well as one-line exchanges militates against this suggestion. Cf. e.g. 1002–3, 1005–6; also 549–56, 572–5. In any case in my experience, masked actors can convey very easily through gesture, posture and movement of body or mask who is speaking and who is listening.

[73] During this exchange the Korinthian draws attention to Oidipous' damaged ankles. This raises the question for the actor: does Oidipous limp? In our production he did not; it was felt that this would be a constant distraction throughout performance and would work against the character's authority. The first actor wore leather strapping around each ankle to provide some verisimilitude. Discussion at Fergusson 1949, 49 and (esp.) Taplin 1983, 155–6. Fagles (1984, 159) would have him enter for Scene 1 'majestic but for a telltale limp'.

that the first actor is required to ask very many one line questions, nowhere in a more concentrated space of time than the ten that follow the Korinthian's own question at 1114. Although variation in delivery of these questions and answers must be contrived to avoid monotony, the pattern imposes its own theatrical character, a sense of moving inevitably towards a momentous revelation.[74]

In blocking this sequence, it was decided in our production to leave the Korinthian marginalized, as he had been in the earlier sequence, in the area between FR and BR. The first actor moved to C as Oidipous explained the dual prophecy of incest and parricide and he stayed in that area, giving visual focus to the consequences on him of the revelations. The second actor responded to these same revelations through a reflective and increasingly agitated journey from EFC to ELC, and eventually to L when the Korinthian delivers the critical (for Iokaste) information that the child rescued from Kithairon was from the house of Laios. At the same time, the supernumeraries in the silent masks of Antigone and Ismene moved to either side of Oidipous as if drawn by the intensity of the exchanges. The first actor then broke from C to confront the Elders gathered EB, when Oidipous sought information about the Herdsman (1047–50). This allowed the second actor to move to C to gain full focus, as the stricken Iokaste tried in vain to prevent Oidipous from pursuing the investigation further.

The Korinthian's information has two violently opposed consequences: Iokaste realizes who Oidipous is while he, and the Elders, are convinced that his birth, though possibly of a line of slaves, is more likely to be divine. Iokaste's anguished exit counterpoints Oidipous' triumphant cry anticipating confirmation from the Herdsman of his glorious birth. But irony abounds as Oidipous' claim that 'bounteous Fortune' (*tychê*) is his mother recalls Iokaste's philosophy that 'Chance rules/ supreme' (977–8) and Oidipous' own prayer that Kreon's arrival might lead to the chance (*tychê*) of deliverance (80).

Choros 4

As in *Aias* (Choros 3), *Young Women of Trachis* (Choros 3) and *Antigone* (Choros 6), the revelation of disaster is preceded by an upbeat song and dance, ironically full of hope and joy (in the original Greek, the dactylo-epitrite metre contributes to a rhythm which is lively and exciting). In AI, the Elders proclaim Kithairon's future fame as

[74] Cf. Rehm 1992, 62–4.

nurturer of their king[75] and, in A2, they cry out the names of gods – Pan, Apollo, Hermes, Dionysos – who might be revealed as the father of Oidipous. Our choreography expressed a search for identity, with dancers travelling as individuals across the *orchêstra* and representing different totems from Oidipous' life-cycle. These totems were associated with different emotions and events in his personal history and recalled earlier representations of animals. Two dancers in particular enacted moments in the histories of Oidipous and Iokaste. This searching reflection on self was presented through fragments of dance, pieces of the jigsaw to which one final piece was to be added. The excitement and joy of this song and dance has barely had time to dissipate before the short, fast scene that follows reaches its devastating revelations.

Scene 5

This is by far the shortest scene in the drama, as the plot unravels towards its terrible conclusion. Oidipous welcomes the Herdsman, ensures he has the right person and, with some gentle nudging from the Korinthian of the Herdsman's conveniently faulty memory, again demonstrates his powers of investigation in eliciting from an unwilling witness the appalling truth.[76] In our production, the first actor remained FC facing the *skene* and announced the arrival at the R *parodos* of the second actor in her fourth role, playing the Herdsman. It was decided that, given the crucial evidence the Herdsman was to provide, the second actor should remain at C throughout the dialogue, vacating the centre point only at the very end when Oidipous realizes the truth. This allowed the first and third actors to approach and withdraw from the second actor as their characters painstakingly sought confirmation and information from the frightened servant.[77]

[75] The Elders name Oidipous *tyrannos*, as did the Korinthian (925, 939). There is no connotation, however, of excessive power or abuse of power; the word is being used precisely, to denote that Oidipous is not king by blood-descent. Of course there is hideous irony in this, since the action is about to show Oidipous all too clearly that he is exactly that. Cf. Knox (1954, 93), O'Neil (1986, 34 and 40) and Pope (1991).

[76] There seems to be a line lost in the Greek text after 1135. Lloyd-Jones and Wilson suggest the appropriateness of surmising one and I have followed their suggestion because the Greek as we have it is very difficult to construe.

[77] Cf. Segal 1980, esp. 126–7 and 140–42, on Sophokles' use of visual effects, notably, as here, when the silent observer in the mask of Oidipous witnesses the Korinthian's interrogation of the Herdsman.

The scene is marked by violence. The long delay in the Herdsman's arrival prompts an entrance in which he is dragged by attendants before Oidipous. His unwillingness to cooperate frustrates Oidipous, who eagerly awaits confirmation of the auspicious birth which, spurred on by the expectations of the Elders, he now fully anticipates. His good temper quickly gives way to threats of torture and actual physical restraint, when he orders attendants to grab hold of the Herdsman's arms. The determination and impatience of Oidipous, as he paced towards and away from the cowed figure, drove the enquiry in our production at a furious pace. When the horrifying truth eventually emerges, it does so with a suddenness that brings the charge towards enlightenment to a dramatic halt mid-line: 'A slave? Or born of the same line as Laios?' (1168). It is only in articulating this question that Oidipous realizes that there might be a worse outcome than descent from a line of slaves – the very outcome that the Herdsman now confirms: 'The child was called the son of Laios' (1171). Iokaste is revealed as the mother of Oidipous, and the oracle that he would kill his father is reiterated. Oidipous, stunned by these monstrous revelations, can only ask: 'Then why'd you pass me over to this man?' (1077) to which the Herdsman can only respond truthfully: 'Out of pity, lord . . .' (1178). Human compassion was the source of acts so shameful that eminent lives have been lost or destroyed, and a long and renowned ancestry brought to its day of reckoning. At Toowoomba, the first actor moved to C for his apostrophe to the 'light of day', a lament that foreshadows the themes of birth, incest and parricide which will occupy much of the last scene of the drama. Then he stumbled towards the *skene* while the second and third actors scurried out down the R *parodos*.[78] The damage has been done.

[78] Although Rehm's meditation (1992, 118) on the triadic themes in the drama and the use here of the three exits is attractive, it can hardly be sustained. Both the Korinthian, who had just come from Korinth, and the Herdsman, who had come from a place where 'he couldn't even lay eyes on Thebes' (762), must enter from the R *parodos*. Neither has any reason or justification to stay in Thebes, which would be the import of an exit by the L *parodos*. Kitto (1961, 141) also seems to imagine exits by both 'side-entrances'; however, he is right in drawing attention to the theatrical effect of the long exits by these two dismayed characters.

Choros 5

If there is a typical tragic choros, this is it.[79] The underlying pessimism of ancient Greek culture, with its proverbs 'not to be born is best' and 'call no one happy until they have passed through life without disaster'[80] informs this entire ode, and is distilled in the person of Oidipous.[81] A1 and A2 are in wholly aeolic metres in the Greek, and this allows for a powerful and melancholic solemnity. B1 and B2 are in more animated, mixed metrical patterns as the Elders recite the rises and falls in the fortunes of Oidipous.[82] The ode concludes with the touching recollection that, thanks to Oidipous, the Thebans, for a little while, 'slept in peace' – a peace that now is gone for ever.

Our choreography was based on a sense of incomprehension in the face of the revelations in the scene. Again (cf. Choros 4), the movements were isolated and fragmented, with individuals rising and falling in grief, staggering in slow, agonized patterns, heads bowed, torsos twisted and bent, gestures contorted, painted faces masks of rejection. The journey of the dance throughout the drama had reached a terrifying truth which fractured the community.

Finale

The so-called messenger-speech is a regular feature of tragedy. Though some scholars have dismissed it as a relic of earlier traditions,[83] others have expressed an appreciation for its continuing theatrical worth.[84] There is of course no possible way of knowing how the ancient Greek

[79] Cf. Hogan 1991, 65–6.

[80] Cf. OKing 1528ff., YWT 1–3, OKol 1224–5 and Herodotos 1.32 for other iterations of this famous sentiment. At Herodotos 5.4, the Trausi, a tribe in Thrakia, were said to mourn the birth of a child by reciting all the human ills it must endure, and to rejoice when someone dies because that person has at last escaped many miseries.

[81] Easterling cites this ode as a particularly telling instance of the witnessing role of the *choros*. They come to 'a new understanding of human nothingness as well as human achievement' (1996, 178) after witnessing what has happened to Oidipous.

[82] 'In the opening strains of the last choral ode, which now ring out, the emotions of the scene are wonderfully expressed. Each one recognizes the solemnity and depth of his own feelings in their pathetic tones' – Jebb (1902, 205) on a production of the drama by members of Harvard University in May 1881.

[83] Cf. e.g. Bremer 1976, 42.

[84] Cf. e.g. Arnott (1989, 94–5) and Rehm (1992, 61–2).

actors performed messenger speeches or indeed even if there was a particular convention that governed them. Perhaps competitiveness drove the actors to seek innovative modes of performance.[85]

The messenger speech in this drama, as in many others, has two principal dramatic features. First, it relies on a lively and explicit narrative to stimulate the spectators to imagine the violent and bloody events that have just taken place inside the palace.[86] Secondly, it prepares for the revelation of the consequences of those events in the person of the blinded Oidipous. Both these features encourage a performance from the second actor that endeavours to continue the acceleration in dramatic intensity evident in the previous Scene and Choros. To allow the impetus to drop at this point would do a disservice both to what has preceded and to what is yet to come.[87]

The performance of this scene in our production was characterized by an explosion of physical and vocal energy and an intense emotionalism from the second actor.[88] Gestures were vigorous and extended, while the visceral language appeared driven by acute agony. She entered with a hurried dash from the *skene* to CL, as if escaping the nightmarish events just witnessed, and directed her impassioned address initially to an Elder at CR, while the other members of the *choros* scurried in apparent fear around the left of the *orchêstra* to huddle, distanced from the *skene*, around EFR to EFL.

The narrative was acted out by the actor through quick, emphatic moves and strong, mimetic gesture. Thus Iokaste's rushing to her bed and slamming of the doors of her room were enacted in mime as were

[85] Cf. Ewans on *Ant* Scene 7 and Ley on *YWT* Scenes 4 and 5, above pp. 238–9, 257–8 and 261.

[86] 'The narrated but unseen events are overwhelming in their specific details and sensory impressions' – Segal 1993, 136.

[87] Gould argues that the absence of direct speech in this narrative, unique in extant messenger speeches, implies the Servant's refusal to become engaged, 'to play out the events of his narrative' so that they pass in 'a kind of appalled silence' (1988, 156–7). However, we found in performance that the rhetorical language and precise descriptions of the horrific actions reported drove the actor to a vigorous, mimetic re-enactment which maintained and intensified the dramatic impetus of the Finale.

[88] The Servant must be played by the second actor. Pavlovskis (1977) rightly argues that the tragedians made ironic use of the fact that an actor could not disguise his voice in playing multiple roles. His suggestion that hearing the Servant speak with the same voice as Iokaste makes the disclosures even more horrifying is borne out in performance. Also, the third actor should continue with the part of Kreon later in this scene.

Oidipous' pacing, lowering the body of his wife/mother to the floor, and stabbing out his eyes with the pins that adorned her garments.[89] Physical and emotional exhaustion was registered in the final lines of the main address (1280f.) before the actor turned to face the *skene* doors on the lines: 'He wants to be cast out of here, and never / live in the house of curses which he's cursed' (1290–91). The actor was in prime position then to announce the entrance of Thebes' destroyed king from the palace.[90]

The 234-line sequence which brings the tragedy to its close places exceptional demands on the first actor, not the least because the portrayal of a blinded character restricts action to the use of mask, hands and torso.[91] It is also superbly conceived psychologically: the *kommos* (1297–368) dramatically exposes Oidipous' physical and mental torture, his address to the Elders (1369–415) is an elaborate defence of his action and a lament on his life's circumstances, while his requests to Kreon to put his house in order, to the extent it can be, and his farewell to his daughters bring him finally to physical and emotional collapse. Throughout the scene, the first actor restricted himself in our production to BC, continuing the general trend of the blocking, as the drama unfolded, from predominant use of the centre/front of the *orchêstra* – 'in the open' – towards the centre/back as the story inexorably came closer to revelations of the *miasma* from inside the palace.

The *kommos* commences with the re-entrance of the first actor, whose mask and motion now signify blindness.[92] Oidipous is consumed

[89] Lloyd-Jones and Wilson (1992) bracket 1278–9, on the grounds that the description is too gory and is likely to be a fourth-century actor's interpolation. I am not convinced that deletion leaves the text in better shape, and I have retained the two lines in the translation.

[90] Poe (1992, 132) suggests that the normal convention of messengers making an exit after their narrative is complete was followed here. However, we found that with Oidipous' immediate entry after 1295 and the subsequent *kommos* there was simply no opportunity for the Servant to depart without causing an awkward distraction.

[91] Cf. Ley (above, pp. 263ff.) on the portrayal of the crippled Herakles in the Finale to *YWT*. Rehm (1992, 120–22) appreciates the demands on the performer in his sound discussion of the sequence in *OKing*.

[92] In our production, blindness for both Teiresias and Oidipous, in a deliberate mirror-image, was signified by each of them wearing a 'blindfold'. This was effective, along with the actions of the actors, in portraying the disability, and in the case of Oidipous, the effects of recent mutilation. A mask streaming with fictitious blood, as Taplin imagines (1978, 89), is not necessary, nor is a change

with the dual agonies of his punctured eyes and the recollection of his parricide and incest. His voice 'flies round and round' (1310) but his 'poor steps' (1309) have no sight to guide him through his 'cloud of darkness' (1313–14). His screams of pain interrupt the efforts to articulate his suffering and his incomprehension. His gratitude to the Elder for his continuing care exposes his new vulnerability. He acknowledges the hand of Apollo in his disaster, but heroically asserts that it was his own hand that meted out the punishment (1332–33). His curse on the Herdsman – who had acted out of pity – precedes the climactic recital of his own cursed condition as father-killer and mother-lover, now god-forsaken (1357–60). The use in the ancient Greek of the dochmiac metre in the strophic pairs (1313–68) clearly instructs the actor to convey in the performance an emotional pain almost beyond the limits of suffering, a pain that defies comprehension and allows only for a desperate pity.[93]

In contrast, Oidipous' extended, spoken response to 1368 is a masterpiece of logical, if harrowing, reasoning.[94] Oidipous confronts in turn the impossibilities of his living with sight: how could he look on his father and mother in Haides, his children, the holy statues of Thebes, and the people before him, given his defilement? The fall from the most cherished in Thebes to the most wretched is complete. He apostrophizes three geographical sites and names a fourth where calamitous events determined his life: Kithairon which sheltered him, Korinth where his childhood bloomed despite the sickness festering underneath, the junction of the three roads which drank his father's blood, and Thebes where his marriage to Iokaste completed the cycle of disaster beyond disaster. The construction of this speech allows the actor to build, step by step, thought by thought, towards Oidipous' final impassioned and demanding plea to the Elders to be hidden away out of sight or be killed. The frightening spectre of the mutilated man reaching out for contact drives the Elders away in their efforts to escape contact with his *miasma*.

When Oidipous and Kreon first faced each other in Scene 1, Oidipous rejected Kreon's suggestion that they speak inside in favour of

---

of mask an absolute requirement (*contra* Ley, above, n. 42 p. 260). For a historical survey of the Aristotelian notion of *opsis* (spectacle) and the need to restore its place in critical discourse, cf. Vince 1990.

[93] For a meditation on metatheatrical devices in the drama, particularly in this appearance of Oidipous, cf. Segal 1986, 459–84, especially 465–7.

[94] Buxton 1980, 24–5 and 36–7.

public disclosure. At the end of this third confrontation, Kreon orders
the polluted man inside to avoid offence to the Sun-god and then
follows him as the inheritor of the throne. It is precisely in his
relationship to Kreon that Oidipous' reversal is seen to be complete.
Even the postures that the actors are prompted to adopt (the upright,
vindicated Kreon and the cowed, condemned Oidipous) reflect the
reversal of status. Acknowledging how wrong he was in accusing
Kreon earlier of treachery, Oidipous must now beg favour: for Iokaste,
whom he asks Kreon to bury as a queen should be buried, for himself,
for whom he begs only immediate banishment, for his two boys, who,
as men, should be left to fend for themselves, and for his two daughters,
who need continuing care. Then there is heart-rending anguish in
Oidipous' sudden realization that his request to be allowed exile and
eventual death on Mount Kithairon, ironically fulfils his parents'
wishes (1451-4) and the Elders' prophetic description of Laios' killer,
roaming the wild with 'stumbling step on stumbling step' (474-81).

In the received text the flow of this speech is halted by a brief
meditation on Oidipous' fate (1455-9);

> Of this I'm certain: I'll not perish by
> disease or any other way. For I've been saved
> from death for some strange, terrible purpose
> But as for my fate, whatsoever it is, let it be.

It is surprising that scholars have not queried the authenticity of these
lines.[95] The passage appears to point so clearly to the events in
Oidipous at Kolonos, which Sophokles wrote some two decades later,
that the hand of an interpolator must be suspected. It is also out of
place to suggest that Oidipous has been 'saved' from death (1457). As
with all other circumstances in this drama, it is human action, in this
case Oidipous' own, that generates a destiny.[96]

[95] Indeed, many have found compelling significance in them; e.g. Roberts
(1988), who argues that this disruption in the closing moments forces us to realize
that our judgement at the end of the drama is 'inevitably provisional' (191),
because the tragic narrative of which this drama is a part is incomplete. Pucci
(1992) considers the passage to be one of 'superb *hybris*' (165) in which the tragic
hero finally recognizes that 'as long as Oedipus encounters woes, he will continue
to live and to perform on stage' (166). Bushnell (1988) suggests Oidipous
articulates but has no clear knowledge of a future. Despite these considerations,
the fact remains that the lines are inconsistent with the rest of the text, and
constitute an acute disjunction for the actor delivering them.

[96] Now a common critical view with respect to tragedy in general. Cf. e.g.

The first action in *Oidipous the King* was the arrival of children, the suppliants led by the old Priest. The first words spoken – and spoken by Oidipous – were 'Oh children'. Oidipous' determination to rid Thebes of the plague was in response to the supplication of Theban children (145–6). And now he calls for his own 'most precious darling children' (1474), Antigone and Ismene, for whom the Theban children's salvation means absolute deprivation. They will now live ostracized lives, condemned to childlessness, reliant entirely on Kreon for a place to live. And that is the prayer that Oidipous enjoins on them: 'to live where time allows' (1513). He then reaches his nadir in his sobbing plea that they might have a better life than that of their father. In this sequence, Sophokles has shaped the theatrical action in a way that elicits a most profound pity. In the passage in which Oidipous begs Kreon to be allowed to touch his children and when he hears them crying, Sophokles includes three lines which comprise, in the Greek, only three syllables each: 'Please, oh lord' (1468), 'What is that?' (1471) and 'Am I right?' (1475). The implication for the actor is to allow these words to linger in silence, and the effect in performance is to underscore Oidipous' utter dependency and to delay momentarily, although the children are clearly present to the spectators, the fulfilment of his plea. In *Oidipous at Kolonos*, when Antigone and Ismene are reunited with the blind Oidipous after they had been abducted, Oidipous calls them to him and says: 'Press close to me, my girls, one on each side. / Graft yourselves on my old trunk and rest / from this lonely separation' (1112–14). It is not hard to envisage a similar grouping here with the two young girls acting as props for their father, a man who now has no strength (1292).[97]

The hurried half-line exchanges between Oidipous and Kreon about the immediate future ends in Kreon having to point out to Oidipous that he has outlived his authority and, exemplifying the point,[98] to take his children from him. In our production, an Elder intervened, thrust a

Reinhardt 1979, 98, Knox 1957, Taplin 1979, 165, Rehm 1992, 109, and Ewans 1996b, 443–5.

[97] Oidipous, though a polluted man, has physical contact with his daughters and with Kreon in this scene. In *OKol* Oidipous, although he himself recoils from touching Theseus at one point (1132–6), directs his daughters, with whom he has been in contact, to clasp hands with Theseus (1631–3). There was apparently a flexible approach to contact with *miasma*. All the same, there seems little reason, despite Taplin's concerns (1978, 66), to suggest that the Elders in either *OKing* or *OKol* go anywhere near Oidipous.

[98] Kaimio 1988, 44.

staff into Oidipous' hand, and directed him towards the palace. In making his exit 'on three legs', the first actor created an image that fulfilled both the Sphinx's riddle and Teiresias' prophecy (455–6). It also demonstrated Oidipous' complete loss of control over his own destiny.[99]

The drama closes with the Elders' reflection on the life of Oidipous and the lesson to be learned.[100] The speech reflects the same sense of resignation as Choros 5.[101] In our production, the *choros* retreated from the perimeter to the centre of the *orchêstra* in a muted 'bowing out' before leaving the playing area.

[99] Taplin 1978, 46; cf. 1983, 169–74. Some scholars (esp. Hester, 1984) doubt the authenticity of the final exchange between Oidipous and Kreon. Scodel (1984) finds this 'refusal of closure . . . disturbing' (71–2) and intentionally so. However, it seems appropriate that, having lost all else, Oidipous is deprived of his preferred future, and must return in shame to the sinister rooms of the palace that housed his *miasma*.

[100] Unusually, this is spoken rather than chanted. The last six lines of the play (1524–30) have been the subject of debate with regard to their attribution (see Jebb 1902 *ad loc.* who adopts the MSS attribution to the *choros* against the Scholiast's attribution to Oidipous) and their authenticity (see Dawe 1982 *ad loc.*). Arkins (1988, 555–8) cites various critical views in his convincing argument for authenticity. Roberts (1988) calls these passages gnomic codas which simplify and universalize the concerns of the drama.

[101] Not a tragic calm but a partial or tempered reconciliation, as Tarvin has it (1990, 22).

GLOSSARY OF PROPER NAMES

ABAI, a city in Phokis, site of a famous oracle of Apollo.

ACHELOOS, a river in Aitolia; the river-god was a suitor of Deianeira.

ACHERON, a river in the underworld.

ACHILLEUS, son of Peleus and the nymph Thetis; king of Pthia in Thessaly. His quarrel with Agamemnon, leader of the expedition against Troy, is the central strand in the plot of Homer's *Iliad*.

   In the ninth year of the war, his friend and companion Patroklos was killed by Hektor, wearing Achilleus' armour; the god of forging, Hephaistos, made him the new, golden armour which the Greek chieftains awarded to Odysseus after Achilleus' own death at the hands of Paris.

AGAMEMNON, son of Atreus, grandson of Pelops; king of Argos, brother of Menelaos and husband of Klytaimestra. Commander-in-chief of the Greek expedition against Troy. His mother Airope was a Kretan girl, the daughter of Katreus. Katreus sent her to Nauplios, king of Euboia, to be drowned (*Aias* 1295ff.); but he spared her, and gave her to Atreus in marriage.

AGENOR, king of Sidon (Tyre) in Phoinikia. Father of Kadmos, the first king of Thebes.

AIAS, son of Telamon, the king of Salamis. Founder of Aiantis, one of the ten tribes of Athens, and worshipped in Attika as a *heros*.

AITOLIA, a region of western Greece, surrounding the river Acheloos.

ALKMENE, daughter of Elektryon king of Mykenai; the mother of Herakles.

ANTIGONE, daughter of Oidipous, sister of Eteokles and Polyneikes.

APHRODITE, the goddess of love.

APOLLO, son of Zeus and Leto, and brother of Artemis; a major Greek god, worshipped especially at Delos and Delphi. God of archery (and so particularly able to protect his friends and send sudden death on his enemies); music and painting; purification from *miasma*; healing from disease; and prophecy.

ARES, the god of war, son of Zeus and Hera.

ARGOS, one of the two most important cities in the Peloponnese, located in a level, fertile plain in the north-east, just west of the river Inachos.

ARTEMIS, sister of Apollo; a virgin goddess, imaged as a huntress. As a female counterpart to Apollo, she both inflicted and could cure diseases in women. She was also the protectress of the young, and the goddess who presided over childbirth.

ATHENA, goddess of wisdom, and patron deity of Athens.

ATHENS, the largest and most important city in mainland Greece.

ATREUS, father by Airope of Agamemnon and Menelaos. He avenged himself on Thyestes, who had seduced his wife and fraudulently claimed the kingship, by murdering Thyestes' children and serving their flesh and vitals to him at a banquet.

BAKCHOS, see DIONYSOS.

BOREAS, the North Wind, father of Kleopatra.

BOSPOROS, the 'cow-crossing' (named in memory of Io's wanderings); the narrowest part of the Hellespont linking Asia and Europe.

CHEIRON, a divine kentaur and a healer, accidentally wounded by Herakles.

DANAE, daughter of Akrisios, king of Argos. He imprisoned her in a tower of bronze, because an oracle foretold that her son would kill his grandfather. Zeus visited her in a shower of gold, and made her pregnant. Akrisios then shut up both mother and child in a chest, which he cast into the sea. She and her son Perseus eventually landed on the island of Seriphos, and were rescued.

DAULIS, a town in Phokis, near the route from Delphi to Thebes.

DEIANEIRA, daughter of Oineus and wife of Herakles.

DELOS, an island in the Aigeian Sea; birthplace of Apollo and Artemis.

DELPHI, a town in Phokis, on the slopes of Mount Parnassos; site of Apollo's principal oracle.

DEMETER, sister of Zeus, goddess of agriculture and of all the fruits of the earth. She had a particularly splendid temple at Eleusis, where the Eleusinian mystery cult initiated worshippers of Demeter, her daughter Persephone, and Iakchos.

DIONYSOS, son of Zeus and Semele; god of ecstatic possession, fertility and the life-force, both creative and destructive – especially as manifested through liquids, the sap of young trees, the blood of young animals and humans, and wine. His followers are called

Bakchantes, after his alternate cult-title Bakchos. 'Euoi' is an ecstatic cry sometimes used in rituals of Dionysiac worship.

DIRKE,   one of the two rivers of Thebes.

DODONA,   a small city in southern Epiros, in north-west Greece; the site of a famous oracle of Zeus, where the god's responses were given by the wind rustling through the branches of oak trees; these were interpreted by priestesses called 'Doves'.

ECHIDNA,   monstrous mother of Kerberos, the three-headed hound of Haides.

EDONIANS,   inhabitants of the part of Thrakia between the river Strymon, the frontier with Makedonia, and the river Nestos.

ELEUSIS,   village west of Athens, near the border between Attika and Megarian territory. Chief centre of the worship of Demeter.

ERIBOIA,   daughter of Alkathoos, king of Megara; wife of Telamon and mother of Aias.

ERYMANTHOS,   a mountain in Arkadia in the Peloponnese, where Herakles killed a wild boar.

ETEOKLES,   son of Oidipous and brother of Polyneikes.

EUBOIA,   long island off the north-east coast of Lokroi, Boiotia and Attika.

EUENOS,   a river in central Greece, descending into the Korinthian Gulf.

EURYDIKE,   wife of Kreon; mother of his first son, not named in *Antigone*, and of Haimon.

EURYSAKES,   son of Aias by Tekmessa; his name means 'broad-shield', after his father's exceptionally large shield.

EURYSTHEUS,   king of Tiryns, responsible for imposing the Labours on Herakles.

EURYTOS,   king of Oichalia, and father of Iphitos and Iole.

HAIDES,   brother of Zeus and Poseidon, husband of Persephone. Zeus' counterpart below the earth, the ruler of the underworld to which human souls pass after death. His kingdom is often called 'Haides', abbreviated from 'Haides' halls'.

HAIMON,   second son of Kreon.

HEKATE,   the sinister goddess (from the underworld, a companion of Persephone) who taught witchcraft and sorcery, and let loose phantoms and evil spirits at night. She haunted crossroads, and places near the blood of corpses.

HEKTOR,   eldest son of Priam of Troy and Hekabe; husband of

Andromache and father of Astyanax. He was killed by Achilleus in the ninth year of the Trojan War, in revenge for his own killing of Patroklos.

HELIOS,   the Sun-god.

HERA,   wife of Zeus and goddess of marriage.

HERAKLES,   son of Zeus by Alkmene, the wife of Amphitryon king of Thebes; the greatest Greek hero.

Laomedon promised to give him his horses if he saved Hesione from the sea-monster which demanded a virgin sacrifice from the Trojans. But he broke his word. Herakles sailed against Troy, killed Laomedon and all his sons except Priam, and gave Hesione to Telamon, who had been the first to enter Troy.

Apollo's oracle ordered him to serve Eurystheus for twelve years. The Labours of Herakles (cf. YWT, esp. 1090ff.) are the superhuman feats that Eurystheus demanded of him.

HERMES,   son of Zeus and Maia, herald and messenger of the gods. He was the god who escorts travellers, and conducts souls between the worlds of the living and the dead; also the guardian of paternal rights, and the god of deception and trickery.

HYLLOS,   eldest son of Herakles and Deianeira.

IAKCHOS,   a god worshipped at Eleusis, often identified with Dionysos. His name means 'shout', and is used as an outcry at the end of Choros 6 in *Antigone*.

IKAROS,   son of Daidalos of Krete; while escaping from Minos, king of Krete on wings made by his father and fastened on by wax, he flew too near the sun and fell into the sea. 'The Sea of Ikaros' normally refers strictly to the part of the Aigeian north-west of Krete, but is used loosely in *Aias* Choros 3 to refer to the part of it between Delos and Troy.

IOKASTE,   sister of Kreon, wife of Laios and mother of Oidipous; later wife of Oidipous.

IOLE,   daughter of Eurytos, raped and taken as his mistress by Herakles.

IPHITOS,   son of Eurytos, a friend of Herakles, whom Herakles hurled to his death from the walls of Tiryns in a fit of rage.

ISMENE,   daughter of Oidipous, sister of Antigone, Eteokles and Polyneikes; probably a fictitious name, created from that of the river Ismenos.

ISMENOS,   the second river of Thebes (cf. Dirke).

ISTER,   the river Danube.

ISTHMIA, the district around Korinth.

ITALIA, Greeks had colonized much of Sicily, and the southern part of the mainland, before the fifth century. Dionysos is Italia's 'guardian' at *Antigone* 1119 because he is the patron god of vines, for which the country was (and still is) famous.

KADMOS, son of Agenor the king of Phoinikia; the founder of Thebes.

KALCHAS, son of Thestor; the prophet who accompanied the Greek expedition against Troy.

KASTALIA, a spring on Mount Parnassos, source of the sacred stream of the same name which flows down past Delphi.

KENAION, north-west promontory of Euboia, sacred to Zeus.

KENTAUR, a creature with a human torso on a horse's body.

KITHAIRON, a mountain on the borders of Attika and Boiotia; it lies between Korinth and Thebes.

KORINTH, the most north-easterly city in the Peloponnnese, controlling the Isthmos.

KORYKIS, a large cave high on Mount Parnassos outside Delphi.

KREON, son of Menoikeus; brother of Iokaste, and therefore brother-in-law to Oidipous.

KRETE, a very large island in the southern Aigeian.

KRONOS, the youngest of the Titanes, son of Ouranos and Ge (Heaven and Earth); he deprived Ouranos of the government of the world, and was himself dethroned by his own son, Zeus.

KYLLENE, the highest mountain in the Peloponnese, marking the frontier between Arkadia and Achaia.

KYPROS, large island off the south coast of Asia Minor; birthplace of Aphrodite, who is often called 'the Kyprian goddess'.

LABDAKOS, son of Polydoros, himself the son of Kadmos, the founder of Thebes, and grandson of Agenor; father of Laios.

LAERTES, king of Ithaka and father of Odysseus by Antikleia.

LAIOS, king of Thebes; son of Labdakos; first husband of Iokaste and father of Oidipous.

LAOMEDON, king of Troy; father of Priam and of Teukros' mother Hesione (see HERAKLES).

LERNA, a district near Argos, with a lake and a small river. Herakles' second Labour was to kill the Lernaian hydra, a monster with nine heads; he used its bile to poison his arrows.

LETO, mother of Apollo and Artemis.

LICHAS, herald and attendant of Herakles.

LOKROI,   a region of central Greece, opposite Euboia.

LYDIA,   central western district of the peninsula of Asia Minor; an early seat of Asian civilization.

LYKOURGOS,   king of the Edonians in Thrakia. The legend of his opposition to Dionysos is the other great myth about resistance to the god and his *mainads*, apart from that of Pentheus of Thebes, which is dramatized in Euripides' *Bakchai*. Lykourgos was the subject of a lost trilogy by Aischylos.

MALIS,   the region of central Greece, directly to the west of Kenaion on Euboia, in which Trachis lies.

MENELAOS,   son of Atreus, king of Sparta and husband of Helene, whose abduction by Paris of Troy caused the Trojan War.

MENOIKEUS,   father of Kreon and Iokaste.

MEROPE,   wife of Polybos and queen of Korinth; from Doris, a small region of central Greece north of Mount Parnassos.

MYSIA,   the north-western region of Asia Minor.

NEMEA,   a small valley in the mountains between Korinth and Argos on the Peloponnese.

NESSOS,   a kentaur, killed by Herakles while attempting to rape Deianeira.

NIOBE,   daughter of Tantalos, and wife of Amphion, king of Thebes. She boasted that she was a better mother than Leto, because she had more children. Apollo and Artemis killed her children in revenge, and she wasted away, gradually turned by Zeus into stone in the manner described at *Antigone* 823ff.

NYSA,   legendary scene of the childhood of Dionysos, located by Sophokles in Euboia.

ODYSSEUS,   son of Laertes and king of Ithaka, husband of Penelopeia and father of Telemachos; the most cunning of the heroes who joined the expedition against Troy (and hence the favourite of Athena, the goddess of wisdom). His adventures after the war, and his return home, are the subject of Homer's epic poem *The Odyssey*. In some accounts he was the son of Sisyphos not Laertes.

OICHALIA,   the city of King Eurytos, sacked by Herakles. Located in the Eritrean region of Euboia.

OIDIPOUS,   son of Laios and Iokaste; ruler of Thebes after he rid the city of the Sphinx, until he discovered that his wife was his own mother.

OINEUS,   king of Pleuron in Aitolia; father of Deianeira.

OINIADAI,   city in western Greece, near the mouth of the river Acheloos.

OITA,   a mountain in southern Thessaly, near Olympos and overlooking Trachis; site of Herakles' self-immolation.

OLYMPIA,   a town in Elis in the west of the Peloponnese; site of a very important cult of Zeus, as well as of quadrennial Games.

OLYMPOS,   a mountain in the north-east of mainland Greece, the dwelling-place of the gods.

OMPHALE,   queen of Lydia, to whom Herakles was enslaved for a year.

ORTYGIA,   'Quail-island', a cult name for Delos, the island where Artemis was born.

PAIAN,   a cult name of Apollo, invoked in hymns to the god (*paians*).

PALLAS,   a cult title of Athena, of unknown origin and meaning.

PAN,   the god of flocks and shepherds; a lover of music, the inventor of the syrinx, the shepherds' flute. Feared by travellers, whom he sometimes startled with sudden terror ('panic').

PARNASSOS,   the great, sacred mountain which rises behind Delphi.

PELOPS,   father of Atreus and grandfather of Agamemnon and Menelaos.

PERSEPHONE,   daughter of Demeter and wife of Haides.

PHASIS,   a river flowing into the east end of the Black Sea.

PHINEUS,   king of Salmydessos in Thrakia, whose second wife Eidaia (or Eidothea) blinded his sons. They were the children of his first wife Kleopatra, daughter of Boreas the north wind by the Athenian princess Oreithyia, whom Boreas once abducted. According to a late source Kleopatra was once imprisoned, and this may be alluded to in the last two lines of Choros 5 in *Antigone*.

PHOKIS,   the region of central Greece surrounding Mount Parnassos.

PHRYGIA,   the region of north-west Asia Minor in which Troy is sited.

PLEURON,   a city in Aitolia.

PLOUTON,   'the giver of wealth'; a name for Haides, since crops and minerals come from below the earth.

POLYBOS,   king of Korinth.

POLYDOROS,   son of Kadmos and father of Labdakos.

POLYNEIKES,   son of Oidipous, and brother of Eteokles. When Eteokles kept the throne, he persuaded the Argives, under his father-in-law Adrastos, to march against Thebes so he could reclaim it as his inheritance.

POSEIDON,   brother of Zeus, god of the sea.

PYTHIA,   cult title of Apollo and name of his priestess at Delphi.

SALAMIS,   an island, separated by a narrow channel from the west coast of Attika; legendary home of the hero Aias, and part of Athenian territory since Solon.

SALMYDESSOS,   a town in Thrakia, on the shore of the Black Sea.

SARDIS,   capital city of Lydia.

SELLOI,   inhabitants of Dodona.

SEMELE,   daughter of Kadmos, the second king of Thebes, and Harmonia. She was loved by Zeus, who promised to give her anything she wanted. Hera was jealous of Semele; she appeared before her in disguise, and persuaded her to ask Zeus to show himself before her in all his majesty as the god of thunder. She did this, and was consumed by lightning; but Zeus saved her son, Dionysos.

SIPYLOS,   a mountain in Lydia.

SISYPHOS,   the deceitful and cunning king of Korinth; in some accounts, the father of Odysseus.

SKAMANDER,   the main river of the Trojan plain.

SOUNION,   cape at the south-east end of Attika; the first Athenian land sighted by sailors returning from Troy.

SPARTA,   the principal city of the southern Peloponnese; kingdom of Menelaos.

SPHINX,   a monster, usually imaged with the head of a woman, the body of a lioness and the wings of an eagle; but referred to as 'bitch-sphinx' at *Oidipous the King* 391.

TEIRESIAS,   the legendary prophet of Thebes.

TEKMESSA,   daughter of Teleutas, king of part of Phrygia; captured by the Greeks on an expedition for plunder early in the Trojan War, and given to Aias as his reward for bravery during that expedition.

TELAMON,   brother of Peleus, who became king of Salamis. Father of Aias by Eriboia, and later of Teukros by Hesione, who was given to him by Herakles in return for his courage in their expedition against her father Laomedon of Troy.

TELEUTAS,   king of part of Phrygia; father of Tekmessa.

TEUKROS,   son of Telamon by the captive Trojan princess Hesione.

THEBE,   daughter of the river Asopos; patron goddess of the fields and groves around Thebes, which was named after her.

THEBES,   the principal city of Boiotia, in central Greece.

THRAKIA, the relatively uncivilized tribal lands north of the part of the Aigeian coastline between the river Strymon and the Hellespont.

TIRYNS, city in the plain of Argos.

TRACHIS, city in Malis in central Greece; near Thermopylai, and below Mount Oita.

TROY, a city in Phrygia in modern Turkey. First sacked by Herakles when it was ruled by Laomedon; then sacked when ruled by his son Priam, after a ten-year siege by the Greek expedition, commanded by Agamemnon and Menelaos, which set out to avenge Paris' abduction of Menelaos' wife Helene.

TYNDAREUS, king of Sparta, restored to the throne by Herakles; husband of Leda, who gave birth to his children Kastor and Klytaimestra, and Zeus' children Pollux and Helene. The suitors for Helene's hand in marriage swore an oath to Tyndareus that they would support her choice of husband and restore her if anyone else attempted to abduct her. Helene married Menelaos.

ZEUS, the most powerful god: son of Kronos and Rhea. Husband of the goddess Hera; father by Alkmene of Herakles. Originally a sky and weather god, his weapon was the thunderbolt. He punished oath-breaking, and some other kinds of wrongdoing; in particular, the table of hospitality was sacred to him as the protector of the rights of guests and hosts. However, Zeus did not make the world, and he was not omnipotent or omniscient. Despite his great and wide-ranging powers, other gods as well as human beings could defy him (at their own risk).

GLOSSARY OF GREEK WORDS

agathos, a good or noble man – head of an *oikos* by virtue of a combination of birth, wealth and military ability.

agora, the market-place or city square; the centre of political, legal and social life in the city-states of ancient Greece.

agôn, a contest, in athletics or warfare; in tragedy, a formally structured scene in which one speaker puts a case, and is answered (usually after a two-line interjection from the *choros*) by another speaker with a speech of approximately the same length. Plural *agones*.

anapaests, the metre of the chanted sections of a Greek tragedy, midway in intensity between speech and lyric song. Often used as the accompaniment for the entrance-march of the *choros*.

antilabe, the division of single spoken lines between different speakers.

antistrophe, see *strophe*.

arete, excellence; the qualities of the *agathos* – good birth, wealth and military ability. Female excellence consisted in good birth and *sophrosyne*, q.v.

bronteion, the machine for producing the special effect of the sound of thunder. Later tradition says that stagehands rattled a barrel of small stones; but shaking a large sheet of thin copper would also have been feasible in fifth-century technology.

choros, literally song (and dance) – denotes either the group of fifteen *choros* members or the odes (songs) that they perform.

daimôn, a god or god-like power; *daimones* are often what we, like later, more rationalist Greeks, would call personifications of abstract forces – e.g. Madness, Fear, Persuasion.

deinos, marvellous, awe-inspiring, strange and/or terrible.

dike, often translated 'justice', *dike* usually means a recompense or fair requital rather than any more sophisticated concept of justice.

dithyramb, a song and dance in the form of a choral hymn, usually including a narrative. These *choroses* were originally connected with the worship of Dionysos; at the Festival each of Athens' ten tribes presented two 'circular *choroses*', one of fifty men and one of fifty boys, to compete with *dithyrambs* in two different competitions.

ekkyklêma, the 'rolling-out machine', used in tragedy when the pressure of events inside the building represented by the *skene* has such implications for the public world outside that they must be seen (as they could not, if simply displayed in the entrance, because of shadows).

epode, a third stanza, sometimes added as a tailpiece after a pair of *strophe* and *antistrophe*; in the same metres but not responding exactly in its structure to those stanzas.

hamartia, an error or mistake of fact; the term used by Aristotle in his explanation of why stories like those of Oedipus and Thyestes make good tragic plots (*Poetics* 53a10). This word was long misunderstood to mean a 'tragic flaw' in the character of a 'tragic hero'.

heros, a legendary ancestor, who was considered to have divine powers, and was therefore worshipped in a cult, especially by his descendants and by residents of his local territory.

hybris, wanton violence, usually against human beings. The neoclassical mistranslation of this word as 'arrogance' or 'pride' which angers the gods and brings down *nemesis* or divine revenge receives no support from the surviving texts.

kentaur, a creature with a human torso on a horse's body.

kommos, a lyric lamentation, sung by the *choros* and one or more solo actors. Plural *kommoi*.

kyrios, a male head-of-household, who had control over the members of his family.

mechane, the crane used in and after the late fifth century to swing into view gods and other characters who are to be imagined as flying into the playing area. (Hence Latin '*deus ex machina*', god from the machine.)

miasma, pollution; the word embraces both literal dirt and what we would call psychic pollution automatically incurred by breaches of taboo, e.g. bloodshed.

mimesis, imitation in or through enactment.

moira, a person's share or lot in life; the 'destiny' which is not a predetermined fate, but gradually takes shape as a human life unfolds, under the guidance of three ancient goddesses, the Moirai.

oikos, the great household, consisting of an *agathos'* family and the dependants who work for him, which was the basic unit of Greek society.

orchêstra, the circular dance-floor on which tragedies were performed.

paian, hymn to the god Apollo as a saviour.

parabasis, the choral ode towards the middle of an Aristophanic comedy, in which the *choros* steps out of the plot of the drama (but not out of character) to address the audience on matters of current political and social concern, in a mixture of seriousness and caricature.

parodos, one of the two entrance-ways, one on each side of the *orchêstra.* By a convention which reflected the reality of the theatre's location, the *skene* left *parodos* was imagined as leading to 'down-town' from the place where the action was set, and the *skene* right *parodos* to the countryside and to other *poleis.* Plural *parodoi.* (Some scholars, following the interpolated ch. 12 of Aristotle's *Poetics,* use this term to indicate the entry-song, the first choral ode of a tragedy or comedy. They favour the synonym *eisodos* for the side entrance-ways.)

parthenos, a young woman who has begun to menstruate but is not yet married.

peripeteia, the moment of 'reversal' where the plot of a tragedy reaches its climax, after which the consequences of the events are dramatized. A technical term employed by Aristotle (*Poetics* ch 11); often, as in Scene 5 of *Oidipous the King,* accompanied by an *anagnorisis* or 'recognition'.

philia, a friendship or alliance, bound by loyalty or blood-relation-ship; it especially included relatives and other members of your own household. A person so bound to you was your *philos;* plural, *philoi.*

polis, a city which, with its surrounding territory, was also an inde-pendent state; the largest social unit in ancient Greece after their formation in the eighth to sixth centuries.

satyr-drama, the farcical and ribald afterpiece to each competitor's offering of three tragedies. The *choros* played the role of the half-animal, half-human satyrs, and their father Silenos was normally one of the characters.

skene,   literally and until *c.* 460 a tent in which the actors changed masks and costumes. After that it was a wooden building behind the *orchêstra*, with a pair of double doors and a practicable roof; it could be used to represent e.g. a palace, house, temple or tent – probably by the use of changeable front panels on which features of the relevant façade could be painted.

stichomythia,   literally 'step-speech'; a dialogue sequence of rapid cut and thrust, in which normally the speaker changes every line.

strophe, antistrophe,   literally 'turn' and 'counter-turn'; the metrically responding stanzas (A1, A2; B1, B2 etc.) in solo and choral lyrics.

sophrosyne,   self-restraint and mental balance. An excellence, especially in women, for whom it included chastity and fidelity.

theatron,   the 'seeing-place' – the part of the theatre in which the audience sat.

time,   honour or status; always in terms of concrete possessions and/or privileges.

tragoidia,   the Greek name for the genre, of wider application than the modern word 'tragedy', since it includes some dramas in which catastrophe is survived, or avoided altogether, and some dramas which modern critics would regard as nearer to melodrama.

tychê,   fortune, chance or luck; a *daimon*.

tyrannos,   a king who has received the throne by other means than by inheritance, and therefore is not connected by blood-descent to the original royal family. The pejorative overtones of the modern English derivative word 'tyrant' appear only rarely in fifth-century Greek; the translation of the title *Oidipous Tyrannos* as 'Oidipous the King' is therefore better than 'Oidipous the Tyrant' – but it fails to do justice to the deep irony of the application of the word *tyrannos* to Oidipous, who turns out to be all too closely connected with the house of Labdakos.

SUGGESTIONS FOR FURTHER READING

Arnott, P. (1989): *Public and Performance in the Greek Theatre*, London. The best book on this subject, covering a wide range of features of the Greek theatre.

Blundell, M. W. (1989): *Helping Friends and Harming Enemies*, Cambridge. A study of the ways in which decisions are reached and choices made in five Sophoklean tragedies, with special reference to the fundamental code of Greek values described by the title.

Burton, R. W. B. (1980): *The Chorus in Sophocles' Tragedies*, Oxford. A thorough, comprehensive analysis of the choral odes.

Easterling, P. E. (ed.) (1982): *Sophocles, Trachiniae*, Cambridge. This is an edition of the Greek text; but its Introduction presents, in a form accessible to the Greekless reader, Prof. Easterling's pioneering interpretation, which inaugurated modern appreciation of *Young Women of Trachis*.

Ewans, M. (ed. and tr.) (1995): *Aeschylus: The Oresteia*, London.

Ewans, M. (ed. and tr.) (1996a): *Aeschylus: Suppliants and Other Dramas*, London. Two companion volumes to this book, containing the work of the first surviving Greek dramatist. The introductions deal in detail with the theatre space and performance style of Athenian tragedy.

Ewans, M. (ed.) (2000): *Sophocles: Three Dramas of Old Age*, London. The sequel to this book, containing Sophokles' last three surviving dramas, and fragments of lost tragedies.

Gardiner, C. P. (1987): *The Sophoclean Chorus: A Study of Character and Function*, Iowa City. An examination of the extent to which the chorus should be perceived as a character in the drama. Less comprehensive than Burton, but containing many valuable insights.

Jones, J. (1962): *On Aristotle and Greek Tragedy*, London and New York. A pioneering book; the chapters on Sophokles are particularly strong on the concept of mutability.

Ley, G. (1991): *A Short Introduction to the Ancient Greek Theater*,

Chicago. The best introduction for students and readers new to the subject.

Rehm, R. (1992): *The Greek Tragic Theatre*, London. The most recent introduction to the nature and context of Greek tragic performance, with a particularly good chapter on *Oidipous the King*.

Seale, D. (1982): *Vision and Stagecraft in Sophocles*, London. This book is limited by its concentration on the theme of vision and on words for seeing; the suggestions for theatre practice were not tested in performance, and are often undermined by the author's belief in a raised stage. However, there are stimulating chapters on all seven dramas, with many worthwhile ideas.

Segal, C. (1981): *Tragedy and Civilization: An Interpretation of Sophocles*, Cambridge Mass. This book is extremely detailed, and has little sense of the scripts as texts for performance; but it is very important as the first reading to develop a sense of the bleakness of Sophokles' tragic vision, and to apply structuralist insights, in particular the antithesis between civilization and barbarism.

Taplin, O. (1978): *Greek Tragedy in Action*, London. This book provides good discussion of gestures, props, tableaux and other important topics.

Walcot, P. (1976): *Greek Drama in its Theatrical and Social Context*, Cardiff. A short and excellent book.

Winnington-Ingram, R. P. (1980): *Sophocles: An Interpretation*, Cambridge. Very good literary interpretations of the dramas.

Other References Cited in the Introduction and Notes

Adkins, A. W. H. (1960): *Merit and Responsibility: a Study in Greek Values*, Oxford.

Ahl, F. (1991): *Sophocles' Oedipus: Evidence and Self-Conviction*, Ithaca and London.

Angas, M. (1995): 'An actor's approach to the role of Haimon in Sophokles' *Antigone*', *Didaskalia*, 2.1.

Arkins, B. (1988): 'The Final Lines of Sophocles, *King Oedipus* (1524–30)', *Classical Quarterly*, ns 38, 2, 555–58.

Arnott, P. (1962): *Greek Scenic Conventions in the Fifth Century* BC, Oxford.

Arnott, P. D. (1989): *Public and Performance in the Greek Theatre*, London.

Arthur, E. P. (1980): 'Sophocles' *Oedipus Tyrannos*: The Two Arrivals of the Herdsman', *Antichthon*, 14, 9–17.

Ashby, C. (1991a): 'The Siting of Greek Theatres', *Theatre Research International*, 16, 181–201.

Ashby, C. (1991b): 'Where was the Altar?', *Theatre Survey*, 32, 3–21.

Aylen, L. (1985): *The Greek Theater*, Cranbury (New Jersey) and London.

Bain, D. (1977): *Actors and Audience: a Study of Asides and Related Conventions in Greek Drama*, Oxford.

Bain, D. (1981): *Masters, Servants and Orders in Greek Tragedy*, Manchester.

Baldry, H. C. (1971): *The Greek Tragic Theatre*, London.

Barnes, J. (1982): *The Presocratic Philosophers*, London.

Beer, D. G. (1990): 'The Riddle of the Sphinx and the Staging of *Oedipus Rex*', *Essays in Theatre*, 8, 107–20.

Belton, J. (1991): 'Language, Oedipus and *Chinatown*', *Modern Language Notes*, 106, 933–50.

Brault, P. (1989): 'Thresholds of the Tragic: A Study of Space in Sophocles and Racine', *Theatre Research International*, 14, 229–41.

Bremer, J. M. (1976): 'Why Messenger Speeches?', in *Miscellanea Tragica in Honorem J. C. Kamerbeek* (ed. J. Bremer, S. L. Radt, C. J. Ruijgh), Amsterdam 29–48.

Burian, P. (1997): 'Myth into *Muthos*: the Shaping of Tragic Plot' in *The Cambridge Companion to Greek Tragedy* (ed. P. E. Easterling), Cambridge.

Bushnell, R. (1988): *Prophesying Tragedy: Sign and Voice in Sophocles' Theban Plays*, Ithaca.

Buxton, R. B. (1980): 'Blindness and Limits: Sophokles and the Logic of Myth', *Journal of Hellenic Studies*, 100, 22–37.

Buxton, R. B. (1996): 'What can you rely on in *Oedipus Rex*?' in *Tragedy and the Tragic: Greek Theatre and Beyond* (ed. M. S. Silk), Oxford, 38–48.

Calame, C. (1986): 'Facing Otherness: The Tragic Mask in Ancient Greece', *History of Religions*, 26, 125–42.

Calder, W. M. (1959): 'The Staging of the Prologue of *Oedipus Tyrannus*', *Phoenix*, 13, 119–29.

Calder, W. M. (1968): 'Sophocles' Political Tragedy: Antigone', *Greek, Roman and Byzantine Studies*, 9, 389–407.

Case, S. (1985): 'Classic Drag: The Greek Creation of Female Parts', *Theatre Journal*, 37, 317–28.

Chancellor, G. (1979): 'Implicit Stage Directions in Ancient Greek Drama: Critical Assumptions and the Reading Public', *Arethusa*, 12, 133–53.

Cohen, D. (1978): 'The Imagery of Sophocles: a Study of Ajax's Suicide', *Greece and Rome* 25, 24–36.

Cropp, M. (1997): 'Antigone's Final Speech (Sophocles, *Antigone* 891–928)', *Greece and Rome*, 44.2,137–60.

Dale, A. M. (1969): *Collected Papers of A. M. Dale* (ed. Turner and Webster), Cambridge.

Damen, M. (1989): 'Actor and Character in Greek Tragedy', *Theatre Journal*, 41, 316–40.

Davidson, J. F. (1986): 'The Circle and the Tragic Chorus', *Greece and Rome*, 33, 38–46.

Davies, M. (1984): 'Lichas' Lying Tale', *Classical Quarterly*, 34, 480–83.

Davies, M. (ed.) (1991): *Sophocles: Trachiniae*, Oxford.

Dawe, R. D. (ed.) (1979): *Sophoclis Tragoediae: Tomus II*, Leipzig.

Dawe, R. D. (ed.) (1982): *Sophocles: Oedipus Rex*, Cambridge.

Dodds, E. R. (ed.) (1960): *Euripides: The Bacchae*, Oxford.

Dodds, E. R. (1983): 'On Misunderstanding the *Oedipus Rex*' (from *Greece and Rome*, 1966) in *Oxford Readings in Greek Tragedy* (ed. E. Segal), Oxford, 177–88.

Drachmann, A. B. (1908): 'Zur Composition der Sophokleische *Antigone*' *Hermes*, 43, 67–76.

Easterling, P. E. (1968): 'Sophocles, *Trachiniae*', *Bulletin of the Institute of Classical Studies*, 15, 58–69.

Easterling, P. E. (1973): 'Repetition in Sophocles', *Hermes*, 101, 14–34.

Easterling, P. E. (1978): 'The Second Stasimon of *Antigone*', in *Dionysiaca: Essays Presented to D. L. Page*, Cambridge, 141–58.

Easterling, P. E. (1996): 'Weeping, Witnessing, and the Tragic Audience: Response to Segal', in *Tragedy and the Tragic: Greek Theatre and Beyond* (ed. M. S. Silk), Oxford, 173–81.

Easterling, P. E. (1997): 'Constructing the Heroic', in *Greek Tragedy and the Historian* (ed. C. Pelling), Oxford.

Edmunds, L. (1981): 'The Cults and the Legend of Oedipus', *Harvard Studies in Classical Philology*, 85, 221–38.

Ewans, M. (1982): 'The Dramatic Structure of *Agamemnon*', *Ramus*, 11, 1–15.

Ewans, M. (1996b): 'Patterns of Tragedy in Sophokles and Shakespeare', in *Tragedy and the Tragic: Greek Theatre and Beyond* (ed. M. S. Silk), Oxford 438–57.

Fagles, R. (tr.) (1984): *Sophocles: the Three Theban Plays* (introduction and notes by B. M. W. Knox), Harmondsworth.

Fergusson, F. (1949): *The Idea of a Theater*, Princeton.

Foley, H. P. (1996): 'Antigone as Moral Agent' in *Tragedy and the Tragic* (ed. M. Silk), Oxford, 49–73.

Francis, E. D. (1992): 'Oedipus Achaemenides', *American Journal of Philology*, 113, 333–57.

Galinsky, G. K. (1972): *The Herakles Theme*, Oxford.

Gellie, G. H. (1972): *Sophocles: a Reading*, Melbourne.

Goheen, R. F. (1951): *The Imagery of Sophocles'Antigone*, Princeton.

Golder, H. (1990): 'Sophocles' *Ajax*: Beyond the Shadow of Time' *Arion, third series*, 1, 9–31.

Golder, H. (1992): 'Visual Meaning in Greek Drama: Sophocles' *Ajax* and the Art of Dying', *Advances in non-verbal Communication* (ed. F. Poyatos), Amsterdam, 323–60.

Goldhill, S. (1986): *Reading Greek Tragedy*, Cambridge.

Goldhill, S. (1997): 'The Language of Tragedy: Rhetoric and Communication' in *The Cambridge Companion to Greek Tragedy* (ed. P. E. Easterling), Cambridge.

Gould, J. (1988): 'The Language of Oedipus', in *Sophocles' Oedipus Rex* (ed. H. Bloom), New York.

Gould, J. (1996): 'Tragedy and Collective Experience' in *Tragedy and the Tragic: Greek Theatre and Beyond* (ed. M. S. Silk), Oxford, 217–43.

Green, J. R. (1991): 'On Seeing and Depicting the Theatre in Classical Athens', *Greek Roman and Byzantine Studies*, 32, 15–50.

Griffith, M. (ed.): *Sophocles: Antigone*, Cambridge (forthcoming).

Halliwell, S. (1986): 'Where three Roads Meet: A Neglected Detail in the *Oedipus Tyrannus*', 106, 187–90.

Hamilton, R. (1978): 'Announced Entrances in Greek Tragedy', *Harvard Studies in Classical Philology*, 82, 63–82.

Havelock, E. (1984): 'Oral Composition in the *Oedipus Tyrannus* of Sophocles', *New Literary History*, 16, 175–97.

Heiden, B. (1989): *Tragic Rhetoric: An Interpretation of Sophocles' Trachiniae*, New York.

Henry, A. (1969): 'Sophocles, *Oedipus Tyrannus* 222–43', *The Classical Review*, 19, 125–6.

Hester, D. (1977): 'To Help one's Friends and Harm one's Enemies: A Study in the *Oedipus at Colonus*', *Antichthon*, 11, 22–41.

Hester, D. (1984): 'The Banishment of Oedipus', *Antichthon*, 18, 13–23.

Hoey, T. F. (1972): 'Sun Symbolism in the Parodos of the *Trachiniae*', *Arethusa*, 5, 133–54.

Hoey, T. F. (1977): 'Ambiguity in the Exodos of Sophocles' *Trachiniae*', *Arethusa*, 10, 269–94.

Hogan, J. C. (1972): 'The Protagonists of the *Antigone*', *Arethusa*, 5, 93–8.

Hogan, J. C. (1991): *A Commentary on the Plays of Sophocles*, Carbondale.

Holt, P. (1989): 'The End of the *Trachiniae* and the Fate of Herakles', *Journal of Hellenic Studies* 109, 69–80.

Jebb, R. (ed. and tr.) (1891): *Sophocles: Antigone*, Cambridge.

Jebb, R. (ed. and tr.) (1902): *Sophocles: Oedipus Rex*, Cambridge.

Jebb, R. (ed. and tr.) (1907): *Sophocles: Ajax*, Cambridge.

Jebb, R. (ed. and tr.) (1908): *Sophocles: Trachiniae*, Cambridge.

Kaimio, Maarit (1988): *Physical Contact in Greek Tragedy: A Study of Stage Conventions*, Helsinki.

Kamerbeek, J. C. (1959): *The Trachiniae*, Leiden.

Kirk, G. S. (1974): *The Nature of Greek Myths*, Harmondsworth.

Kirkwood, G. M. (1958): *A Study of Sophoclean Drama*, Ithaca.

Kitto, H. D. F. (1956): *Form and Meaning in Drama*, London.

Kitto, H. D. F. (1961): *Greek Tragedy: A Literary Study* (3rd edn), London.

Kitto, H. D. F. (1966): *Poiesis: Structure and Thought*, Berkeley.

Kitto, H. D. F. (tr.) (1994): *Sophocles: Antigone, Oedipus the King, Electra*, Oxford.

Knox, B. M. W. (1954): 'Why is Oedipus called *Tyrannos?*', *Classical Journal*, 50, 97–102.

Knox, B. M. W. (1956): 'The date of the *Oedipus Tyrannus* of Sophocles', *American Journal of Philology* 77; reprinted in Knox 1979, 112–24.

Knox, B. M. W. (1957): *Oedipus at Thebes*, New Haven.

Knox, B. M. W. (1964): *The Heroic Temper: Studies in Sophoclean Tragedy*, Berkeley and Los Angeles.

Knox, B. M. W. (1979): *Word and Action: Essays on the Ancient Theater*, Baltimore and London.

Knox, B. M. W. (1980): 'Sophocles: *Oedipus Tyrannus* 446: Exit Oedipus?', *Greek, Roman and Byzantine Studies*, 21, 321–2.

Knox, B. M. W. (1984): *see* Fagles, R. (1984).

Kovacs, D. (1993): 'Zeus in Euripides' *Medea*', *American Journal of Philology*, 114, 45–71.

Lattimore, R. (1964): *Story Patterns in Greek Tragedy*, London.

Lewis, R. G. (1988): 'An Alternative Date for Sophocles' *Antigone*', *Greek, Roman and Byzantine Studies*, 29, 35–50.

Lewis, R. G. (1989): 'The Procedural Basis of Sophocles' *Oedipus Tyrannus*', *Greek, Roman and Byzantine Studies*, 30, 41–66.

Ley, G. and Ewans, M. (1985): 'The Orchestra as Acting Area in Greek Tragedy', *Ramus*, 14, 75–84.

Ley, G. K. H. (1988): 'A Scenic Plot of Sophocles' *Ajax* and *Philoctetes*', *Eranos*, 86, 85–115.

Ley, G. (1989): 'Agatharchos, Aeschylus and the Construction of a Skene', *Maia*, n.s. 1, 35–38.

Ley, G. K. H. (1991): *A Short Introduction to the Ancient Greek Theater*, Chicago.

Ley, G. K. H. (1994): 'Performance Studies and Greek Tragedy', *Eranos*, 92, 29–45.

Lloyd-Jones, H. and Wilson, N. G. (1990): *Sophoclea: Studies on the Text of Sophocles*, Oxford.

Lloyd-Jones, H. and Wilson, N. G. (1992): *Sophoclis Fabulae* (corr. ed.), Oxford.

McCart, G. (1991): 'Implied Action in Sophocles' *Oidipous at Kolonos*', *Proceedings of the International Symposium on Ancient Greek Drama: A World Heritage*, Cyprus Centre of the International Theatre Institute, Nicosia.

McCart, G. (1999): 'Seen and Unseen: Sophokles' *Aias* in Production', *Study Book: Pre-Renaissance Drama*, Toowoomba.

Macintosh, F. (1994): *Dying Acts; Death in Ancient Greek and Modern Irish Drama*, Cork.

McKinnon, J. K. (1971): 'Heracles' Intention in His Second Request of Hyllus: *Trach.* 1215-16', *Classical Quarterly*, 21, 33–41.

Manton, G. R. (1982): 'Identification of Speakers in Greek Drama', *Antichthon*, 16, 1–16.

March, J. (1991–3): 'Sophocles' *Ajax*: the Death and Burial of a Hero', *Bulletin of the Institute of Classical Studies*, 38, 1–35.

Mastronarde, D. J. (1979): *Contact and Discontinuity*, Berkeley.

Mikailson, J. D. (1989): 'Unanswered Prayers in Greek Tragedy', *Journal of Hellenic Studies*, 109, 81–98.

Moore, J. (tr.) (1952): 'Ajax', in *Sophocles II* (ed. D. Grene and R. Lattimore) Chicago, 1957.

Moore, J, (1977): 'The Dissembling-Speech of Ajax', *Yale Classical Studies* 25, 47–66.

Mogyoródi, E. (1996): 'Tragic Freedom and Fate in Sophocles' *Antigone*: Notes on the Role of the "Ancient Evils" in "the Tragic"', in *Tragedy and the Tragic* (ed. M.Silk), Oxford, 358–76.

Müller, G. (ed.) (1967): *Sophokles' Antigone*, Heidelberg.

Neuburg, M. (1990): 'How Like a Woman: Antigone's "Inconsistency"', *Classical Quarterly*, 40, 54–76.

Nussbaum, M. C. (1986): *The Fragility of Goodness. Luck and Ethics in Greek Tragedy and Philosophy*, Cambridge.

O'Neil, J. L. (1986): 'The Semantic Usage of *tyrannos* and Related Words', *Antichthon*, 20, 26–40.

Oudemans, C. W. and Lardinois, A. (1987): *Tragic Ambiguity: Anthropology, Philology and Sophocles' Antigone*, Leiden.

Perotta, G. (1935): *Sofocle*, Messina.

Pickard, J. (1893): 'The Relative Position of Actors and Chorus in the Greek Theatre of the v Century BC', *American Journal of Philology*, 14, 68–89.

Pickard-Cambridge, A. W. (1946): *The Theatre of Dionysus in Athens*, Oxford.

Pickard-Cambridge, A. W. (1988): *The Dramatic Festivals of Athens* (2nd edn rev. by J. Gould and D. M. Lewis), Oxford.

Poe, J. P. (1992): 'Entrance-Announcements and Entrance-Speeches in Greek Tragedy', *Harvard Studies in Classical Philology*, 94, 121–56.

Pope, M. (1991): 'Addressing Oedipus', *Greece and Rome*, 38, 156–70.

Pound, E. (tr.) (1969): *Sophocles: Women of Trachis*, London.

Pucci, P. (1992): *Oedipus and the Fabrication of the Father: Oedipus Tyrannus in Modern Criticism and Philosophy*, Baltimore.

Reinhardt, K. (1979): *Sophocles* (trans. of 1933 book by H. and D. Harvey), Oxford.

Rigsby, K. J. (1976): 'Teiresias as Magus in *Oedipus Rex*', *Greek, Roman and Byzantine Studies*, 17, 109–14.

Roberts, D. (1987): 'Parting Words: Final Lines in Sophocles and Euripides', *Classical Quarterly*, 37, 51–64.

Roberts, D. (1988): 'Sophoclean Endings: Another Story', *Arethusa*, 21, 177–96.

Schlegel, A. W. von (1846): *Dramatic Art and Literature* (tr. J. Black), London.

Scodel, R. (1982): 'Hybris in the Second Stasimon of the *Oedipus Rex*', *Classical Philology*, 77, 214–23.

Scodel, R. (1984): *Sophocles*, Boston.

Scott, W. (1996): *Musical Design in Sophoclean Theater*, Hanover and London.

Seaford, R. (1986): 'Wedding Ritual and Textual Criticism in Sophocles' "Women of Trachis"', *Hermes* 114.1, 50–59.

Seaford, R. (1987): 'The Tragic Wedding', *Journal of Hellenic Studies* 107, 106–30.

Seaford, R. (1990): 'The Imprisonment of Women in Greek Tragedy', *Journal of Hellenic Studies*, 110, 76–90.

Seaford, R. (1994): *Reciprocity and Ritual: Homer and Tragedy in the Developing City-State*, Oxford.

Segal, C. (1964): 'Sophocles' Praise of Man and the Conflicts of the *Antigone*', *Arion*, 3.4, 46–66.

Segal, C. (1977): 'Sophocles' *Trachiniae*: Myth, Poetry, and Heroic Values', *Yale Classical Studies*, 25, 99–158.

Segal, C. (1980): 'Visual Symbolism and Visual Effects in Sophocles', *Classical World* 74, 125–42.

Segal, C. (1986): 'Time, Theater, and Knowledge in the Tragedy of Oedipus', in *Edipo* (ed. B. Gentile and R. Pretagostini), Rome.

Segal, C. (1993): *Oedipus Tyrannus: Tragic Heroism and the Limits of Knowledge*, New York.

Segal, C. (1994): 'Bride or Concubine? Iole and Herakles' Motives in the *Trachiniae*', *Illinois Classical Studies*, 19, 59–64.

Segal, C. (1995): *Sophocles' Tragic World*, Cambridge, Mass.

Segal, E. (1983): *Oxford Readings in Greek Tragedy*, Oxford.

Shisler, F. (1945): 'The Use of Stage Business to Portray Emotions in Greek Tragedy', *American Journal of Philology*, 66, 377–97

Sicherl, M. (1977): 'The Tragic Issue in Sophocles' Ajax', *Yale Classical Studies*, 25, 67–98.

Sidwell, K. (1992): 'The Argument of the Second Stasimon of *Oedipus Tyrannus*', *Journal of Hellenic Studies*, 112, 106–22.

Sifakis, G. M. (1979): 'Children in Greek Tragedy', *Bulletin of the Institute of Classical Studies*, 26, 67–80.

Silk, M. S. (1985): 'Heracles and Greek Tragedy', *Greece and Rome*, 32, 1–22.

Silk, M. S. and Stern, J. P. (1981): *Nietzsche on Tragedy*, Cambridge.

Slater, K. F. (1976): 'Some Suggestions for Staging the *Trachiniae*', *Arion* n.s. 3, 57–68.

Slater, P. (1992): *The Glory of Hera: Greek Mythology and the Greek Family*, Princeton.

Sorum, C. (1978): 'Monsters and the Family: The Exodos of Sophocles' *Trachiniae*', *Greek, Roman, and Byzantine Studies*, 19, 59–73.

Sourvinou-Inwood, C. (1989): 'Assumptions and the Creation of Meaning: Reading Sophocles' *Antigone*', *Journal of Hellenic Studies*, 109, 134–48.

Stanford, W. B. (ed.) (1963): *Sophocles: Ajax*, London.

Steiner, G. (1983): 'Variations sur Créon', Fondation Hardt, Entretiens 29, 77–96.

Steiner, G. (1984): Antigones, Oxford.

Stinton, T. C. W. (1990): Collected Papers on Greek Tragedy, Oxford.

Tanner, R. G. (1966): 'Sophocles, O. T. 236–41', The Classical Review, 16, 259–61.

Tanner, R. G. (1975): 'Goats, Pity and Fear', Hetairos 2. 3–6 and 21.

Taplin, O. (1977): The Stagecraft of Aeschylus, Oxford.

Taplin, O. (1983): 'Sophocles in his Theatre', in Sophocle (ed. J. Romilly) (Fondation Hardt, Entretiens 29), Geneva, 155–83.

Taplin, O. (1984): 'The Places of Antigone', Omnibus 6, 13–16 = Omnibus Omnibus 1987, 56–9.

Taplin, O. (1986): 'Fifth-century Tragedy and Comedy: A Synkrisis', Journal of Hellenic Studies, 106, 163–74.

Tarvin, W. L. (1990): 'Tragic Closure and "Tragic Calm"', Modern Language Quarterly, 51, 5–24.

Taylor, D. (tr.) (1986): Sophocles: The Theban Plays, London.

Trendall, A. D., and Webster, T. B. L. (1971): Illustrations of Greek Drama, London.

Vernant, J-P. (1983): 'Ambiguity and Reversal: On the Enigmatic Structure of Oedipus Rex', in Oxford Readings in Greek Tragedy (ed. E. Segal), Oxford, 189–209.

Vernant, J-P, and Vidal-Naquet, P. (1981): Tragedy and Myth in Ancient Greece, Sussex.

Vickers, B. (1973): Towards Greek Tragedy, London.

Vince, R. W. (1990): 'Opsis as a Term in Dramatic Theory', Assaph C, 6, 89–102.

Waldock, A. J. A. (1951): Sophocles the Dramatist, Cambridge.

Walton, J. Michael (1980): Greek Theatre Practice, Westport, Connecticut.

Walton, J. Michael (1984): The Greek Sense of Theatre, London.

Weiss, P. (1966): The Investigation, London.

Whitman, C. (1951): Sophocles: A Study of Heroic Humanism, Cambridge, Mass.

Wilamowitz-Moellendorf, U. von (tr.) (1923): Griechische Tragödien Ubersetzt, Vol. 4, Berlin.

Wiles, D. (1997): Tragedy in Athens, Cambridge.

Williams, B. (1993): Shame and Necessity, Berkeley and London.

Winnington-Ingram, R. P. (1969): 'Tragica', Bulletin of the Institute of Classical Studies 16, 44–7.

Zeitlin, F. (1986): 'Thebes: Theater of Self and Society' in Edipo (ed. B. Gentili and R. Pretagostini), Rome, 343–78.

Aias

In the tenth year of the war against Troy, Achilleus has died in battle. The Greek chiefs award his armour to Odysseus rather than to Aias. Offended by this slight to his excellence, Aias goes out in the night to kill the other officers; but he is sent mad by Athena, goddess of wisdom, and brings back animals from the fields instead, which he kills and tortures under the delusion that they are his enemies in the camp.

The drama opens at dawn; Odysseus is hunting for traces of Aias, and the trail leads him to Aias' tent. Athena appears to him, and exhibits the maddened Aias as a warning of how suddenly even the great and powerful can fall.

Aias' Sailors appear, disquieted by rumours. Aias' mistress, the captive princess Tekmessa, comes out and tells them that he went out in the night, and returned with animals which he then killed and tortured. Aias is revealed, sitting in the middle of the slaughtered animals. He is sane again, and sunk in misery. He sends for his son Eurysakes, and speaks to him as if making his will. But then he reappears, carrying the sword that he won from Hektor, and seems to be at ease with the world again. He goes off to the seashore, apparently to wash off the pollution.

A Soldier comes with the news that the prophet Kalchas has told Aias' half-brother Teukros that the goddess Athena is angry with Aias for boasting that he did not need her help; for twenty-four hours Aias must be kept inside his tent. Led by Tekmessa, the Sailors hastily disperse to try to find Aias.

The scene changes to a deserted part of the seashore. Aias appears, farewells this life and commits suicide. He is found by Tekmessa, and soon afterwards Teukros appears. A bitter wrangle develops between Teukros and the two chief commanders of the expedition: first Menelaos, and then Agamemnon; they want to deny Aias burial because he had attempted to kill them. The dispute reaches an impasse; but Odysseus appears, and talks Agamemnon into allowing the burial. The

drama ends as Teukros, Tekmessa, Eurysakes and the Sailors form
Aias' funeral procession.

Antigone

The sons of Oidipous, Eteokles and Polyneikes, have quarrelled about
the throne of Thebes. Polyneikes has gone to Argos and brought back
a fighting force to take the city by storm. It has failed, but the two
brothers have died in hand-to-hand combat with each other.

Their uncle Kreon inherits the throne. His first decree is that Eteokles, who has defended his native city, should have a full state funeral;
but Polyneikes' body is to be cast out for dogs and birds to eat; if
anyone tries to bury him, they will suffer death.

Before dawn on the night when the siege is lifted, Oidipous' daughter
Antigone finds out about this decree, and seeks out her sister Ismene to
tell her about it, and gain her assistance in burying Polyneikes. Ismene
refuses.

Kreon summons his Council, and tells them about the decree. A
terrified Guard, one of several whom Kreon placed near the body to
make sure nobody violates his edict, comes in to report that Polyneikes
has been ritually buried, with a light sprinkling of dust all over his
body. Kreon is enraged, and tells him he must return with the culprit
or suffer death himself.

The Guard departs, and returns later with Antigone, whom he
caught trying to bury Polyneikes again after they scraped off the dust.
She defies Kreon, and tells him the unwritten laws of the gods commanded her to bury her brother in defiance of his edict. Ismene tries to
share in her guilt, but Antigone rejects her. Kreon nevertheless condemns both sisters to death.

Kreon's son Haimon is engaged to Antigone. He tries to reason with
his father, telling him that public opinion is on her side, and he should
yield. Kreon instead threatens to kill Antigone before Haimon's eyes;
Haimon leaves in great distress.

Antigone is led out to die, entombed in a cave. The prophet Teiresias
arrives, and tells Kreon that there are disturbing omens in the sacrifices
because he has left Polyneikes unburied and condemned Antigone to
death. Kreon finally relents, and leaves to obey the gods.

But he is too late. By the time he has buried Polyneikes and gone on
to the cave to free Antigone, Haimon has got there before him and
forced his way in. Rather than starve to death, Antigone has hanged

herself; Haimon is found embracing her corpse. He first threatens his father with his sword, and then turns it on himself.

When Kreon's wife Eurydike hears this news, she goes into the palace in silence. Kreon returns, bearing the body of his son. He is confronted with the corpse of his wife as well; she has cursed him, and stabbed herself. Kreon is taken away, a totally broken man who has learned wisdom too late.

Young Women of Trachis

Herakles has left his wife Deianeira and his son Hyllos in Trachis while he performs his Labours. She has an oracle which prophesies that at this time his Labours would end, and he would either die, or live in peace for the rest of his days.

Herakles' herald Lichas arrives, bringing some captive women, and news that Herakles has sacked Oichalia, and is on his way home. Deianeira is strangely drawn to one of the captive girls, Iole. When Lichas takes the women and girls into the house, an Old Man detains Deianeira, and tells her the truth about the capture of Oichalia: because the king would not give him his daughter Iole, Herakles sacked the city and raped her; he has now sent her back to be his mistress. Deianeira at first accepts this news without a qualm – it is not the first time Herakles has had an affair; but then she resolves to use a love-potion which the kentaur Nessos once gave her – the blood from his veins, as he died, shot by Herakles with a poisoned arrow when he attempted to rape her. She smears the ointment on a robe, and gives it to Lichas to take back as her gift to Herakles.

Soon she comes back terrified; a shaft of sunlight lit on the tuft of wool she used to smear on the ointment, and it burned up at once. Hyllos runs home in agony, and accuses his mother of murdering his father; the robe began to consume him with fire when he put it on for his homecoming sacrifice. Deianeira goes without a word into the house.

Hyllos' Nurse appears, telling the Young Women of Trachis that Deianeira has stabbed herself in the womb on her marriage-bed, and is dead.

Herakles is now brought in, suffering terrible death-agonies. When he hears what Deianeira did, he recognizes that certain oracles have been fulfilled, and he is dying through the revenge of the kentaur. He commands Hyllos to place him on a funeral pyre, to have him burned alive on Mount Oita, and to marry Iole. Hyllos reluctantly consents, and the cortège moves off.

Oidipous the King

Thebes is being destroyed by a plague on the fertility of its crops and its women. Oidipous tries to solve his city's problem; he sends his brother-in-law Kreon to the oracle at Delphi, which says that the Thebans must drive out the murderers of Laios. Teiresias, the prophet, at first refuses to tell Oidipous who this is, then tells him that this very day will show him to be a parricide, living in incest with one whom he should not; he will lose the throne, and become a blinded beggar.

Oidipous accuses Kreon of plotting with Teiresias to bring him down. Kreon argues that he has a much better position now, as the queen's brother, than if he had the responsibility of being king. His sister Iokaste overhears their quarrel, successfully pleads for Kreon's life, and after he has left asks her husband what their quarrel was about. When Oidipous tells her, she tries to prove to him that oracles are nonsense, mentioning an oracle given to herself and her first husband Laios that their son would kill his father.

Oidipous is terrified by this, as he had been given an oracle at Delphi that he would kill his father and marry his mother. He questions Iokaste as to when and where Laios died, and learns that it was in the same place and at roughly the same time as he got into a quarrel with an older traveller, and killed him. They send for the Herdsman who survived the massacre of Laios' attendants, to find out if he still sticks to his story that not one solitary man, but many robbers attacked the former king.

A messenger from Korinth arrives, with the news that King Polybos is dead, and Oidipous has inherited the throne there. Oidipous and Iokaste are delighted that Oidipous' father is apparently dead, and the oracles have therefore been disproved: but then the Korinthian reveals that Queen Merope of Korinth is not Oidipous' natural mother; the baby Oidipous was given to the Korinthian long ago by a Theban shepherd on Mount Kithairon, and adopted by the royal couple.

Iokaste now knows the truth. She begs Oidipous to search no more, and when he refuses goes into the Palace.

The Herdsman arrives, and Oidipous forces him to reveal whose baby he gave to the Korinthian. It was the son of Laios and Iokaste. Oidipous realizes who he is and what he has done.

A Servant comes out to tell how Iokaste hanged herself, and Oidipous blinded himself with the brooch-pins from her dress. Oidipous himself now appears, and in an extended scene tries to come to terms with having violated two of mankind's most fundamental taboos. Kreon grants Oidipous the favour of touching and speaking to his daughters, Antigone and Ismene; then he makes him go back into the palace, away from the sunlight which he pollutes by his presence.

ACKNOWLEDGEMENTS

The translators would like to thank the Universities of Exeter, Newcastle (Australia) and Southern Queensland for financial, material and other support given to the practical research for this book. We also wish to thank all those who worked with us on the workshops and productions that made this edition possible.

Michael Ewans in particular wishes to name Frances Gordon and Shona Spence (Assistant Directors, *Antigone* and *Aias*), Constance Colley (composer) and Christine Smith (choreographer); Helen Atkinson (Antigone), Tom Bonjekovic (Kreon), Ben Kirkwood (Haimon) and Lauren Eade (Ismene); Duncan McKensey (Aias), Emma Fuller (Tekmessa) and Patrick Bryson (Teukros).

Graham Ley would like to thank Lindsay Buchanan for typing the first draft of the translation of *Young Women of Trachis*, and those students of the Drama Department at the University of Exeter who took part in the workshop in the early months of 1997.

Gregory McCart would specially like to thank Helen Howard (assistant to the director and actor), Sharmon Parsons (choreographer and dancer), Rod Boschman (didjeridoo), Graham Moodie (dancer), David Moran (actor) and Kristan Robinson (leader of the *choros*).

ACKNOWLEDGMENTS

The author would like to thank the Department of the Navy, naval Air establishment, and Sea-Air Operations Command, as well as personnel at ... to ... for ... their help. It is a pleasure to wish to thank all those who read chapters of the text in draft and proffered thoughtful insights throughout.

...